T0122467

Progress in IS

"PROGRESS in IS" encompasses the various areas of Information Systems in theory and practice, presenting cutting-edge advances in the field. It is aimed especially at researchers, doctoral students, and advanced practitioners. The series features both research monographs that make substantial contributions to our state of knowledge and handbooks and other edited volumes, in which a team of experts is organized by one or more leading authorities to write individual chapters on various aspects of the topic. "PROGRESS in IS" is edited by a global team of leading IS experts. The editorial board expressly welcomes new members to this group. Individual volumes in this series are supported by a minimum of two members of the editorial board, and a code of conduct mandatory for all members of the board ensures the quality and cutting-edge nature of the titles published under this series.

More information about this series at http://www.springer.com/series/10440

Mikael Lind • Michalis Michaelides •
Robert Ward • Richard T. Watson

Editors

Maritime Informatics

 Springer

Editors
Mikael Lind
Research Institutes of Sweden (RISE)
and Chalmers University of Technology
Göteborg, Sweden

Michalis Michaelides
Department of Electrical Engineering,
Computer Engineering and Informatics
Cyprus University of Technology
Limassol, Cyprus

Robert Ward
Pymble, NSW, Australia

Richard T. Watson
Department of MIS
University of Georgia
Athens, GA, USA

ISSN 2196-8705   ISSN 2196-8713   (electronic)
Progress in IS
ISBN 978-3-030-50894-4   ISBN 978-3-030-50892-0   (eBook)
https://doi.org/10.1007/978-3-030-50892-0

This Springer imprint is published by the registered company Springer Nature Switzerland AG.
The registered company address is: Gewerbestrasse 11, 6330 Cham, Switzerland

Foreword

Informatics, the study of the structure, behaviour, and interactions of natural and engineered computational systems, including the science of processing data and information for storage and retrieval, is very important in ensuring that the shipping and transport community obtains the full benefits of new and vast digital data sources and information technology developments.

The Transport and Logistics Domain team within the United Nations Centre for Trade Facilitation and Electronic Business (UN/CEFACT) has observed that the so-called *fourth industrial revolution* is now arriving in the shipping world and includes digitalisation, robotics, artificial intelligence, and big data. It is important that these developments are carefully integrated into shipping and transport, balancing their benefits against safety and security concerns, the impact on the environment, and the impact on international trade and contributing positively to the United Nations 2030 Agenda on Sustainable Development. It is also important in ensuring a sustainable maritime transport sector—including shipping and ports—supporting world trade and facilitating the global economy. For all these reasons, the newly emerging specialism of maritime informatics becomes particularly relevant.

Artificial intelligence, big data, automation, and the Internet of Things are set to have a profound impact on shipping—not just in terms of navigation but across the full spectrum of ship operations and the logistics chain.

So, it is without doubt, an exciting time to be in shipping, and transport in general. Thanks to digitalisation and other new technology emerging in so many areas—like clean fuel and renewable energy, smart sensors, just-in-time arrivals, robotics, AI, new materials, smart containers, and construction techniques—shipping is entering a new era. This also puts emphasis on the efforts made for standardisation, such as those of UN/CEFACT.

The only real certainties are that the next 10 or 20 years will see as much change in shipping as has been experienced in the past 100 years, and that whatever those changes may be in the future, they will have to be ever efficient, cost-effective, and environmentally friendly. In this regard, maritime informatics has an important part to play in ensuring that the changes for the future are effective, successful, and beneficial.

We congratulate and encourage the distinguished authors who have contributed to this, the first consolidated academic text on maritime informatics, and we hope that, through this book, all those who are now becoming involved in bringing the fourth industrial revolution to the maritime transportation sector will be all the more wiser.

UN/CEFACT   Sue Probert
London, UK

UN/CEFACT – United Nations Economic Commission   Lance Thompson
for Europe
Geneva, Switzerland

Preface

Over the last few years, as a result of our involvement in the shipping industry and in several European Union projects to improve the safety, efficiency, and the sustainability of shipping, the editors of this book have been developing the idea of maritime informatics as a specific thematic topic. We recognised that there are characteristics of the maritime sector that require a specific approach to its digital transformation through information systems. Before we discuss these characteristics and their implications, we will first define maritime informatics and then go on to present our perspective on its development and application.

> Maritime informatics is the application of information systems to increasing the efficiency, safety, and ecological sustainability of the world's shipping industry.
>
> Maritime informatics is an applied science. Developed by data scientists to meet the needs of practice and applied by practitioners and data scientists cooperatively.

Shipping, the most efficient way of transporting goods across the globe, handles about 90% of the world's trade. It enables regions and countries to exploit their comparative advantage and thus improves the lot of many citizens. Trade facilitated by shipping and application of Ricardo's comparative advantage principle has created a global economy. The last few years, however, have demonstrated its fragility. Trade wars have flared, and the Covid-19 pandemic has demonstrated the brittleness of a highly interconnected society. As we have learned, a digital society can be quite agile in some regards, such as the use of video conferencing and webinars for meetings, but we still rely on people performing physical actions, such as stocking supermarket shelves, for many tasks. As a result, it is likely that robots will take on many critical physical operations to increase societal resilience, and also there could be localisation of some operations that currently take advantage of labour arbitrage. The localisation possibilities of robots and such things as 3D printing will have an impact on shipping volumes.

The sea has fascinated people for centuries. It has long been a source of transport, food, and entertainment. However, with rising ocean temperatures, sea level increases, and massive plastic waste in the ocean, we are endangering a major source of food and seaside cities will have to spend billions on adjusting to more frequent flooding. At the same time, aquaculture and windfarms are adding to our dependency on the seas. All these developments support the case for maritime informatics. The quality of maritime decision-making needs to improve in efficiency, so we do more with less, sustainability, and safety and minimise the environmental impact, thereby protecting human lives and the environment.

Maritime informatics takes a holistic approach to shipping. Consequently, information requirements are strongly influenced by the self-organising nature of the shipping industry and the spatial-temporal data needed to manage a voyage and a port visit. Digital data streams are the fulcrum of coordination, because the many actors involved in a voyage and a port visit must share data in real time to organise the many associated activities. Strong voices in the shipping industry are also pushing for a digital transformation that will result in higher levels of transparency, predictability, and visibility of all transport operations connected with shipping. There is a drive for enhanced situational awareness across the full spectrum of activities in the movement of goods from origin to destination.

Because of the high level of actor autonomy in this competitive industry, those who own and generate data want complete control over when they grant data access to others. Data owners tend only to authorise sharing of data when it is in their self-interest.

Much of the knowledge and practices for developing information systems is based upon building systems for internal use by an enterprise's employees. Data access authorisation is stable. For example, an employee's data access rights might persist for years, whereas, in shipping, authority to access particular data will likely be limited to a port visit or a portion of a visit. Thus, you have to set aside notions of building centralised databases and focus on digital data streams whose flow and attributes could be precisely managed.

The automatic identification system (AIS) is the seed innovation for maritime informatics. It was the first widespread adoption of digital data stream technology within the shipping industry, and in this case, the stream is openly accessible to those with a receiver. If the industry is to advance its digital transformation and for maritime informatics to bloom, it needs more standardised digital data streams to create shared information systems, such as a common situation awareness, which improve coordination and raise the capital productivity of transportation fleets and hubs. The industry is on the way to leaving behind non-standard data sharing using a variety of different media, from voice to fax to email, to settle upon standardised digital data exchange across the communication networks, something that creates the foundation for the next era of shipping.

An early and very beneficial digital innovation for the shipping industry was the Morse code and associated telegraphy equipment. Invented around 1837, the Morse code was the first international digital standard. Since the 1950s when General Electric (GE) purchased the first business computer, there has been a steady conversion of systems from analogue to digital. An early label was automated data processing (ADP) later followed by management information systems (MIS), and more recently a variety of terms, such as digitisation, digitalisation, and digital transformation, have been applied. Over this period, the essential goal of converting analogue to digital to lower the cost of business and improve customer service has not changed. It seems, however, that talking about a digital "something" currently gets managers more engaged than "ADP" or "MIS".

The analogue to digital conversion has been the major force for productivity improvement for over half a century, and every business needs to stay on this track to remain competitive. Thus, in this book we have not been too concerned whether authors choose to use the words digitisation, digitalisation, or digital transformation. While there are pundits who write about the difference between these three terms, they do not always agree on their definitions. Consequently, people confuse them, and authors sometimes use them interchangeably. We do not think the difference matters that much. What matters is that businesses continue to use advances in information technology and network connectivity to transform business processes to raise efficiency and create a sustainable world. Whether you describe your goal as digitising, digitalising, or a digital transformation will unlikely make too much difference to the outcome.

In setting the scope for this book, we excluded the data communication layer. Also, while we include data exchange standards, we do not delve into their structure and features. We do not intend to imply that secure standardised data exchange is not important. Indeed, it is the foundation on which maritime informatics is built. We want, however, to focus attention on the processing of communicated data.

The first objective of maritime informatics is to promote standardised digital data sharing to achieve high levels of coordination and resource utilisation. The ultimate goal is to use the data that accumulates through data sharing to develop and implement new types of shipping analytics, which will advance operational performance and strategic planning to further raise the capital productivity of the shipping industry. Maritime informatics is about enabling understanding, predicting, advising, and improving maritime activity by digital means.

This work is the product of many minds across practice, academia, and the world. The contributors are from 20 countries; they include 46 from industry or government and 34 from universities or research institutes. With so many contributors, there is inevitably some repetition of key ideas and critical facts. As we expect that some might read only a few chapters, we decided it would be appropriate to leave some repetition in place to ensure that each chapter has the necessary context to meet its goals and does not require a linear reading of all prior chapters.

The purpose of this book is to give you insights into the current status and future directions of maritime informatics. We provide charts for you to successfully navigate your digital transformation through a waterway of connected ships, ports, and cargoes. Our vision is that maritime informatics will help you reach higher levels of operational performance and sounder strategic visions so that you reap the full benefits of digital transformation of the industry and your organisation in particular.[1]

Göteborg, Sweden	Mikael Lind
Limassol, Cyprus	Michalis Michaelides
Pymble, NSW, Australia	Robert Ward
Athens, GA, USA	Richard T. Watson

---

[1]To keep current on developments in maritime informatics, see http://maritimeinformatics.org/

Contents

Contributors

A. Alexandrou Queen Mary University of London/Jackson Parton Solicitors, London, UK

S. Alexandrou Cyprus University of Technology (CUT), Limassol, Cyprus

T. Andersen NOFO, Sandnes, Norway

J. Askvik ShortSea Promotion Centre Norway, Oslo, Norway

S. Aslam Cyprus University of Technology (CUT), Limassol, Cyprus

M. L. Bartosiak Università di Pavia, Pavia, Italy

H. Becha UN/CEFACT Transport and Logistics Vice Chair, Marseille, France

M. Bergmann BM Bergmann-Marine, Grosskrotzenburg, Germany

N. Bjørn-Andersen Copenhagen Business School, Copenhagen, Denmark

S. Breitenbach Port of Hamburg Marketing, Hamburg, Germany

A. B. Brendel University of Göttingen, Göttingen, Germany

T. Christensen Maritime Connectivity Platform Consortium, Daejeon, South Korea

A. Chrysostomou MarineFields Holding Ltd., Limassol, Cyprus

Chye Poh Chua ShipsFocus Group, Singapore, Singapore

J. C. Croston Manzanillo International Terminal, Colón, Panama

N. Delmeire European Inland Waterway Transport, Brussels, Belgium

E. Eklund Dubai Maritime City Authority, Dubai, United Arab Emirates

F. von Elern Swedish Maritime Technology Forum (SMTF) a part of Research Institutes of Sweden (RISE), Gothenburg, Sweden

C. L. Forcellati Risk Consulting/Sustainability, Singapore, Singapore

T. Frazier FedEx Express, Los Angeles, CA, USA

X. Fu IHPC A*Star, Singapore, Singapore

J. Gahnström CompetenSEA AB, Gothenburg, Sweden

C. Georgeson Cass Business School at City University of London, London, UK

A. González Barcelona Port Authority (APB), Barcelona, Spain

L. Göthberg GIGS by Lena G, Gothenburg, Sweden

L. Green ShortSea Promotion Centre Sweden, Stockholm, Sweden

S. Green Swedish Shipowners' Association, Gothenburg, Sweden

M. Greve University of Göttingen, Göttingen, Germany

M. Hägg Research Institutes of Sweden (RISE), Gothenburg, Sweden

S. Haraldson Research Institutes of Sweden (RISE), Gothenburg, Sweden

C. Harnischmacher University of Göttingen, Göttingen, Germany

D. Hayes Cyprus Subsea Consulting and Services C.S.C.S. Ltd., Lakatamia, Cyprus

H. Herodotou Cyprus University of Technology (CUT), Limassol, Cyprus

G. Hirt HVCC Hamburg Vessel Coordination Center, Hamburg, Germany

J. Hoffmann UNCTAD, Geneva, Switzerland

H. Holm Svenska Beräkningsbyrån AB, Torslanda, Sweden

H. Hvid Jensen DXC Technology, Copenhagen, Denmark

V. Jayaraman IHPC A*Star Computing, Singapore, Singapore

J. Karlsson ABB Marine & Ports, Gothenburg, Sweden

M. Karlsson Research Institutes of Sweden (RISE), Gothenburg, Sweden

L. M. Kolbe University of Göttingen, Göttingen, Germany

I. Kyriakides University of Nicosia Research Foundation, Nicosia, Cyprus

F. Liesa ETP-Alice, Brussels, Belgium

M. Lind Research Institutes of Sweden (RISE) and Chalmers University of Technology, Gothenburg, Sweden

M. Michaelides Department of Electrical Engineering, Computer Engineering and Informatics, Cyprus University of Technology, Limassol, Cyprus

F. Olindersson Chalmers University of Technology, Gothenburg, Sweden

E. Olsson Research Institutes of Sweden (RISE), Gothenburg, Sweden

S. O'Malley Analytical Innovative Solutions, LLC, Atlanta, GA, USA

N. B. Othman IHPC A*Star, Singapore, Singapore

J. M. Pagés Sánchez AIVP – The Worldwide Network of Port Cities, Hamburg, Germany

P. M. Panayides Cyprus University of Technology (CUT), Limassol, Cyprus

J. H. Park KRISO, Daejeon, South Korea

S. Paulsen Pragmatique Denmark, Copenhagen, Denmark

T. Penttinen Attracs/Ahola Transport, Kokkola, Finland

F. W. Pot BM Bergmann-Marine, Seattle, WA, USA

O. Primor Windward, Tel-Aviv, Israel

P. Rudolfsson Kvarken Ports, Umeå, Sweden

T. Rydbergh Marine Benchmark, Västra Frölunda, Sweden

T. Rygh The City of Stavanger, Stavanger, Norway

P. Schmitt BearingPoint GmbH, München, Germany

M. Schröder Hapag-Lloyd AG, Hamburg, Germany

B. Sengupta OSM Maritime Group, Singapore, Singapore

A. Simha MSC Mediterranean Shipping Company, Geneva, Switzerland

S. Singh The University of Trinidad and Tobago, Chaguaramas, Trinidad and Tobago

Z. Siokouros Cyprus Marine and Maritime Institute (CMMI), Cyprus

C. Sjöberger Chalmers University of Technology, Gothenburg, Sweden

S. Theodossiou Tototheo Maritime, Limassol, Cyprus

D. P. Theodosiou Tototheo Maritime and WISTA International, Limassol, Cyprus

D. Thomas Kennesaw State University, Kennesaw, GA, USA

M. Tichavska MarineTraffic, London, UK

P. Tsiantis University of Nicosia Research Foundation, Nicosia, Cyprus

J. M. Voorspuij GS1 AISBL, Brussel, Belgium

R. Ward Pymble, NSW, Australia

R. T. Watson University of Georgia, Athens, GA, USA

J. Woxenius University of Gothenburg, Gothenburg, Sweden

B. Wulff HHLA Container Terminal Altenwerder GmbH, Hamburg, Germany

Z. Xiao IHPC A*Star, Singapore, Singapore

H. Xu IHPC A*Star, Singapore, Singapore

A. Zerem Research Institutes of Sweden (RISE), Gothenburg, Sweden

About the Editors

Mikael Lind is Associate Professor and Senior Strategic Research Advisor at Research Institutes of Sweden (RISE). He has initiated and headed a substantial part of several open innovation initiatives related to ICT for sustainable transports of people and goods. He is also part-time at the Chalmers University of Technology (M2), Sweden, exploring the opportunity of maritime informatics as an applied research field. Lind also serves as an expert for the World Economic Forum, Europe's Digital Transport Logistic Forum (DTLF), and UN/CEFACT. He has been the lead author of more than 30 concept notes associated with maritime informatics, and with over 8500 LinkedIn connections and well published in maritime trade press, he has become a recognised thought leader in maritime informatics. He is based in Gothenburg, a major Scandinavia shipping centre with a number of companies already offering information services to the maritime sector. Lind and Watson have been mini-track chairs for maritime informatics at the major regional IS conferences in Europe and the Americas for several years.

Michalis Michaelides is an Assistant Professor with the Department of Electrical Engineering, Computer Engineering and Informatics at the Cyprus University of Technology. Michalis' research interests include communication systems, wireless sensor networks, event detection and localisation, fault detection and diagnosis, fault tolerance, collaborative signal and information processing, computational intelligence with applications to environmental monitoring, intelligent systems, and maritime informatics. Michalis has been involved as a principal investigator in many research projects, both local and European, including the Sea Traffic Management Validation (EU, 2016–2019) and STEAM (RPF, INTEGRATED/0916/0063, 2019–2021). In 2014, he received the Elsevier Building and Environment Journal Best Paper Award.

Robert Ward was the Secretary-General of the International Hydrographic Organization (IHO) until his retirement in late 2017. Prior to that, he was the Deputy Hydrographer of Australia. For more than 20 years, he represented Australia and subsequently the IHO at the highest international levels and has played an influential role in the development and implementation of global digital data exchange standards for nautical charting services that now also underpin the IMO's e-Navigation concept of a maritime digital information environment.

Richard T. Watson is a Regents Professor and the J. Rex Fuqua Distinguished Chair for Internet Strategy in the Terry College of Business at the University of Georgia. He is a former President of the Association for Information Systems (AIS). In 2011, he received the AIS's LEO award, which is given for exceptional lifetime achievement in information systems. He has written books on *Data Management*; *Electronic Commerce, Internet Strategy, Energy Informatics*; and *Capital, Systems, and Objects and* published nearly 200 journal articles, including articles in the major IS journals and practitioner journals such as *Harvard Business Review* and *California Management Review*. He was educated at the University of Western Australia (BSc, Dip. Comp), Monash University (MBA), and the University of Minnesota (PhD).

Acronyms and Initialisms

A-CDM	Airport Collaborative Decision Making
AACV	Automatic Access Control of Vehicle
AAV	Autonomous Aerial Vehicle
ACCS	Automatic Customs Control System
AFS	Anti-Fouling System
AI	Artificial Intelligence
AIS	Automatic Identification System
AIVP	Association Internationale Villes et Ports
AMQP	Advanced Message Queuing Protocol
API	Application Programming Interface
ASS	Autonomous Stationary System
ASV	Autonomous Surface Vehicle
ATA	Actual Time of Arrival
AUV	Autonomous Underwater Vehicle
BAU	Business as Usual
BCO	Beneficial Cargo Owner
BIC	Bureau International des Containers et du Transport Intermodal
BIMCO	Baltic and International Maritime Council
BMW	Ballast Water Management
BRS	Business Requirements Specification
CapEx	Capital Expense
CCBI	Customs Cross Border Interoperability
CCL	Core Components Library
CEP	Courier, Express, and Parcel
CIRM	Comité International Radio-Maritime
CM	Condition Monitoring
CMDS	Common Maritime Data Structure
COSCO	China Ocean Shipping Company
CSSC	China State Shipbuilding Corporation
DCS	Data Collection System
DCSA	Digital Shipping Container Association

DDS	Digital Data Stream
DEA	Data Envelopment Analysis
DFS	Distributed File System
DPF	Deep Profiling Float
DSME	Daewoo Shipbuilding & Marine Engineering
DTLF	Digital Transport Logistics Forum
EAI	Enterprise Application Integration
ECA	Emission Control Area
ECDIS	Electronic Chart Display and Information System
ECS	Electronic Chart System
EDI	Electronic Data Interchange
EDR	Enterprise Data Replication
EEDI	Energy Efficiency Design Index
EEOI	Energy Efficiency Operational Index
EEZ	Exclusive Economic Zone
eFTI	Electronic Freight Transport Information
EIS	Environmental Information System
EMS	Environmental Management System
EMSO	European Multidisciplinary Seafloor and Water Column Observatory
EMSW	European Maritime Single Window
ENC	Electronic Navigational Chart
EPCIS	Electronic Product Code Information Service
ESG	Environmental Social and Governance
ETA	Estimated Time of Arrival
FAIR	Findable Accessible Interoperable and Reusable
FAL	Facilitation Committee
FF	Financial Flow
GHG	Greenhouse Gas
GI	Geospatial Information
GIA	Global Industry Alliance
GIS	Geographic Information System
GLN	Global Location Number
GMA	General Morphological Analysis
GMDSS	Global Maritime Distress Safety System
GML	Geography Markup Language
GNSS	Global Navigation Satellite System
GOOS	Global Ocean Observing System
GSCM	Green Supply Chain Management
GT	Gross tonne
GTD	Global Trade Identity
HDFS	Hadoop Distributed File System
HFSW	High Frequency Surface Wave
HTS	High Throughput Satellite
IACS	International Association of Classification Societies

IALA	International Association of Marine Aids to Navigation and Lighthouse Authorities
IATA	International Air Transport Association
IC	Integrated Circuit
ICAO	International Civil Aviation Organization
ICT	Information and Communications Technology
IEC	International Electrotechnical Commission
IHMA	International Harbour Masters Association
IHO	International Hydrographic Organization
IMO	International Maritime Organization
INS	Integrated Navigation System
IOC-UNESCO	Intergovernmental Oceanographic Commission-UNESCO
IoT	Internet of Things
IPCC	Intergovernmental Panel on Climate Change
IPCDMC	International PortCDM Council
IPCSA	International Port Community Systems Association
IS	Information System
ISO	International Standards Organization
ITF	International Transport Forum
ITPCO	International Taskforce Port Call Optimisation
ITS	Intelligent Transport System
ITU	International Telecommunications Union
JCOMM	Joint WMO-IOC Commission for Oceanography and Marine Meteorology
JDP	Joint Development Project
JIT	Just in Time
KML	Keyhole Markup Language
KPI	Key Performance Indicator
LAS	Location Aware System
LCCA	Life-Cycle Cost Analysis
LPR	Licence Plate Recognition
LR	Lloyd's Register
LRIT	Long-Range Identification and Tracking
LSP	Logistic Service Provider
MCP	Maritime Connectivity Platform
MEPC	Marine Environment Protection Committee
MESIS	Maritime Environment and Safety Information Service
MMOP	Marine Meteorology and Oceanography Programme
MMSI	Maritime Mobile Service Identity
MMT	Multi-Modal Transport
MoS	Motorways of the Sea
MoU	Memorandum of Understanding
MR	Minute Reserve
MRN	Maritime Resource Name
MSI	Maritime Safety Information

MTCC	Maritime Technology Cooperation Centre
NAMAS	Navigation Monitoring and Assistance Service
NetCDF	Network Common Data Form
NFS	Network File System
NGO	Non-Governmental Organization
NII	Non-Intrusive Inspection
OpEx	Operational Expense
OSI	Open System Interconnection
OU	Ornstein-Uhlenbeck
P2P	Port-to-Port
PACT	Pilot Action for Combined Transport
PAYS	Pay As You Sail
PCA	Principal Component Analysis
PCC	Point of Common Coupling
PCMF	Port Call Message Format
PCR	Primary Control Reserve
PCS	Port Community System
PIM	Port Information Manual
PITAS	Pilot & Tugs Assistance Service
PM	Particulate Matter
PMS	Planned Maintenance System
PortCDM	Port Collaborative Decision Making
PSC	Port State Control
PSSA	Particularly Sensitive Sea Area
RDBMS	Relational Database Management System
REDSS	Real-Time Electronic Navigational Chart Distribution and Streaming Service
RFD	Reporting Formalities Directive
RISE	Research Institutes of Sweden
RORO	Roll-on, Roll-off
SaaS	Software-as-a-Service
SAR	Synthetic Aperture Radar
SBMS	Ship-Borne System Monitoring Service
SCMP	Single-Consumer-Multiple-Provider
SCR	Secondary Control Reserve
SDG	Sustainable Development Goal
SDO	Standards Development Organization
SECA	Sulphur Emission Control Area
SEEMP	Ship Energy Efficiency Management Plan
SEO	Search Engine Optimization
SES	Ship Earth Station
SFA	Stochastic Frontier Analysis
SIP	Strategic Implementation Plan
SIR	Sampling Importance Resampling
SMDG	Ship Planning Message Development Group

SME	Small to Mid-Sized Enterprise
SOA	Service-Oriented Architecture
SOE	Self-Organizing Ecosystem
SOLAS	International Convention for the Safety of Life at Sea
SORPS	Safe and Optimal Route Planning Service
SSF	Small-Scale Fisheries
SSI	Sustainable Shipping Initiative
SSLS	Ship Software Logging System
SSS	Short Sea Shipping
SST	Sea Surface Temperature
STEAM	Sea Traffic Management in the Eastern Mediterranean
STM	Sea Traffic Management
SUMP	Sustainable Urban Mobility Plan
SV	Shared Visibility
T&E	Transport and Environment
TCO	Total Cost of Ownership
TCS	Traffic Control System
TEN-T	Trans-European Transport Network
UKC	Under Keel Clearance
ULCS	Ultra Large Container Ship
ULD	Unit Load Device
UN	United Nations
UN/CEFACT	United Nations Centre for Trade Facilitation and Electronic Business
UNECE	United Nations Economic Commission for Europe
VDR	Voyage Data Recorder
VHF	Very High Frequency
VLCC	Very Large Crude Carrier
VOS	Voluntary Observation Ship
VPP	Virtual Power Plant
VSAT	Very-Small-Aperture Terminal
VTS	Vessel Traffic Service
WCO	World Customs Organization
WFL	Web Feature Layer
WMO	World Meteorological Organization
ZB	Zettabyte

Part I
Maritime Informatics as a Better Glue

Richard T. Watson

The maritime industry is a global self-organizing ecosystem that has been glued together by information for centuries. Information enables traders and shippers to overcome national differences and permits the myriad actors in the worldwide maritime system to request and receive the necessary services to transit oceans, fairways, inland waters, rivers, and lakes and handle cargo and passengers in a multitude of ports of varying size and resources.

For centuries, the industry has continually upgraded its glue to improve safety, efficiency, and reliability. The leading navies of each era invested heavily in charting the oceans to improve safety and navigation. The need to measure longitude accurately was fostered by a national competition for a precise and sea-worthy chronometer (Sobel, 1995). In the digital era, the global navigation satellite system and satellite communication have become essential information sources for modern navigation.

As well as charting a safe course, each shipping company has to keep track of the content of its cargo and its destination, as well as plans for future voyages and their cargoes and destinations. Each needs to manage its human capital needs, market price competitive services to exporters and importers, keep its ships safe and reliable, and organize the many other activities that enable a level of capital productivity comparable to that of its key competitors. While doing all this, a shipping company needs to obey local, regional, national, and international regulations.

Like all organizations, a shipping company is a capital creation system (Watson, 2019). It converts capital from one form to another. Primarily, it converts an exporter's products, economic capital, into higher value economic capital by getting them closer to the final customer. This is the age-old business of trading that existed thousands of years ago around the Euphrates and Tigris rivers. It is the same capital creation model; except today it is far more capital, energy, and information intensive.

R. T. Watson
Department of MIS, University of Georgia, Athens, GA, USA

Shipping companies now need the new glue of Maritime Informatics to tie together the many components through digital data exchange. This new field will enhance a shipping company's capacity to compete with others in the maritime sector and the sector to integrate and contend with alternative transport modes to provide the best combination of modes across the overall transport chain. The global capital creation system does not care about history and customs. It ruthlessly weeds out the inefficient whose capital productivity is low relative to their rivals.

Each of the nine chapters in this first section is now briefly summarized.

Chapter "The Origins of Maritime Informatics" reviews the history of the maritime industry with a particular emphasis on its long search for accurate data that improves the safety and efficiency of voyaging and port visits. The need for captains to know where they are when at sea led to the development of detailed nautical charts, accurate clocks, and other supports for navigation. Very early on, many countries realized that reliable charts and clocks were a competitive advantage in war and in trade. Thus, recent digital developments such as global navigation systems, electronic charts, the automatic identification system (AIS), and marine satellite communication are today's answer to the need for accurate location and depth data.

Chapter "Shipping: A Self-Organizing Ecosystem" introduces some key concepts for understanding the nature of the shipping industry and how it operates as a foundational worldview for maritime informatics. It describes the shipping industry as a self-organizing ecosystem that uses episodic tight coupling to coordinate actions. The chapter also discusses the nature of innovation and how it follows a path of seeding, standardizing, and sequencing, such as with containerization and now in the form of a digital transformation. This may be the most academic of the chapters, because the concepts it discusses are important for developing a vocabulary and understanding of critical characteristics of the maritime sector that determine the nature of information systems required and the evolution of Maritime Informatics.

Chapter "The Necessity of Standards for Maritime Informatics in Ship Operations" reports five maritime incidents to endorse its arguments for digital data exchange standards for onboard equipment. In today's digital era, nearly all products have embedded digital capabilities and data streaming features. However, unless there are common standards, a digital babel of data streams is generated that means a ship's bridge can become overwhelmed by data from multiple sources without sufficient integration. In a crisis situation, a flood of data can interfere with quality decision-making and contribute to safety breaches and accidents.

Chapter "The Port as a Set of Socio-Technical Systems: A Multiorganizational View" explores issues arising in port operations because of the myriad organizations that need to coordinate and cooperate for a successful port visit. A port is a continually evolving collection of socio-technical systems, each subject to different levels of change induced by the digital transformation of shipping, simultaneously serving a multitude of different trades relying on different business models. The multiple organizations within a port need to collaborate to create value through a value network, and understanding this process is core to the design of systems to support port collaboration and the collection and analysis of data aimed at raising the performance of each organization and thus the port collectively.

Chapter "Digitalization in Maritime Regional and Global Supply Chains" addresses the need to improve connectivity across the entire supply chain. It argues that maritime transportation is a laggard in many supply networks because of its slow adoption of digital business practices. The proposed solution is founded on the acceptance of global standards to meet each of the stakeholders' needs and the adoption of common technology and process building blocks to ensure systems integration.

Chapter "Sustainable Maritime Transport and Maritime Informatics" is concerned with the absolute necessity to create a sustainable society. As the producer of around 2.5% of global greenhouse gas emissions, the shipping industry has a social responsibility to reduce its carbon footprint. Most people and organizations want to be environmentally responsible, but without information many are unaware of their current and future ecological impact. Thus, the industry needs the support of Maritime Informatics to improve its sustainability so that it can identify opportunities to reduce waste, pollution, carbon emissions, and energy efficiency. There is also a need for Maritime Informatics to help raise capital productivity, so we learn to do more with less ships, cranes, and other maritime hardware.

Chapter "Connecting Cities and Ports via Maritime Informatics" details the need for ports and their associated cities to jointly develop a cooperative smart city and port environment. Increasing global urbanization is leading to many of the world's population living and working in port cities; it is essential for this to duet to working together to deploy technology to achieve the United Nations' sustainable development goals. The need for connected cities and ports broadens the scope of Maritime Informatics because it recognizes that the port is a transportation hub connecting multiple modes of transportation, such as road and rail, that are typically integral to a city's environmental footprint and efforts to reduce it. The flow of information across transport modes can support the reduction of a supply chain's impact upon the environment, a city, and its citizens.

Chapter "Maritime Informatics for Increased Collaboration" is a summary of the current situation in the Maritime industry. It establishes the importance of the industry and describes its different business models. In particular, it describes the complexity of the port call operation and introduces the "Metro Map" to show the many episodes of tight coupling that can occur in a port visit. The chapter is comprehensive coverage of the existing state of the industry and complements chapter "The Future of Shipping: Collaboration Through Digital Data Sharing".

Chapter "The Future of Shipping: Collaboration Through Digital Data Sharing" gives us an overview of likely future directions with respect to digital system and technology and associated changes in the shipping industry. You will likely find particularly useful and though provoking the final paragraph in the chapter that list seven expected significant transformations that flow from greater collaboration enabled by digital data sharing. For shipping executives, this is set of waypoints for charting your enterprises' future.

References

Sobel, D. (1995). *Longitude: The true story of a lone genius who solved the greatest scientific problem of his time*. New York: Walker.
Watson, R. T. (2019). *Capital, systems and objects: The foundation and future of organizations*. Athens, GA: eGreen Press.

The Origins of Maritime Informatics

Robert Ward ⓘD and **Niels Bjørn-Andersen** ⓘD

Collecting and recording information that supports maritime operations and trade is not new. However, sharing that information is a much newer phenomenon; collecting the information using technology is newer still, and collecting and sharing that information using digital technology and ubiquitous communications is the most recent development. Recent developments in collecting, recording, analysing and sharing relevant data using digital technology and communications have resulted in the emergence of maritime informatics.

The basic need for access to vital maritime information is very old indeed. Early civilisations were all fundamentally based on and located near natural water. Water was needed for gathering food, hunting and agriculture, and for most of human history, water was by far the most effective mode of transport of people and goods. The location of practically all major cities at river mouths, large lakes and oceans bears witness to the fact that water was the prerequisite for living, trade and war. In all of human history, water has been connecting people rather than separating them.

From the earliest of times, seafarers' knowledge of how to navigate rivers and oceans must have been acquired through learning-by-doing and, once learned, passed down by word of mouth and demonstration from generation to generation, from seafarer to seafarer. Among that information, knowledge about the depth of the sea, seasonal variations, weather threats and the hazards that lie below the surface was and continues to be the most fundamental requirements for effective maritime operations and trade.

R. Ward (✉)
Pymble, NSW, Australia
e-mail: robert.ward1@gmail.com

N. Bjørn-Andersen
Copenhagen Business School, Copenhagen, Denmark
e-mail: nba.digi@cbs.dk

M. Lind et al. (eds.), *Maritime Informatics*, Progress in IS,
https://doi.org/10.1007/978-3-030-50892-0_1

It is known that mariners have measured water depth in support of navigation as far back as 1800 BCE and probably much earlier, as indicated by the dating of models of sailing ships recovered from Egyptian tombs.[1] Key to making this information useful is to know what are the hazards, where they are located and the safe passages around them.

Until the sixteenth century, the main utility of water was for human subsistence and agriculture. There were of course early sea explorers like Leif Eriksson, Marco Polo and Zheng He, but it was not until the time of the great explorations heralded by Columbus in 1492 and followed by many others like Vasco da Gama and Ferdinand Magellan that the whole world became "internationalised".

The Netherlands is a particularly interesting case of a geographical region exploiting the oceans for trade in order to grow economically. Originally called "Les Pays Bas" (low lands) by the French and Spanish, the region became an economic powerhouse, based on the opportunity for seafaring trade after being freed from the rule of the Spanish throne at the time of the Habsburg King Philip II of Spain. The wealth created is visible today in the beautiful architecture from that period.

It is also interesting to observe how the position as the leading country in the Western hemisphere changed almost every hundred years to a large extent due to the superiority of naval forces. In the 1500s, it was the Spanish/Portuguese dominating. However, the Anglo-Spanish war 1585–1604, which was mainly a naval war, resulted after many encounters in the defeat of the Spanish Armada by the British, and this ended the Spanish supremacy. This left room for the Dutch as described above, who became the leading nation in Europe in the 1600s. In the 1700s, the French were the leading nation until the end of the Napoleonic wars, where the supremacy of the British naval forces made it possible for Britain to "rule the waves" in the 1800s. Finally, after the First World War, Britain had lost its superiority on the open seas and left the role as the leading nation in the Western hemisphere to the USA in the 1900s. For more than 500 years, shipping, trade and military power based on superior fleets has played an enormous role.

Two types of information are necessary to navigate the sea effectively, a reliable account of the location of the ship and reliable maps of the sea and coast that indicate all the hazards to shipping.

Location of the ship out of sight of land was particularly problematic, since one needed to know position both in terms of latitude and longitude. With regard to latitude, as far back as we can record, seafarers have used the stars. The observation of the North Star, the Southern Cross or the height of the Sun at noon makes it possible to determine latitude.

However, measuring longitudinal position was for centuries a huge challenge, and leading seafaring nations like Spain, Portugal, Netherlands and Britain offered significant prizes to those who could provide solutions. The most effective were the offers made by the British Board of Longitude established in 1714, which lasted more than one century. Eventually, by the mid-eighteenth century, the ability to

---

[1] https://www.metmuseum.org/en/art/collection/search/544214

confidently determine longitude at sea was achieved through the perfection of the marine chronometer, in particular made possible through the work over 45 years of John Harrison (Sobel 1995). During the second half of the twentieth century, various radio-based positioning systems made the determination of position ever more accurate. Finally, these were surpassed by the global navigation satellite system (GNSS), which by 2020 provides mariners with their position to a typical accuracy of 2–3 m under good conditions.

The second very important source of information for seafarers is from maps and nautical charts. No one knows when the first map representation was created. The earliest cartographic representation known, dated as between 2000 and 1500 BCE, is the village plan of Bedolina incised on a rock face in Camonica Valley in northern Italy (Lloris 1972, pp. 121–158). The earliest portable map is one inscribed on a small clay tablet from near Babylon, Mesopotamia, now Iraq, dated from approximately 3800 BCE. The earliest nautical charts, none of which showed much detail, are the Portolan charts of the thirteenth century, which were navigational charts compiled by Italians, probably in Genoa, where a school of marine cartography had been established. The charts were subsequently supplemented by portolan pilot guides that provided navigators with written guidance for navigation into unknown waters (Campbell 2002).

The introduction of printing techniques in the mid-1450s considerably facilitated the reproduction of nautical charts, which until then were copied by hand. In the late 1790s, the invention of lithography offered a cheaper alternative. Printed charts then became more readily available to mariners from their national hydrographic offices. Further steps were taken with the development of plastics and zinc printing plates in the 1950s, and the advent of computer-based processes from the 1980s provides the digital nautical chart of today.

Prince Henry "the Navigator" of Portugal, although neither a sailor nor a navigator, was the sponsor of many exploratory sea voyages, particularly to the west coast of Africa, and founded the first school for navigation in the fifteenth century. In this school, people were trained in navigation, map-making and the scientific methodology that underpins the concept of systematic surveying. Thus, systematic acquisition of hydrographic data became a part of the exploration of new territories and trade areas. But for a time, nations, such as Portugal, withheld their important hydrographic and charting information from competing exploring and trading nations for economic and military advantage as well as for territorial gain (Beding 2016, p. 106). In those times, a seaman's geographic knowledge meant power and advantage to those that knew; so, knowledge was generally not on display to share.

However, this attitude began to change by the eighteenth century. Regular and catastrophic losses through shipwreck meant that the centralised capture and subsequent compilation of hydrographic data acquired by ships to make nautical charts became an obvious necessity, and the first national hydrographic offices came into being to provide mariners all that was known in the way of hydrographic data and information. It is estimated that during the Napoleonic wars, the British Royal

Navy lost twice as many men through shipwreck, drowning and fire than were killed in action (White 2011).

In 1720, France created the first official national hydrographic office. This was followed by the Government of England in 1795, of Spain in 1797 and several other nations in the following centuries. Today, there are national hydrographic offices in more than 90 countries producing nautical charts and supporting information.[2] Almost all of them now provide this information both in printed and in digital form. The world's larger ships engaged on international voyages are now obliged to use digital rather than paper charts for navigation (*International Convention for the Safety of Life at Sea (SOLAS)* Chapter V, Regulation 19).[3]

With the advent of national hydrographic offices, ship owners were encouraged to file records of safe voyages and to share this information with the relevant administrative bodies to facilitate safe passage for other ships bound by the same routes and destinations. The International Hydrographic Organization (IHO),[4] established in 1921, is the intergovernmental organisation that ensures the global standardisation of nautical charts and related hydrographic information. Under the auspices of the IHO and through the international agreements made in the International Maritime Organization (IMO) (*International Convention for the Safety of Life at Sea (SOLAS)*, Chapter V, Regulations 4, 9, 28 and 31), coastal states are obliged to identify shipping hazards and to update the affected nautical charts accordingly. Regular iceberg reporting is required, and information on buoyage and navigation lights are promulgated in a standardised manner. General information on tides, waves and currents derived from ships' logs and reports were included in official *sailing directions* from France as early as 1763. This is an early example of data sharing for a common and ultimately mutual benefit.

Similar to the handling of beneficial navigational information, which has moved from being treated as exclusive knowledge to being made more readily accessible to all those that could benefit, the sharing of information related to trade and trading schedules has also become more common—albeit only relatively recently. Other than for ships engaged on regular, scheduled routes, it is only recently that the arrival and departure times for ships and even their destinations have been made known widely. This became common practice, when, as a measure for improving collision avoidance, the automatic reporting of a ship's position and details, including its destination, was made mandatory by the IMO in 2002 for most ships through the fitting of an automatic identification system (AIS). In 2008, a regime of long-range identification and tracking (LRIT) was also introduced by the IMO to ensure a thorough tracking system for ships across the world. As a result, the whereabouts, progress and destination of ships became much more accessible through electronic and largely automatic means.

---

[2] www.iho.int, retrieved September 2019.

[3] http://www.imo.org/en/About/Conventions/ListOfConventions/Pages/International-Convention-for-the-Safety-of-Life-at-Sea-(SOLAS)-1974.aspx

[4] https://iho.int/uploads/user/pubs/misc/M-10_2019_EN.pdf

The remote monitoring of engines and equipment is another recent development that relies on digitalisation and informatics. Remote monitoring now occurs in about one in ten ships. It is said to deliver savings in service costs of anything from 10% to 30% when measured against traditional preventive maintenance (Latarche 2017).

These and other recent informatics developments have well and truly exposed the possibilities and benefits of sharing an ever-increasing range of information concerning the operations of ships. In the last decade, the IMO, supported by the IHO and its successful work with the digitalisation of chart and chart-related information, has promoted the concept of e-Navigation. This involves the digital sharing of relevant information between ships and relevant shore-based organisations to improve the efficient and safe passage of ships from port to port.

The ongoing EU-sponsored Sea Traffic Management (STM)[5] project seeks to achieve better overall decisions resulting in increased efficiency and improved safety in the maritime industry. Its vision is a world where all the information needed is at the fingertips of the decision-maker, wherever they might be, and updated in real time. Ideally, no data are entered manually. Data are collected from various data sources as digital data streams to ensure their timeliness. The STM project is an important example of the growing interest and the implementation of maritime informatics.

The shore-side maritime infrastructure is being re-formed along similar lines through digitalisation. Most of the large bulk and container shipping lines are now pursuing ways to collect information systematically from all those involved in their processes, in order to optimise processes and minimise the use of resources around port operations.

For ports, the Port Collaborative Decision Making (PortCDM) concept, which was validated from 2015 to 2018 as part of the STM project, seeks to optimise the port call process by encouraging digital data sharing between all the different actors involved so that they share a common situational awareness. According to PortCDM, all parties involved in a port call should generate standardised digital timestamps that describe the time and progress of their various component activities that they are involved in, especially reporting status changes. These data are shared in near real time with others in the maritime transportation chain, thereby enabling other actors to revise or adjust any dependent plans as necessary.

Another initiative in the maritime digital data exchange framework is the Single Window concept that allows parties involved in trade and transport to lodge standardised information and documents with a single-entry point to fulfil all import, export and transit-related regulatory requirements. The EU Reporting Formalities Directive (RFD) in force since 2015 simplifies and harmonises the administrative procedures applied to maritime transport through National Single Windows for reporting formalities from ships arriving in and/or departing from ports. The RFD is planned to be superseded by the European Maritime Single Window environment (EMSWe) that it is currently expected to apply from 2025.

---

[5]For a more detailed description, see https://www.stmvalidation.eu/

Maritime informatics is all about providing the *what*, the *where* and the *when* concerning matters of vital interest to those involved in maritime activities and who have a legitimate reason to know. It can cover all types of information including the support of an increase in the efficiency, safety and ecological sustainability of the world's shipping industry.

To do this successfully in a straightforward, timely, reliable and trustworthy way has taken a long time. There have been progressive improvements over the centuries in obtaining information, for example, improved navigational information and most recently the details of ships' loading plans and the tracking of shipping containers.

The willingness to share information has improved too. Acknowledging that the actions of one player in the maritime transportation chain are likely to have a trickle-down effect for others provides an incentive to share relevant data for mutual benefit rather than acting in isolation and suffering the consequences of being reactive to information that others have withheld until the last possible moment.

Pinpointing and tracking the location associated with information has also improved, particularly through the now almost ubiquitous access to cheap, reliable global satellite-based positioning. This is intrinsically tied to the ability to provide precise and unambiguous timestamps for the data events that are being captured digitally in real time.

However, by far the biggest improvement has occurred as a result of the so-called digital revolution that provides the ability to collect, store, manage, analyse and make information available using digital technology. This in turn has changed society from the first two eras of being an agricultural and then an industrial society into a post-industrial society which is now being given titles such as the information society, digital society or new media society.

American mathematician Claude E. Shannon, a 32-year-old researcher at Bell Laboratories, published a landmark paper in 1948 proposing that information could be quantitatively encoded as a series of ones and zeroes. Shannon showed how all information media, from telephone to radio to television, could be transmitted digitally without error using this single building block.

Central to the digital revolution was the mass production and widespread use of digital logic, MOSFETs (MOS transistors) and integrated circuit (IC) chips and their derived technologies, including computers, microprocessors, digital cellular phones and the Internet (Debjani 2014). The sweeping changes brought about by accessible digital computing and communication technology during (and after) the latter half of the twentieth century transformed traditional production and business techniques.

The digital revolution moved the hitherto analogue technology into a digital format. By doing this, it became possible to make copies that are identical to the original. In digital communications, for example, repeater hardware is now available to amplify a digital signal and pass it on without loss of information in the signal. Of particular importance to informatics and access to information is the ability to move easily the digital information between media and to access or distribute it remotely.

Growth in the amount of data that can be stored and handled and the speed with which it can be processed and distributed has been particularly spectacular in the last two decades. Computer processing power continues to increase—albeit at rates less than the 20 or so years when Moore's Law predicting computer processing speeds doubling every 2 years prevailed (Bentley 2018). In 2010 the estimate of the world's digital data holding was about 1 zettabyte (ZB), by 2018 it was 33 ZB, and by 2025 it is estimated to be at least 175 ZB.[6]

The network speeds and capacity to handle the growth in digital data have also grown impressively to meet the ever-growing demand to transfer data. The world's average for download speed over fixed broadband increased 37.4% from 46.48 Mbps in July 2018 to 63.85 Mbps in July 2019. In the same very short time span of 1 year, the mean upload speed over fixed broadband increased 48.9% from 22.52 Mbps to 33.53 Mbps (McKetta 2019).

The recent advances in telecommunications and digital technology now mean that data and information from all parts of the maritime transportation chain can be collected, analysed and distributed among those with the need to know. This is helping to improve existing methods and practices and, in some cases, even led to innovative new ones. It is providing both economic and environmental benefits through the analysis of recorded activities, the monitoring of current events and the use of data analytics to predict likely future outcomes. All these topics and more are covered in greater detail in the subsequent chapters of this book.

The era for maritime informatics to thrive has well and truly arrived.

References

Beding, S. A. (2016). *The Christopher Columbus encyclopedia*. Springer. ISBN: 1349125733.
Bentley, P. (2018, December 3). The end of Moore's Law: What happens next? *Science Focus*. Retrieved from https://www.sciencefocus.com/future-technology/when-the-chips-are-down/
Campbell, T. (2002). Map history/history of cartography: The gateway to the subject.
Debjani, R. (2014). Cinema in the age of digital revolution. *International Journal of Interdisciplinary and Multidisciplinary Studies (IJIMS), 1*(4), 107–111.
Latarche, M. (2017, May 10). The pros and cons of remote monitoring on ship. *ShipInsight*. Retrieved from https://shipinsight.com/articles/the-pros-and-cons-of-remote-monitoring-on-ship
Lloris, M. B. (1972). *Los grabados rupestres de Bedolina (Valcamonica)* (Vol. VIII). Centro camuno di studi preistorici.
McKetta, I. (2019). *In-depth analysis of changes in world internet performance using the speedtest global index*. Retrieved from https://www.speedtest.net/insights/blog/global-index-2019-internet-report/
Sobel, D. (1995). *Longitude: The true story of a lone genius who solved the greatest scientific problem of his time*. New York: Walker. ISBN: 0802713122 (hc).
White, M. (2011). *Statistics of wars, oppressions and atrocities of the nineteenth century (the 1800s)*. (Last modified March).

---

[6] www.datanami.com/2018/11/27/global-datasphere-to-hit-175-zettabytes-by-2025-idc-says

Shipping: A Self-Organising Ecosystem

Richard T. Watson (iD)**, Mikael Lind** (iD)**, Nik Delmeire** (iD)**,
and Fernando Liesa** (iD)

1 The Sharing Economy

The sharing economy is celebrated as a phenomenon of information and communications technology (ICT) and a networked society (e.g., Hamari, Sjöklint, & Ukkonen, 2016). Technology, such as online platforms, have simplified the sharing of goods and services and created entities such Uber and AirBnB. This exuberant embrace of the shiny new has overlooked an old, established, and more important sharing economy—the maritime industry—one of the world's largest and longest-lived sharing economies. Ports have operated as a sharing ecosystem for millennia. Anchorages, berths, and cargo handling capacity have been pooled for thousands of years, because in most cases it makes little economic sense for a ship owner to own all the resources required to move a cargo safely and efficiently between ports. It is extremely difficult to effectively manage the utilisation of a wide span of resources located in different countries, and it is more effective to have distributed

R. T. Watson (✉)
University of Georgia, Athens, GA, USA
e-mail: rwatson@terry.uga.edu

M. Lind
Research Institutes of Sweden (RISE) and Chalmers University of Technology, Gothenburg, Sweden
e-mail: mikael@realsearchers.com

N. Delmeire
European Inland Waterway Transport, Brussels, Belgium
e-mail: n.delmeire@inlandwaterwaytransport.eu

F. Liesa
ETP-Alice, Brussels, Belgium
e-mail: fliesa@etp-alice.eu

M. Lind et al. (eds.), *Maritime Informatics*, Progress in IS,
https://doi.org/10.1007/978-3-030-50892-0_2

ownership. If there were a better solution, market forces would have fashioned it over time. While ownership of a port's resources can be spread across multiple parties, collectively a port requires the resources necessary to meet the needs of visiting ships. A major challenge for all concerned in a port visit is to connect these resources seamlessly in the right sequence for high levels of resource efficiency for all involved parties. While the ship's agent was, and still is in many cases, the information and communication hub of the maritime sharing economy to ensure integration of these shared resources to service a port call, developments such as the Physical Internet[1] (Economist, 2006) could be transformational (see Voorspuij & Becha, 2020; Becha, Schroeder, Voorspuij, Frazier, & Lind, 2020).

Life on earth is characterised by increasing levels of complexity both in the natural and built environments. Simple single-cell life evolved into manifold ecosystems capable of supporting life in some of the globe's harshest settings. Over millennia, humans have created a complex network of economic structures and relationships that have increasingly produced more complex products and services. Trade was one of the earliest of these complex structures because it had to deal with distance, navigation, and differences in language and culture to exploit the principle of comparative advantage (Ricardo, 1817).

Today, the global shipping industry's complexity arises from several features. First, there are multiple diverse autonomous stakeholders operating in a competitive global market. Second, there are both international and sovereign state rules and regulations governing shipping. Third, there are many various and dynamic interactions between participants from different cultures, often speaking different languages. Fourth, the industry is simultaneously under adaptive pressure to digitise and reduce carbon emissions. Thus, it can be readily classified as a complex adaptive system (CAS) (Holland, 1995, p. 20; Caschili & Medda, 2012). In particular, as we show in this chapter, it is a self-organising ecosystem (SOE).

1.1 Why an Ecosystem?

When humans settled in the Fertile Crescent of the Middle East about 11,000 years ago, they set in motion a capital creation system that is the progenitor of our current life style (Watson, 2019). They were able to convert the propitious natural capital of the area (cereal crops and domesticable animals) (Diamond, 1997) into other forms of capital. They also created economic structures for capital creation, namely, hierarchies and markets. We see hierarchies in the command and control structures of kingdoms and farms. Trading, an early form of a market, is at least 8000 years old (Bernstein, 2008).

Capital is a durable and transforming factor of production resulting from prior capital investments (Dean & Kretschmer, 2007). An economy, and its component

---

[1] For recent thinking, see https://www.youtube.com/watch?v=O-8OQZYqNi4

structures (such as hierarchies and ecosystems), is a capital creation system that generates capital through capital conversion. This conversion of capital from one form to another to create more capital is the foundation of all economies, irrespective of their political or technological structure. A country or an organisation's capability for capital conversion creates for it a distinctive market position. The maldistribution of wealth illustrates the varying facility of nations and economic structures to create capital. The earth's current natural, social, and built environments are the result of tens of thousands of years of capital creation.

Organisations of all forms and purpose are in the business of capital creation. Universities concentrate on creating human (graduates) and organisational (knowledge and intellectual property) capital. Religions produce social (the community of believers) and symbolic (prestige and authority) capital. Government agencies fund economic (e.g., through highways) and organisational (e.g., via regulation of electronic communication) capital, for example, which in turn provide critical capital for other organisations to incorporate in their capital creation processes.

The capacity to convert and create capital is not constant. The firm that requires more capital than its competitors to produce goods or services receives less profit, and it will likely disappear unless it can soon match or exceed its competitors' skills. For the last five or six decades, information systems have been the major driver of productivity improvement (Stiroh, 2002). They have been the agent for raising capital conversion capabilities. The underlying technology that spawns information systems is ever evolving, and its innovative deployment changes the nature of capital conversion.

There are six foundational types of capital (Table 1). Natural capital was the seed capital for the birth of human civilisation and continues to support capital creation (e.g., agriculture, fishing, logging, and mining). In shipping, natural capital, such as open waters and protected bays, are needed for the capital creation process.

An organisation is a capital conversion and creation system (see Fig. 1). For example, it might borrow funds (economic capital) to retain engineers (human

Table 1 Capital typology (Watson, 2019)

Capital	Definition
Natural	Natural resources, living systems, and ecosystem services
Economic	Financial, physical, and manufactured resources
Human	Skills, knowledge, and abilities of an individual that can be used to generate income or other useful outputs
Organisational	Institutionalised knowledge and codified experience stored in databases, routines, patents, manuals, structures, etc.; essentially, the knowledge, skills, and information that stays behind when an organisation's people go home at night
Social	The ability of an individual or group to benefit from their social connections; includes structural, cognitive, and relational dimensions
Symbolic	The amount of honour or prestige possessed within a given social structure; includes aspects such as reputation, legitimacy, authority, status, and rank

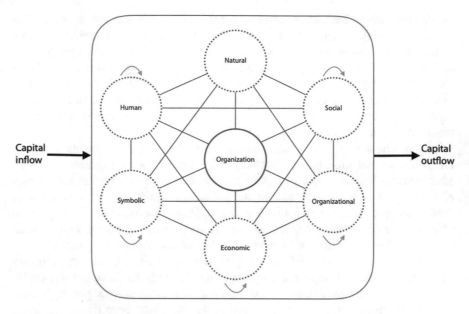

Fig. 1 The organisation as a capital conversion and creation system (Watson, 2019)

capital) to develop a product (organisational capital) for sale (economic capital). An economy's capital conversion mechanisms (e.g., firms, governments, universities), except for failed states, collectively generate more output than input capital and contribute to long-run economic growth and social progress. New technologies, such as 3D printing, and phenomenon, such as digitisation, are opportunities for changing the methods of capital creation and uplifting capital creation productivity. The Web, for example, galvanised new capital creation mechanisms that added significantly to society's capital. In a competitive economy, those whose capital conversion rates below market leaders will likely soon fail. Consequently, firms need to be continually scanning the environment for new technologies and procedures that enable them to rejigger their capital creation system for greater efficiency and effectiveness.

The maritime ecosystem is a capital creation process. It creates capital by moving products from the producer to consumer, the same function performed by early traders. The economic value of a product increases the closer it gets to the final consumer. Each stage of the shipping industry is designed to fulfil this purpose. This value, however, is only realised when a product is purchased at a price that enables competitive returns to all involved in its manufacturing, shipping, and storage at various stages. Now that we have established that the purpose of the shipping ecosystem is to create economic capital, we can question why it is an ecosystem.

In the long run, an organisation must use its capital more productively than its competitors. In the case of a shipping company, it makes a major investment in a ship and then seeks to recoup this investment based on the cash flow difference, in gross terms, between cargo fees and operational costs.[2] It can gain a competitive advantage by having the fastest port turnaround time so that it needs to invest in fewer ships. Alternatively, it might invest in energy efficient ships and practices to reduce operational costs.

Galvanised by the Brundtland (1987) report and the evidential multiple impacts of global change, many increasingly recognise the importance of natural capital to the successful operation of the global capital creation system. Natural capital is the ultimate source of all energy, including the food we eat. The shipping industry relies on natural capital, the world's waterways, to conduct its business. Preserving and restoring natural capital requires society to improve energy efficiency and capital productivity (Watson, 2019). For the shipping industry, this includes actions such as just-in-time arrival, to conserve fuel, and raising equipment utilisation so more is done with less. For example, reducing ship turnaround times across many ports will mean less ships are built and operated, with less impact on our natural capital.

Circumstances and regulations change. For example, if the IMO mandates a speed reduction to decrease greenhouse gas emissions, then every shipping company will likely find its capital productivity lowered because it requires more ships to handle the same volume of cargo because voyages take longer, though operational costs will be lowered. Provided such mandates are enforced fairly, then all are affected, but the competitive advantage of the capital productivity leader does not change. Analysing the financial implications of such industry wide changes and determining new operating parameters, such as cargo pricing, is a role for Maritime Informatics.

Each stakeholder has a specific productivity bias, and in an SOE, there can be conflicts among these goals. For example, a cargo owner typically wants to minimise payment time, and any lengthening of voyage time, such as ship speed reduction or port delays, extends the payment period and reduces ROI. Speedy conversion of capital from one form to another is everyone's goal, but goal conflicts or regulatory requirements can impede this conversion. Prior to the implementation of any major change in the shipping SEO, there should be an analysis of the financial implications for each of the affected stakeholders. Maritime Informatics should aim to produce tools and models that facilitate such an analysis.

2 What Economic Organisational Problems Does an Ecosystem Solve?

In the twentieth century, clarifying the distinction between hierarchies and markets (Coase, 1937), and their origins (O. E. Williamson, 1979), was considered a breakthrough in economic thinking, for which Coase and Williamson were both awarded the Nobel prize in Economics. However, hierarchies and markets are not

---

[2]See Forcellati et al. (2020) for a detail discussion of financial analysis methods.

the only structures for wealth creation. The ecosystem is an additional form (Iansiti & Levien, 2004), and the community is a fourth structure for capital creation (Watson et al., 2005).

Electronic networks enable the various capital generating structures to interact in multiple and diverse ways to create capital building ecosystems. The net-enabled organisation (Straub & Watson, 2001) has and is transforming the creation of capital (Goodwin, 2015). For example, the launch of the Apple Watch was accompanied by the release of over 3500 apps for it,[3] something Apple could not have managed within its hierarchical confines. Instead, it relied on the many coders competing to sell their creations via the App Store market. Hierarchies have become very dependent on ecosystems to create value around their core products and extend their reach, and ecosystems are arising to compete with hierarchies. Airbnb, for example, competes with every hotel, from the large global chain to the local inn, by matching properties and travellers.

In a dynamic competitive environment, adaptation is a central problem for many organisation (Tadelis & Williamson, 2012) and reflects similar thinking by influential economists (Hayek, 1945) and organisational theorists (Barnard, 1938). However, Hayek sees markets as the mechanism for adaptation, whereas Barnard views adaptation as the result of the deliberative managerial action embedded in a hierarchy. Both markets and hierarchies are designs for addressing adaptation of the capital creation system, but they are not the only possibilities.

Ecosystems (Moore, 2006; P. J. Williamson & De Meyer, 2012), also sometimes called networks (Jarillo, 1988; Uzzi, 1996), are an additional form of economic structure to handle adaptation in complex environments. An ecosystem is a set of relationships among different organisations that interact with varying degrees of an arm's length relationship typically found in a market.

Ecosystems are not just a phenomenon of recent times. The shipping industry, for example, has operated as an ecosystem for thousands of years (Fayle, 2013) whereas ICT has spawned the *coordinated ecosystem* (P. J. Williamson & De Meyer, 2012), where there is a keystone partner (e.g., Apple) (Iansiti & Levien, 2004) harmonising the activities of the other members of the ecosystem. Coordinated ecosystems are like supra-hierarchies that adapt as directed by the keystone's leadership. They are possibly the most significant change in organisational structure since the industrial revolution (Moore, 2006). In the case of a coordinated ecosystem, the relationships among the different members are well-established, might last years, and they can interact many times during a day. Consequently, a coordinated ecosystem will typically invest in specific systems to support close integration among and between members.

In contrast, shipping is an example of a *self-organising ecosystem* (SOE), because there is no single keystone and control is distributed (Caschili & Medda, 2012). Ships, collectively, are a keystone, because the system does not exist without ships, but no particular ship, or shipping company, is sufficiently powerful to determine

---

[3] http://techcrunch.com/2015/04/27/apple-boasts-over-3500-apple-watch-apps-already-available/

the activities of the various members. SOEs are collections of loosely coupled organisations and individual that adapt in response to the environmental forces they experience or anticipate. For example, a shipping and tug company might have a contract for towing services for one or more ports, and it is through such service contracts and ad hoc transactions that the SEO operates.

SOEs are more like naturally occurring CASs because adaptation is not centrally directed but organic. Their adaptation, sensibly, is most influenced by the keystone players because the ecosystem exists to serve them. An SOE can also include markets, other SOEs, and coordinated ecosystems. For instance, a port's administration coordinates operations within the port, which is an ecosystem within the larger SOE. Thus, an SOE can differ from a coordinated ecosystem in several ways: relationships might be ad hoc (such as existing only during a port visit), might occur infrequently, and might not warrant specific investments to support coordination because of the short-lived nature of relationships. Shipping is characterised by episodic tight coupling, which we further examine in the next section.

In summary, ecosystems arise because of complexity costs. In the case of coordinated ecosystems, hierarchies reduce complexity costs by forming ecosystems to work collectively and synchronously with other hierarchies. In contrast, in an SOE, autonomous organisations emerge to meet the various needs of a central, but not coordinating, entity. SOEs emerge when the timing and spatiality of interaction is varied or episodic, whereas coordinated ecosystems feature routine tight coupling. Ecosystems continually adapt to provide the most economic current solution for meeting the overriding goal, such as moving cargo from producer to consumer.

2.1 Episodic Tight Coupling and Data Sharing

Coupling requires two or more entities to coordinate their actions for an episode or an event, which is known as *episodic tight coupling* (Watson & Boudreau, 2011), and it is helpful in understanding a distinctive characteristic of SOEs.

Earlier we proclaimed that shipping is perhaps the original sharing economy, because assets, such as cargo handling equipment, have been shared for centuries. Sharing of physical assets requires coordination through the exchange of data about those episodes, defined by time and location, when the asset owner and the would-be customer can Tightly Couple their actions, such as unloading a ship. The form of data sharing might be passive, such as a ferry's timetable indicating when it will depart, or active, such as when a passenger gets an electronic message about the expected departure of a ferry. In the case of a ferry, the passenger has no say in when episodic coupling occurs. Coupling is dictated by the ferry company. As a result, the ferry company needs minimal visibility about the intended actions of the various passengers, other than they have purchased a ticket. A passenger missing a ferry is most unlikely to affect the episodic tight coupling between the other passengers and the ferry.

Alternatively, the various parties can negotiate the occurrence of episodic coupling. Thus, a ship's captain and pilot service can decide jointly when and where they will meet so the pilot can board and guide the ship into the harbour. Coupling is negotiated by the ship's captain, or someone acting on behalf of the shipping company (such as a shipping agent), and the pilot service. If one party fails to appear at the designated place at the specified time, then episodic tight coupling fails, and one-party wastes time and resource waiting for the other. Ideally, a port visit is a series of successful episodic tight couplings.

Episodes can be regular (such as the arrival of a car ferry serving two ports on a published schedule) or irregular (the use of a tug to berth a cargo ship). Tight coupling means that two or more parties must closely synchronise their activities, such as discovering the specific time and place when a car ferry departs or setting a specific time and place for linesmen to be in place to fasten a ship at its assigned berth). The ability to learn what other entities are doing across a wide variety of timelines, from seconds to years away, enables people and enterprises in a highly decoupled society to coordinate their actions. It will often be the case that dominant activities, such as container ship visits, will get resource precedence over others, such as a bulk cargo ship visit, because ports learn what increases their competitiveness.

When two entities want to coordinate their actions for an episode or an event, they must share data about their intentions, such as when a certain waypoint is expected to be reached. Episodic tight coupling is dependent on data sharing relevant to the episode. Furthermore, it is important to recognise that data can reveal competitive information. For example, a ship might not want to reveal details of its cargo size and contents to competitors. Thus, data sharing needs to be controlled by the data owner and turned on or off for specific data streams to particular parties at the owner's discretion. The default will typically be non-sharing, unless there is a legal requirement, such as with AIS. A ship owner has an incentive to share data when it is to their advantage. During a port visit, a ship should share those data that ensure all parties associated with episodic tight coupling during the visit have all the required resources available when and where required. Because a port visit requires multiple such couplings, their coordination is often complex and can easily become more complex when one of the couplings is delayed or extends beyond the planned completion time.

The members of an SOE synchronise their actions through episodic tight coupling. The efficiency of such coupling is determined by data sharing prior to each coupling. A key purpose of Maritime Informatics is to advance digitisation of the maritime ecosystem.

3   The Components of a Digitised Self-Organising Ecosystem

From an informatics perspective, a digitised SEO is a network of objects, where each object provides application programming interfaces (APIs) that facilitate its sending and receipt of electronic messages in the form of standardised digital data streams (DDSs) (see Fig. 2).

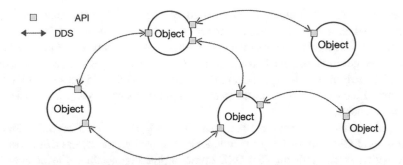

Fig. 2 Components of a self-organising ecosystem

The term object is derived from the object-oriented (OO) design principles of computer science, which are commonly used for designing software (Booch, 1991) and organisational systems (Taylor, 1992). OO is a general design principle (Pancake, 1995) and as such is applicable to the design of organisations and ecosystems (Watson, 2019; Watson, Zinkhan, & Pitt, 2004). In the shipping domain, an object is an organisation with a memory (e.g., database) and business logic (e.g., software), which enable it to transact with other organisations.

For an informatics specialist, an API is a set of definitions and protocols for building and integrating software. APIs are essential for data sharing as they define the way to locate and request data from a public or private third party. When an API is private, the protocol must include the required authentication data. Think of an API as a managed electronic gateway to an organisation's data. It can manage what data are accessed by whom and when.

Efficient data sharing across many potential ecosystem objects or partners requires a digital data exchange standard based on a language for data exchange, such as XML. In the case of the shipping industry, because there can be typically 25 actors involved in a port visit (Lind, Watson, Bergmann, Haraldson, & Maldonano, 2017), there is a need for an industry message standard within and across ports, such as the International Association of Aids to Navigation and Lighthouse Authorities (IALA)'s S-211 standard for the support of Port Collaborative Decision Making (PortCDM).[4] A ship can send an S-211 compliant message to the appropriate API of a pilot service specifying its estimated time of arrival (ETA) at a specific location. The pilot service might then respond using S-211 to the ship's API confirming the time and place of their meeting.

A DDS is the continuous digital encoding and transmission of data generated as events occur or states change (Pigni, Piccoli, & Watson, 2016). Automatic Identification System (AIS)[5] is an example of a DDS. When organisations put their

---

[4]https://www.iala-aism.org/technical/data-modelling/iala-s-200-development-status/s-211/
[5]http://www.imo.org/en/OurWork/Safety/Navigation/Pages/AIS.aspx

assets online, they can create an associated API and DSS so that their ecosystem partners, and authorised others, can continually monitor an asset's status.

Efficient data sharing across many potential ecosystem partners requires a digital data exchange standard based on a language for data exchange, such as XML. In the case of the shipping industry, because there can be typically 25 actors involved in a port visit (Lind et al., 2017), there is a need for an industry message standard within and across ports.

Digitising an ecosystem requires that the various involved parties adopt the principles of OO design. They can reconceive themselves as objects that coordinate their activities through an API/DSS combination that enables the standardised digital exchange of messages to facilitate episodic tight coupling.

4   Maritime Informatics for a Self-Organising Ecosystem

The Internet of Things (IoT) will enable realisation of the promise of the Physical Internet. It will mean that the shipping industry can fully digitise its assets so that each resource emits a time-stamped digital data stream of its current status, which is core to seamless integration of physical resources. AIS turned ships into digital data streams, and this innovation can be extended to all assets. For example, a berth could stream its status so that a port is not reliant on a person entering data about a berth's status, but rather optical imaging, for example, recognises what ships are berthed where, every few minutes.

When ports are extensively digitised, then there are opportunities for the real-time merging and processing of the digital data streams by advanced data analytics tools and machine learning applications to identify the scope of various improvements in port handling efficiencies. New levels of situational awareness for all actors are possible. Most importantly, the real-time processing of digital data streams permits *look-now* situational awareness to optimise current activities. Data analytics can support *look-ahead* situational awareness to explore likely port operations in the immediate future if involved actors (such as shipping companies and terminal operators) publish their plans, and it can support *look-back* situational awareness to learn how to improve operations by identifying efficiency shortcomings revealed by historical data.

5   Innovation in SOEs

Innovation within an SOE is particularly challenging because there is usually no central player who can direct change. Occasionally, there can interventions, such as the IMO dictating the adoption of AIS or the introduction of a new data standard, such as S-211. Rather, innovation starts with one organisation and then is adopted by others in an ad hoc fashion as they recognise its potential to improve their capital productivity. An examination of the adoption of containers by the shipping industry, gives us a closer understanding of innovation in an SOE (Watson, Lind, & Haraldson, 2017).

5.1 Physical Innovation

The first load of 58 containers, shipped on a converted tanker from Newark, New Jersey, to Houston, Texas, in 1956, initiated a set of complementary innovations that drove freight costs to the point of irrelevance (Levinson, 2010). The container was the seed innovation that gestated my other related innovations that first transformed the shipping of goods by sea and then later by land and air (Fig. 3).

This created a requirement for other innovations that were necessary to make containerisation efficient: (1) establishment of an industry standard to support transhipment, (2) design of an efficient means of stowing containers on a ship, and (3) development of equipment for efficient loading and unloading.

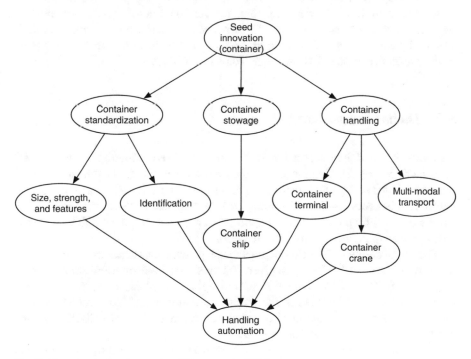

Fig. 3 Containerisation innovation (Watson et al., 2017)

ISO 668,[6] standards for the size and construction of containers to enable global interoperability and meet IMO requirements were introduced in 1968. IMO also appointed the Bureau International des Containers et du Transport Intermodal (BIC)[7] to uniquely identify and register each container. Standards for construction and identification in an SEO generally require an industry body to manage their design and introduction.

In the case of innovations that do not require industry wide agreement, competitive invention is the usual practice. Thus, various parties designed and operationally tested designs for the new class of dedicated container ships, developed equipment for loading and unloading a ship's containers and handling them within a port, and created the container terminal as a new port facility. Standardisation was also the gateway to efficiency gains in multi-model transport. The railroad and trucking industries developed equipment and procedures for the efficient movement of containers between modes and automated container handling within and across modes.

Development and adoption of these innovations would have been unlikely without ISO 668. An SOE needs industry-wide coordination mechanism for episodic tight coupling and cargo handling. Universal standards and practices enhance the operations of an SOE. In shipping, standards for containers have dramatically cut the cost of sea transport, so that "It is better to assume that moving goods is essentially costless than to assume that moving goods is an important component of the production process" (Glaeser & Kohlhase, 2004, p. 4).

5.2   Digital Innovation

AIS was the seed innovation for kickstarting digitised shipping. In 2000, IMO mandated that by 2005 all cargo ships above a certain gross tonnage and all passenger ships had to implement AIS. AIS generates a DDS about a vessel's state automatically every 3–10 s, depending on its speed. The DDS for individual ships can be detected by anyone with an appropriate receiver and made public since the data are open (e.g., www.marinetraffic.com).

The IMO defined 27 different types of top level messages that can be sent by a ship's onboard AIS transceiver (International Telecommunications Union (ITU), 2010). This laid a foundation for the digitisation of the maritime ecosystem by creating standardised DSSs for ships, the major asset. However, ecosystem digitisation is not complete until every asset can stream a standardised DDS and can be managed digitally as appropriate.

The availability of AIS data has since provided opportunities to use the digital data for several green innovations. Two examples are *green routing* (the determi-

---

[6]https://www.iso.org/standard/59673.html

[7]https://www.bic-code.org

nation or optimisation of the most energy efficient and safe distance for a voyage) (Kontovas, 2014) and *green steaming* (determination of the lowest operational speed during a voyage to arrive on schedule) (Watson, Holm, & Lind, 2015).

PortCDM (Lind, Haraldson, Karlsson, & Watson, 2015) established a new innovation branch by developing a message standard, S-211, and a conceptual foundation for data sharing within a port to improve coordination and synchronisation in pursuit of advancing port efficiency and reducing ship turnaround times. PortCDM looks like becoming the standard for realising the notion of the connected port, and it connects the environment within the port.

We can envisage a path of digital innovation over the next decade or so (see Fig. 4).

In late 2015, two leading communication companies signed an agreement to create the *connected ship*. Inmarsat and Ericsson plan to provide a managed cloud solution for ship-to-shore communication that will facilitate the sharing of cargo, logistics, and vessel operational data to improve the efficiency of the maritime supply chain.[8] By 2017, they had added additional partners.[9]

AIS streams current data about a ship's locations, but it does not indicate its future path. Since nearly all commercial shipping uses digital navigation systems to chart courses, a future path in digital format is available, and the RTZ format[10] supports exchange of these data to support digital ship-to-ship coordination, which is a critical safety concern when ships are passing or operating in congested or confined waters. Software can ensure that collisions are avoided and environmentally friendly routes followed.

Autonomous shipping is the penultimate next big innovation that we can foresee at this point.[11] An autonomous ship will require no crew and use less fuel, because of the removal of human-related facilities. Just like other autonomous vehicles, the unmanned ship will be reliant on DDSs to determine its speed and route. The ultimate goal is to create a sustainable and efficient transport system that enables the world to reap the benefits of trade while minimising carbon emissions. All aspects of transport must be sustainable. Containerisation created the model for driving down the costs of multimodal transport and digital innovations can drive down carbon emissions and costs to create efficient sustainable multimodal transport.

As with physical innovation, we see that digital innovation requires collaborative development of industry standards to create a foundation for efficient cooperation across the ecosystem. Once these guidelines are in place, innovators can exert their creativity and knowledge with the assurance that the entire maritime ecosystem is their potential market.

---

[8]http://www.inmarsat.com/news/transforming-the-future-of-the-connected-ship/

[9]http://emag.nauticexpo.com/article-long/ericssons-vision-of-connected-shipping/

[10]http://cirm.org/rtz/index.html

[11]https://www.digitaltrends.com/cool-tech/autonomous-ships-are-coming/

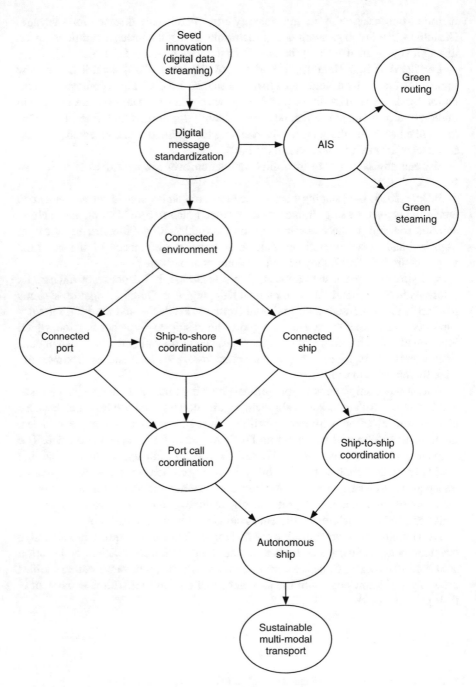

Fig. 4 Digital innovation in maritime shipping (Watson et al., 2017)

6   The Maritime Informatics Stack

It is common parlance in the Information Technology domain to talk of a stack, which is discrete layers of connected hardware and/or software that communicate with their immediate neighbour layers via standard messages. The seven-layer Open System Interconnection (OSI) model is an example of a stack (Yemini, 1993). Stacks simplify the design and development of complex solutions because they divide it into parts, and provided the parts follow data exchange standards, they can talk to their immediate neighbours above and below them in the stack. The efficiency of Maritime Informatics might be improved by developing an appropriate stack.

Morphology, the study of the form of things (OED), is the investigation of the structural relationships among the different parts of an object of interest (Álvarez & Ritchey, 2015), such as an MI stack. Its original use was to study the interrelationship among existing structural relationships in areas such as anatomy, geology, and botany. Zwicky (1969) generalised the concept by applying it to the design of the structural relationships of new systems. He asserted that general morphological analysis (GMA) was applicable to any sociotechnical problem where the factors of consideration (e.g., social, technical, and ecological) created a complex or difficult task beyond the capabilities of one or a small group of experts. The first step of GMA is to identify and define the primary components. Based on our analysis, we propose a seven-layer model for advancing Maritime Informatics (Table 2).

Table 2 Layers of the Maritime Informatics stack

	Layer	Design questions
1	Global	Industry-wide international standards for digital data exchange within the maritime sector
2	Regional/national	Design and implementation of policies to support a digitally enhanced maritime sector and a regional/national excellence in Maritime Informatics
3	Structural	Design of structures, such as markets, organisations, and partnerships to implement efficiently frequently occurring maritime decisions in a digital era. These include shipping conferences and long-term contracts between shipping companies and terminal operators
4	Decision support	Design of decision processes and associated actions to implement frequently occurring maritime industry decisions
5	Data stream mining	Design of techniques for dynamic identification of model parameters to support real-time decision processes in the maritime sector
6	Data exchange	Design of message formats and content for data exchange between elements of a maritime system to support decision-making
7	Data communications	Design of data communication networks to capture data for decision making at the appropriate level of granularity and frequency and transmit control commands to connected maritime equipment and devices

Each layer should communicate with its immediate neighbour(s) in a standardised method to enable a high degree of interdependence between layers. This division of decision rights enables developments in each layer to occur relatively independently provided communication protocols with adjacent layers are obeyed. In the case of an SOE, we might well see the most activity in the structural layer as the ecosystem dynamically adjusts to changing trade patterns and environmental threats. As a result, bordering layers might also have to adjust to accommodate these perturbations. Thus, an MI stack should not cement relationships in place but rather be designed to support a resilient ecosystem with some separation among distinct activities to confine the effects of a major change to one layer and allow the others to gradually adjust as required.

6.1   Global

Four hundred years ago, the Dutch jurist Hugo Grotius defined the notion of *Mare Liberum* and introduced to the concept of the 'Freedom of the Seas' (Russ & Zeller, 2003). He proclaimed that the sea was international territory and should be free to all nations for seaborne trade. Since then, this concept has underpinned the global maritime industry. Now, AIS has made the ocean a digital territory, and the free exchange of its standardised messages has improved the shipping industry's safety and provides massive volumes of data for analysis to improve efficiency. Further standards development, such as those promoted or developed by the IMO, the IHO, IALA,[12] and others will create a foundation for extending the scope of Maritime Informatics.

6.2   Regional/National

Regions or nations can develop policies that promote Maritime Informatics. For example, the EU's MonaLisa and Sea Traffic Management[13] projects have promoted the development of PortCDM, green routing, and green steaming, which are examples of Maritime Informatics in action. A country that invokes policies to encourage Maritime Informatics research and education has the opportunity to build a new service industry for a global market. A country or a region can also pass laws to enable new structural arrangements, such as with the SESAME (Secure, Efficient, and Safe maritime traffic Management in the Straits of Malacca and Singapore) testbeds in the Malacca straits.[14]

---

[12]https://www.iala-aism.org/about-iala/

[13]https://www.stmvalidation.eu

[14]http://sesamesolution2.org/about.html

6.3   Structural

The structural layer is concerned with the design of organisations that take advantage of new data sources to create new industry services. Markets, in particular, are dependent on information, and Maritime Informatics will create new data sources. For example, if berth booking data were standardised across a region or internationally, it would enable a market for berth space to emerge. Thus, when a ship is delayed, the captain could sell their berth space to another captain who has a need for a berth at the same time and location as the booking. Markets, generally acknowledged as the best way to allocate scarce resources, can only emerge when information about an asset can be standardised.

An SOE can self-organise in the form of alliances and partnerships to enhance the capital productivity and efficiency of the members. In the case of the maritime sector, shipping conferences are a major structural feature that some assert reduce competition because they are oligopolistic (Sys, 2009). Digitisation will likely make it easier and less costly to form such relationships.

6.4   Decision Support

There are some decisions that are common across many actors in the shipping industry, such as the optimum route between two ports. One goal of Maritime Informatics is to build tools to support efficient decision processes and associated actions for frequently occurring maritime industry decisions. In particular, there is a need to develop spatial-temporal analytics and visualisation because decisions in the shipping industry often relate to a location and time.

6.5   Data Stream Mining

Digital data streams, real-time encoding of events or state changes, can be mined as the data are received to identify critical changes that need immediate action. Collison detection and avoidance are candidates for data stream mining. The identification of anomalous ship behaviour is another application for data stream mining. Maritime Informatics should aim to develop spatial-temporal data stream mining procedures to support such uses.

6.6 Data Exchange

Decision support and data stream mining are dependent on the generation of standards compliant data. Imagine how useless AIS data would be if there were 50 or more different national standards. Defining standards for data exchange across the industry is a necessary first step for unlocking the gains from data analytics. Such standards need to be developed and adopted for every facet of the industry, including cargo and personnel reporting to port and customs administrations and the recording of financial transactions for port services.

6.7 Data Communications

Data communication networks are necessary for data exchange. Fortunately, there are worldwide standards, such as TCP/IP and LTE, upon which industry specific platforms can be built, such as the Maritime Connectivity Platform (MCP),[15] which is a communication framework for efficient, secure, reliable, and seamless electronic information exchange among maritime stakeholders. The MCP provides open source maritime-focused registries for identity, services, and messaging. Data exchange standards could be built on top of the MCP.

7 Conclusion

Defining the shipping industry as a self-organising ecosystem does not mean that it is a static collection of highly independent operators. Rather, it is an evolving cluster of changing alliances and ownership structures that emerge, often over a long period, to generate higher levels of capital productivity. For instance, some shipping lines have purchased terminals because owning a combination of vessels and terminals potentially provides a higher return on investment than purely operating ships.

While this chapter focuses on sea shipping, other transport systems, such as inland navigation and road, are also self-organising ecosystems. However, their degree of control over self-organising might be constrained because they often operate within national or regional boundaries, where governments are more able to exercise their sovereign powers than on the open seas.

Digitisation and Maritime Informatics create opportunities for new structures for capital creation. It can enable alliances to achieve high levels of coordination through real-time data sharing. It can give early adopters an advantage that they can extend by acquiring the laggards and giving them state-of-the-art information systems. This means shipping ecosystem members need to be vigilant and continually

---

[15] https://maritimeconnectivity.net

search for opportunities to use digitisation to bundle shipping services in new ways to provide superior customer service.

References

Álvarez, A., & Ritchey, T. (2015). Applications of general morphological analysis. *Acta Morphologica Generalis, 4*(1).

Barnard, C. I. (1938). *The functions of the executive.* Cambridge, MA: Harvard University Press. ISBN: 0674328035.

Becha, H., Schroeder, M., Voorspuij, J., Frazier, T., & Lind, M. (2020). Global data exchange standards: The basis for future smart container digital services. In M. Lind, M. P. Michaelides, R. Ward, & R. T. Watson (Eds.), *Maritime informatics.* Heidelberg: Springer.

Bernstein, W. J. (2008). *A splendid exchange: How trade shaped the world.* New York, NY: Atlantic Monthly Press.

Booch, G. (1991). *Object oriented design with applications.* Redwood City, CA: Benjamin/Cummings.

Brundtland, G. H. (1987). *Our common future: Report of the World Commission on environment and development.* Oxford: Oxford University Press.

Caschili, S., & Medda, F. R. (2012). A review of the maritime container shipping industry as a complex adaptive system. *Interdisciplinary Description of Complex Systems, 10*(1), 1–15.

Coase, R. (1937). The nature of the firm. *Economica, 4*, 386–405.

Dean, A., & Kretschmer, M. (2007). Can ideas be capital? Factors of production in the postindustrial economy: A review and critique. *The Academy of Management Review, 32*(2), 573–594.

Diamond, J. M. (1997). *Guns, germs, and steel: The fates of human societies.* New York: W.W. Norton.

Economist. (2006). The physical internet. *The Economist.* Retrieved from https://www.economist.com/special-report/2006/06/17/the-physical-internet.

Fayle, C. E. (2013). *A short history of the world's shipping industry.* Routledge. ISBN: 1136606386.

Forcellati, C. L., Georgeson, C., Lind, M., Singh, S., Sjöberger, C., & Woxenius, J. (2020). Support for financial decision making. In M. Lind, M. P. Michaelides, R. Ward, & R. T. Watson (Eds.), *Maritime informatics.* Heidelberg: Springer.

Glaeser, E. L., & Kohlhase, J. E. (2004). Cities, regions and the decline of transport costs*. *Papers in Regional Science, 83*(1), 197–228.

Goodwin, T. (2015). The battle is for the customer interface. *Technocrunch.* Retrieved from http://techcrunch.com/2015/03/03/in-the-age-of-disintermediation-the-battle-is-all-for-the-customer-interface/#.gk4jly:ynOm.

Hamari, J., Sjöklint, M., & Ukkonen, A. (2016). The sharing economy: Why people participate in collaborative consumption. *Journal of the Association for Information Science and Technology, 67*(9), 2047–2059.

Hayek, F. A. (1945). The use of knowledge in society. *The American Economic Review, 35*(4), 519–530.

Holland, J. H. (1995). *Hidden order: How adaptation builds complexity.* Basic Books. ISBN: 0201442302.

Iansiti, M., & Levien, R. (2004). *The keystone advantage: What the new dynamics of business ecosystems mean for strategy, innovation, and sustainability.* Cambridge, MA: Harvard Business Press. ISBN: 1591393078.

International Telecommunications Union (ITU). (2010). *Recommendation 1371-4,"Technical characteristics for an automatic identification system using time-division multiple access in the VHF maritime mobile band".* Retrieved from http://www.itu.int/rec/R-REC-M.1371-4-201004-S/en.

Jarillo, J. C. (1988). On strategic networks. *Strategic Management Journal, 9*(1), 31–41.

Kontovas, C. A. (2014). The green ship routing and scheduling problem (GSRSP): A conceptual approach. *Transportation Research Part D: Transport and Environment, 31*, 61–69.

Levinson, M. (2010). *The box: How the shipping container made the world smaller and the world economy bigger*. Princeton University Press. ISBN: 1400828589.

Lind, M., Haraldson, S., Karlsson, M., & Watson, R. T. (2015). *Port collaborative decision making – closing the loop in sea traffic management*. Paper presented at the 14th International Conference on Computer Applications and Information Technology in the Maritime Industries, Ulrichshusen, Germany.

Lind, M., Watson, R. T., Bergmann, M., Haraldson, S., & Maldonano, J. (2017, Autumn). Empowering mega-terminals with gigabytes. *Port Technology, 104*–106.

Moore, J. F. (2006). Business ecosystems and the view from the firm. *Antitrust Bulletin, 51*, 31–75.

Pancake, C. M. (1995). The promise and cost of object technology: A five-year forecast. *Communications of the ACM, 38*(10), 33–49.

Pigni, F., Piccoli, G., & Watson, R. T. (2016). Digital Data Streams: Creating value from the real-time flow of big data. *California Management Review, 57*(4), 5–25. https://doi.org/10.1525/cmr.2016.58.3.5.

Ricardo, D. (1817). *On the principles of political economy and taxation*. London: G. Bell & Sons.

Russ, G. R., & Zeller, D. C. (2003). From mare liberum to mare reservarum. *Marine Policy, 27*(1), 75–78.

Stiroh, K. J. (2002). Information technology and the US productivity revival: What do the industry data say? *American Economic Review, 92*(5), 1559–1576.

Straub, D. W., & Watson, R. T. (2001). Transformational issues in researching IS and net-enabled organizations. *Information Systems Research, 12*(4), 337–345.

Sys, C. (2009). Is the container liner shipping industry an oligopoly? *Transport Policy, 16*(5), 259–270.

Tadelis, S., & Williamson, O. E. (2012). Transaction cost economics. In R. Gibbons & J. Roberts (Eds.), *Handbook of organizational economics*. Princeton, NJ: Princeton University Press.

Taylor, D. A. (1992). *Object-oriented information systems*. New York, NY: Wiley.

Uzzi, B. (1996). The sources and consequences of embeddedness for the economic performance of organizations: The network effect. *American Sociological Review, 61*, 674–698.

Voorspuij, J., & Becha, H. (2020). Digitalisation in maritime regional and global supply chains. In M. Lind, M. P. Michaelides, R. Ward, & R. T. Watson (Eds.), *Maritime informatics*. Heidelberg: Springer.

Watson, R. T. (2019). *Capital, systems and objects: The foundation and future of organizations*. Athens, GA: eGreen Press.

Watson, R. T., & Boudreau, M.-C. (2011). *Energy informatics*. Athens, GA: Green ePress.

Watson, R. T., Boudreau, M., Greiner, M., Wynn, D., York, P., & Gul, R. (2005). Governance and global communities. *Journal of International Management, 11*(2), 125–142. https://doi.org/10.1016/j.intman.2005.03.006.

Watson, R. T., Holm, H., & Lind, M. (2015). *Green steaming: A methodology for estimating carbon emissions avoided*. Paper presented at the International Conference on Information Systems.

Watson, R. T., Lind, M., & Haraldson, S. (2017). *Physical and digital innovation in shipping: Seeding, standardizing, and sequencing*. Paper presented at the HICSS. https://scholarspace.manoa.hawaii.edu/handle/10125/41741.

Watson, R. T., Zinkhan, G. M., & Pitt, L. F. (2004). Object orientation: A tool for enterprise design. *California Management Review, 46*(4), 89–110.

Williamson, O. E. (1979). Transaction-cost economics: The governance of contractual relations. *Journal of Law and Economics, 22*(2), 233–261.

Williamson, P. J., & De Meyer, A. (2012). Ecosystem advantage: How to successfully harness the power of partners. *California Management Review, 55*(1), 24–46.

Yemini, Y. (1993). The OSI network management model. *IEEE Communication Surveys and Tutorials, 3*(1), 20–29.

Zwicky, F. (1969). Discovery, invention, research through the morphological approach.

The Necessity of Standards for Maritime Informatics in Ship Operations

Dominic Thomas (iD) **and Steven O'Malley** (iD)

1 Introduction

In this age of high-speed technology creation and proprietary systems driving competitive advantage, why are standards needed for developing maritime informatics? Indeed, standards take time to develop, because they require consensus on shared expectations and norms. They often communicate core technical requirements and solutions, the opposite approach from proprietary alternatives based on trade secrets. We present a developing case study focused on creating a global standard for software monitoring and maintenance on larger vessels to address the increasing digital transformation of shipboard equipment. In the process, we provide insight into what standards do and how organisations in the industry can and should participate. The data reported here derive from first-person experience gathered by the authors who are organising and participating in this process as ISO TC 8 members. As a result, this chapter is more of a direct report on an important aspect of technological advancement in shipping that will shape maritime informatics, because it and projects like it will define the information architecture aboard ships for the next 30 or more years.

The maritime industry is the oldest industry-focused group in the International Standards Organization (ISO), housed in Technical Committee (TC) 8 founded in 1947 (ISO, 2020b). Shortly thereafter, the industry worked with the nascent United Nations at the UN Maritime Conference of 1948 to found the International Maritime Organization (IMO), which came into effect in 1958 (Britannica, 2020). At the time, many countries had a clear understanding that cooperation and coordination

D. Thomas (✉)
Kennesaw State University, Kennesaw, GA, USA
e-mail: dominic.thomas@kennesaw.edu

S. O'Malley
Analytical Innovative Solutions, LLC, Atlanta, GA, USA

© The Editor(s) (if applicable) and The Author(s), under exclusive licence
to Springer Nature Switzerland AG 2021
M. Lind et al. (eds.), *Maritime Informatics*, Progress in IS,
https://doi.org/10.1007/978-3-030-50892-0_3

33

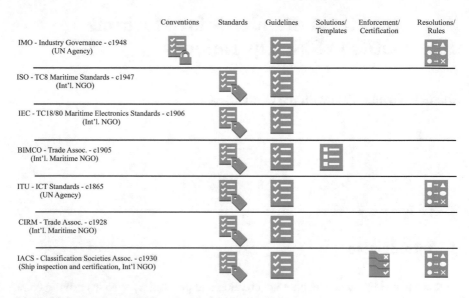

Fig. 1 Major maritime standards organisations and their roles

would be required in order to develop safe shipping, global partnerships, and
shared commercial interests. These two organisations provided a means and remain
centres for coordinating the shipping industry, with one of their principle tools
being developing and publishing agreements that enable cooperation. They are
both international organisations. While IMO is part of the UN and draws its
membership therein, ISO membership is comprised of official national standards
organisations from countries around the world. A primary difference among them
is that IMO creates conventions and sets industry technical requirements (Fig. 1).
Conventions are international treaties, which signatory countries agree to follow
and enforce. The conventions establish policy and set rules to be followed by the
industry. These conventions may be revised by resolutions. A recent example is IMO
Resolution MEPC.320(74) that lowered the maximum sulphur content allowable
in marine fuels to 0.5% unless a ship was equipped with emission scrubbers.
ISO creates standards, which get implemented in industry but have no specific
force of law or penalties for non-compliance on their own. ISO standards may
however be referenced by national or international regulations or be incorporated
into business contracts as a requirement, allowing for indirect enforcement. ISO
TC 8 has been designated as ISO's representative to the IMO, and the ISO has
been granted consultative status with IMO as a non-governmental international
organisation. Interestingly, both organisations follow an almost identical process
of standards-making based on committees and volunteer participation. A third type
of industry-shaping mechanism is a policy or procedure guideline. Both IMO and
ISO and all of the subsequently mentioned organisations in this chapter produce

guidelines from time to time. Guidelines are non-binding, and they need not have specific mechanisms for assessing compliance with requirements unlike standards.

In addition to IMO and ISO, several notable non-governmental industry associations and organisations have large standardisation roles within the maritime informatics domain. These include the Baltic and International Maritime Council (BIMCO), Comite´ International Radio-Maritime (CIRM), the International Telecommunications Union (ITU), and the International Electrotechnical Commission (IEC). BIMCO is the largest single industry association dedicated to policy and guidance in the shipping industry with over 1900 company members from 120 countries (BIMCO, 2020). BIMCO convenes various meetings annually and provides members with guidance on contracting, insurance, and other critical issues facing shipowners. CIRM was formed by maritime manufacturers in 1928, restarted after 1948, became an accredited IMO consultant by 1961, and a liaison organisation to ISO and IEC as well. The latter two pre-date the IMO and ISO TC 8 and have formal groups focused on maritime technologies that collaborate within this space to issue guidelines and standards. In the case of the IEC, for example, subgroups TC 18 and TC 80 both focus on aspects of the shipping and maritime industry. While efforts existed prior to World War II, shipping and maritime industry standards work has increased subsequent to 1945 as globalisation has increased. For any given guideline or standard, there are typically revisions over time. Many different organisations might participate. With the advent of standards organisations, participation has become easier to coordinate.

ITU, founded in 1865, is the oldest of these organisations, created to standardise telecommunications protocols. It exists today as a UN agency founded by way of an international convention. It released the earliest guidance on ship-to-ship communications but with only a limited uptake; this led to major issues when ships were in distress. The International Convention for the Safety of Life at Sea (SOLAS) was created in response to the failure of these early efforts and was one of the first major commercial shipping conventions. It was created subsequent to the sinking of RMS Titanic in 1912 by an ad hoc group of leaders from 14 countries at a specially called conference completed in 1914. Its modernised format was accomplished by the IMO in 1960 with amendments in 1974. At present, 164 countries are signatories to the SOLAS convention representing at least 99% of all international ship traffic and then drop globally, effectively making SOLAS an international law governing, among other things, message transfer and response protocols in cases of maritime emergency and related safety events.

From an informatics point of view, the SOLAS convention requires various transmission protocols as well as message content as laid out in SOLAS chapters IV and V. These chapters are foundations for systems such as the Global Maritime Distress Safety System (GMDSS) as they enable coordinated production, installation, and interaction among GMDSS devices on the many ships at sea at any given time. While conventions carry the force of international law, they require ratification and more coordination than standards (Ponte & Gibbon, 2005). As a result, convention theory as explained by Ponte and Gibbon indicates that as the need for industry innovation speeds up and increases, the usefulness of more agile regulatory mechanisms like standards will increase. Meanwhile, the theory also indicates that larger companies will attempt to embed their specific capabilities and needs into the standards to make themselves more dominant in their sectors. Thus, the process of standards creation will require careful attention to ensure that finalised texts are optimised for the overall well-being of any given industry.

2   The Need for an ISO Software Governance Standard Aboard Ships

The international fleet of commercial ships exceeding 400 gross tonnage currently lies around 55,000 vessels (Wagner, 2020). Among the commercial shipowners and operators, Maersk is the largest in the cargo sector (the largest sector within global shipping) with approximately 350 ships providing about 18% of the global capacity (Alphaliner, 2020). As a result, this industry has fairly low consolidation as measured by a Herfindahl-Hirschman Index even when applied to the more consolidated container shipping sub-sector (Drewry, 2018). Low consolidation means no specific service provider has overwhelming power to determine technical standards. Shipbuilders are even less consolidated (Christian Steidl, Daniel, & Yildiran, 2018). In the subsector of shipping engines and navigation equipment, for example, the market is slightly more consolidated (Marine Propulsion Engine Market | Growth, Statistics, Industry Forecast 2019-2024, 2019). What this means for developing a standard is that there are many different solutions being created and implemented. No major player in the ecosystem can unilaterally define the platform standards for interoperability and data exchange. And, shipowners face a complex problem if they want to develop and deploy unified solutions to reduce the complexity of managing the many systems in their ships.

One might wonder what sorts of problems may arise aboard modern ships in relation to informatics, thereby driving the need for standards. Several short stories collected from industry reports and direct experience of the authors should suffice to illustrate five major problems maritime informatics can help address in conjunction with standards:

- Miscalculation
- Information asymmetry
- Confusion
- Wilful negligence
- Unintended consequences of computer systems integration

Beginning with miscalculation, consider the developing story of the USD300M vessel Golden Ray. On September 8, 2019, with over USD400M of luxury car cargo onboard, this roll-on, roll-off car carrier ship capsized leaving the port of Brunswick, GA, USA (Bacon, 2019). A ship of this nature has an automated ballast management system (a few large ships have manual ballast systems) to calculate ship stability based on its design, cargo loaded, fuel (bunkers) load, and water ballast to ensure it does not capsize. The ship's captain receives an alarm if there is a stability issue. However, a ship operating in protected waters (such as a port) does not need the same degree of stability as a ship operating out at sea. Furthermore, due to the water depth being less in port than at sea, crews sometimes wait to fill the ship's ballast tanks until they reach open seas so as not to exceed draft restrictions and to keep muddy water and marine animals from being drawn into the tanks. In these cases, the alarm must therefore be overlooked if the system is active, because it could not account for such factors at present levels of system automation. In the case of the Golden Ray, the ship was in protected waters, and there were clear skies and calm conditions. The US Coast Guard reported that the Golden Ray was making a turn before it capsized. Satellite data recorded by the ship-tracking website Marine Traffic shows an inbound ship was passing the Golden Ray around the same time it overturned. "If the ship was turning at a high enough speed, the Golden Ray may have listed just enough to set off a chain reaction of events that ultimately pulled the ship down," according to Brandon Taravella, a professor at the University of New Orleans' school for naval architecture and marine engineering (Bynum, 2019). In the case of the Golden Ray, unless the accident investigation process uncovers a material failure or unsecured cargo, the cause will probably be attributed to a miscalculation or inability to take all of the relevant factors into account when navigating, resulting in a USD1B+ salvage operation (including cutting up and removing the ship, which cannot be righted due to its grounding in a shallow part of the shipping channel). It follows that the relevant stability data interfaces should be easier to read and monitor for critical navigation information like this. Predictive algorithms could detect differing conditions that would make a given approach extra risky using real-time sensing, traffic, and weather information.

Another common problem is information asymmetry. Fires aboard cargo ships are more frequent than would be expected (Dupin, 2019). For this reason, cargo ships have fire suppression systems that can, for example, flood a cargo bay with carbon dioxide when a fire is detected. Unfortunately, some fires are harder to extinguish, particularly chemical fires. The MSC Flaminia, a Swiss ocean cargo carrier, experienced such a fire after leaving the port of New Orleans in July 2012. The incident killed three crew members and caused a loss of thousands of loaded cargo containers. The cause of the fire was reported to be containerised shipments of a chemical, divinylbenzene (DVB), which after being exposed to high ambient temperatures began autopolymerising causing an explosion and fire. The New York District Court ruled that the fault for the casualty lies with the freight forwarder (Stolt) and the manufacturer (Deltech) of a potentially hazardous cargo. The ruling stated that "Stolt and Deltech are incorrect in their positions that generalised knowledge MSC possessed regarding DVB's heat sensitive nature eliminates Stolt's responsibility to effectively warn MSC about known dangers for these particular ISO containers (out of thousands upon thousands of cargo containers it was carrying) or shifts the burden to MSC ... MSC's actions were consistent with industry practice, its prior practices, and the reasonable (versus unreasonable) expectations of the parties" ("Court", 2018).

While shippers are required to declare what they are shipping, it is difficult for ocean carriers, especially those operating containerships, to verify if the declarations are correct due to the vast number of shipments involved. While containers can be scanned using non-intrusive inspection (NII) methodology such as gamma or X-rays, NII information is generally not shared with the ocean carriers. In addition, while NII can identify the shapes of cargo contained in a shipping container and density differences, it cannot detect generally the chemical composition of the cargo being shipped or if the product has begun to chemically react.

In the absence of specific information on any limitations or special precautions about the cargo being shipped in containers, an ocean carrier will load the containers to facilitate their unloading at destination. Often ships will call upon more than one port, so the containers destined for the first port would be placed so that they can be removed without the need to rearrange containers destined for later ports. Dangerous goods ("hazardous materials") require additional documentation and often require special handling and placement on the ship. For these reasons, ocean carriers will normally charge extra for shipping dangerous goods. Unfortunately, while the international rules for shipping dangerous goods [i.e. the IMO International Maritime Dangerous Goods Code (IMDG)[1]] are very good, there are situations where all the necessary information needed to properly ship a particular dangerous good may not be conveyed to all those that need to see or consider it in the supply chain. In addition, the extra charge discussed previously can incentivise some people to hide the fact that the contents are dangerous goods from time to time to save money. In cases such as these, the information asymmetry can lead to huge losses ("Court", 2018) that could have been avoided if a sensor had picked up the nature of the cargo or load management software had predicted the hazardous load due to prior similar shipments and the nature of cargo often sent by that client. Further, algorithms could lower the cost of customising the individual container loading, which could remove or reduce the cost barrier to disclosure.

A third type of problem is confusion, distinguished from miscalculation as a problem faced by crew members attempting to execute an order. The example here comes from an incident investigated by one of the authors directly, though similar incidents are not unusual (Press, 2002). Some years ago, a cargo ship came into harbour and was being loaded with containers. Suddenly after container loading operations had stopped, the ship listed and smashed into the cargo crane.

The crew claimed they were properly ballasting when it suddenly listed. Furthermore, the crew was certain that they had secured the pumps before evacuating the ship. The simple observation of attaching a pendulum to the side of the ship and seeing the shadow keep moving toward the dock indicated that the pumps were actually still running. This case illustrates that the crew must directly manage processes that can be complex. Ships can have multiple ballast tanks, which in turn must be loaded or unloaded in order. In this case the ship was righted after the accident by slowly adding water to the specific ballast tanks in a proper sequence.

---

[1] http://www.imo.org/en/Publications/IMDGCode/Pages/Default.aspx

This type of confusion due to non-integrated controls and little to no feedback leads to such incidents.

A fourth type of problem is wilful negligence. Among the most recent and notable example of this nature is the wrecking of the Carnival cruise ship Costa Concordia in January of 2012. In this case the captain claimed that he had taken the ship very close to the coastline for "commercial reasons" in a bid to please his passengers and those ashore. He rejected rumours that he had wanted to impress an accompanying companion, who was with him on the bridge. The captain was sentenced after a court found him guilty of manslaughter, causing a maritime accident, and abandoning ship ("Concordia skipper's sentence upheld", 2016). The route taken by the ship ran through an area with a shallow rock outcrop that ended up gashing the hull, triggering a series of events ultimately leading to the scrapping of the ship and costing over USD2B in damages. Remote sensing, as well as properly configured onboard navigation systems, can potentially geo-fence a ship and alert shore oversight when boundaries are exceeded.

Finally, unintended consequences of computer systems integration remind us that systems can interact in unexpected ways with bad results. In March 2019, the Viking Sky cruise ship lost engine power at sea. The Norwegian Maritime Authority (NMA) investigating the incident announced at a news conference that "low oil levels were the direct cause of the engine failure... sensors detected the low levels and automatically shut down the engines to prevent a breakdown. Although the amount of oil was relatively low, ... it was 'within set limits'...." "The heavy seas probably caused movements in the tanks so large that the supply to the lubricating oil pumps stopped. This triggered an alarm indicating a low level of lubrication oil, which in turn, shortly thereafter, caused an automatic shutdown of the engines" ("Nightmare at Sea: Viking Cruises faces class-action lawsuit after high-seas nightmare off Norway", 2019). As noted in the subsequent investigation, while the lubricating oil levels were relatively low, they were adequate. It appears the fault was that the sensor system used to measure the lubricating oil levels did not take into account any movement of the oil in the tanks due to turbulent seas and therefore generated a false low-level signal. The software programme upon receipt of the false low-level signal then executed an unnecessary engine shutdown sequence that in turn caused the ship to drift and come dangerously close to grounding on rocks. Subsequently, after many passengers were airlifted to safety, the ship's three other engines were safely restarted, and the ship was navigated to a port. However, the chain reaction shutdown was unexpected, and there was no way to double-check the logic as it was happening. Designers had not anticipated this set of conditions, and the results were disastrous.

These examples illustrate the central importance of standardised digital data exchange to ship safety. Maritime informatics needs to be concerned with onboard human-to-machine, machine-to-human, and machine-to-machine communication to advance safety at sea and in port. Additionally, it can analyse these data to improve ship performance. Recognising increasing problems, like those discussed, facing ships as well as the opportunity to use integrated, computerised systems to solve them, BIMCO undertook a project to define a standard for shipboard software maintenance in 2013 in cooperation with CIRM. Notable in this initial effort was the rationale:

> The industry has been living in a world of hardware. But software has been integrated into most physical equipment on the vessels, and the systems and procedures to manage the software has not kept up with technical developments, and it creates problems [Angus Frew, Secretary General and CEO at BIMCO]
>
> BIMCO has seen incidents, where ships for example, suffer complete blackouts, and malfunctions in radar and other related systems, as a result of unforeseen difficulties with a software update. (Rasmus Nord Jorgensen, 2017)

This first effort culminated in a guideline, which was released as an industry "standard" by the cooperating workgroup through BIMCO in December 2017. Development and pilot testing of the guideline included companies such as BP Shipping, Emarat Maritime, Furuno, Kongsberg Maritime, Maersk Line, MAN Diesel & Turbo, Radio Holland, and Sperry Marine. This guideline while a significant step forward would not support a determination of conformity, and as such its principal authors requested ISO to develop standards that could be used to implement all or parts of the guideline. In addition, they realised that compliance with its requirements would require far more companies to agree to a new cooperative ecosystem approach to periodic servicing and maintenance as well as equipment manufacturing. The largest manufacturers already had proprietary systems for software maintenance and reporting and could perhaps claim compliance, but the majority had not started on this type of work. Compliance for them would require quite a lot of redesign, and the guideline gave little technical guidance on what direction the data transfer protocols and packages should take. Thus, the likelihood of further proprietary systems increased, and the dream of using a standard to *standardise* in order to integrate and coordinate software maintenance remained distant after this effort. As members of the initial working group realised this problem following pilot tests, they decided they needed to make this guideline into an ISO standard so that it could have industry-wide effects and broad legitimacy across the globally dispersed industry.

3 Development of the ISO Standard and the Smart-Shipping Future

The ISO 24060 standard project ("Software Maintenance of Shipboard Equipment") was born early in 2018 with the Intermodal and Short-Sea Shipping subcommittee of ISO TC 8 (ISO, 2020a). The selection of ISO to house the standard was not accidental. Among the various potential organisations, ISO offers the benefit of being able to focus on a ship-wide standard because it does not share the history of separating the bridge and the rest-of-ship communities, unlike CIRM, ITU, and IEC. Additionally, its domain extends to the entire maritime stakeholder community including shipowners, manufacturers, government regulators, service organisations, port operators, etc. Committee members included working group members from the prior effort representing CIRM (manufacturers), BIMCO (shipowners), and some additional industry experts. Also, due to the nature of the ISO, the new committee project was advertised to the global standards community and drew interest from a larger global community including Asian organisations. Additionally, the chairman of the new effort recognised that the problem it faced was complex and technological from an information systems perspective and one that existing members were not experienced in handling. So, he sought assistance from those with skills in international industry technology ecosystems development. With this new team in place by May 2018, the group began assessing the state of the initial guideline and analysing how it could result in an enforceable ISO standard.

One of the first issues noted by the new committee was that existing information technology (IT) infrastructure aboard ships was unlikely to be consistent. Standards for shipboard networking such as ISO 16425:2013 or IEC 61162-1, -450, and -460 were rarely implemented in more than just single locations, such as on the bridge, and even when implemented did not seem to specify clear methods for inter-connection that would enable transmission of software maintenance data. Actual networking solutions for the rest of a ship at best included RS232 connections between proprietary systems, setup by individual manufacturers. Thus, a control or box on the bridge might have a screen on which software status could be displayed, but the ability to aggregate these messages into a single log as required in the emerging standard would have to be a manual process. Given that crews tend to be trained primarily for the jobs in hand and existing process requirements in their jobs are high, pilot testing had already shown that compliance with adding such a manual system would likely be very low in the long run. In effect, this effort to create a software maintenance standard would require an industry-wide movement toward smart shipping, ships in which devices are networked and able to safely and securely talk to each other, thereby enabling digital data stream processing and decision-making (Pigni, Piccoli, & Watson, 2016).

To illustrate the larger problem, ships currently have an IT infrastructure on the bridge comprising a variety of isolated boxes. A small percentage of ships have integrated navigation systems (INS) that connect some of these boxes and allow limited coordination but only on the bridge. However, equipment across the industry is increasingly becoming digitised and hosting updatable software. Some manufacturers and port authorities are already checking for software statuses and updates remotely, because out-of-status software can cause problems. For new ships, the International Association of Classification Societies (IACS), a technical advisor to IMO and the principle coordinator for official groups conducting ship inspections and certifying them as seaworthy around the world, recognised as early as 2006 that usage of computer systems aboard ships would be an issue beyond just the bridge. Their revised standard for On Board Use and Application of Computer Based Systems (IACS 2006 rev 2 2016) requires software quality procedures and documentation during construction and stipulates three categories of equipment based on criticality to ship operations. Unfortunately, the requirements are very general. According to interviews with current IACS members, at this point even during construction certification, their ability to truly assess software quality and status is very limited, because the number of devices spread about a ship has increased drastically in the past few years.

Figure 2 illustrates part of this problem. While it shows a design solution is an ongoing development in the standards process, imagine if all of the gateways and connection lines were not there. That is the present situation. Thus, current ships may have digitised equipment in the various categories, but to check if they are up to date, people have to physically visit the equipment in many cases and conduct a process that may require powering down the unit. Such processes take down systems and require ships to be in port and out of service for some of the time. Software problem diagnoses alone sometimes require individual service people from manufacturers to fly to a disabled ship from the other side of the world, further extending the out-of-service time.

As noted in Watson, Lind, Delmeire, and Liesa (2020), the shipping industry is a fragmented self-organising ecosystem. As illustrated in Fig. 2, many types of equipment are becoming digitised and software-operated, even down to pumps and sensors within water and safety systems. At the same time, without a specific technical solution that is at once clear and inspectable and at the same time flexible enough to accommodate fairly low-tech devices, such as pumps, a requirement to log and update software on all devices will be impossible to accomplish manually. And, manufacturers will not implement any solution that significantly increases the costs of their devices. The future of smart ships, ships with networking and the capacity to be automated and controlled or monitored from shore, has become a top future topic within TC 8, but without networking and data transfer standards, solutions for such future systems will be proprietary and fragmented. The broad range of manufacturers will not be able to coordinate their products into integrated cross-manufacturer systems, thus slowing down innovation.

By April 2020, ISO 24060 had been through three major revisions. What was becoming clear was that the software maintenance standard would have both procedural as well as technology requirements. For procedural requirements to gain industry buy-in, they would need to be formally accepted as technical requirements by an organisation such as IMO, where member states would vote on accepting them. Later, the technology designs could be added as the means to address the procedural requirements. As the group realised this strategic need, the standard got split into multiple pieces. The first focuses on getting the procedures recognised as a need by the IMO. The second focuses on describing how a Ship Software Logging System (SSLS) would work. Subsequent pieces focus on how compliant equipment would communicate and connect. This current staged approach offers a means to evolve the industry at a speed more likely to succeed.

Finding a pragmatic initial design for the SSLS remains a challenge without a settled solution. Perhaps this design can rely on IEC 61162-1. In that standard, internetworking via UDP packets includes a requirement that manufacturers of bridge equipment produce something called a VER message. This message indicates details about the equipment, including software, manufacturer, version, operational status, etc. Many bridge devices already integrate this capability, and it can be added at low cost and bridged from serial connections to Ethernet with existing devices

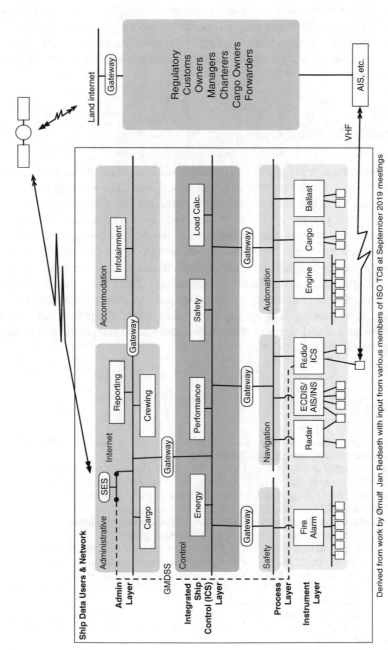

Fig. 2 Current systems and possible future shipboard network design

available on the market if needed. Small steps such as broadening the usage of this existing standard could lead to an effective industry transformation. Many will be needed just to enable automated software version logging aboard ships. Once logging is in place, a future step may be enabling remote updates and optimisation in systems involving devices from heterogeneous manufacturers. As this work is still in progress, we do not yet know how it will look at completion, but the future direction is clear.

4 Towards the Future

Global standards currently govern how ships are built, how ports operate, and how cargo is stored and transferred. Much recent work has focused on how to network within ships and between ships and ports, satellites, buoys, etc. with the understanding that the day is coming when ships' systems may be making more autonomous decisions, governed by software or remote operators. Still, the costs of integrating network technologies have slowed progress, and the lack of standards has led to poor interoperability. For maritime informatics, the implication is that data will soon become much more available for any number of analyses. In the meantime, the informatics and IS community can do a significant service within the industry by assisting in the process of designing these emerging standards to be effective at growing the future, smart-shipping ecosystem desired among shipowners, operators, consumers, and producers.

References

Alphaliner. (2020, February). *Top 100 shipping companies.* Retrieved from https://alphaliner.axsmarine.com/PublicTop100/index.php

Bacon, J. (2019, September 10). "It's perplexing." How did the Golden Ray ship capsize? Here's a look at possible answers. *USA TODAY.* Retrieved from https://www.usatoday.com/story/news/nation/2019/09/10/why-did-golden-ray-cargo-ship-capsize-possibilities/2272699001/

BIMCO. (2020). *BIMCO home.* Retrieved from https://www.bimco.org/

Britannica. (2020). *International Maritime Organization.* Encyclopedia Britannica. Retrieved from https://www.britannica.com/topic/International-Maritime-Organization

Bynum, R. (2019). Why did a ship the size of a 70-story building capsize in the Brunswick shipping channel? | 11alive.com. *11Alive News.* Retrieved from https://www.11alive.com/article/tech/science/why-did-ship-capsize-georgia/85-1ae68ea5-f007-4698-a03a-9cd9346e2d48

Concordia skipper's sentence upheld. (2016, May 31). *BBC News.* Retrieved from https://www.bbc.com/news/world-europe-36421474

Court: MSC Not Liable for Losses from MSC Flaminia Fatal Fire. (2018, September 14). *Offshore energy.* Retrieved from https://www.offshore-energy.biz/court-msc-not-liable-for-losses-from-msc-flaminia-fatal-fire/

Drewry. (2018, January 22). *Drewry: Container Market Still Competitive—Global Trade Magazine.* Retrieved from https://www.globaltrademag.com/drewry-container-market-still-competitive/

Dupin, C. (2019, March 2). Number of containership fires is 'shocking.' *FreightWaves*. Retrieved from https://www.freightwaves.com/news/number-of-containership-fires-is-shocking

ISO. (2020a). *ISO/AWI 24060*. ISO. Retrieved from https://www.iso.org/cms/render/live/en/sites/isoorg/contents/data/standard/07/76/77678.html

ISO. (2020b). *ISO/TC 8—Ships and marine technology*. ISO. Retrieved from https://www.iso.org/cms/render/live/en/sites/isoorg/contents/data/committee/04/57/45776.html

Marine Propulsion Engine Market | Growth, Statistics, Industry Forecast 2019-2024. (2019). Mordor Intelligence. Retrieved from https://www.mordorintelligence.com/industry-reports/marine-propulsion-engine-market

Nightmare at Sea: Viking Cruises faces class-action lawsuit after high-seas nightmare off Norway. (2019, March 9). *ABC News*. Retrieved from https://abcnews.go.com/International/viking-cruises-faces-class-action-lawsuit-high-seas/story?id=62926477

Pigni, F., Piccoli, G., & Watson, R. T. (2016). Digital data streams: Creating value from the real-time flow of big data. *California Management Review, 58*(3), 5–25. https://doi.org/10.1525/cmr.2016.58.3.5.

Ponte, S., & Gibbon, P. (2005). Quality standards, conventions and the governance of global value chains. *Economy and Society, 34*(1), 1–31. https://doi.org/10.1080/0308514042000329315.

Press, A. (2002, October 27). Weyco ship rights itself. *Longview Daily News*. Retrieved from https://tdn.com/business/local/weyco-ship-rights-itself/article_adfb829f-b31f-5241-851e-c4ed146f58fb.html

Rasmus Nord Jorgensen. (2017, December 14). BIMCO and CIRM propose software maintenance standard for shipping [Industry Association]. *News and Trends*. Retrieved from https://www.bimco.org/news/priority-news/20171214_software-maintenance

Steidl, C., Daniel, L., & Yildiran, C. (2018). *SHIPBUILDING MARKET DEVELOPMENTS Q2 2018* (Directorate for Science, Technology and Innovation (STI), p. 23) [Industry Analysis]. Organisation for Economic Co-operation and Development. Retrieved from https://www.oecd.org/sti/ind/shipbuilding-market-developments-Q2-2018.pdf

Wagner, I. (2020, February). *Global merchant fleet—Number of ships by type 2019*. Statista. Retrieved from https://www.statista.com/statistics/264024/number-of-merchant-ships-worldwide-by-type/

Watson, R. T., Lind, M., Delmeire, N., & Liesa, F. (2020). Shipping: A self-organising ecosystem. In M. Lind, M. P. Michaelides, R. Ward, & R. T. Watson (Eds.), *Maritime informatics*. Heidelberg: Springer.

The Port as a Set of Socio-technical Systems: A Multi-organisational View

Sandra Haraldson (ID)**, Mikael Lind** (ID)**, Stefan Breitenbach** (ID)**,
Juan Carlos Croston** (ID)**, Mathias Karlsson** (ID)**, and Gerald Hirt** (ID)

1 The Port as a Conglomerate

While we might think of a port as if it were an organisational entity, it is a conglomerate of different organisations acting within a certain geographical area, such as a harbour. Due to the geographical concentration of infrastructure and capabilities for delivering services to enable transhipments and supporting intermodal transfer, we commonly use the word port to describe this conglomerate. It is also possible that there exist ports within ports.

Ships as regular and episodic port visitors, to some extent, often need to use and share the same infrastructure, such as the waterways under the control of the port authority. Therefore, it is important that the various organisations within a port

S. Haraldson (✉) · M. Karlsson
Research Institutes of Sweden (RISE), Gothenburg, Sweden
e-mail: sandra@realsearchers.com; Mathias.Karlsson@ri.se

M. Lind
Research Institutes of Sweden (RISE) and Chalmers University of Technology, Gothenburg, Sweden
e-mail: mikael@realsearchers.com

S. Breitenbach
Port of Hamburg Marketing, Hamburg, Germany
e-mail: breitenbach@hafen-hamburg.de

J. C. Croston
Manzanillo International Terminal, Colón, Panama
e-mail: JuanCarlos.Croston@mitpan.com

G. Hirt
HVCC Hamburg Vessel Coordination Center, Hamburg, Germany
e-mail: hirt@hhla.de

© The Editor(s) (if applicable) and The Author(s), under exclusive licence
to Springer Nature Switzerland AG 2021
M. Lind et al. (eds.), *Maritime Informatics*, Progress in IS,
https://doi.org/10.1007/978-3-030-50892-0_4

47

do not act in isolation. Port actors are part of the port ecosystem defined by their respective roles in the planning and realisation of a port's value creation process. The port ecosystem is delimited by a shared common object of interest, which is to enable transhipment and intermodal transfer as efficiently and sustainably as possible as part of berth-to-berth sea transport and the larger multimodal transportation system. Importantly, ports are entry and exit points for worldwide trade and raw material supply linking the maritime trade dimension with other modes.

In international, regional, and local arenas, a lot of effort is placed on integrating ports into the larger transportation system, by connecting what happens at sea with that ashore. This has driven the need for ports to upgrade their capabilities to become information hubs as well as utilising different means for automation. The business landscape of port operations is also highly competitive. Nevertheless, we should not exclude the people factor, and we need understand that ports are socio-technical systems (Bostrom and Heinen 1977a, b).

To cater for alignment among the various actors involved in a port's operations, this chapter explores the foundations for viewing a port as a multi-organisational set of socio-technical systems.

2 Ports as Socio-technical Systems

Digital collaboration, electrical connectivity to ships, land vehicles and equipment, autonomous shipping and automated operations, port-city integration, digital control rooms and digital service towers, digitally twinned physical infrastructure such as bollards, digitally twinned waterways, and auto-mooring are all initiatives now high on the agenda for upgrading a port's operations to respond to the needs of its clients. These changes occurring in the maritime sector are designed to integrate a port's socio-technical systems into the inevitable changes occurring in the global transport system, as well as increasing its efficiency and ecological sustainability.

The most important property of system thinking is that a system is more than the sum of its parts, and these parts are interconnected into complex structures (Meadows 2008; Seiffert and Loch 2005). The basis of system thinking is thus seeing "wholes": investigating entire systems within a boundary, understanding their components, functions, and interconnections (Senge 1991).

Socio-technical refers to the interrelatedness of the *social* and *technical* aspects of an organisation. Socio-technical theory is founded on two main principles: that the interaction of social and technical factors creates the conditions for successful (or unsuccessful) organisational performance and that optimisation of each aspect alone (socio or technical) tends to increase not only the number of unpredictable, "un-designed" relationships but those relationships that are injurious to the system's performance. Therefore, socio-technical theory is about *joint optimisation* (Cooper and Foster 1971), that is, designing the social system and technical system in tandem so that they work together smoothly.

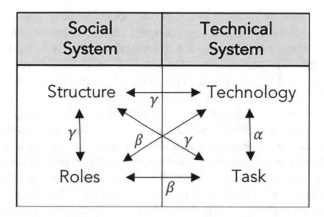

Fig. 1 Three levels of change in socio-technical systems (O'Hara et al. 1999)

Building upon O'Hara et al. (1999), the technical system includes the technology and the tasks performed to achieve organisational goals, while the social system includes structure and the roles assumed to comprise the social system. In the model depicted in Fig. 1, these four interacting elements and their inter-relations facilitating three types of change are illustrated. *Alpha* change is when a task is automated; *beta* change when roles and tasks are redesigned or transformed; and *gamma* change when structure, roles, and tasks are redesigned or transformed in a coordinated manner. For example, introducing enhanced interactions between fleet operation centres and port operators is an alpha change, as technology automates the interaction between the operators in the different domains. A beta level change could, for example, be when fleet operation centres conduct some of the tasks that historically were conducted by the ship's master, such as ordering a pilot. Enhanced digital interaction capabilities of a fleet operation centre could also create structural (gamma) change because of the improved ability to monitor and act upon the progress of a port call enabled by real-time data sharing resulting in a redistribution of roles and new tasks and, as a result, the restructuring of port relationships.

A port environment is social in the sense that it relies on people acting on behalf of organisations, collaborating with each other in patterns that are defined by the logic of agreed assignments and fulfilled. Each port is an ecosystem embedded in the maritime self-organising ecosystem (See Watson et al. 2020). On the technology side, we need to assess the value that technology contributes to the performance of a port ecosystem, both at the common organisational level and in providing individual support to multiple organisations.

The ongoing process of digitalisation and other technical upgrades are putting pressure on each of the actors engaged in maritime transport, including regulators, to upgrade their capabilities. At the same time, few out of the thousands of ports have the resources or capabilities to keep up to date with the latest developments. Most small to mid-size enterprises (SMEs) that are active in ports do not have the capability to push forward with innovations in the same way as state-owned terminal operators. Differences in the various socio-technical systems exacerbate collaboration, knowledge sharing, and co-utilisation of solutions among ports.

Ports have historically developed distinct local practices, but in order to ensure integrated capabilities within a global transport chain, individual ports must recognise that they are also part of a global network of sea transportation and therefore they should align their practices wherever possible. There will always be some diversity. Some smaller ports act only on a national level, for example, serving the outlying regions of one country such as the Orkneys in the north-west of the United Kingdom, where vessels engaged in international trade are rare visitors.

Digital and autonomous innovations are enablers for increasing the competitiveness of sea transport. For example, new technology enables enhanced coordination and highly efficient transhipment operations through information transparency among involved actors in the transport system. A port, as a hub consisting of a large number of actors, requires that all those engaged in a port call deliver vital components of value by acknowledging a common object of interest, such as a consignment passing through the port transferring between different modes of transport.

As of today, the strongest argument for sea transport is its overall transport cost between two hubs being the lowest compared to other modes of transport. Ensuring that ports operate as well-coordinated hubs is key to maintaining a high level of attractiveness for those choosing sea transport. This ensures a competitive advantage for ports (in relation to other ports) and its more permanent actors, creates incentives for cargo owners to choose sea over other transport modes (when applicable), meets the demands of increased cargo flows, and contributes to the realisation of the United Nation's Agenda 2030 for sustainable development.

Ports are more attractive for cargo owners if their transhipment/multimodal solutions linking maritime to land-based transport are of better quality and price ratio compared to competitors. Shipping companies can change a port of call relatively easily if the total costs of a visit or the quality of services are better at an alternative port. Therefore, a port's ability to optimise its port operations and compete is of highest concern. However, to do this it is now necessary to look at applying a collaborative strategy among the actors in a port, in order to jointly gain the benefits from technology-driven innovation.

Since the origins of information systems, a lot of attention has been paid to understanding the "object system" that an information system is aimed at supporting (Checkland 1981; Engeström 1991; Haraldson and Lind 2011a, b). Taking a purely logistics perspective on a port and a strict focus only on the flow of goods, we might overlook contextual issues. It is necessary to take into account how different chains of action, structures, and the people involved in the different organisations associated with port operations work (or do not work) together. A multi-organisational perspective is the foundation upon which to conceptualise the actions performed by the many organisations within a self-organised ecosystem and to account for how the different actors, with diverse roles and tasks, provide value through predefined structures, possibly enabled by technology, to the common aim.

The rest of this chapter considers a port as a set of socio-technical systems in a global network of sea transport and explores the characteristics of an organisation's social phenomena having technical capabilities, but regarding each of their value contributions as part of a multi-organisational business. We elaborate on the potential opportunities to make such a multi-organisational business more efficient and environmentally sustainable through different technical means by exploring and positioning contemporary technological trends. The chapter concludes by summarising some of the development trends for ports as socio-technical systems within the global transport chain.

3   Conceiving Multi-organisational Business Entities

In this section, we view a port's business as a multi-organisational business and elaborate on how value is created and the roles undertaken by the different involved organisations.

3.1   Foundation: Value Creation in Multi-organisational Business Processes

Multi-organisational businesses build upon the notion that different organisations, by undertaking different actor roles, co-produce value (Haraldson and Lind 2011a). A multi-organisational perspective adopts an integrated or synthesised view of value creation by taking identified strengths from both the value chain and the value network perspective (Fig. 2) (Haraldson and Lind 2011b). In a multi-organisational business, value is created by actor relationships (i.e. capabilities to perform future actions are established), through interaction among actors (i.e., value creation through interaction) and through the actions performed by the actors in the value network (i.e. value creating activities). Value creation is often described and structured as value chains or value networks, which are contrasting views on value creation. Meanwhile, a multi-organisational perspective conceives value creation structured as value chains in value networks, meaning that value is created both in actor relationships and in the actions performed. Thus, from a port actor's point of view, this would, for instance, recognise that a ship agent's social capital is highly valued by its client because it enables the provision of particular services that need to be agreed upon and delivered through the agent's and the service providers' cooperative actions. An actor in a multi-organisational business is an entity where people and technology act on behalf of the organisation. In Fig. 2 the strengths of the value chain and value networks perspectives are identified as foundational to the perception of value creation in such settings of which multiple organisations co-produce value.

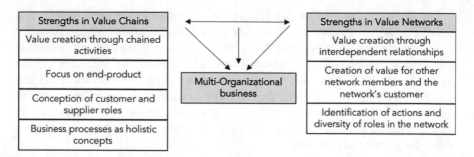

Fig. 2 A multi-organisational analysis of value chains and value networks (Haraldson and Lind 2011b)

The value chain perspective states "the logic being that every company occupies a position in the chain; upstream suppliers provide inputs before passing them downstream to the next link in the chain—the customer". A value network on the other hand consists of specific roles and value interactions oriented towards the achievement of a particular task or outcome. The notion of relationship is key in value networks (Peppard and Rylander 2006; Allee 2009).

"The active agents of any organisation are real people who play particular roles to convert both tangible and intangible assets into negotiable offerings and fulfil different functions" (Allee 2009, p. 429). A value network is therefore to be seen as "any purposeful group of people or organisations creating social and economic good through complex dynamic exchanges of tangible and intangible value" (Allee 2009, p. 429). Multi-organisational businesses are coordinated through the establishment, fulfilment, and evaluation of assignments (Haraldson and Lind 2011a, b) by interactions among the different actors (Haraldson 2008). Taking a viewpoint of a business as multi-organisational, integrating elements of the value chain and value network perspective, value is conceived as created through *actions performed by actors based on their relationships in a multi-organisational business network*.

Consequently, in order to conceive the logic of how assignments are established, fulfilled, and concluded in a multi-organisational setting, a repertoire of actor roles and their relationships needs to be reflected. This is in order to understand which role different organisations, as socio-technical systems, would have in the multi-organisational business. By regarding the organisation in the context of a multi-organisational business, requirements and opportunities would be put upon its socio-technical interacting elements. In the next section different actor roles in different value chain and value network approaches are discussed.

3.2   Actor Roles in a Multi-organisational Setting

Multi-organisational businesses need to be arranged such that action logics are defined, and role relationships are established and formalised. Their business processes need to be planned and coordinated in order to be successfully realised. Multi-organisational businesses are logically structured as assignment processes, consisting of both integrated and embedded business transactions; there is a need to distinguish the interaction patterns that create transactions. Such interaction patterns form the basis for identifying the role of actors as value creators and value consumers in the realisation of multi-organisational business transactions.

In a multi-organisational business, four types of generic actor roles are distinguished; *end-customer* (which is divided into two types, *potential* and *particular*, of beneficiaries), *main actor* (responsible for the relationship to and the value propositions aimed towards end-customers), and *co-producing actor* (taking assignments from the main actor and ensuring the realisation of these). In the realisation of business transactions, the end-customer can be a co-producer (e.g. a customer taking their car to the car wash and washing it). A main actor is normally the *coordinating actor* that undertakes the role of managing different assignments in the co-production of value.

In a multi-organisational business, assignment relationships (and the realisation of assignments) are the basis for the conception of actor roles. Role relationships are the conditions for the realisation of assignments (based on that they create an action capability for future actions). Action relationships are the outcome of the interaction required to realise the assignment which also becomes an important part of the creation of the structure and the task of each of the engaged organisations. Role relationships can be conceived in value networks, and action relationships can be conceived based on value chain structures. To enable an appropriate coordination of a multi-organisational business, actions need to be understood in the context of established actor roles and the recognition of different assignments. Those actions need to be reflected in the structure ingredient of the organisation to ensure that the roles undertaken by people and technology in their performance of their tasks are aligned with the organisation in the multi-organisational value creation.

In a port setting, business interactions need thus to be understood from a holistic point of view to ensure a successful realisation of the multi-organisational business. The roles that multi-organisational actors can undertake are based on a logic of interaction (i.e. interaction patterns). This logic builds upon that action relationships are established related to different assignments, in giving rise to patterns of interaction.

Organisations undertake different roles in a port business. As ports constantly need to change due to contemporary developments, there is also a need for the involved organisations, as entities of the port as a multi-organisational business, to respond to such changes. Each organisation, as a socio-technical system, needs to be continuously aligned with the expectations of the multi-organisational business, defined by the common object of interest. A socio-technical view thus can be used to

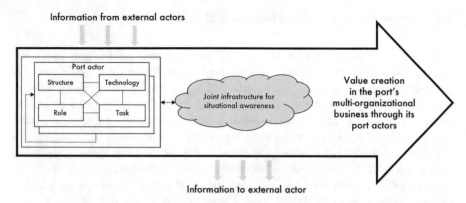

Fig. 3 The multi-organisational business of a port composed of multiple socio-technical systems

understand the organisational change of each collaborating organisation emerging from a changing digital landscape.

This relationship between the multi-organisational businesses, as composed by different socio-technical systems, is depicted in Fig. 3. The figure shows that the port depends on information provided from and to external actors (such as authorities, shipping companies, hinterland operators, cargo owners, and transport buyers) as well as the potential need of an digital infrastructure (technology) providing foundations for each socio-technical system to be aligned in the value creation that is pursued jointly by the port actors. An example of such an environment is the port community system (PCS) or tools for coordination relying on, for example, the principles of Port Collaborative Decision Making (PortCDM) or similar initiatives (see Chapter "Maritime Informatics for Increased Collaboration" in this book by Lind, Ward, Bergmann, Haraldson, Zerem, Hoffman, and Eklund).

4 Towards a Multi-organisational Conception of a Port

Building upon actor roles in multi-organisational businesses, this section elaborates on the role that the port, through its actors, undertakes in being part of the larger transport chain. This is followed by taking this role as the basis for depicting the assignment logic foundational for port operations.

4.1 The Port Framed in a Multi-organisational Transport Context

Everything in a port originates with the cargo owner or transport buyer making an agreement with a transport coordinator. They place transport assignments with a

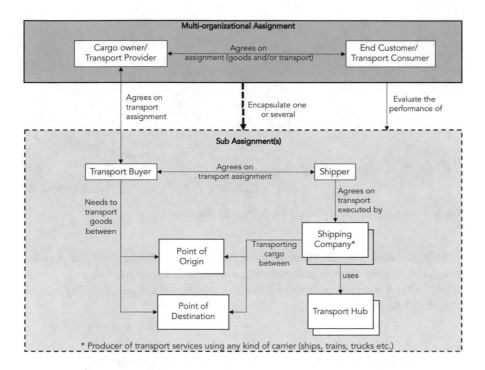

Fig. 4 The roles involved in transports

shipper, an organisation designed to meet the needs of moving goods or passengers from an origin to a destination for a customer.

All underlying agreements for a shipment should be settled and fulfilled by co-producers such as shipping companies (operating at sea and on land), infrastructure providers, and transport hubs enabling transhipments between the same or different means of transport. Figure 4 depicts these relationships, positioning the role of a port as a transport hub in the larger transport chain.

By adopting a multi-organisational view of the transport chain, the cargo owner or transport buyer can be regarded as the main actor with all others involved in coordinating or enabling transport being co-producers, who jointly create value for the customer. Depending on the INCO term[1] chosen, the agreement between the cargo owner and the end-customer may mean that the end-customer could take the role as cargo owner depending on the business agreement associated with the different phases of the transport necessary for bringing the goods from one location to another. Operations performed throughout the chain of transport events by a multitude of actors (co-producers) are performed on behalf of somebody else, such as the cargo owner (Fig. 5).

---

[1]https://iccwbo.org/resources-for-business/incoterms-rules/

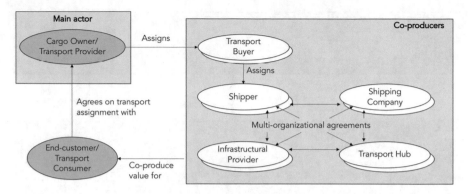

Fig. 5 The transport chain realised in a multi-organisational setting

In Figs. 4 and 5, the transport provider and transport consumer are also depicted associated to cargo owner and end-customer. This is to acknowledge the special case of when a business agreement is made on a transport product requiring a multi-organisational realisation.

4.2 Assignment Logic of the Port as a Transhipment Hub

Ports are multi-organisational business entities, but without an overall commanding body. Coordination is the glue that makes a port work. The foundational logic that ports build upon for any visiting ship is an inbound passage, operations performed at one or several physical location(s), and an outbound passage. These foundational three process steps determine the business logic of a ship's port visit (Fig. 6). Multiple assignments are agreed upon and fulfilled during a port visit, and these need to be aligned to ensure a smooth flow of activities.

The common object of interest for all actors is the end-to-end supply chain. In the larger transport chain, the shipper supports the coordination of the action pursued by the different port operators serving a port call. The shipper or their agent, as a co-producer, must thus take the responsibility of coordinating the other co-producers to fulfil the assignment agreed with the main actor to fulfil the needs of the receiver. However, it is also necessary to acknowledge that transport hubs (Fig. 7) exist in a societal context, which means that the coordination has to be aligned with societal goals such as being as safe as is feasible and with a carbon footprint in line with the UN and other public environmental and climate-change goals.

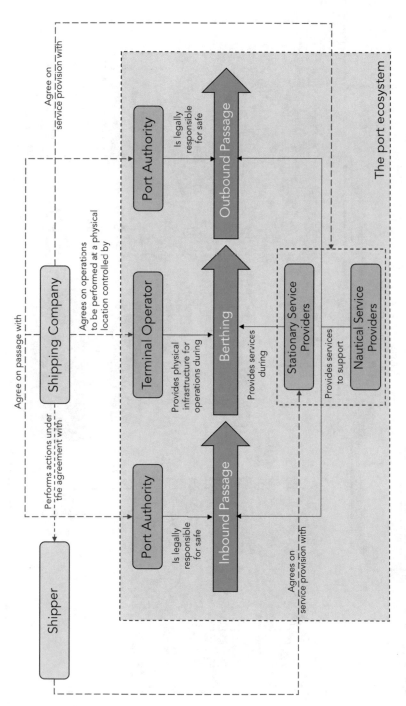

Fig. 6 Assignment logic associated with maritime port visits

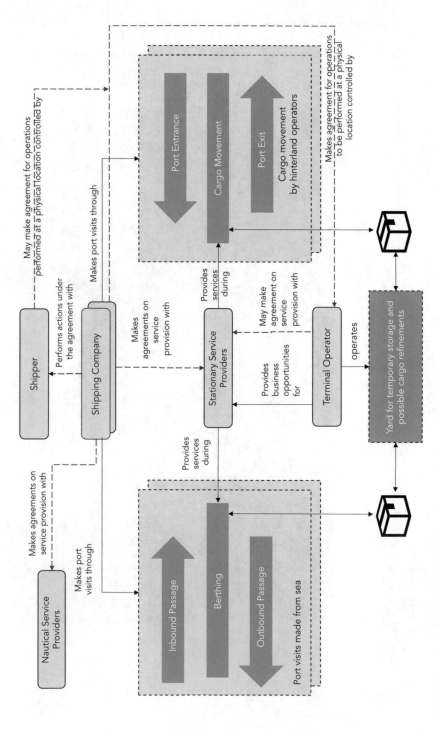

Fig. 7 The port as a multi-organisational transhipment hub

5 Technology and Port Operations

In a multi-organisational transport system, each actor should contribute to and benefit from up-to-date situational awareness for their decision-making. From a maritime informatics point of view, a socio-technical system uses digital communication to enable a common understanding of the intentions of the various actors. As information does not exist without communication, one needs to identify what information is needed for each participant in the ecosystem to create value for the entire system. This can be achieved through the different types of fundamental system (engagement, production, records, inquiry, and framing) that are combined to create value (Watson 2019).

Ports are an important source of capabilities to generate and manage data. A port is a system of engagement as it requires coordination and collaboration between different port actors. A port is also a system of production as it conducts routine operations on passengers and cargo delivered and picked up by visiting ships and other transport carriers. Both systems of engagement and production generate data for a system of records, such as data on agreements made for services and reports on the productive fulfilment of these agreements, as well as the status of goods, infrastructure used, and resources. These data may then be used in a system of inquiry, such as data analytics, to generate knowledge to enable more efficient use of a port's capacity. The system of framing uses the information produced by a system of inquiry to position its role in the transportation system in terms of the services it provides and how it refines these over times to meet changing needs. A virtuous interrelation among these different systems levels is depicted in Fig. 8.

As we now see that many ports and their actors, in the light of digitalisation, are starting to reframe their business, this also changes the expectations for the other organisations in a port. In a multi-organisational setting, there can be a fourth level of change, *delta*, when the changes by one party force critical changes on the others. In a period of digital transformation, these delta changes require considerable mutual adjustment.

To respond to these requirements, in a multi-organisational context, digitalisation may have four distinct roles:

- Sharing of digital transformation plans to ensure mutual accommodation of each other's plans
- Providing digital interfaces among participants
- Ensuring necessary data are shared in a common standard form to create a situational awareness useful to all parties
- Supporting distributed coordination through prediction of expected actions based on standardised data exchange

There are also numerous sources of information that the port and its actors need for planning. For this purpose, predictive analytics, as part of the system of inquiry, may be used. Sensors attached to containers generate data about their location and conditions; connected ships and connected port operations generate data about status

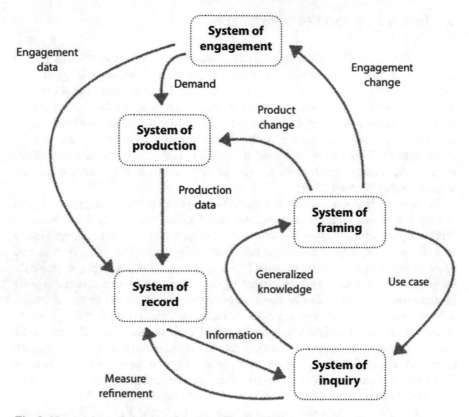

Fig. 8 Virtuous interrelationship of systems (Watson 2019)

changes. All of these data can be firstly stored in a system of record and then processed by a system of inquiry to enable a port and its actors to execute the system of production in a very efficient and sustainable way. The key is to create a virtuous linkage between all systems to gain the most value from digitalisation.

The well-connected port is thus both a data consumer and a provider to external parties. The smart port and its constituent members should have established capabilities to make intelligent evidence-based decisions. This requires everyone to be able to access raw data in a system of record and information generated by a system of inquiry while acknowledging that privacy and competitiveness should not be compromised.

At the same time, there are also expectations for a connected port to be an information hub for others. The port of the future should be providing data streams captured within the port to external parties, such as administrations, shipping companies, hinterland operators, transport buyers, cargo owners, and upstream and downstream transport hubs as their foundation for their planning. Again, data access must be arranged so as not to infringe competitiveness.

From a socio-technical point of view, there is a need to ensure that information systems are based upon agreed message formats, interfaces, and processes. This is to enable joint coordination between the actors involved in the transport of goods. By taking a multi-organisational point of view, requirements can be stipulated as to what data are needed for ensuring coordination and synchronisation among involved actors and when these should be shared.

Digital data sharing is key to coordination and synchronisation in a multi-organisational setting. The data made available contributes to the efficient utilisation of resources required to complete a port visit, even including such things as the planning and use of electrical equipment for shore-based power for ships and hinterland carriers. It may also include detailed data streams about the status of particular infrastructure (such as bollards or moving vehicles within the port) or the environmental parameters (such as current, water level, and wind).

Within the ecosystem of digital services, there are a number of phenomena that ease the coordination process, such as:

- Standardised message formats and machine-to-machine interfaces generating data streams necessary for coordination and situational awareness
- Digitally twinned objects such as the connected container and connected fairways
- Approaches to increased supply chain visibility
- Block-chain technology for capturing sub-agreements, such as bills of lading
- Data-sharing environments within different parts of the transport chain, such as for fleet operations
- Inter-country collaboration enabling smooth import and export processes
- Discovery services providing access to a repertoire of potential services offered by port service innovators

These technical opportunities influence the tasks, roles, and structures of organisations, and these need to be continually assessed to ensure that a port is responding to the needs of its customers. This can be achieved only if data are shared within all the modes of the transport ecosystem.

6 Change and Maritime Informatics

The socio-technical system perspective emphasises the interaction between structures, roles, tasks, and technologies. Mostly, people think of technology driving change, but organisations can also change structures, roles, and tasks. Maritime informatics has the capacity to facilitate change in all four components in response to industry trends and initiatives. New alliances and structural changes will typically require new information systems to support coordination. For example, the ship agent's role could be transformed when digital data exchange reduces their role as local information providers and increases their role as local service coordinators (Lind and Croston 2020). Data analysis will become a more common task because of the greater availability and depth of data provided by standardised data exchange, a technological change. Another example is the establishment of Hamburg Vessel Coordination Centre (HVCC) in Port of Hamburg, which is a separate organisation designated to handle the coordination of vessel visits by being connected to terminals, carriers, service providers, and authorities (Hirt 2018). Such an establishment is itself a socio-technical system which by establishment can cause a change of other involved organisation's socio-technical systems and thus is a delta change across the port's conglomerate of organisations.

It is important to realise that the level of change is an order of magnitude more difficult as we go from task, to role, to structural, to ecosystem. Thus, maritime informatics exponents must exercise skills in change management comparable to the level of change to be implemented.

High on the IMO transformation list is just-in-time shipping. This will likely require technology-facilitated change at all levels. Maritime informatics can enable such a change, but the more difficult challenge is to successfully change the social system elements, such as deeply embedded customs, practices, and relationships. Developments in technology are relatively easy, but changing well-established structures and behaviours in a self-organising ecosystem can be very hard. The first step on the path is to openly examine the full ramifications of digitalisation on the multiple socio-technical systems and their relationships that it is designed to change.

References

Allee, V. (2009). Value-creating networks: Organisational issues and challenges. *The Learning Organization, 16*(6), 427–442.

Bostrom, R. P., & Heinen, J. S. (1977a). MIS problems and failures: A socio-technical perspective: Part I: The causes. *MIS Quarterly, 1*(3), 17–32.

Bostrom, R. P., & Heinen, J. S. (1977b). MIS problems and failures: A socio-technical perspective: Part II: The application of socio-technical theory. *MIS Quarterly, 1*(4), 11–28.

Checkland, P. (1981). *Systems thinking. Systems practice*. Chichester: Wiley.

Cooper, R., & Foster, M. (1971). Sociotechnical systems. *American Psychologist, 26*, 467–474.

Engeström, Y. (1991). *Developmental work research: Reconstructing expertise through expansive learning*. Proceedings of human jobs and computer interfaces conference, University of Tampere.

Haraldson, S. (2008). *Design principles for action quality in collaboration – a multi-organizational perspective on third party logistics (in Swedish)*. Licentiate Thesis, Linköping University, Sweden.

Haraldson, S., & Lind, M. (2011a). *Value chains in value networks: A multi-organizational business process definition*. Australian Conference on Information Systems, Australia.

Haraldson, S., & Lind, M. (2011b). *Challenging dyadic interaction in the context of multi-organizational business processes*. Australian Conference on Information Systems, Australia.

Hirt, G. (2018). Port partnerships in practice, Ed. 79. *Port Technology Journal*. Retrieved from www.porttechnology.org

Lind, M., & Croston, J. C. (2020). *Rethinking maritime businesses for the digital age: The evolving role of ship agents*. Article No. 49 [UNCTAD Transport and Trade Facilitation Newsletter N°85 – First Quarter 2020]. Retrieved from https://unctad.org/en/pages/newsdetails.aspx?OriginalVersionID=2306

Meadows, D. (2008). *Thinking in systems: A primer.* Sustainability INstitute.

O'Hara, M. T., Watson, R. T., & Kavan, C. B. (1999). Managing three levels of change. *Information Systems Management, 16*, 63–70.

Peppard, J., & Rylander, A. (2006). From value chain to value network: Insights for mobile operators. *European Management Journal, 24*(2–3), 128–141.

Seiffert, M., & Loch, C. (2005). Systemic thinking in environmental management: support for sustainable development. *Journal of Cleaner Production, 13*, 1197–1202.

Senge, P. M. (1991). *The fifth discipline: The art and practice of the learning organization.* Wiley Online Library.

Watson, R. T. (2019). *Capital, systems and objects: The foundation and future of organizations.* Athens, GA: eGreen Press.

Watson, R. T., Lind, M., Delmeire, N., & Liesa, F. (2020). Shipping: A self-organising ecosystem. In M. Lind, M. P. Michaelides, R. Ward, & R. T. Watson (Eds.), *Maritime informatics.* Heidelberg: Springer.

Digitalisation in Maritime Regional and Global Supply Chains

Jaco Voorspuij ⓘ and Hanane Becha ⓘ

1 Introduction

The maritime mode of transport is an essential component in all value and supply chains that need to transport physical products of any kind at any stage of these chains. Think of raw materials, parts and components, sub-assemblies, assemblies, sub-systems, systems and finished goods items.

The International Transport Forum (ITF) report (OECD/ITF, 2019) highlights two important facts that are important background for this chapter. First, today (2020) the maritime mode carries twice as much freight as all other modes of transport combined, over any distance anywhere in the world. Second, maritime transport is set to grow very quickly. By 2050, the transported volume will be three times what it is in 2020.

Furthermore, value chains and thus the supply chains that support them have been growing ever more global and complex over the past decades. There have been many incidents that seriously affected the availability of essential materials for entire industries, value chains or parts thereof. Beneficial cargo owners (BCOs) are acutely aware of the need to take more control of their supply chains in order to stay in control of their value chains. BCO first focussed on digitalisation of their own operations and then started to look at the wider supply chain. Traditionally the BCOs have looked at modes of transport other than maritime as their first step towards taking control of their supply chains. BCO tended to regard the freight

J. Voorspuij (✉)
GS1 AISBL, Brussel, Belgium
e-mail: jaco.voorspuij@gs1.org

H. Becha
UN/CEFACT Transport and Logistics Vice Chair, Marseille, France
e-mail: hbecha@gmail.com

M. Lind et al. (eds.), *Maritime Informatics*, Progress in IS,
https://doi.org/10.1007/978-3-030-50892-0_5

carried over the maritime mode as lower priority and often perceived the maritime mode as too difficult to try to improve.

More and more however, the BCOs and their logistic service providers (LSPs) are turning their attention to the maritime mode of transport. In the next section of this chapter, we will cover in more detail the interests and drivers for various stakeholders in this mode. We will also look at how these translate into requirements for improvements in information exchanges (or in other words further digitalisation in the maritime transportation system). For now, it is important to know the BCOs have started to realise the following:

- Customer and commercial pressures make it imperative to know more about what happens to goods. BCOs do not think in terms of freight or cargo; they think in terms of the goods or products that they need to run their value chains in a profitable fashion, irrespective of the mode of transport.
- Regulatory requirements force BCOs to keep better track of their goods and products, as well as the materials used to create them.
- The maritime mode is moving to levels of digitalisation that will enable it to meet the needs of BCOs in terms of providing them with the information they need to meet the challenges outlined in the previous two bullets.

Additionally, in the past stakeholders in maritime transport focussed mostly or exclusively on the questions "Where is my shipment?" or "When will my shipment arrive?" Nowadays, BCOs are also increasingly interested in the question "What condition are my goods in?" As indicated previously, customers and authorities are demanding increasing levels of quality of both the goods and the information related to these goods. BCOs can meet this demand only if they also keep track of the condition of the goods. We will return to this question later in this chapter.

The "Just-In-Travel Arrival Guide", published by the "Global Industry Alliance to Support Low Carbon Shipping" (IMO/MEPC, 2020) also identifies this increased need for sharing information among all stakeholders relying on maritime transportation. It states:

> Stakeholders across the supply chain need to share up-to-date, reliable information about each vessel's location, its speed and the shipments it carries—as well as data on the terminals and locations where the shipments may be collected (or delivered) in order to efficiently connect maritime vessels with other modes of transport such as road, rail or inland waterways.

However, the draft also recognises that there are stakeholders who may not be eager to share the information required to meet the challenges identified:

> Nowadays, and in most ports, stakeholders are not equally eager to share information. This may be, for example, because of concerns that third parties could deduce commercially sensitive information (e.g., berthing windows, terminal productivity, type/location of commodities loaded and discharged, and which ships are given berth priority at which terminals).

This observation serves as a reminder that the challenges around sharing information go beyond the technical ones. That said, we will focus on the technical aspects in this chapter.

2 Stakeholders and Their Key Drivers

We will now take a closer look at the various stakeholders related to supply chains relying on maritime transportation and the key considerations that drive the requirements and demands (in terms of information exchanges) that they place on the LSPs (logistic service providers) they use to handle and manage the maritime transportation for them.

To better understand the context, let us look at a simplified depiction of a supply chain relying on maritime transportation (Fig. 1).

The example supply chain in Fig. 1 does not aim to be comprehensive. It merely aims to demonstrate what is very common in today's maritime-based transport and logistics environments. We may split the overall process logically into four main segments: pre-carriage, main carriage, onward carriage and intra-port operations. Pre-carriage covers all logistics tasks required to transport goods from the sender and to make them available to the port operations. Main carriage covers the transportation of the freight between ports. Onward carriage takes care of all logistic tasks taking the goods from the ports to their final destination (the receiver).

Information exchanges among stakeholders will need to cross over all segments of the supply chain seamlessly.

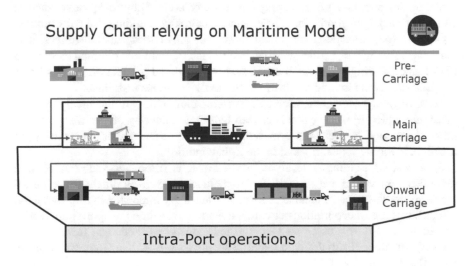

Fig. 1 A supply chain relying on the maritime mode

From the prior description, it will be obvious there is a large number of different kinds of stakeholders. We should also stress that the sample supply chain is trade independent. It applies to container shipping, wet and dry bulk, chemicals as well as other cargo types.

In the following paragraphs, we will cover some of the different kinds of stakeholders and their interests and key considerations/concerns when they use supply chains that rely on maritime transportation.

Note: The key considerations generally apply over the entire supply chain, but below we highlight the impact on maritime transportation and requirements for information exchange.

The first set of stakeholders are BCOs. Many more stakeholders than we include below may be classified as BCOs, but we focus on stakeholders who together reflect the most common demands on maritime transportation. At the start and at the end of the process, we have senders and receivers of goods/products. We will look at manufacturers, retailers, online sales (web shops, marketplaces) and commodity trading each of which may act as a receiver or sender of goods.

The second set of stakeholders we will look at are the LSPs involved in this process and their key challenges and considerations. We cover both the non-ship-oriented LSPs and the ship-oriented LSPs (actual carriers).

After that, we will cover organisations that regulate/control the flow of cargo/goods such as port authorities and governmental agencies (e.g. customs).

2.1 Manufacturers

There are manufacturers in all supply chains based around physical product such as consumer-packaged goods, food, healthcare, electronics, building and construction, equipment (e.g. transport) and many more. For all of these manufacturers, it is very expensive when production stops due to lack of materials required as input to their manufacturing process. To avoid such unscheduled production interruptions, manufacturers tend to hold levels of "buffer stock" of those materials.

That way, they protect themselves against the unreliability of the supply of these materials, which in many cases is caused by the unreliability of the transportation networks needed to make those materials available at the right time, at the right location, in the right quantity and in the right condition.

The cost of holding a level of buffer stock is often very substantial, and manufacturers would very much like to reduce or even eliminate those buffer stock levels. Therefore, manufacturers are increasingly interested in improving the reliability of the transportation networks, including maritime transportation. Buffer stocks are determined using well-established industry methods and formulae that are very sensitive to variability in material supply (See A.R. Van Goor, Kruijtzer, & Esmeijer, 1990).

2.2   Retailers

Within the context of this chapter, the retailers are medium to large enterprises with distribution centres, where they receive generally large quantities of the goods/products they plan to sell through their sales channels. Due to the large quantities handled and because some of the products are sourced from locations far away, retailers often rely on maritime transportation for those products to be delivered to their distribution centres.

The distribution centres have functions similar to those for maintaining buffer stocks for manufacturers, but there are also significant differences. In the traditional retail models, physically located shops sell a retailer's products to the customer. The customer then takes the product home or has it delivered.

Retail shops generally hold low stock levels for specific products, so a delay in replenishment from a retailer's distribution centre will generally quickly cause significant issues in the shop such as lost sales, loss of consumer satisfaction or even reduced loyalty.

To handle fluctuations in supply and demand, retailers and, to a lesser extent, manufacturers require more information at a more granular level than is currently customarily provided by LSPs active within the maritime mode of transport.

2.3   Online Sales, Web Shops and Marketplaces

Online sales have had a profound effect on global supply chains, and it will likely continue to transform these supply chains for many more years to come. Organisations like Amazon, Alibaba, Zalando and many similar others did not exist three decades ago. They are now responsible for hundreds of billions of shipments every year. A significant proportion of those shipments are international or even global (e.g. China to Europe) (GS1 Last Mile, 2018).

Many of the traditional retailers now offer online sales to their customers also. Some of the pure online players have started to offer products in physical shops also. Therefore, the lines between the organisations are blurring. The logistic processes associated with online sales differ greatly from those for the traditional retailer.

Traditionally, postal, courier, express and parcel (CEP) carriers carry the online sales shipments. Those carriers may in turn consolidate those shipments into larger consignment over the main carriage stage of the end-to-end transportation process. These CEP carriers often outsource the main carriage to third-party carriers.

Nowadays we see several of the online sales organisations taking control of the supply chains that transport goods sold to customers. Some have built their own logistics execution capability (e.g. becoming a carrier and/or building distribution centres); some have built logistics and management capability (but refrained from investing in execution capacity). In some cases, they offer these capabilities to third parties who could benefit from those capabilities even though these third parties are not directly involved in the online sales done within the online ordering systems of the online sales organisation (such as Fulfillment by Amazon, Cainiao).

Because the customer in the online sales model does not visit a physical shop, the online sales organisation has only two main means at its disposal to deliver an experience that will ensure the customer will return to the online sales organisation frequently. First, they need to make their online ordering system as easy to use and as conducive to making a sale as they can. Second, they need to make sure the customer will receive the goods they purchased at exactly the right time, at exactly the right place and in perfect condition. Clearly the online sales organisations have a higher than average interest in reliable logistic execution. In addition, the customer will also demand much more traceability regarding the (planned) delivery of their purchase. The result is many tens and possibly hundreds of billions of small shipments to households. The requirements for the related information exchanges are several orders of magnitude more in volume and complexity than what maritime transportation has traditionally handled (Hvid Jensen, H. (2020); Logistic Internet #2: Shared Visibility (SV)).

One of the main reasons that online sales organisations have taken more control over their supply chains is that their customers require visibility of where their orders are and where the goods ordered come from (often referred to as traceability). The online sales organisations have apparently lost patience with the LSPs, including those in maritime environments, and decided they need to ensure they can provide the required levels of traceability to their customers.

2.4 Supply Chain Improvements by BCOs

BCOs that have already significantly improved their own operations will turn their attention to optimising the supply chain they are a part of. Many BCOs are involved in long, complex supply chains. In addition, these supply chains are too often very inefficient and costly. Many BCOs have recognised these shortcomings, and they seek improvements by taking full control or working with a partner. They generally adopt one or several of the following approaches.

They decompose the supply chain identifying the individual legs or lanes that make up the network (see also Fig. 1). They then select the most appropriate mode of transport and carrier for each of those legs. This may mean they will shift transportation of certain types of products from one mode of transport to another, such as from road to short sea or from road to inland waterways or rail.

They implement a logistic control centre that will take care of all of the transportation movements throughout the transport and logistics network they use. Instead of booking transportation end to end with a single LSP, they will book transportation for each of the linked transportation movements required to move goods from original source to ultimate delivery location. They can select the most appropriate mode and carrier for each of those movements based on all relevant information available at that time.

They implement methods and systems to gather much more information regarding the execution of transportation and the condition of their goods whilst in transit to ensure their product arrives in good condition at the right place at the right time more and more often.

Clearly, to do this BCOs need more information regarding their goods and shipments from the individual LSPs handling the transportation legs. Among other things, BCOs require reliable information from the LSP related to estimated time of arrival (ETA) at a specified location. We will cover this in more detail below.

We need to stress here that this need for reliable estimates regarding future events is common to all stakeholders in the supply chain in order to better plan and align activities among stakeholders especially where the activities of those stakeholders are directly dependent upon the activities of the other stakeholders.

2.5 Commodity Trading

Commodities include goods, such as oil and gas, and materials traded in the wet and dry bulk sectors of maritime transportation. Commodities are traded in large quantities and are often transported using the maritime mode using large and extremely large ships. A challenge for a commodity trader is to find a ship that can safely enter the port where the cargo is located, load the cargo and then navigate out of the port safely to the port of destination. At the destination, there are similar challenges in terms of making sure the ship can safely enter the port and unload.

Whether or not a ship can enter a port is largely dependent on its draught, which is dependent on reliable information regarding the ship and its payload and reliable depth information regarding the relevant sections of the voyage route. Currently stakeholders in bulk commodity trading tend to insist on very high margins for the safe passage of their ships to ensure the safety of the cargo and minimise the risk of environmental damage and loss of reputation if an incident occurs. It is sometimes the case, particularly for less frequented destinations, that the depth information available from nautical charts along the voyage route is either not available or deemed unreliable. As a result, ships can only plan routes based on whatever data are available and then add a safety margin to avoid risks to the ship, the crew and the cargo. Planning with a wide safety margin for depth means that a ship cannot load as much cargo as it could if more reliable depth information was available.

A particular interest of the commodity trading stakeholders is therefore on reliable spatial information (e.g. depths and navigational dangers related to geographical features) that may also be dependent on the time of day, time of year, weather conditions, winds, currents or tidal conditions.

The next two sections cover logistic service providers. We distinguish LSPs that operate ships versus LSPs that do not. The main reason is the way they use and create capital (see also Watson, Lind, Delmeire, & Liesa, 2020). The ship-oriented LSPs tend to use economic capital (the ships) predominantly; the non-ship-oriented LSPs tend to use human, social and/or organisational capital predominantly.

2.6 Logistic Service Providers: Not Ship Oriented

Currently most transport service providers will manage and handle cargo at the level of the consignment. A consignment is a collection of transport units or cargo to be carried between two specified locations. Nowadays, the consignment will often have an identification code issued by the carrier. The transport units belonging to the consignments may also be identified. Many transport service providers will not record the transport unit each time it is handled; instead, they will generally record that they handled the consignment.

For road transport—where a consignment is often a single container or transport unit—this tends to work well enough. For other carriers in modes connecting with the port and maritime mode such as rail and inland waterways, this practice causes issues in traceability for BCOs, who in most cases have packaged the goods in small transport units. Stakeholders at any point in the pre-carriage stage may then consolidate these smaller transport units in larger transport units (e.g. pallets), and these larger transport units may be consolidated into even larger transport units (e.g. containers).

Warehousing and storage service providers manage and handle transport/storage units based on unique identifiers. These identifiers may be based on global standards that are commonly used across the supply chain or the service provider issues proprietary identifiers. Therefore, the warehousing and storage providers are in principle capable of providing full traceability of all units that they handle as well as traceability on how they have consolidated smaller units into larger units.

Freight forwarders often take care of the end-to-end transportation on behalf of the BCO. As a result, they face many of the same challenges a BCO faces. In fact, the BCO often engages the freight forwarder so that the BCO does not have to face those challenges. Freight forwarders will often combine or consolidate shipments and transport units received from several of their logistic services clients into a consolidated consignment, and in the process, they may create larger transport units to facilitate their transportation (GS1 LIM, 2019). Many transportation service providers do not routinely capture exactly how that consolidation process was executed, and unfortunately, this is an issue with many freight forwarders as well. They may capture that information in part of their networks, but for most freight forwarders, they do not capture it throughout their entire network.

Terminals—be they in ports, inland/dry ports or rail networks—are responsible for transferring transport units from one mode of transport to another. Terminals, like warehouses, routinely capture what transport units they handle (and the applicable identifiers). In fact, they generally need to know in advance what transport units they need to handle and other relevant data such as weight, dimensions, type of cargo inside the transport unit and so on. Given that the transport units they receive may have been created by service providers, the terminals will not always receive reliable information related to the transport units they will receive.

Warehouse and other storage service providers also appreciate detailed information regarding the transport units they will receive. Quite often, warehouses will deconstruct the transport units and store the goods contained in those units rather than the transport units themselves. That means that they should be able to access detailed information on the contents of those transport units.

We also need to point out here that some of the LSPs covered in this section (e.g. inland warehouses) may be responsible for cross-border procedures such as customs clearance. To be able to take care of their responsibilities, they need detailed information regarding the shipments/purchases, transport units and their contents.

2.7 Logistic Service Provider: Ship Oriented

LSPs involved in operating ships tend to need less information regarding the cargo carried than other stakeholders in maritime-based supply chains. Even so, they need some information about the transport units and their contents for the safety of the ship, the crew and the environment.

2.8 Port Authorities

Port authorities are interested in ensuring that their port is attractive to those stakeholders who decide how to route cargo through supply chains and hopefully through their port. Ports often decide to focus on a particular kind of cargo, so they can invest in specific projects that will make the port more attractive for that kind of cargo. These investments may cover realising better handling/processing within the port or creating better hinterland connections. They may also focus on cargo-related information, for example, offering more reliable information to the stakeholders wishing to use the port. Providing reliable and accurate information on depths for all elements making up a port's navigable waters may enable the stakeholders to carry more payload. Gathering and analysing information regarding traffic, congestion and cargo movements in and around the port area may enable a port to offer stakeholders a more predictable and reliable lead time for cargo moving into or coming in from the hinterland.

2.9 Government/Authorities

Many different authorities and government agencies have an interest in the maritime mode of transport. Multiple agencies might need to receive information regarding products, goods and shipments. For example, agricultural products may carry a wide range of biohazards that are of interest to pest and environmental control agencies.

An important government agency in the maritime transportation chain is customs. Most cargoes are subject to taxes and duties when imported into a country.

Furthermore, prohibitions and restrictions may apply for certain kinds of products meaning that they cannot be imported or there are limits on the quantity. The customs service therefore requires that it receives sufficient information to perform its tasks, including assessing what taxes and duties are applicable and what rates and tariffs to apply.

2.10   Summary of Stakeholder Information Exchange Needs

We summarise the various business requirements for information exchanges in four functionality groups:

1. Information related to the traceability of goods and shipments
2. Information to improve the efficiency and reliability of operations within the maritime-based supply chains
3. Information related to cross-border procedures
4. Information for aggregation and analysis of many transportation movements

3   Technologies and (Lack of) Standards

In this segment, we will look at the building blocks needed to meet the business requirements previously identified. First, we need to be aware of the extremely diverse and fragmented landscape of stakeholders. The Port Information Manual[1] provides the following statement "Ports can receive up to 55,000 different ships and the global shipping industry operates in a network of up to 9,000 different ports".

A large number of different companies operate those 55,000 ships. The technical capabilities of both the ports involved and the companies operating the ships vary considerably. Furthermore, they may be subject to different sets of regulations that apply in the countries and regions in which they operate. It is clear that establishing information exchange among these stakeholders will not be an easy task and one that may take many years to achieve. Considering the end-to-end supply chain, the numbers of involved stakeholders is very large. Within the EU alone, it is estimated there are well over one million LSPs. Global numbers are not known or highly unreliable, but GS1 estimates there are probably over ten million LSPs.

The majority of these stakeholders currently have few if any automated information exchanges in place. In order to meet the business requirements identified in this chapter, it is imperative that far more stakeholders become integrated in a network of information exchanges that can easily connect these stakeholders on an as-needed basis and is affordable for those stakeholders.

---

[1] https://portcalloptimization.org/images/Port%20Information%20Manual%201.4.4%20-%20final%20(2).pdf

Table 1 International Taskforce on Port Call Optimisation agenda[a]

1	Agree on business process of port calls
2	Agree on minimum scope of data
3	Agree on functional definitions
4	Use of functional definitions by industry
5	Agree on data model and formats
6	Use of data model and formats by industry
7	Agree on ISO quality label
8	Use of ISO quality label by industry
9	Local roll out by industry
10	Global roll out by industry

[a]https://portcalloptimization.org/images/Flyer%20port%20call%20optimization%2020090719.pdf

To enable a much more efficient and effective exchange of information, it is necessary to start using common semantics and apply those semantics in common syntaxes (Morton & De Cauwer, 2019). Whereas semantics tend to be stable and fixed over long timeframes, syntaxes are technology dependent and thus tend to be subject to technology changes.

The International Taskforce on Port Call Optimisation[2] (ITPCO) has formulated an agenda to achieve common semantics and syntax (Table 1).

ITPCO recognises that it is necessary to start with a specific target area within the end-to-end supply chain process in order to be able to mobilise relevant stakeholders and to deliver results within a timeframe that is acceptable to the stakeholders. The specific target area for ITPCO is optimising the business process related to a ship visiting a port (port call for short), (Hvid Jensen, H. (2020); Logistic Internet #3: Port Call Optimisation) which is a similar target for the Port Collaborative Decision Making (PortCDM) concept (Lind et al., 2018) described elsewhere in this book (Lind et al., 2020).

The agenda starts with an analysis of the existing business process and agreeing among the relevant stakeholders what the essential and most common elements are. Stakeholders then determine jointly what the minimum sets of data are, required to make the business process function properly. In both steps, the objective is to ensure the stakeholder group can deliver common best practices for the target business process ensuring business benefits that make it well worthwhile for the stakeholders to invest in the efforts for developing those common best practices.

The next step is to agree on semantics for the target business process. ITPCO develops so-called functional definitions that unambiguously describe each of the key terms in the port call process. Where needed the functional definitions also describe relationships between some of the terms. Additionally, standards are defined for the format of each of the concepts or terms. This results in a data model that may be understood unambiguously by stakeholders in the target process.

---

[2]https://portcalloptimization.org/

Several other organisations active in the maritime domain or in the wider supply chain have adopted similar agendas, such as the Digital Container Shipping Association.[3] These organisations build upon international or global standards developed and maintained by robust official standardisation organisations such as ISO (International Standards Organization),[4] UN/CEFACT (United Nations Centre for Trade Facilitation and Electronic Business),[5] GS1,[6] IALA (International Association of Marine Aids to Navigation and Lighthouse Authorities),[7] IHO (International Hydrographic Organization)[8] and others (Morton & De Cauwer, 2019).

The technologies and the building blocks required to establish common best practices that will massively help improve processes in maritime-based supply chain already exist. What is lacking are agreed ways (or best practices) to combine the building blocks in affordable and easy-to-use "fabrics" to deliver a solid, safe and comfortable environment for the maritime industry, its customers and other stakeholders to collaborate and massively improve current processes.

In the remainder of this chapter, we briefly cover a number of the main building blocks, describe how they work and indicate how they may help deliver the improvements in maritime-based supply chains. To be able to put things into context, it is important we consider the below framework developed by GS1 (Fig. 2).

The framework identifies three layers that must link together to enable digitalisation of cargo movement.

1. *Identification*

   Information systems require the unique identification of each entity that they need to manage. The layer depicts a number of different kinds of entities and some examples of identifiers that may be used for them. The identifiers come from various different global data standard organisations such as the International Maritime Organization (IMO) (the IMOVN or IMO vessel number), BIC (Bureau International des Containers) (BIC code for intermodal containers) as well as GS1/ISO.

2. *Automatic identification and data capture*

   Each physical object must display or have embedded in it a unique identification code that can be read automatically without error.

3. *Information sharing*

   As goods or cargo travel through the supply chain, different stakeholders will handle them using different information systems. To make use of unique identifiers, it is imperative that all stakeholders involved exchange information

---

[3] https://dcsa.org/

[4] https://www.iso.org/home.html

[5] https://www.unece.org/cefact/

[6] https://www.gs1.org/

[7] https://www.iala-aism.org/

[8] https://iho.int/

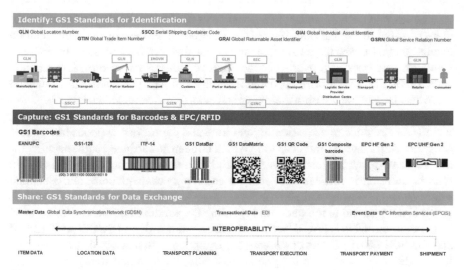

Fig. 2 GS1 framework for digitalisation of cargo movement

regarding these entities use the standardised identifiers for each class of object, such as a container.

Within the information sharing layer, GS1 also distinguish between three kinds of information:

1. *Master data*

    Data elements for a given entity that remain stable over relatively long times (e.g. a ship may be used for several decades; its main characteristics such as beam[9] and length overall[10] remain the same over its lifetime).

2. *Transactional data*

    Transactional data relates to business transactions, such as sales of goods or transport orders. These transactions tend to have relatively short lifetimes.

3. *Event data*

    Event data that is related to observations regarding physical (or virtual) entities that have occurred for the entity. An example is a ship departing from a berth at a specific date and time.

These building blocks create the means for answering four common traceability questions:

- What entity is this event for?
- Where did the event take place?
- When did it happen?
- Why (in what business context) did it happen?

---

[9]https://portcalloptimization.org/images/Functional%20definitions%205.5.pdf

[10]https://portcalloptimization.org/images/Functional%20definitions%205.5.pdf

The ISO/IEC 19987 and 19988 standards (EPCIS and Core Business Vocabulary)[11] provide the building block to enable common best practice information exchanges that cover the above questions. The first versions of these traceability standards date back well over a decade. First versions of the identification/capture standards in Fig. 2 were developed half a century ago. Many industries implemented these standards widely within their supply chains (e.g. healthcare and retail).

Another data exchange building block is AIS (automatic identification system), which enables ships to be tracked in real time and therefore any goods transported on those ships can be tracked, too. AIS has been a carriage requirement[12] for the majority of commercial ships since 2004, so there is a huge data set of ship tracking information available for analysis and supply chain planning and execution improvements (Watson et al., 2020).

To better respond to the question regarding the condition of the goods, we need to mention the UN/CEFACT "smart container" standards.[13] UN/CEFACT (2019) and UNECE (2019) Smart containers are equipped with sensors that can capture the conditions under which the goods are stored, handled and transported. Using common global standards, it is possible to get (real-time) access to the sensor information, gain situational awareness and take appropriate action (if needed). Here too, over time the available data set will grow to be very large and may be analysed to improve supply chain operations (Becha, Schroeder, Voorspuij, Frazier, & Lind, 2020).

Finally, we need to stress the paramount importance of the unambiguous identification of locations (the *where* traceability question posed earlier) as well as reliable and accurate information for the location. Currently, there is much fragmentation in this area with many different and partly overlapping location master data services. The result is that sometimes there are more than a dozen different identifiers for the exact same location (and potentially as many different data sets for it). This is confusing and potentially dangerous. The ISO/IEC 6523 standard—*Structure for the identification of organizations and organization parts*—provides for a global identifier that may be used across all locations anywhere in the supply chain. Adding this common identifier to the current location databases will allow the unambiguous linking of all those databases and ensuring stakeholders can easily share the data available in those databases, use them in operations and compare the data sets to improve data quality. The GS1 Global Location Number (GLN) is ISO/IEC 6523

[11] https://www.gs1.org/standards/epcis

[12] http://www.imo.org/en/About/Conventions/ListOfConventions/Pages/International-Convention-for-the-Safety-of-Life-at-Sea-(SOLAS),-1974.aspxhttp://www.imo.org/en/KnowledgeCentre/ReferencesAndArchives/FocusOnIMO(Archives)/Documents/Focus%20on%20IMO%20-%20SOLAS,%20the%20International%20Convention%20for%20the%20Safety,%20of%20Life%20at%20Sea,%201974%20(October%201998).pdf

[13] http://www.unece.org/tradewelcome/tradepublications/cefact/2019/trade-facilitation-white-paper-on-smart-containers-ecetrade446/doc.htmlhttps://www.unece.org/fileadmin/DAM/cefact/brs/BRS-SmartContainer_v1.0.pdf

compliant. The Port Information Manual (PIM)[14] prescribes the use of the GLN for a range of different locations within ports.

4 Conclusions

The maritime industry is subject to massive pressures to transform the way supply chain stakeholders relying on maritime transportation will share data and information in the future. The industry can no longer afford to ignore the legitimate demands from these stakeholders for much improved information exchanges. Should the industry not do so, it will risk its key stakeholders taking control of their supply chains and replace the traditional maritime operators with mechanisms that will meet their information needs and efficiency goals.

The good news is that the maritime industry and the stakeholders relying on maritime-based supply chains can make use of many building blocks that are already available to improve information sharing rapidly to meet the business requirements of the end-to-end stakeholders much better. Furthermore, many developments ongoing currently aim to deliver even more building blocks that will help all stakeholders to improve the information exchange and their business process and operations even further. A well-established foundation is available, and so are skilled practitioners able to transfer their knowledge to the shipping sector and produce the raw material to enable maritime informatics to take the industry to a higher level of efficiency, safety and sustainability.

References

Becha, H., Schroeder, M., Voorspuij, J., Frazier, T., & Lind, M. (2020). Global data exchange standards: The basis for future smart container digital services. In M. Lind, M. P. Michaelides, R. Ward, & R. T. Watson (Eds.), *Maritime informatics*. Heidelberg: Springer.

GS1 Last Mile. (2018). *Transforming the Last Mile. Emerging innovations and solutions in the challenging world of customer-centric logistics*. Brussels, Belgium. Retrieved from https://www.gs1.org/sites/default/files/gs1_customer-centric_logistics_wp_a4_081018_hi-res.pdf

GS1 LIM. (2019). *GS1 logistics interoperability model application standard*. Brussels, Belgium. Retrieved from https://www.gs1.org/docs/EDI/GS1_Logistics_Interoperability_Model_Application_Standard.pdf

Hvid Jensen, H. (2020). *5 ways to digitalize logistics and boost trade*. World Economic Forum. Retrieved from https://www.weforum.org/agenda/2020/02/how-the-global-logistics-industry-can-collaborate-to-increase-trade-and-reduce-poverty/

IMO/MEPC. (2020). *Just in time arrival guide – barriers and solutions*. Retrieved from https://portcalloptimization.org/images/JIT%20Guide%20Final.pdf

---

[14]https://portcalloptimization.org/images/Port%20Information%20Manual%201.4.4%20-%20final%20(2).pdf

Lind, M., Ward, R., Watson, R. T., Haraldson, S., Zerem, A., & Paulsen, S. (2020). Decision support for port visits. In M. Lind, M. Michaelides, R. Ward, & R. T. Watson (Eds.), *Maritime informatics*. Heidelberg: Springer.

Lind, M., Watson, R. T., Ward, R., Bergmann, M., Bjørn-Andersen, N., Rosemann, M., Haraldson, S., & Andersen, T. (2018). Digital *data sharing: The ignored opportunity for making global maritime transport chains more efficient*. Article No. 22 [UNCTAD Transport and Trade Facilitation Newsletter N°79 – Third Quarter 2018]. Retrieved from https://unctad.org/en/pages/newsdetails.aspx?OriginalVersionID=1850

Morton, R., & De Cauwer, N. (2019). *Why standards matter*. Edition 85. Retrieved from www.porttechnology.org, https://www.porttechnology.org/technical-papers/why_standards_matter/

OECD/ITF (International Transport Forum). (2019). *ITF Transport Outlook 2019*. Retrieved from http://www.oecd-ilibrary.org/transport/itf-transport-outlook-2019_transp_outlook-en-2019-en

UN/CEFACT. (2019). *The UN/CEFACT Smart Container Business Specifications (BRS)*. Retrieved from https://www.unece.org/fileadmin/DAM/cefact/brs/BRS-SmartContainer_v1.0.pdf

UNECE. (2019). *The UNECE Trade Facilitation*. White Paper on Real-time Smart Container data for supply chain excellence. ECE/Trade/446. Retrieved from https://www.unece.org/index.php?id=53347

Van Goor, A., Kruijtzer, A., & Esmeijer, G. (1990). *Goederenstroombestruing, voorraadbeheer en materials handling*. Leiden, Netherlands. ISBN 9020722778.

Watson, R. T., Lind, M., Delmeire, N., & Liesa, F. (2020). Shipping: A self-organising ecosystem. In M. Lind, M. P. Michaelides, R. Ward, & R. T. Watson (Eds.), *Maritime informatics*. Heidelberg: Springer.

Sustainable Maritime Transport and Maritime Informatics

Sukhjit Singh ⓘ and Bhaskar Sengupta ⓘ

1 Introduction

Shipping is a crucial and strategic sector, by providing the link via maritime supply chains; shipping is the backbone of international trade. The maritime transport industry is also recognised as one of the cleanest modes of global transport. Being an economic, reliable and safe mode of transport, ships providing sea mode of transportation are key enablers of globalisation. Driven by the growing world population and economic activity, the demand for shipping services is set to grow (UNCTAD, 2018). Maritime transport accounts for the largest share of tonne-kilometres and in the baseline scenario of ITF study (OECD/ITF, 2017); this is predicted to grow from 71% of total transport in 2015 to 75% by 2050.

Maritime shipping remains the most carbon efficient and cost-effective medium of transport for long-distance trade. The predictions of increased trade raise concerns for the associated GHG emissions caused by the combustion of fuel on-board ships. The business as usual (BAU) scenarios raise concerns over the negative externalities from the sector such as environmental degradation, including air emissions. The potential damage of these negative externalities will intensify if BAU is maintained (IMO, 2015). Although shipping is the most carbon efficient mode of transportation, according to the IMO's Third GHG Study (IMO, 2015), between the years 2007 and 2012, international shipping was responsible for an annual average of approximately 866 million tonnes of CO_2 emissions, which was about 2.4% of global greenhouse gas (GHG) emissions. These emissions are a

S. Singh (✉)
The University of Trinidad and Tobago, Chaguaramas, Trinidad and Tobago
e-mail: sukhjit.singh@utt.edu.tt

B. Sengupta
OSM Maritime Group, Singapore, Singapore
e-mail: bhaskar.sengupta@outlook.com

© The Editor(s) (if applicable) and The Author(s), under exclusive licence to Springer Nature Switzerland AG 2021
M. Lind et al. (eds.), *Maritime Informatics*, Progress in IS,
https://doi.org/10.1007/978-3-030-50892-0_6

direct consequence of the fuels (maritime bunker) used to power a ship's internal combustion engines and particulate matter (PM) released. The IMO has played the leading role in taking several measures to reduce the GHG from ships in collaboration with shipowners/operators and shipbuilders.

The global nature of shipping and climate change mitigation requires coordinated solutions at the international level. International commitment and cooperation are key in achieving sustainable development. The role of maritime transport in addressing the global sustainability imperative is increasingly recognised. Safe, secure, energy-efficient, affordable, reliable, low-carbon, climate-resilient and rule-based maritime transport systems contribute to achieving an economically efficient, socially equitable and environmentally sound development (UNCTAD, 2018). However, for this role to effectively materialise, unsustainable maritime transport practices that result in wide-ranging external costs need to be addressed.

As early as 1992, Langlois argued that using technology "is not an end-product but a means to an end or to a variety of ends" (Langlois, 1992). In this respect, the current capabilities of conventional maritime information systems (IS) are only sufficient to fulfil the needs of the customers of traditional service providers. In these context initiatives of information sharing platforms, collecting and dispersing data and information from multiple stakeholders, in a logical framework, needs adoption at large scale to meet the targets of diverse stakeholders in relation to the efficiency, safety and sustainability of the industry.

2   Sustainable Development and Impact of Shipping

The concept of sustainability first appeared in the Brundtland Report published in 1987. This document, which was also referred to as Our Common Future, was elaborated for the United Nations in order to warn about the negative environmental consequences of economic development and globalisation. It was written with the aim of offering solutions to the problems arising from industrialisation and population growth. Today, sustainability attempts to secure present needs without compromising the future generations. Sustainable development embraces environmental, social and economic objectives, to deliver long-term equitable growth which benefits current and future generations. Sustainability means understanding the future risks and acting on these risks (Fig. 1).

To achieve sustainable development, it is crucial to harmonise three core elements: *economic growth, social inclusion and environmental protection*, which are interconnected and are equally crucial for the well-being of individuals and societies. Environmental protection, to many, is the primary concern of the future of humanity. It defines how we should study and protect ecosystems, air quality, integrity and sustainability of our resources and focusing on the elements that place stress on the environment.

Sustainability demands that day-to-day operations must now routinely consider the UN Sustainable Development Goals (SDGs) in decisions and actions. Envi-

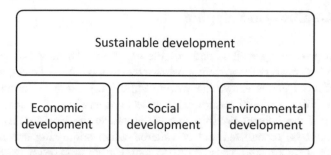

Fig. 1 Three elements of sustainable development

ronmental sustainability is awareness of risks associated with carbon emissions, ocean health and other impacts influenced by the associated operations. Moving towards more sustainable patterns of production and consumption was globally agreed upon as an essential part of the United Nations' Agenda 2030 on Sustainable Development and its 17 associated SDGs, which provide an important driver for progressing from a linear to a circular economy.

Of the three, the environmental dimension is widely addressed in the maritime sector and has been at the forefront of recent global issues, mostly in relation to ships and port equipment. Ships generate emissions at sea and within ports, while port equipment adds to the emissions within ports. While in port, ships engaged in cargo operations emit GHGs, such as NOx, SOx, CO_2 and particulate matter. The negative impact from these emissions on the health of adjacent urban and coastal populations is estimated in various studies (Bouman, Lindstad, Rialland, & Strømman, 2017; Huang, Wen, Geng, Zhou, & Xiao, 2018). The maritime sector has been less active in dealing with environmental issues in the past due to a lack of visibility and interaction with society when compared to the aviation and land transportation sectors. Among the several international organisations, the IMO has played the leading role in taking measures to reduce GHG emissions from ships and ports in collaboration with shipowners/operators, shipbuilders and ports.

With 12 of the 17 SDGs depending directly on the sustainable use of natural resources, increasing resource efficiency is a key strategy. The contemporary maritime sector is faced with the challenge of understanding the economic, social and environmental benefits of achieving the SDGs and minimising climate change. As a matter of urgency and driven by regulatory and economic factors, various solutions have been adopted at different levels in isolation from a global standardised approach. Several international developments continue to contribute to the implementation of the 2030 Agenda for Sustainable Development. The Paris Agreement under the United Nations Framework Convention on Climate Change and various IMO instruments provide the foundation for sustainable, low-carbon and resilient development in a changing climate (UNCTAD, 2019).

3   Sustainability in Shipping

In order to provide a seamless and reliable service in the most efficient manner, the maritime transportation system must deliver safe, secure, efficient, and reliable transportation of goods across the world, while minimising pollution, maximising energy efficiency, and ensuring resource conservation. To achieve this, the complexity of the interrelationships among actors in the maritime transportation system should be recognised and considered when addressing specific actions. Benamara, Hoffmann, and Youssef (2019) identify the linkages between shipping and sustainable development and highlight the stakeholders, trade-offs, policy issues, obstacles and enablers of sustainable shipping and the role of international institutions, including the IMO and UNCTAD (Fig. 2).

Underlying requirements for a sustainable maritime transportation system are well-organised maritime administrations that co-operate internationally and promote compliance with global standards through proactive participation. To achieve a high efficiency, the coordination and support from shore is intrinsic for shipping. And most importantly, the data required to achieve the sustainability will need digital data sharing in standardised format across a common platform. Trust among stakeholders is a must to have completeness and transparency of shared data (Fig. 3).

Maritime transportation involves many stakeholders, where one decision and action can affect the whole logistic chain. Ships and ports are two crucial entities, and their operational performance determines the level of efficiency achieved. Information exchange across the maritime logistic chain is still very traditional in the majority of the developing world. As a result, all associated activities are often exposed to last minute changes and negatively impact planned actions and their

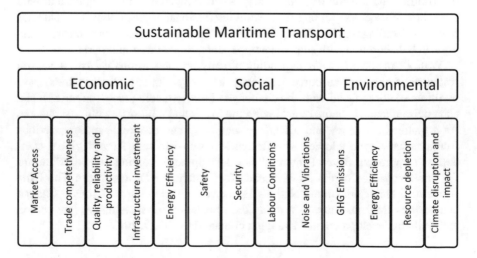

Fig. 2 Sustainable maritime transport (adapted from Benamara et al., 2019)

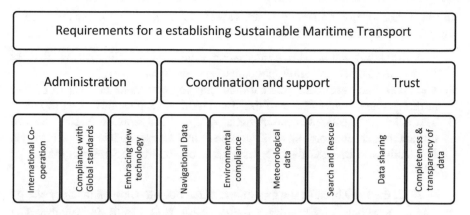

Fig. 3 Underlying requirements to achieve sustainability in shipping

efficiency. Such lack of coordination in data exchange among all involved actors usually results in a significant waste of time, which leads to a decrease in efficiency. This has direct impact on the environmental and economic sustainability aspects.

4   IMO and Its Role in Environmental Sustainability

The IMO is the UN specialised agency responsible for setting global standards for the safety, security and facilitation of international shipping and the prevention of pollution by ships. The IMO's regulatory framework covers various technical matters pertaining to the safety of ships and of life at sea, efficiency of navigation and the prevention and control of marine and air pollution from ships.

The Paris Agreement, signed in 2016, is an agreement within the United Nations Framework Convention on Climate Change, dealing with greenhouse gas emissions mitigation, adaptation, and finance, signed in 2016. It appeals for a global response to combat the threat of climate change. Efforts from every industry are being structured around reducing GHG emissions through the use of alternate fuels or energy efficiency measures. While the Paris Agreement does not include international shipping, the preceding UN Kyoto Protocol recognised the significantly increasing contribution of shipping emissions to the global climate change, and a mandate was given to the IMO to deal with maritime GHG emissions. The IMO has implemented a number of strategies formulated and implemented through the organisation's Marine Environment Protection Committee (MEPC), such as the development of MARPOL (The International Convention for the Prevention of Pollution from Ships) Annex VI-Prevention of Air Pollution from Ships and IMO

Initial GHG Strategy adopted by MEPC (MEPC 72) in April 2018. The IMO has so far published three greenhouse gas studies:

1. The 2000 study estimated that international shipping in 1996 contributed about 1.8% of the global total anthropogenic CO_2 emissions.
2. The 2009 study estimated international shipping emissions in 2007 to be 880 million tonnes, or about 2.7% of the global total anthropogenic CO_2 emissions.
3. The 2015 study estimated international shipping emissions in 2012 to be 796 million tonnes, or about 2.2% of the global total anthropogenic CO_2 emissions. The study also updated the CO_2 estimates for 2007 to 885 million tonnes, or 2.8%.

In 2011, the IMO became the first international body to adopt mandatory energy efficiency measures for an entire industry sector with a suite of technical and operational requirements for new and existing vessels entering into use on and after 2013. By 2025 new ships built must be 30% more energy efficient than those built in 2014. The initial IMO strategy, which will be revised in 2023 and reviewed in 2028, includes an overall vision for decarbonisation, GHG reduction targets through to 2050, a list of potential short-, mid- and long-term measures to meet these targets, barriers to achieving the targets and supportive measures to help achieve them, and criteria for future review. The strategy incorporates quantitative carbon intensity and GHG reduction targets for the international shipping sector, including:

- At least a 40% reduction in carbon intensity by 2030 and pursuing efforts towards a 70% reduction by 2050, both compared to 2008 levels
- Peak GHG emissions from international shipping as soon as possible and reduce them by at least 50% by 2050 compared to 2008 levels while pursuing efforts towards phasing them out consistent with the Paris Agreement temperature goals
- New phases of the EEDI, to be reviewed within MEPC

5   Accounting for GHG Emissions from Shipping

The Kyoto Protocol, adopted in 2007, is an international treaty which extends the 1992 UN Framework Convention on Climate Change (UNFCCC) that commits state parties to reduce GHG emissions, based on the scientific consensus that global warming is occurring, and it is extremely likely that human-made CO_2 emissions have predominantly caused it. The Protocol calls for GHG emissions from fuels used for both international aviation and maritime transportation (bunker fuels) to be accounted for and reduced through initiatives from the International Civil Aviation Organization (ICAO) and the IMO, respectively. However, the Intergovernmental Panel on Climate Change (IPCC) guidelines for the preparation of GHG inventories requires that emissions from international aviation and maritime transport (international bunker fuel emissions) be calculated as part of the national GHG inventories of parties but should be excluded from national totals and reported separately. This is due to the nature of shipping where a vessel plying trade for a country might opt to register with country's registry (flag). The emissions of the vessel will be accounted for by the flag state of the vessel. The IMO's Data Collection System (DCS) will collect international bunker consumption figures from the flag states for the vessels registered to them regardless of their region(s) of operation.

IMO Mandatory Data Collection and Reporting MARPOL Annex VI Chapter 4 Regulation 22A adopted by MEPC (MEPC 70) in October 2016 entered into force on March 1st, 2018 with a mandatory requirement that all commercial ships of 5000 gross tonnage and above collect data on their fuel oil consumption (each type of fuel used) and transport work parameters. These data are to be submitted in annual reports to their flag state. Once the flag state has verified that the Ship Energy Efficiency Management Plan (SEEMP) and the data reported are in accordance with the requirements outlined in Regulation 22A and the 2017 Guidelines for Administration Verification of Ship Fuel Oil Consumption Data, it will issue a Certificate of Compliance to the ship. The flag state will subsequently transfer the data to the IMO Ship Fuel Oil Consumption Database, and the data will then be used to produce an annual report to MEPC. The Data Collection System (DCS) is the first step of a three steps approach (data collection and reporting → data analysis → decision-making) by the IMO for developing a comprehensive strategy on the reduction of GHG emissions from ships.

The DCS is expected to provide the IMO with reliable data which, when analysed, will inform relevant decisions and policies in the MEPC. The data can also be used by ship operators to improve their ships' Energy Efficiency Operational Index (EEOI). Data collection began on January 1, 2019, with first reporting for calendar year 2019 by Spring 2020, as shown in Fig. 4.

The mandatory data collection system for ship fuel oil consumption will provide a robust dataset on which future decisions on additional measures, over and above those already adopted, can be made. These data can then be analysed applying Maritime Informatics techniques discussed in the third section of this book.

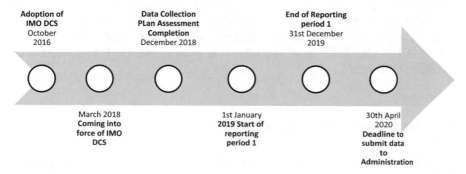

Fig. 4 IMO DCS roadmap

The IMO has set ambitious targets for the shipping industry. In addition to the recently enforced 2020 Global Sulphur Cap and carriage ban, shipowners and operators must consider the GHG targets for 2030 and even more ambitious emissions goals for 2050. The IMO contributes to international cooperation to facilitate access to clean-energy research and technology, in particular energy efficiency and advanced, cleaner fossil-fuel technology, and promotes investment in energy infrastructure and clean-energy technology. In response to increasing concerns about the IMO's effort to mitigate climate change from the impact of shipping, the IMO, through its Marine Environment Division, has undertaken bold initiatives aimed at supporting the uptake and implementation of energy-efficient measures in shipping.

6 Global Maritime Energy Efficiency Partnerships: A GEF-UNDP-IMO Project

The Global Maritime Energy Efficiency Partnerships (GLoMEEP) project supports 10 lead pilot countries for the purposes of championing:

- Legal, policy and institutional reforms
- Awareness raising and capacity building activities
- Establishment of public private partnerships to encourage technology transfer

The lead pilot countries are Argentina, China, Georgia, India, Jamaica, Malaysia, Morocco, Panama, the Philippines and South Africa. The GLoMEEP project offers considerable assistance in form of toolkits to the global community in the technical requirements for energy efficiency in shipping. Focussing on developing countries, where shipping is increasingly concentrated, GloMEEP has created global, regional and national partnerships to build capacity to address maritime energy efficiency and for countries to bring this issue into the mainstream within their own development policies, and dialogues. GloMEEP recently launched the Global Industry Alliance to Support Low-Carbon Shipping, in which a group of world-leading private companies from different sectors of the industry are coming together to contribute to tackling the challenges of decarbonizing the shipping sector (IMO, 2018). GloMEEP is an opportunity to demonstrate the power and use of Maritime Informatics.

7 The Global MTCC Network Project

Another key initiative is the Global MTCC Network (GMN) project, formally entitled 'Capacity Building for Climate Mitigation in the Maritime Shipping Industry'. This project enables developing countries, especially least developed countries and small island developing states, in five target regions (Africa, Asia, Caribbean, Latin America and Pacific), to effectively implement energy efficiency measures through technical assistance, capacity building and promoting technical cooperation. The project is funded by the EU and implemented by the IMO through contractual partnerships with five centres of excellence across the developing world. The Maritime Technology Cooperation Centres (MTCCs) act as regional focal points for a wide range of activities including (IMO, 2017):

- Building compliance with existing and future international energy efficiency regulations
- Help participating countries develop national energy efficiency policies and measures for their maritime sectors
- Promoting the uptake of low-carbon technologies and operations in maritime transport
- Establishing voluntary pilot-data collection and reporting systems to inform the global regulatory process

The individual MTCCs are positioned to have considerable impact in their respective regions through pilot projects, capacity building and stakeholder engagement with all level of industry including policymakers and operational personnel within governmental bodies. Many of the MTCCs have created academic, government and private sector industry partnerships. For example, The Caribbean region is impacted by the operations of MTCCs, which provides a significant opportunity for the region to make strides in addressing the complex issues of climate action in the maritime industry (Singh & Rambarath-Parasram, 2018). The MTCC Caribbean established an online voluntary reporting system in June 2017 as a pilot. Data were collected on the use of equipment and machinery on-board, including air emissions abatement and energy efficiency technologies. Ships of 400 GRT and above are encouraged to submit fuel oil consumption and voyage data on a voluntary basis at each port of call while operating in the region. The reporting system provided the baseline of energy-efficient technology and fuel consumption for ships trading in the Caribbean region.

8   The Role of Data in Maritime Transport Sustainability

In shipping, digitalisation and the use of data is continuing to have a huge impact. Digitalisation is shaping the shipping industry's future in every aspect, whether on-board or ashore, taking advantage of new designs and technologies to improve efficiency and safe operations. Environmental sustainability has become a top priority for regulators and shipowners alike. Decarbonisation in the maritime space is not achievable in the absence of consequential operational data. An understanding of a ship's operational output requires measurement and analysis of fuel efficiencies before it can be used as an influence within carbon reduction strategies. The number of possible interactions between a ship and its environment are significant and harnessing this information is critical. Data is essential to understand, optimise and ensure compliance within day-to-day activities. Ships are becoming sophisticated sensor hubs and data generators, producing and transmitting data in real time. Regulatory mandates, such as IMO DCS and EU MRV require the collation and reporting of emissions data. Digital innovation with various information technology (IT) solutions has supported the shipping companies with compliance to advance decarbonisation in the industry.

The improvement in availability and connectivity of satellite communication has increased the ability to transfer large volumes of data at ever-lower cost. These digital data flows are driving the automation of processes and functions, and they can have a positive impact on safety and commercial and environmental performance. Therefore, combining data streams from multiple sources allows the maritime industry to be more efficient and responsive. The sustainability impact of digitalisation with respect of economic implication is considered more important than the other dimensions (Kayikci, 2018). The environmental implications of digitalisation have most impact on reducing waste, pollution, and the emission of greenhouse gases. Digitalisation of logistics is still in an early maturation phase. However where implemented, digitalisation and improved connectivity on-board ships and between shore and ship offered improved environmental footprint and safety performance. Data continues to play a significant role in ship operations specially in reducing operating costs. Route and arrival optimisation has helped vessels reduce fuel consumption. However, the data can vary from simple estimated time of arrival (ETA) required for port scheduling to very complex data on specific components on-board vessels. To explore maximum benefits, some form of standardisation is required. For this reason, the role of data in sustainability can be further explored, and we expect such developments in the future.

9   What's Next

Since the IMO's announcement of its initial GHG strategy in April 2018 with the ambition of reducing total annual GHG emissions by at least 50% by 2050 compared to 2008, digitalisation has been viewed as a key enabler to meet this goal. Industry action has been driven by this ambitious target. More and more shipping companies are taking a long-term perspective focused on decarbonisation. Shipowners and operators are continuously exploring optimum technical solutions to meet the decarbonising needs for their fleets. Digitalisation can make decarbonisation faster and more effective. Energy efficiency gains in shipping operations can be achieved only by data-enabled decisions. Digitalisation will provide the means to measure energy efficiency by providing management of data allowing informed decisions on decarbonisation. Digitalisation is imperative in the journey to zero carbon shipping. Sustainable maritime transport will also be essential in the achievement of the UN's vision for sustainable development by providing an energy efficient, reliable and economical means of freight transport.

Maritime transport has been identified as a laggard sector in the Industry Digitalisation Index (Morgan Stanley, 2016). But recent regulatory and sustainability demands have provided the momentum to fully embrace digital transformation. While implementation has been slow in relation to other sectors various industry stakeholders are collaborating towards implementing digital transformation. Digitalisation and joint collaborative platforms and solutions enabled by new technologies and innovations are increasingly used by the shipping industry, transforming business and partnership models. ABS and Daewoo Shipbuilding & Marine Engineering (DSME) have signed a joint development project (JDP) agreement to explore decarbonisation and digitalisation strategies for very large crude carriers (VLCC) and ultra large container ships (ULCS). The JDP aims for DSME to develop ABS approved VLCC and ULCS vessel designs, which offer potential solutions to the IMO's 2030 decarbonisation goals. The JDP also covers onshore remote monitoring, SMART criteria (specific, measurable, achievable, relevant and time-bound) and autonomy technology, as well as the development and review of cybersecurity aspects associated with the DSME Smart Ship platform (Digital Ship, 2019). In a similar way, the Lloyds Register (LR) and China State Shipbuilding Corporation (CSSC) collaborative research programme will look at the use of blockchain and digital twin technologies and will evaluate ship propulsion systems, including various clean-energy sources and their certification. FPSO, FLNG and FSRU design concepts will also be assessed (NafsGreen, 2019). Pilot projects utilising new technologies have demonstrated tangible results and offered new opportunities to achieve greater sustainability in shipping and ports and improved performance and efficiency.

Digitalisation and automation are transforming the shipping sector. To achieve digitalisation uniformly in the maritime world, it is essential that ships and ports are data enabled and data ready. Recognising the growing need for well-managed big data connectivity on merchant vessels, Ship Earth Station (SES) networks are working in tandem with shipping companies to ensure that their digital strategies are achieved in a simple, cost-effective way. High-quality satellite broadband underpinned by superior ground infrastructure and optimal VSAT (very small aperture terminals) can make a difference by having the capability and realising the full potential of the investment in digital solutions. New technologies on the horizon for the coming 10 years include cellular networks in coastal areas; VDES (new data service on the VHF band); Wi-Fi in ports; and, most importantly, satellite communications, improving coverage and bandwidth. Currently, the maritime industry contributes to the growth in deployment of VSAT equipment on-board ships. According to COMSYS, the number of active maritime VSAT installations quadrupled from 2008 (6001) to 2014 (21,922) and the number exceeded 40,000 by 2018. By 2020, most classed vessels were broadband capable. Also, the VSAT network capacity is increasing owing to the introduction of new high throughput satellite (HTS) systems, with 2–10 times higher throughput than classical satellites. The overall VSAT network capacity covering maritime regions will experience at least a tenfold growth to some 200 Gbps in 2025, implying a massive increase in data transfer rates and decreased costs per bit for the connected vessels. Ships, systems and components are already accessible from almost any location. At the same time, combining data streams from multiple sources will boost performance management (including fleet utilisation, routing, trim, fuel consumption, emission management) and asset integrity management, building on remote condition monitoring as well as allowing for an increased level of automation. This could reduce lead times and fuel consumption by optimising arrival times and allow related efficiencies on the shore side too (and vice versa) (DNV GL, 2020). The aim is to promote efficient and secure trade, including offering greater supply-chain visibility and use of electronic documents, ultimately benefitting customers who rely on shipping industry services (UNCTAD, 2019).

Forecasting remains an inexact science, and the data it depends upon can be inconsistent and incomplete. Lack of transparency leads to failure of understanding among supply-chain stakeholders. However, increased transparency not only enables stakeholders to respond efficiently to disruptions but also provide capability to anticipate them. In addition, the further development and study of Maritime Informatics will be most important in prescribing how the supply chain should operate. For example, the aim is not simply to achieve optimal environmental efficiency by route and arrival optimisation but to enhance the capability to proactively inform the many stakeholders across the entire chain as applicable to circumstances and enable them to operate in a dynamic mode to modify plans accordingly.

Industry action, aligned with similar principles as the IMO's Global Industry Alliance to Support Low-Carbon Shipping (GIA), is already focusing on the vessels that can implement Just In Time (JIT) arrivals at a global level (IMO, 2018). Currently JIT is not a common industry practice, and IMO's Facilitation Committee discussed the idea of providing vessels with regular updates concerning the availability of berths, mostly in the 12 h prior to a port arrival. By timing their arrival, ships would be able to optimise their speed; by slowing down for JIT arrival, they reduce the carbon footprint of shipping as well as saving fuel. The GIA discussions also concluded that JIT arrival is not a problem, but operationally unreliable/inaccurate data is a major impediment to securing a reliable berthing window. Contractual solutions are required in the case of tankers and bulk ships to allow a ship to arrive during a 12-h berthing window.

Other ongoing developments include the PortCDM concept, for maritime services based on standards and open interfaces. The concept is built on information sharing and collaborating to optimise the maritime transport chain while increasing safety and sustainability. In addition to supporting the key performance indicators (KPIs) of duration time, waiting time, berth productivity, capacity utilisation, predictability and punctuality, the various timestamps that are shared include the arrival and the departure times of ships and/or the duration of the services provided to ships during their port calls. These data are a very valuable contributor to the data set needed to measure the efficiency of resources. Wherever possible, the data required to evaluate the KPIs and to provide data for other useful efficiency analyses should be shared by machine-to-machine interaction using a standard data format such as the S-211 port call message format and the timestamps that underpin

PortCDM and data sharing (Lind et al., 2019). Monitoring performance through the KPIs and associated analyses enables the different actors to improve their operations and utilisation of physical infrastructure and variable resources.

10   Issues for Discussion

In summary, embracing digitalisation prepares the maritime sector for the demands of future. Extensive understanding of Maritime Informatics and its role in keeping maritime transport sustainable is a relevant imperative for the industry. This understanding of digital transformation is beyond technology and improving processes. It is more about change management, "a company's ability to evolve its corporate culture to not only take advantage of emerging technology but to also critically embrace the new business strategies that those technologies drive" (Accenture, 2016), especially in the maritime sector which has been very traditional and lagged behind in many aspect of its operations.

Further research on the implementation of sustainability in the maritime sector is obligatory, and it must consider peculiarities in shipping and the port sector covering intermodal transport, port governance, development strategy, and policies because they will influence implementation and policies of sustainability and intervention policy (Lee, Kwon, & Ruan, 2019). The decision-making and planning processes often lack sufficient coordination, and they create potential for conflicts. Policy coherence can be enhanced by using common platforms to take advantage of interrelationships. This can be further enhanced by conducting comprehensive policy analysis, defining institutional mechanisms for monitoring and collecting data and proposing strategies that will take advantage of identified interrelationships (Singh & Rambarath-Parasram, 2018). Research and data collection for enhancing sustainability, particularly in developing economies, is at an embryonic stage and voluntary in nature. Despite a body of knowledge, the adoption of best practices, lessons learnt, modern technologies, and sustainability continues to remain a challenge as part of mainstream shipping practices. Countries will need to combine a wide range of policies, from support to technology, research and development to behavioural measures, adequately supported by the required legal and institutional framework. In our opinion the solution may be in understanding the philosophy.

The significant restrictions put in place during the Covid-19 outbreak reduced GHG emissions dramatically. Are we ready to continue with drastic steps to help maintain this reduction or will we wait until we are forced to do so? Can the industry develop the required trust or streamline its principle to be an ethical and ecologically sustainable business?

References

Accenture. (2016). *Accenture Technology Vision 2016*. Retrieved from https://www.accenture.com/t20170227t030304__w__/us-en/_acnmedia/pdf-20/accenture-technology-trends-technology-vision-updated.pdf

Benamara, H., Hoffmann, J., & Youssef, F. (2019). Maritime transport – The sustainability imperative. In H. N. Psaraftis (Ed.), *Sustainable shipping: A cross-disciplinary view*. Berlin: Springer.

Bouman, E. A., Lindstad, E., Rialland, A. I., & Strømman, A. H. (2017). State-of-the-art technologies, measures, and potential for reducing GHG emissions from shipping—A review. *Transportation Research Part D: Transport and Environment, 52*, 408–421.

Digital Ship. (2019). *ABS and DSME sign digitalisation and decarbonisation agreement*. Retrieved from https://thedigitalship.com/news/maritime-software/item/6327-abs-and-dsme-sign-digitalisation-and-decarbonisation-agreement

DNV GL. (2020). *Digitization of shipping*. Retrieved from https://to2025.dnvgl.com/shipping/digitalization/

Huang, L., Wen, Y., Geng, X., Zhou, C., & Xiao, C. (2018). Integrating multi-source maritime information to estimate ship exhaust emissions under wind, wave and current conditions. *Transportation Research Part D: Transport and Environment, 59*, 148–159.

IMO. (2015). *Third IMO Greenhouse Gas Study 2014* [Online]. Retrieved from http://www.imo.org/en/OurWork/Environment/PollutionPrevention/AirPollution/Documents/Third%20Greenhouse%20Gas%20Study/GHG3%20Executive%20Summary%20and%20Report.pdf

IMO. (2017). *Global MTCC Network*. Retrieved from https://gmn.imo.org/about-gmn/

IMO. (2018). *IMO holds Roundtable on Just-in-Time Operation of Ships*. Retrieved from https://glomeep.imo.org/news/imo-holds-roundtable-on-just-in-time-operation-of-ships/

Kayikci, Y. (2018). Sustainability impact of digitization in logistics. *Procedia Manufacturing, 21*, 782–789. https://doi.org/10.1016/j.promfg.2018.02.184.

Langlois, N. (1992). Transaction-cost economics in real time. *Industrial and Corporate Change, 1*(1), 99–127.

Lee, P. T., Kwon, O. K., & Ruan, K. (2019). Sustainability challenges in maritime transport and logistics industry and its way ahead. *Sustainability, 11*, 1331. https://doi.org/10.3390/su11051331.

Lind, M., Bjørn-Andersen, N., Bergmann, M., Ward, R., Haraldson, S., Michaelides, M., Zerem, A., Angelov, V., Karlsson, M., Andersen, T., Gimenez, J., & Ferrus, G. (2019). *Maturity Level 7 in implementing PortCDM – Continuous improvement of PortCDM principles*. Retrieved from http://fathom.world/wp-content/uploads/2018/09/Implementation-Note-5-Reaching-Maturity-Level-7.pdf

Morgan Stanley. (2016). *Morgan Stanley's digitalization index in riding the long tail of the digital revolution*. Retrieved from https://www.morganstanley.com/ideas/digital-revolution-big-data-iot-productivity.html

NafsGreen. (2019). *CSSC and LR to collaborate on decarbonisation and digitalisation research*. Retrieved from https://www.nafsgreen.gr/green-sea/environment/7528-cssc-and-lr-to-collaborate-on-decarbonisation-and-digitalisation-research.html

OECD. (2017). *ITF Transport Outlook 2050*. Retrieved from https://read.oecd-ilibrary.org/transport/itf-transport-outlook-2017/transport-demand-and-co2-emissions-to-2050_9789282108000-5-en#page21

Singh, S., & Rambarath-Parasram, V. (2018). Considerations for the Latin American and Caribbean region in light of the global move towards low carbon shipping. In J. García Alcaraz, L. Rivera Cadavid, R. González-Ramírez, G. Leal Jamil, & M. Chong Chong (Eds.), *Best practices in manufacturing processes*. Cham: Springer.

UNCTAD. (2018). *Sustainable freight transport in support of the 2030 Agenda for Sustainable Development*. Retrieved from https://unctad.org/meetings/en/SessionalDocuments/cimem7d17_en.pdf

UNCTAD. (2019). *Review of Maritime Transport 2019*. Retrieved from https://unctad.org/en/PublicationsLibrary/rmt2018_en.pdf

Connecting Cities and Ports via Maritime Informatics

Terje Rygh ⓘ, José Manuel Pagés Sánchez ⓘ, Albert González ⓘ, and Patrik Rudolfsson ⓘ

1 Introduction

Digitalisation and smart technologies open up immense possibilities for innovative solutions for connecting ports and cities. This is also crucial for achieving the United Nations (UN) 2030 Agenda for Sustainable Development, in which the cities and their ports are key players for handling the global challenges due to increased urbanisation and the unsustainable use of resources. To achieve a sustainable future for the world, ports and cities will have to cooperate with the quadruple helix, the "stakeholders that represent key local actors from government, research and scientific institutions, companies and citizens" (Igi-global.com, 2020).

We have to break down existing barriers between actors. We need to improve collaboration and co-creation with citizens in the cities and regions who consume and use services and goods. We need to invest in better technology and discuss which methods and standards we need. This has to be done in a collaborative way, not on an individual basis as it is often done at present. This discussion cannot be

T. Rygh (✉)
The City of Stavanger, Stavanger, Norway
e-mail: terje.rygh@stavanger.kommune.no

J. M. P. Sánchez
AIVP – The Worldwide Network of Port Cities, Hamburg, Germany
e-mail: jsanchez@aivp.org

A. González
Barcelona Port Authority (APB), Barcelona, Spain
e-mail: albert.gonzalez@portdebarcelona.cat

P. Rudolfsson
Kvarken Ports, Umeå, Sweden
e-mail: patrik.rudolfsson@kvarkenports.com

M. Lind et al. (eds.), *Maritime Informatics*, Progress in IS,
https://doi.org/10.1007/978-3-030-50892-0_7

held without mentioning the Smart Cities and the Smart Ports that are working to achieve these outcomes. We need to have a transition where we do not look at this exclusively from the maritime side but from several perspectives. If information systems (IS) governance in cities and ports is to be successful in solving and improving these tasks, we need joint efforts.

For the reader to better understand how cities and ports can be connected through digitalisation in the present situation, it is crucial to understand the context of the historical evolution of the port-city relationship and port-city collaboration.

During the twentieth century, the port-city relationship faced serious problems that still have to be resolved. Before this relationship is improved, it will be hard to pinpoint any universal quick fix or solution. We will therefore first discuss the history leading to the present situation and what collaborative challenges need to be overcome before we look at some of the opportunities that can be gained.

To improve the collaboration and co-creation between the ports, cities and the quadruple helix of stakeholders, all stakeholders will have to define their common goals and develop a joint roadmap. These will have to be clear and unbiased. They will need objective and universal definitions, standards and methods, to reach a future where Maritime Informatics creates more value for ports and cities.

1.1 Port and City Cooperation in the Industrial and Modern Era

Ports have always been an important part of society because they connect the land across the sea, and they connect many of the world's major cities. Many of the world's most thriving cities are situated within a short distance of the sea or have direct access to one or more ports. Ports, because they handle the import and export of goods and frequently are services centres, are the economic engines of cities and the hinterland that they service. Ports are also a base for a city's identity, social structure and interaction with global markets.

From the beginning of the industrial revolution, ports and cities have evolved at a rapid pace as a result of increased urbanisation and new technology, until the industrial revolution port and cities evolved in organic symbiosis (Bird, 1963; Hoyle, 1989; Hayuth, 1982). The new technologies that drove the industrial revolution changed the scale of production and of transportation systems. These innovations modified the port-city relationship. To respond to extended supply chains and logistic demands, ports modified their layouts, including industrial-scale expansion through landfills and the introduction of physical infrastructure, such as railways and roads that can act as barriers, separating a port from its city.

In the second phase, in the 1960s, the transport container introduced a change in the scale, further separating port and city. However, port and city remained in contact both on the port-city interface that gradually extended to the regional scale and in an ecosystem formed around the port and urban activities. Today, the port-city relationship remains unbalanced, the local externalities caused by ports contrast with the benefits this infrastructure provides to locations hundreds of kilometres away in the hinterland (Merk, 2013). Further, some question the competitive advantage ports bring to their port cities (Zhao, Xu, Wall, & Stavropoulos, 2017). While others question if the economic resources ports require, can or cannot provide better results if invested in other urban sectors (Grossmann, 2008).

While the physical decoupling of ports and their cities took place, governance and social issues emerged. Ports had been historically the economic engines of port cities, the base for their identity and social structure. Entire families worked in ports (Mah, 2014), neighbourhoods with characteristic atmospheres grew next to the docks (Schubert, 2008), as well as large corporations developed representative buildings or contributed to the urban development (Hein, 2014). However, this social connection gradually faded as ports became automated, introduced no-go areas, provided fewer jobs and increasingly quarantined themselves from the city. Ports turned their back on their cities. The social disconnection is also visible in the unbalanced power relationship established in the governance of ports (Hesse, 2017). Port authorities are no longer the "gatekeepers" they used to be, being today just a "pawn in the game" (Slack, 1993) against multi-national corporations with considerable investment capacity and influence.

Against this backdrop, architects and planners initially focused on waterfront regeneration projects of abandoned waterfront areas. The dominant idea was treating both elements, port and city, as separate areas, only interacting with the interface (Hayuth, 1982). However, port and city remain connected, albeit in different ways than before. There are increasing efforts to develop joint planning solutions, tackling major problems, discussed in global forums such as the UN, but only solvable by acting on the local scale. The UN 2030 Agenda for Sustainable Development together with its 17 Sustainable Development Goals (SDGs) puts a spotlight on the challenges ports and cities will face in the coming decade. Global organisations such as the international association of cities and ports [Association International Villes et Ports (AIVP)] has led efforts to provide a general guideline for sustainable port-city relationships, reflecting the SDGs. These efforts have resulted in the AIVP Agenda 2030 (AIVP, 2019), a document translating the SDGs into ten goals for port cities, fostering the cooperation between partners, including port authorities, municipalities, private companies and citizens.

The ten goals of the AIVP Agenda 2030 strive for climate change adaptation, energy transition, circular economy, substantial mobility, innovative governance, a vibrant port culture, human capital development, protecting biodiversity and reducing the impact of negative externalities on a port city's inhabitants. Although the smart port city approach is not explicitly mentioned in the document, it is a necessary strategy to tackle the different challenges these goals include. Smart technologies increasingly play a crucial role in facilitating the interaction between port and city activities across different fields.

The new technologies that emerged in the late twentieth and the first decades of the twenty-first century offer now the opportunity to recover from the lack of symbiosis and improve the port-city relationship.

1.2   The Environmental Strain

Since the first use of water and steam power in the late eighteenth century, we have experienced the implementation of electricity, the mass production assembly line, standardisation, computers and automation, which have been crucial to the mass production of goods. There has been an increasing consumption, which in turn has driven the value of global exports up almost exponentially (Fig. 1).

As we can see from Fig. 1, the growth of exports and the output of goods produced in cities and regions all over the world has increased nearly exponentially in the last century. This, in turn, increases the need for capital, energy, logistics, and surveillance and control systems. This growth and exploitation of natural resources is not sustainable. Cities and ports have both grown and benefited from the investment and are themselves growing and contributing to the environmental impact. A major digital transformation might be able to rectify past environmental damage, and Maritime Informatics can potentially contribute to improving port cities.

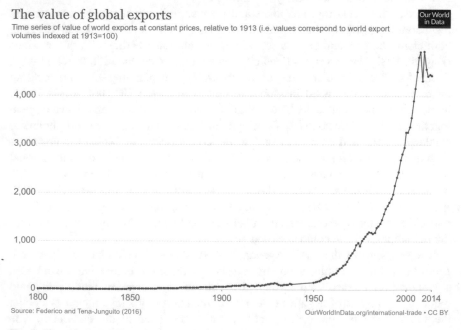

The value of global exports

Time series of value of world exports at constant prices, relative to 1913 (i.e. values correspond to world export volumes indexed at 1913=100)

Source: Federico and Tena-Junguito (2016)

OurWorldInData.org/international-trade · CC BY

Fig. 1 The value of global exports (Our World in Data, 2019)

1.3   The Complexity of the Smart Ports and Smart Cities

While ports may appear similar, and we sometimes talk about them as if they were identical, they are all different, as are the cities. The complexity ranges from the individual socioeconomic aspects, geo-location, market opportunities, the needs, and available solutions, as well as political focus, transparency, flexibility, and area of interest. The "mix" will vary by location and may cause unwanted tension and instability.

The Smart City focus of interacting cities and ports may influence an individual port so much that an "identical twin" port, situated somewhere else in the world, may actually look completely different. As stated earlier, what is "good" for one entity may not be good for another. Smart Ports and Smart Cities can have different performing characteristics, dependent on city size (inhabitants), demography, politics, policies, geographical location, and other city-specific characteristics.

Even so, the main goals of a Smart City and a Smart Port are to improve collaboration with their partners and the citizens. They want to achieve solutions that follow the Smart City principle of ensuring a positive "impact on issues of Urban Quality such as housing, economy, culture, social and environmental conditions" and supporting a port's surroundings (TU Wien, 2020a, b).

Both ports and cities have the common aim to be as attractive, efficient and socially beneficial as possible. They want to improve citizens' quality of life and support all their stakeholders sustainably and profitably. The goal should, therefore, be to find the best way to work together to govern the challenges of complex entities and help achieve the best solution to the Smart City goals and help identify common indicators and information sharing platforms.

2   Digital and Non-digital Cooperation Between Stakeholders

In the present era, cyber-physical systems are connected electronically, a complete supply and value chain can be visualised, and some systems make decisions without human intervention. This fourth industrial revolution is not just Internet of Things (IoT), computers and robotics but also "[...] encompasses areas which are not normally classified as industry, such as **smart cities** for instance" (Wikipedia.org, 2019).

If we are to mitigate the environmental footprint of humankind and achieve the UN SDGs, we need information systems that contribute to reducing poverty and mitigating the gap between the rich and poor nations and regions. Ports will be important partners in this endeavour. Cities and ports need to find the right methods and information systems for handling and using of data in a "smart" manner.

2.1 The Challenging Task of Defining "Smart"

What do we mean when we use the term "smart" in "smart solutions", "Smart Cities" and "Smart Ports"?

The answer to what *smart* is will undoubtedly be as different and ambiguous as the background of each person we might ask and will most likely vary over time. As individuals, we will over time have new or changed needs, views or priorities. In this chapter, we work on the assumption that a smart solution is one benefiting one or more individuals or stakeholders, by using technology, tools and methods in a Smart City or Smart Port, or actors who come in contact with these entities. A smart solution may be to digitalise the SDGs and the Key Performance Indicators (KPIs) as mentioned in the section "Defining Smart in the Ports" and "Smart City and Smart Port indicators". Solving mobility issues in cities and ports by reducing queues may be another smart solution. But we need to recognise that in solving one problem, we might create unanticipated negative consequences. A Smart City or a Smart Port will most likely also change over time, as will their symbiosis.

A smart solution is perhaps best defined as "a good solution" for the person experiencing it, while remaining well aware of the subjectivity in "good", which can be as ambiguous and difficult to interpret and define as "smart". A good solution needs the whole process to be transparent and people-centric and be driven by co-creation. It is an almost impossible task to create solutions that "fit" everybody. Making all happy and content can perhaps be done, but it will most certainly be very costly and resource-intensive at best, if not unachievable, with today's technology.

"Good enough" may be the best solution we can develop and manage at present. Moreover, "smart solutions" should continuously be tested to demonstrate that they solve real problems. This can be done by early prototyping where we can quickly test interventions. Many Smart Cities were initially very technology-driven and often failed. As a result, there is now an increased focus on cooperation and citizen involvement.

We should not build solutions that only benefit a few. We need to test if the present solutions are "good enough" and challenge them if they are not (Can we defend the cost, or can we save time and money?). If new solutions will produce more or better services and goods, we must have a good reason not to swap to them. We should always seek new knowledge, new methods and ways to use them better for humankind and secure the future on our planet, sustainably and economically.

2.2 Defining Smart in the Ports

There are many definitions for the word "smart" in the context of the global port and terminal network. Some industry experts believe that being smart relates more to the mind-set of a given port or terminal, where policy decisions and smart use of resources takes precedence over technology and innovations (Port Technology International, 2020).

We firmly believe in this line of thinking, as does the port of Barcelona as an example. Smart people can deploy the technology that orientates a port towards a "smart" model that improves competitiveness and ensures its long-term survival. A smart port is an automated port that uses nascent technology, such as IoT and blockchain technology, and other technology-based methods to improve performance, economic competitiveness and environmental sustainability.

2.3 What Is All This "Fuss" About Being Smart? Why Bother?

Urbanisation creates demand for goods and services, causing a heavy strain on nature when humans are using the resources of the Earth in an unsustainable way. The UN sees this as a major problem, as we risk handing over an unbalanced planet to future generations. It states that "Understanding the key trends in urbanisation likely to unfold over the coming years is crucial to the implementation of the 2030 Agenda for Sustainable Development, including efforts to forge a new framework of urban development" (UN.org, 2018). Many parts of the UN's list of 17 SDGs are central to the future issues Smart Cities and Smart Ports will have to solve collectively (UN, 2019).

2.4 What Is a Smart Port and a Smart City?

Since ports and the maritime industry often are self-organising and unique ecosystems, operating somewhat independently from the many cities they may serve, they also have the opportunity to define their version of a Smart Port. Catalina Grimalt at the Port of Barcelona (Spain) says that "[...] each port is a unique ecosystem that must aspire to develop its own Smart Port model[...]" (Grimalt, 2019). The Port of Barcelona and the City of Barcelona have come far with citizen involvement and has done much to improve this including a digital transformation strategy, where "citizen participation and transparency" play a key role with the best of intentions (Bria et al., 2020). We need to acknowledge that the majority of ports do not sufficiently engage with their cities, citizens and other ports, and even the ones that do often want to do it in their way. Each port seems to develop independently, and we need to be aware of the strong wishes of many ports to define "smartness" using their terms and conditions. This may result in a low level of collaboration and co-creation among cities, ports and citizens. Ports may see it as natural that they should be the ones to define what a Smart Port is, and it may seem the correct way, but they should not do it alone. They need to cooperate with their corresponding cities and other ports and where possible in a global way. Not learning from other ports leads to a duplication of effort and a waste of resources.

There may be many reasons why the ports want to independently define a Smart Port. Historically, ports and the maritime industry have been exposed to complex international regulations and global trade agreements and international politics. They handle goods and freight from all corners of the world. They own much of their infrastructure and can be substantial "landlords", where they rent out their properties for full market value. They are also a source of jobs for the citizens and generate direct or indirect tax income for the cities they serve. This has led to an uneven power relationship with cities and made it possible for ports to decouple from their surroundings. The maritime industry has been afforded a different economic and political position, agenda and framework. A position which they may still want to keep as a strategic advantage.

2.5 Smart City and Smart Port Indicators

Sustainable "Smart Port" strategies and models will need a common governance plan with port and hinterland cities to succeed in defining and pursuing common goals. Having the same KPIs can support a common understanding.

The Smart City Model created by the European Smart Cities states: "A Smart City is a city well performing in six characteristics, built on the 'smart' combination of endowments and activities of self-decisive, independent and aware citizens" (TU Wien, 2020a, b). The six smart characteristics relate to the economy, mobility, environment, people, living and governance.

According to Suresh Patare, today's cities have eight pillars of interest. They are:

- Mobility
- Energy
- Infrastructure
- Technology
- Buildings
- Governance and Education
- Healthcare
- Citizens

We will have to make these pillars smart. Making all of them smart is certainly not an easy task. Hence, a city that meets at least five out of these eight "smart" parameters will be treated as a "Smart City" (Patare, 2019).

To make the picture even more complex, the United 4 Smart Sustainable Cities (U4SSC) initiative has divided the UN SDG's into the three areas of Economy, Environment and Society & Culture. The U4SSC KPIs initiative started in the city of Ålesund supported by the county government (regional government) of *Møre og Romsdal* in Norway. These main areas are in turn divided into sub-areas in which the whole model has a total of 133 KPIs that cities have to report on for their current sustainability profile.

We can see similarities between the indicators from the European Smart Cities and Patare's eight pillars. In the U4SSC KPIs initiative, the three major areas are mentioned. Which approach should we choose? Most cities already have a strategic city plan, with KPIs connected to the SDGs. So, most will likely have a relationship between the SDG and the U4SSC initiatives and methods. Consequently, we expect that most ports will use a method similar to the SDGs or the U4SSC KPIs model. There are, however, several goals that the SDGs or U4SSC KPIs do not address because they are city specific.

For smaller ports or cities, the U4SSC KPI method might be too complex or resource intensive, so they will probably choose a simpler method. Also, many of the KPIs rely on data in non-digital format, which means a lot of manual work. This may, in turn, make it difficult to compare cities or ports. In the long run, all cities and ports should make their KPI and SDG data available in digital format. This will automate analysis and comparison between port and cities.

3   The Challenges

We now elaborate on the other challenges for making cities and ports "smarter" using Maritime Informatics and what potential this interaction may have for industry and its customers. We will also take a look at some examples of the areas where cities and ports are cooperating, connecting their services and goods to their customers and citizens who are integrated parts of a global value and supply chain.

Maritime Informatics and IS can contribute to reducing global emissions, increasing and improving the quality of services and goods and reduce trade's environmental impact. They can reduce the usage of non-sustainable logistics, services, and goods and will be essential if we want to maintain, and even increase, our present living standards, without producing more pollution or ruining the future of our planet.

Ports and the cities will likely make mistakes in determining their future, but they should adopt decision making processes that aim to minimise endangering life, the environment or the economy. This needs to be a balancing act in cooperation with others, so that we can learn from each other and hopefully avoid the same mistakes.

3.1   The Main Functional Axis at the Port of Barcelona and Examples of Applied Solutions

As an example of Smart Port development, we will describe briefly the experiences of the Port of Barcelona and some of the needs discovered. The port has identified the main functional axis as consisting of People, Environment, Governance, Mobility, Logistics and Economy, and after identifying the main axis, it applied the needed technology.

The most important area for a smart port is typically logistics, which must implement Information and Communication Technologies (ICT) solutions that solve among others, traceability, real-time information, automation and robotisation, physical and technological integration infrastructure, efficiency and predictability, seamless freight transport, smart maintenance and non-intrusive inspection. Another important field of action for a smart port is mobility, in terms of mobility management, smart traffic management, connected vehicle, sustainable transport, autonomous transport, intermodality and syncromodality and advanced parking.

To solve some of these needs, the Port of Barcelona has developed two custom platforms solutions:

The Automatic Customs Control System (ACCS) for Terminals, which uses OCR (Optical Character Recognition) and LPR (Licence Plate Recognition) at the gates to read the container reference number and truck licence plate. Before arriving at the terminal each truck has registered the reference number of the container to be collected. The system communicates with Customs to check if it can authorise an automatic exit and then automatically modifies the registration of the container in the customs system, via a web service, so that the barriers at the exit gates are operated automatically by the system without any human interaction.

The Automatic Access Control of Vehicles (AACV) for the port territory has been deployed in all access gates and at the entrances and exits gates of the terminals, also in the logistic activity area (ZAL) annexed to the port of Barcelona. The AACV system in its different layers of TIC architecture integrates LPR control, wireless RFID personal card control, vehicle fleet licence plate access control and also remote request for external visits with access control via QR code. All access controls automatically activate barriers and access gates can work without human assistance.

The AACV allows calculation of vehicle travel times between entry and exit gates, and terminal gates of the port, and can therefore determine the size of truck queues, which can be consulted online by truck drivers to optimise their arrival time. To help improve road congestion inside the port, a truck buffer project is currently under construction, and integrated with AACV will allow smart regulation of traffic between terminals and the port's access.

To develop ACCS and AACV, a service-oriented architecture (SOA) was used, which is a style of software design where services are provided to the other layers by application components, through a communication protocol over a network. The customised ACCS SOA application is a discrete unit of functionality that can be accessed remotely and acted upon and updated independently; it is also intended to be independent of vendors, products and technologies.

Micro services architecture is now gaining prominence as an evolution of SOA, with an approach that was designed to overcome the disadvantages of traditional monolithic architectures (Cloud Academy, 2020). Further development in software architecture, the IoT, and sensor technology will enable ports to get smarter and create digital data streams to fuel Maritime Informatics.

3.2   The First Movers

Many major ports have a Smart Port model, based on the issues discussed previously, and are trying to digitalise and share data and infrastructure to be more sustainable. Many small ports, however, are dependent on bigger ports being "first movers" and do not have the luxury of making significant investments that might fail. It is therefore important for all actors, both upstream and downstream, to help each other to build a competitive, profitable and sustainable maritime industry. The maritime ecosystem, with ports, cities, citizens, goods owners and other stakeholders, needs everyone to act smarter. Sharing knowledge of tested and proven solutions and solving the root causes of problems is essential for a smart ecosystem. Using open data exchange standards, such as the S-211—Port Call Message Format, is important. The market needs to be sufficiently profitable to attract a range of Maritime Informatics solution providers.

3.3   APIs, Data Value and Data Quality

In a global network, ports and cities are very dependent on high-quality data, well-planned usage of the data and data sources, good API governance and the correct data interpretation and data security. Having a well-functioning transport and data security will be important in all areas where services or goods are produced, shipped, sold or maintained and throughout the life span of a product or service. Well-governed APIs will enable them to make the best possible usage of the collected data. In the end, analysed data will be used by humans or Artificial Intelligence (AI) for decision-making.

3.4   Governance, Planning, and Cooperation in Cities and Ports

The applications of smart technology responding to the goals set by AIVP are visible, for example, in the use of civic tech for inclusive governance processes (Gilman, 2017; Schrock, 2019). Recent social tensions around the globe show citizens' discontent with current governance systems. Although these social movements have been aimed mostly at national governments, it is clear that they are demanding a role in a range of decision-making processes. This principle is behind the civic-tech approach that is increasingly discussed in port cities (AIVP, 2019). Emerging solutions include combining traditional citizen consultation processes (e.g., focus groups, open debates, etc.) with online platforms that facilitate the discussion of ideas and citizens' concerns for the port-city relationship or the externalities generated by ports in their cities. Although still incipient, one possible example of these approaches is in the port city of Halifax in Canada (Port of Halifax, 2019), where the port authority pursued a public consultation process from 2016 to 2019, explaining the different options for port expansion, while taking into consideration inputs from the citizens. Although these kinds of processes and technology are today common practice in urban settings, they remain a novelty, for the moment, in port planning and governance.

Smart technologies have lowered port area traffic congestion to improve port-city sustainability by reducing negative externalities such as polluting emissions. For example, in the Port of Hamburg the Green4Transport project tests intelligent traffic systems that facilitate the outflow of cargo from port terminals to the hinterland, reducing its impact in the urban environment (HPA, 2019). Further on, several European projects have focused on sustainable mobility in port cities, coordinating actions destined to reduce the negative impact of port activities. For example, the Civitas Portis Project, funded by the European Union (EU), shares best practices of urban mobility in port cities. For this project, port cities, like Trieste and Antwerp, are developing several initiatives, including coordinating freight movements and transport systems to reduce their impact in the city and facilitating multimodality for commuters working in port companies. Other EU-funded projects, like SUMPORT (Sumport, 2019) or LOCATIONS (Locations, 2019), are focused on Mediterranean port cities. The first intends to facilitate the drafting of Sustainable Urban Mobility Plans (SUMP), while the second targets the impact of cruise ship tourism. In the guidelines of both projects, smart tech plays a major role, including solutions such as smart bike-sharing for tourists and facilitating access to information to improve their experience. Another example of smart tech for cruise ship passengers is the app developed by the port authority of Cádiz, in Spain, providing cruise passenger visiting the city with first-hand information and allowing them to be more independent from organised excursions.

These examples show that smart technologies are increasingly being applied to solve issues affecting the interaction between ports and cities. However, these technologies also imply certain challenges that we will now explore. We will demonstrate how these solutions offer the opportunity to recover a certain symbiosis and improve port-city relationships. While at the same time, we also question if the institutions and decision-makers can adapt to the new demands and take maximum advantage from all the new possibilities.

4 The Opportunities

Future Smart City and Smart Port opportunities lie in new technology, in developing new methods, smart spaces and people-centric areas, where cities and ports are "allowed to make mistakes" in trying to solve the present and future challenges in cooperation and co-creation among themselves and with citizens and others.

Many of the tools and principles used to improve Smart Cities and Smart Ports rely on the correct use of sensors, big data, data collection, data mining, analyses, automation of operations and use of AI in an ethical, lawful and resilient way. By enabling and building spaces where triple helix and quadruple helix constellations interact, cities and ports can experiment and innovate. By prototyping as soon as possible in the Smart City or Smart Port process, design flaws due to misinterpretation of the real needs can be mitigated or removed before going into the pilot or implementation phase.

We need to actively share experiences, so that "smartness" or the best method found by one actor, can benefit all humankind and not just one city or region. Different Smart Cities and Smart Ports and their organisations should meet and exchange knowledge in an inclusive and complementary manner independent of geographical region, culture, size or type of city or port.

4.1   The Value of Open Data

In combination with other data, open data can result in better quality and easier access to services or goods. It can also reduce costs, through better and cheaper maintenance, higher throughput or better sales and operations. For example, in Stavanger a LoraWAN network collects data from battery-driven temperature sensors at six different beaches and bathing places to measure bathing temperatures. The city has saved money by eliminating hours of travel to beaches for onsite measurement. Now, sensor data are reported through the year. Within less than a year, 50 water temperature sensors in other parts of Norway were installed (Altibox, 2019).

The LoraWAN network was originally installed solely for water temperature sensing, but now it is used for many other measurements including from waste bins, street drain sensors and sea-level monitors, with more to come. 5G communications technology will enable faster and more sensor-based services for the Smart City and Smart Port. Open data sensors can create much value if managed and governed correctly, including tracking ships/containers/goods or solving mobility issues, healthcare logistics and services and other sustainability issues. *Data lakes*, where free and open quality data are shared in a secure manner using open standards, will be essential to extract the full value potential. Open data is a key source input to Maritime Informatics projects.

4.2   Scalability

One of the major obstacles that many ports and cities have identified and experienced in different areas is the "lack of a big enough market". For private SMEs (Small and Medium Enterprises) and other investors, building solutions for only one city, or one port, is often too costly for them to obtain a viable return on investment. Therefore, many cities and ports have created business area clusters for those with similar needs. In doing so, they can create common solutions, even in a competitive market. These clusters cooperate across industries and sectors, avoiding the silos of before. The LoraWAN network water temperature sensor example in Norway shows how a growth market for private actor solutions can emerge from a public investment.

Using new technology and methods to address the UN SDGs through combination, collaboration, and co-creation will be critical, but it will not necessarily guarantee scalability or successful solutions. Technology has to be deployed wisely to create Smart Cities and Smart Ports. Furthermore, it must be accompanied by a willingness for joint experimentation and learning in order to deliver high-quality goods and services for citizens and customers.

5   Summary and Conclusion

Ports and cities around the world have many differences but also many similarities, and the same can be said for port-city collaboration. They are often isolated from each other in organisational and power relations, lacking cooperation due to geography, different digital standards or digital platforms. These silos need to be eliminated to facilitate digital innovation and promote collaboration. We need to mitigate misunderstandings or lack of knowledge in how to build and use information systems to solve common problems together, in order to achieve the best possible outcomes for all parties and stakeholders.

According to Kai B. Westre (personal communication, November 20, 2019) the Managing Director of NMK—Norwegian Maritime Competence Centre—when ports and cities "build maritime and city infrastructure together", the infrastructure can be used by many parties not only one, the financial benefits can be substantial and the solutions are most likely more sustainable.

For example, maritime shore power stations for charging ships at berth should also be accessible to the full range of electrical vehicles within the port area. Investment cost should be amortised over the largest feasible base of customers. Similarly, we should seek to build decentralised digital infrastructures, such as data lakes, using open standards to raise the level of benefits from sharing open data.

By using international standards, cities and ports can have tools to predict and govern maritime operations as well as increasing the quality of the city services and products to private local, regional and national governments, researchers, universities and schools and supporting citizens with their needs in a co-creational way "aiming for an efficient global reach" and together be "The leading maritime cities of the future" (Menon and DNV-GL, 2020).

We will need robust and resilient solutions for connecting cities with ports, ports with ports and cities with cities. Digital transformation will require an inclusive governance process that embraces many viewpoints and produces economically and social viable outcomes. It needs to also engender trust through transparency, facilitate innovation, support the development of standards and focus on generating sound, scalable, sustainable socio-technical solutions for present and future generations. Smart technologies have much potential to improve port-city relationships, and their successful implementation is dependent on extensive collaboration and citizen involvement.

References

AIVP. (2019). *aiVP Agenda 2030*. Accessed December 15, 2019, from https://www.aivpagenda2030.com.

Altibox. (2019). *Sjekk badetemperaturen*. Accessed November 25, 2019, from https://badetassen.no.

Bird, J. H. (1963). *The major seaports of the United Kingdom*. Hutchison. Accessed from http://books.google.pt/books?id=PhYwAQAAMAAJ.

Bria, F., Rodríguez, P., Bain, M., Batlle, J., Vila, A., Fernández, X., Pla, M., Marpons, G., Vilalta, X., Segovia, X., Collazos, J., Bas, J., García, O., Mesegur, C., Frisach, L., Crespo, A., Calza, T., Ruiz, J., Galdon, G., Michaelides, J., & Bretschneider, E. (2020). *Ajuntament de Barcelona. Barcelona City Counsil Digital Plan*. Accessed January 25, 2020, from https://ajuntament.barcelona.cat/digital/sites/default/files/LE_MesuradeGovern_EN_9en.pdf.

Cloud Academy. (2020). *Cloud training that drives digital transformation*. Accessed March 28, 2020, from https://cloudacademy.com/.

Gilman, H. (2017). Civic tech for urban collaborative governance. *Political Science & Politics, 50*(3), 744–750. https://doi.org/10.1017/S1049096517000531.

Grimalt, C. (2019). *The Smart Port model at the Port of Barcelona — PierNext*. Accessed December 15, 2019, from https://piernext.portdebarcelona.cat/en/technology/the-smart-port-model-at-the-port-of-barcelona.

Grossmann, I. (2008). Perspectives for Hamburg as a port city in the context of a changing global environment. *Geoforum, 39*(6), 2062–2072. https://doi.org/10.1016/j.geoforum.2008.04.011.

Hayuth, Y. (1982). The port-urban interface: An area in transition. *Area, 14*(3), 219–224. https://doi.org/10.2307/20001825.

Hein, C. (2014). Port cities and urban wealth: Between global networks and local transformations. *International Journal of Global Environmental Issues, 13*(2–4), 339–361.

Hesse, M. (2017). Approaching the relational nature of the Port-City interface in Europe: Ties and tensions between seaports and the urban. Tijdschrift Voor Economische En Sociale Geografie. https://doi.org/10.1111/tesg.12282.

Hoyle, B. S. (1989). The Port-City interface: Trends, problems and examples. *Geoforum, 4*, 429–435.

HPA. (2019). *Hamburg Port Authority*. Accessed December 15, 2019, from https://www.hamburg-port-authority.de/fileadmin/user_upload/HPA_Imagefolder_WEB_PDF.pdf.

Igi-global.com. (2020). *What is quadruple helix model | IGI Global*. Accessed January 25, 2020, from https://www.igi-global.com/dictionary/quadruple-helix-model/66791.

Locations. (2019). *Interreg Mediterranean | LOCATIONS*. Accessed December 15, 2019, from https://locations.interreg-med.eu.

Mah, A. (2014). *Port Cities and global legacies – urban identity, waterfront work, and radicalism* (1st ed.). London: Palgrave Macmillan. https://doi.org/10.1057/9781137283146.

Menon, & DNV-GL. (2020). *The leading maritime capitals of the world 2019*. Accessed March 27, 2020, from https://www.menon.no/wp-content/uploads/Maritime-cities-2019-Final.pdf.

Merk, O. (2013). *The competitiveness of global Port-Cities: Synthesis report*. Paris: OECD.

Our World in Data. (2019). *The value of global exports*. Accessed December 15, 2019, from https://ourworldindata.org/grapher/world-trade-exports-constant-prices.

Patare, S. (2019). *8 pillars of a Smart City*. Accessed December 15, 2019, from https://www.linkedin.com/pulse/8-pillars-smart-city-suresh-patare.

Port of Halifax. (2019). *PortCityHFX | Building our port for the future.* Accessed December 10, 2019, from https://www.portcityhfx.ca.

Port Technology International. (2020). *Home.* Port Technology International. Accessed March 9, 2020, from https://www.porttechnology.org.

Schrock, A. (2019). What is civic tech? Defining a practice of technical pluralism. In P. Cardullo, C. Di Feliciantonio, & R. Kitchin (Eds.), *The right to the Smart City* (pp. 125–133). Emerald Publishing.

Schubert, D. (2008). Transformation processes on waterfronts in seaport cities-causes and trends between divergence and covergence. In W. Kokot, M. Gandelsman-Trier, K. Wildner, & A. Wonneberger (Eds.), *Port Cities as areas of transition: Ethnographic perspectives.* Transcript Verlag.

Slack, B. (1993). Pawns in the game: Ports in a global transportation system. *Growth and Change, 24*(4), 579–588. https://doi.org/10.1111/j.1468-2257.1993.tb00138.x.

Sumport. (2019). *Goals of the project.* Interreg Mediterranean | Sumport. Accessed December 15, 2019, from https://sumport.interreg-med.eu/index.php?id=5933.

TU Wien. (2020a). *European smart cities 4.0 (2015).* Accessed March 28, 2020, from http://www.smart-cities.eu/?cid=01&ver=4.

TU Wien. (2020b). *The smart city model.* Accessed March 28, 2020, from http://www.smart-cities.eu/model.html.

UN. (2019). *The sustainable development goals report 2019.* Accessed December 15, 2019, from https://unstats.un.org/sdgs/report/2019/The-Sustainable-Development-Goals-Report-2019.pdf.

UN.org. (2018). *2018 Revision of world urbanization prospects.* Multimedia Library – United Nations Department of Economic and Social Affairs. Accessed December 15, 2019, from https://www.un.org/development/desa/publications/2018-revision-of-world-urbanization-prospects.html.

Wikipedia.org. (2019). *Industry 4.0.* Accessed December 15, 2019, from https://en.wikipedia.org/wiki/Industry_4.0.

Zhao, Q., Xu, H., Wall, R. S., & Stavropoulos, S. (2017). Building a bridge between port and city: Improving the urban competitiveness of port cities. *Journal of Transport Geography, 59*, 120–133. https://doi.org/10.1016/j.jtrangeo.2017.01.014.

Maritime Informatics for Increased Collaboration

Mikael Lind ⓘ, Robert Ward ⓘ, Michael Bergmann ⓘ, Sandra Haraldson ⓘ, Almir Zerem ⓘ, Jan Hoffmann ⓘ, and Erik Eklund ⓘ

1 Introduction

Shipping serves the trade patterns of the world with a mixture of short-sea shipping feeding larger vessels transiting the oceans (Fig. 1). Short-sea shipping (Lind, Michaelides, Ward, Herodotou, & Watson, 2019a; Michaelides, Herodotou, Lind,

M. Lind (✉)
Research Institutes of Sweden (RISE) and Chalmers University of Technology, Gothenburg, Sweden
e-mail: mikael@realsearchers.com

R. Ward
Pymble, NSW, Australia
e-mail: robert.ward1@gmail.com

M. Bergmann
BM Bergmann-Marine, Grosskrotzenburg, Germany
e-mail: Michael.bergmann@bergmann-marine.com

S. Haraldson · A. Zerem
Research Institutes of Sweden (RISE), Gothenburg, Sweden
e-mail: sandra@realsearchers.com; Almir.Zerem@ri.se

J. Hoffmann
UNCTAD, Geneva, Switzerland
e-mail: Jan.Hoffmann@unctad.org

E. Eklund
Dubai Maritime City Authority, Dubai, United Arab Emirates
e-mail: erik@eklund.com

M. Lind et al. (eds.), *Maritime Informatics*, Progress in IS,
https://doi.org/10.1007/978-3-030-50892-0_8

113

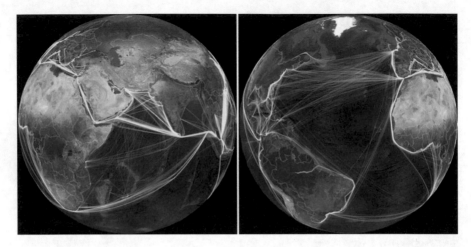

Fig. 1 Patterns of world trade sea voyages (Source: Marine Benchmark, www.marinebenchmark.com)

& Watson, 2019) accounts for about 70% of sea transport in the world through a network pattern of transhipment hubs.[1]

Over the coming years, organisations involved in the maritime logistics chain will continue to look for ways to innovate their business models. These will inevitably involve digital technologies. So, for most, the next wave of innovation will come from turning their attention outward into the business ecosystem of digital communications and information exchange with customers, partners, suppliers and other actors to create new services, products and experiences. See also Lind, Ward, Bergmann, Haraldson, and Zerem (2019b).

For many ports, there is limited anchorage space outside the port, and the absence of a "port line-up" system in previous and next ports reduces the ability for terminals and carriers to increase efficiency and deliver customer satisfaction. In some ports, tanker terminals are operated by different operators, which often results in low flexibility and longer wait time, partially also due to the lack of data sharing among them. Terminals, berths, shippers and carriers tend to work in silos without either long-term, near-time, or real-time sharing of scheduling data. This often is a cause of knock-on effect delays. This inherently inefficient type of port call regime leaves the maritime network in a very difficult and unpredictable position to deliver its resources optimally.

Enhanced collaboration and instant data sharing among stakeholders within and outside the port, leading to synchronisation, coordination and harmonisation of maritime operations associated with the tanker industry, are now beginning to appear. The Port Collaborative Decision Making (PortCDM) concepts, as developed by the

---

[1] https://ec.europa.eu/eurostat/statistics-explained/index.php/Maritime_transport_statistics_-_short_sea_shipping_of_goods#Total_short_sea_shipping

Research Institutes of Sweden (RISE) and tested in the Sea Traffic Management (STM) validation project[2], can bring benefit to all types of trade—not just dry and liquid bulk cargo transport. Recent proposals presented to the International Maritime Organization (IMO) by the Baltic and International Maritime Council (BIMCO) relating to the easier exchange of data and just-in-time arrivals are further examples.

2 Different Types of Trade and Different Business Models

2.1 Container Traffic and Liner Services

Container traffic mostly follows a predefined pattern of scheduled and recurrent visits. It is arranged as a liner service (like a scheduled bus or an underground metro service) where different stakeholders plan their operations in relation to a fixed and repeating schedule. This schedule may be revised periodically or seasonally. This follows a similar concept to passenger traffic in aviation—with a predictable and fixed schedule and travel plan covering the present and the medium-term future. Unlike in air transport, which is mostly between two airports, containerised liner shipping services usually call at several ports during the same service.

This means that the port call actors can expect that a ship (or ships from a shipping company) will arrive at particular time intervals and can prepare for that accordingly. In reality though, maintaining punctual ship arrivals in accordance with the pre-set schedule is sometimes hard to achieve, not because ships have difficulties in making their sea passages but resulting from delays in upstream ports making it hard or impossible for a ship to make its next port call on time. This is especially the case for short-sea shipping arrivals or when ships require repositioning in a port after cargo operations in one terminal prior to further work in another.

Many of the largest container shipping companies, such as Maersk, MSC, CMA/CGM, and Hapag-Lloyd, also own terminal facilities (e.g. the Maersk-owned APM terminals) and may operate in different alliances. These alliances can then have the effect of blocking others in making optimal or desired port calls if the relevant shipping company is not part of the same alliance as the terminal operator. Chinese shipping companies, such as China Ocean Shipping Company (COSCO), are also involved in investing in seaports, including in the context of China's Belt and Road Initiative, or more specifically the Maritime Silk Road part of this initiative.[3]

Recent years have seen the introduction of super large container ships carrying up to 24,000 containers. However, confronted with physical limitations in ports and access channels, combined with changes in global trading patterns, their size may

---

[2]https://www.stmvalidation.eu

[3]https://www.forbes.com/sites/wadeshepard/2017/09/06/chinas-seaport-shopping-spree-whats-happening-as-the-worlds-ports-keep-going-to-china/#1cfb78b14e9d

have peaked, as reflected by the reduction in global order books for these super large vessels.

2.2 The Dry and Liquid Bulk Industry and Irregular, Often Short-Notice Port Calls

The dry and liquid bulk sea transport sector operates most times as a tramp service (more like a taxi or charter bus than a scheduled bus or metro service) with fixed, semi-fixed or flexible routes and without a predetermined timetable. Ships may be engaged on either a voyage or a time charter basis.

A voyage charter means that the charterer pays a fixed price for the carriage of specific goods from one port to another, with the ship operator carrying the risks and expense for any delays or diversions caused by such things as weather, strikes, or variations in the cost of bunkers (fuel). For a time charter, the charterer in effect takes a lease on the operation of a ship for a certain period and, with it, the risks and costs of any late-notice variations in a number of the operating expenses. In either case, this leads to unpredictable and short-notice port visits because at least one of the charter parties is always seeking to minimise or avoid the impact of the mostly unpredictable and variable short-notice changes in voyage expenses.

The tanker industry in particular is governed by freight contracts made by traders who often decide the load date and destinations based on diverse factors and in particular fluctuating cargo-oil prices. Due to the fluctuations in prices and availability, there are often very late changes of schedule, which puts pressure on port call actors and their resources to respond on time and still preserve the financial and environmental benefits for all involved. Some of the liquid bulk cargoes are actually traded while the ship is on passage, and the new cargo owner may then reroute the ship to a new destination.

2.3 RORO Trade and the Need for Detailed Tracking and Scheduling

The so-called RORO (roll-on/roll-off) trade is the maritime part of the dual-modal transport mechanism of road-ship-road. At the port of origin, motor vehicles drive on the ship (roll-on), and in the destination, they drive off the ship again (roll-off). The RORO concept is intended to reduce cargo handling as the cargo does not leave the land carriage vehicle, and, as such, dismounting of such things as containers or other bulky items for loading and remounting at the port of arrival is not necessary. This method also avoids individual storage and rearrangement of cargo. RORO includes "unaccompanied trailer transport". Here the trailers of a truck are positioned on a cargo vessel, but the tractor units and drivers do not travel with the ship. With unaccompanied trailer transport, another tractor unit meets the ship on arrival, or the next modal transport could be a train, where the unaccompanied trailers are carried further on as part of a multimodal transport chain. RORO vessels normally follow the same regime as container shipping by following a fixed liner schedule.[4] The complexity of this highly integrated dual or multimodal transport needs careful and detailed planning and coordination for optimal results to be achieved. This sector is also quite concentrated, with a few shipping companies including common names such as Wallenius Wilhelmsen, Stena and Grimaldi dominating the supply. RORO is also used for the bulk import and export of new motor vehicles. For larger RORO ships, dedicated parking and assembly points are required in ports to manage and synchronise vehicle loading movements.

2.4   The Cruise Industry and Its Long-Term Planning of Port Visits

Presently there are about 390 cruise ships in operation globally, and there are 120 more on the order books with no reported plans for taking any of the existing ships out of service,[5] though this can now be expected to change in view of the Covid-19 pandemic. There are several dominant shipowners, such as Carnival Cruise Line and Royal Caribbean International, together having up to 70% of the market passenger wise.[6]

Seen from a port's point of view, a cruise (port) call is most often initiated two to three years in advance to settle everything that is related to the port visit. The proposed timetable is then used to assign different locations within the port to enable possible parallel cruise calls at the same time. In a popular cruise destination, there is a desire to manage as many cruise calls as possible during the season. A challenge, however, is coordinating a number of calls on the same day; any deviations of a cruise ship's arrival and departure times will influence excursion options as well as passengers joining or leaving the ship.

As the cruise season approaches, contracts related to passenger excursions, linesmen, security and third-party service providers are settled and then planned precisely by the port, agent and cruise line. Cruise lines do not want anything to go wrong and thereby fail to meet the expectations of their passengers. Cruise excursions, for example, require high levels of coordination and understanding of the current situation to function well. This enables cruise ship passengers to schedule their excursions precisely.

Even though actors have an individual focus on delivering their services, there is a need for joint delivery from all actors for a successful cruise call. In order to

---

[4]https://www.marineinsight.com/types-of-ships/what-are-ro-ro-ships/

[5]https://www.cruiseindustrynews.com/cruise-news/cruise-ship-orderbook.html

[6]https://cruisemarketwatch.com/market-share/

provide a high-quality joint delivery, actors must know and understand all involved parties' plans and outcomes and their role in making a cruise call a success for each passenger (Lind et al., 2018b).

Disruptions can happen, such as a local tour operator missing a return deadline for passengers returning to their ship. In most cases, when tours are delayed, then the departure of a cruise ship is delayed, which can then have consequences for other ships in the area, including other cruise ships. There might be several cruise ships arriving on the same day, having the same types of needs for services, physical infrastructure and sea passages. Unplanned changes can cause serious delays, bottlenecks or cancellations, which then requires replanning and execution. In the worst case, the passenger experience is inferior or non-existent.

2.5   The Need for Collaboration and Digital Data Sharing Independent of Trade

As many ports use the container ship or other dominant trade scheduling models as their foundational base for planning, other nonrecurrent visits are then left to fit around the basic plan based on the predominating ships. This exposes an obvious need to provide a more flexible system that provides sufficient information to allow ports to plan, optimise and execute port visits, independent of the type of trade. The PortCDM concepts and the port call optimisation principles laid out by the International Taskforce on Port Call Optimization (ITPCO) have been developed specifically to address this problem.

In the future, there will be an enhanced data stream originating from many different sources, where ship-to-port collaboration becomes increasingly more synchronised. Upstream ports will provide information to downstream ports, where many more physical objects (down to the level of containers, bollards, etc.) are digitally twinned, allowing for remote data streams to be generated and kept up to date with minimal human intervention. All of this requires standards for data sharing, such as the International Association of Marine Aids to Navigation and Lighthouse Authorities (IALA) standard S-211 Port Call Message standard. The Electronic Product Code Information Services (EPCIS) standard that enable data exchange and the sharing of time stamp data ship-to-port, port-to-ship, port-to-port, as well as port actor-to-port actor is another example. S-211 is part of the S-100 family of data exchange standards that underpin the IMO Common Maritime Data Structure (CMDS). The S-100 standards, in turn, are based on the ISO 19100 series of geographic information standards.[7] EPCIS is a standard used for exchanging event information among supply chain partners across all modes of transport and is also an official ISO standard (ISO/IEC 19987).

---

[7]https://www.ipcdmc.org/standards-and-guidelines

Enhanced information sharing, especially regarding the crucial parameters of estimated time of arrival and estimated time of departure, as well as estimated time of operations commencing and completing, is necessary to enable any optimisation effort before a vessel visits a port. This is key to satisfying all port actors, including terminal operators and shipping lines, and it is also relevant to hinterland operators and the final recipient of the cargo (the consignee).

There are different types of challenges that need to be handled in relation to the different types of trade and its shipping services, for example, liner versus tramp services. Independent of trade, there is also a need for enhanced collaboration and data sharing within ports and along the maritime transport chains providing each of the participants with up-to-date real-time information.

3 The Ports of the World and the Complexity of Port Call Operations

3.1 The Ports of the World

There are close to 100,000 commercial ships [>100 gross tonnage (GT)].[8] The ones that are above 1000 GT conduct about 4.1 million port visits per year,[9] and the figure for the amount of port calls made to several thousands of active ports in the world if all commercial ships are taken into consideration is very much higher. These ports are arranged in structures of feeder ports and transhipment hubs. Some of the major ports of the world desire to become *the* gateway into their particular region (such as the Port of Rotterdam into Europe),[10] which both drives competition and also heavy investment in hinterland connectivity.

As physical infrastructures are costly long-term investments, it is highly essential for high-throughput ports to secure sufficient traffic to profit from their investments. For ports, this is highly sensitive because the decision for a shipping company to alter its destination is relatively easy, while relocating the physical infrastructure of a port is costly. This has driven ports to specialise in different segments, such as establishing advanced capabilities for managing containers, providing services that add value to the incoming trade, offering storage facilities or making the port an attractive cruise destination. As much of the world's trade originates in Asia, the majority of the largest specialised ports are also in Asia. Out of the ten largest ports in the world, seven of them are in China and one each in Korea, Singapore and

---

[8]There are 96,295 commercial ships of 100 GT and above (c.f. http://stats.unctad.org/maritime) and 51,684 commercial ships of 1000 GT and above (c.f. https://unctad.org/en/PublicationsLibrary/rmt2019_en.pdf)

[9]In 2018, there were 4,112,944 port calls made of ships of 1000 GT and above (c.f. http://stats.unctad.org/maritime)

[10]https://www.esri.com/en-us/see/stories/port-of-rotterdam/port-digitalization-article

Europe (Rotterdam).[11] This list is complemented with other notable ports such as
Hamburg, Houston, Dubai and Antwerp which have been singled out as growing
proactively.[12]

Ports are a conglomerate of actors working together. Most often the port
"company" or the port authority becomes the landlord providing space for others
to perform operations. This provides opportunity for the larger shipping companies
to own terminals, including locating them at strategic places around the world.

There exists strong competition between ports that carefully consider their
development, promoting local industry and access to the hinterland. As in other
transport sectors, large transhipment hubs are becoming the first line of interaction
for the larger ships to make port calls, while numerous feeder ports follow the
rules of operations stipulated by those transhipment hubs. However, some ports
in the world, such as the Port of Stavanger, take a stronger community approach,
where the actors take a more regional approach, which builds upon the Norwegian
collaborative culture. These ports become the business environment for the local
industry, including supporting start-ups. PortXL,[13] which was initiated in Rotterdam
and now has been brought also to Singapore and Antwerp, are examples of such an
approach.

3.2   The Complexity of Port Call Operations

Port call operations involve a substantial number of actors. Upon reaching the
coastal area, the maritime authority is involved; to enter the port, the port authority
needs to give its approval; often there are pilots and tug operators and other
supporting nautical services required to bring a ship from the port area to berth;
mooring personnel make fast the ship to the berth; terminal operators and stevedores
are engaged in loading and unloading; other providers deal with such things as waste
and security; and agents are there to ensure that everything goes according to plan.
And the same group of organisations are needed to get the ship ready to depart from
berth, leaving the port area, and back to the open sea. The complexity of port call
operations and the need for collaboration and synchronisation can be seen in the
generic PortCDM metro map (Fig. 2).

The diagram of the port call process indicates the wide variety of services for
the ship, the crew and the movement of cargo that all have to be in place during
a port call and often must take place over a short period of time. Not shown in
the diagram are such things as bunkering, maintenance, repair or customs, all of
which serve to further complicate the overall goal of effective coordination and
synchronisation, which more often than not requires complex levels of collaboration

---

[11] https://www.ship-technology.com/features/feature-the-worlds-10-biggest-ports/
[12] https://www.menon.no/wp-content/uploads/Maritime-cities-2019-Final.pdf
[13] www.PortXL.org

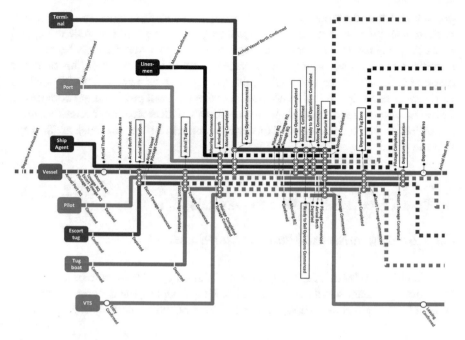

Fig. 2 Core events and engaged actors in the port call process (Lind, Haraldson, Karlsson, & Watson, 2016)

and communication between the crew, owner, agent, the terminal and others, including administrative stakeholders such as border control, customs, immigration and the port authority.

Even the relatively simple metro map in Fig. 2 indicates that nothing is going to be better than the weakest link in the port call process, particularly if every actor acts on its behalf, pursuing only its interests. The risk of sub-optimisation is high. Collaboration with others in the port call chain is the key to enhanced operations and underpins the PortCDM concept and port call optimisation.

3.3 One Size Does Not Fit All

Most ports are also logistical environments, in other words, logistical hubs in the larger transport system that manage different types of trade and modal changes built around different requirements. Handling and other requirements in container transport are very different from those required for liquid bulk transport. As a result, there are often distinct differences in a port ecosystem with the concept of "ports within the port" being common.

Traditionally, ships are served on a first-come-first-served basis upon their arrival to a port, which often leads to "hurry and wait" behaviour for ships steaming towards ports. It is also evident that many ports base their organising approach on serving one predominant type of trade, leaving ships engaged in other types of trade to depend upon the same traditional approach. For many, container transport has become the dominating concept for arranging the schema within the port. Often this does not respond optimally to the needs of liquid and dry bulk or passenger traffic such as ferries or cruise ships. It is also not desirable that port call processes are completely different for each trade (and potentially conflicting with each other) because vessels, regardless of their trade, also need to share common infrastructure, such as fairways into the port.

4 New Opportunities Due to Digitalisation

4.1 Benefits for a Multitude of Stakeholders

If the multitude of actors engaged in the maritime supply chain were to join forces, there are significant beneficial effects to be shared among the different actors and stakeholders (Lind et al., 2018a) (Table 1). These benefits are relevant for ports and

Table 1 Benefits from enhanced digital collaboration for different stakeholders

For shipping companies/ships	For shipping agents
• Saved bunkers due to just-in-time arrivals • Saved bunkers due to just-in-time departures avoiding chasing the time window at the next leg • Fleet optimisation and saved bunkers due to shorter turnaround times	• Enhanced basis for planning and easier coordination of port call operations • Less time spent on chasing different actors, more time for other services to the ships
For terminal operators	**For VTS operators**
• Enhanced possibilities for berth management • Enhanced capacity utilisation (resources and infrastructure) • Better planning horizons for approaches to be served	• Possibilities to digitally log entrance and departures • Better coordination of ship movements • Increased capability to synchronise the traffic dependent on the status in the port
For port authorities	**For port control/pilot planning, tug operators, mooring companies, and service providers**
• Safe and efficient port approaches • A long- and short-term overview of port visits	• Enhanced basis for planning • Optimised capacity utilisation • Enhanced capacity utilisation (resources and infrastructure)
For hinterland operators	**For digital service providers**
• Enhanced capacity utilisation (resources and infrastructure) • Better planning horizons for loading/offloading at ports • Enhanced predictability	• Low entry barriers to provide digital innovations • Enhanced capabilities in existing systems by being connected to the "outside"

maritime stakeholders in other regions, including developing countries. In addition to benefits for specific stakeholders, the international community as a whole will benefit from reduced emissions of greenhouse gases when sailing at optimal speeds and through port call optimisation.

4.2   The Role of Maritime Authorities in Collaborative Data Sharing

The National Maritime Authorities

Key shore side actors in shipping are the national maritime authorities. The national maritime authority is usually responsible for maritime safety and a range of navigational services within its waters. Maritime authorities are often responsible for VTS (Vessel Traffic Services) where established, mostly following the recommendations and standards of IALA. They organise and guide traffic through confined and congested waters, through channels or for approaches and through departures of the port limits and associated sea areas. How these and any other roles are coordinated and executed often differ from country to country, even from port to port within the same country.

Local legislation usually supplements or enacts the relevant international rules, covering such things as border control, customs clearance, immigration control and others. Besides these state duties, the maritime authority usually holds also the responsibility for Port State Control, ensuring that ships meet the requirements of IMO regulations as assigned by ships' flag state, as well as any specific requirements of the coastal state.

The Port Authorities

When it comes to ports and their detailed operation, the relevance and influence of the national maritime authorities can vary greatly. There are centralised ports, where the maritime authority is also responsible for the majority of activities in a port and has decision and ordering rights on port operations. In other words, there is one centralised controlling authority. In other ports, the maritime authority focuses only on state activities, and all operations are executed by individual actors, who are free to organise their cooperation in serving a ship call as they deem appropriate. This gets more complicated in some ports, where the "port within a port" concept is in place. A classic example here is the Scheldt Ports with Antwerp as a central port.

Maritime Governance Structures and the Role of Associations

Most of the world's commercial ships and particularly those engaged on international voyages are subject to regulations established by the IMO. These regulations are adopted by the flag states who together with coastal and port states enforce them which leads to all states following a global harmonised standard.

Meanwhile, shore-based infrastructures, such as the operation of ports, port services and logistical activities, are normally governed by the relevant national regulations. This, of course, can vary from country to country and is an example of how the lack of global standards or practices makes it more complex and less efficient for the trade.

Who Watches Over the Ports and Infrastructure?

Other than for the specific requirements to conform to IMO regulations and to meet any national requirements in each country, the actors in the shipping industry have tended to operate mostly as a self-organised ecosystem where each of the actors makes decisions independently, with only limited consideration of how their decisions might affect other actors further up or down the maritime transportation chain. However, digitalisation, as well as commercial and competitive pressure from other forms of transportation, such as air and land bridges, is forcing key actors in the maritime industry to acknowledge that better coordination and synchronisation is key to improving reliability, customer satisfaction and profitability.

The maritime transportation chain comprises a multitude of actors, each performing often specific and specialised tasks as part of transporting goods from consignor to consignee. Each may be subject to different requirements, regulations and profit drivers. What tends not to be acknowledged well enough is that many if not most of the actors in the transportation chain have at least some dependency on the activities and the actions of others in the chain. This is particularly so in terms of the timing of events and ensuring the availability of appropriate supporting resources.

Just-in-Time Operations and e-Navigation

The IMO, while still considering the operation of ships as its primary focus, is now encouraging initiatives for just-in-time operations together with other regulations such as emission controls to combat environmental pollution and to promote sustainable development (IMO, 2018). One key initiative in this regard is the IMO's e-navigation strategy, which seeks to enhance marine safety as well as efficiency by establishing open digital data exchange standards. e-Navigation is intended to provide digital information and infrastructure for the benefit of maritime safety, security and protection of the marine environment, reducing the administrative burden and increasing the efficiency of maritime trade and transport. To do this, a Common Maritime Data Structure (CMDS) has been established, based on the ISO-compliant S-100 Universal Hydrographic Data Model data exchange standard managed by the International Hydrographic Organization (IHO). e-Navigation goes hand in hand with PortCDM and other standardised digital data exchange arrangements that are now coming in to use. The IMO is also developing a reference data model where the data elements required for ship reporting and associated activities are defined. Great care is being taken to ensure that the definitions are harmonised and consistent with any similar terms being used in other data exchange regimes. The United Nations Centre for Trade Facilitation and Electronic Business (UN/CEFACT) is playing an important role in these endeavours.

Single-Window Data Exchange

Another digital information initiative that sits under the growing maritime digital data exchange framework is the single-window concept that allows parties involved in trade and transport to lodge standardised information and documentation with a single entry point to fulfil all import-, export- and transit-related regulatory requirements. The European Union (EU) Reporting Formalities Directive (RFD) in force since 2015 simplifies and harmonises the administrative procedures applied to maritime transport through National Single Window for reporting formalities from ships arriving in or departing from ports. The RFD is planned to be superseded by the European Maritime Single Window environment (EMSWe) that is expected to be applied in 2025.

At the same time, the IMO member states agreed on a mandatory requirement[14] for national governments to introduce electronic information exchange on 8 April 2019 to make cross-border trade simpler and the logistics chain more efficient for the more than 10 billion tons of goods traded by sea annually across the globe between ships and ports. In support of this, the IMO Facilitation Committee (FAL) is ensuring that the digital data exchange process is supported by appropriate and compatible international standards and definitions. In line with this, the EU VAT eCommerce Regulations will come into effect in 2021.

Taking their lead from the vision of intergovernmental organisations such as the IMO and the supranational organisation of EU, other intergovernmental and international organisations are also proceeding with detailed implementations to improve data sharing and effectiveness in the maritime transportation chain. This includes the IHO, the World Meteorological Organization (WMO) and IALA.

Tackling Environmental Concerns
The IMO, co-financed by EUR10 million from the EU, has implemented an initiative for five Maritime Technology Cooperation Centres (MTCCs), under the umbrella of the Global MTCC Network (GMN)—formally titled "Capacity Building for Climate Mitigation in the Maritime Shipping Industry" in targeted regions as part of a global network.[15] Together, they are promoting technologies and operations to improve energy efficiency in the maritime sector and help move shipping into a low-carbon future.

BIMCO is an example of an industry representative organisation that is actively seeking to improve the environmental performance of shipping and the port call process. As well as submitting proposals to IMO on slow-steaming, it has also submitted proposals to IMO related to port logistic operational data (BIMCO, 2019) in support of the just-in-time concept.

Other Complementary Initiatives
More governmental-focused organisations working on the topic, including the earlier mentioned organisations like IHO and IALA, associations in the private sector as well as those with mixed memberships, are starting to get engaged in the

---

[14]Amendments to the Facilitation Convention were adopted in 2016 and entered into force on 1 January 2017. The FAL Convention amendments make it mandatory for ships and ports to exchange FAL data electronically from 8 April 2019.

[15]https://gmn.imo.org

aforementioned concepts. The International Harbour Masters' Association (IHMA) has developed the definition for IMO Maritime Service 4—Port Support Service which, in effect, places PortCDM and port call optimisation within the IMO's e-navigation initiative.[16]

The International PortCDM Council (IPCDMC)[17] is an example of an association that has combined both governmental and industry players to further develop PortCDM and help in its implementation. IPCDMC was initiated by RISE to provide global guidelines to be used for regional and local implementations of PortCDM.

The Port Call Message Standard S-211, which is the underpinning data exchange format for PortCDM, was created under the auspices of the IPCDMC, adopted as an international standard by IALA and registered in the IHO S-100 Geospatial Information (GI) Registry.

The principal international association for marine electronics companies[18] CIRM is another industrial association supporting the development of e-navigation services, and its members are engaged in the work of the International Electrotechnical Commission (IEC) supporting the development of IALA standard S-421 for route exchange to enable interoperability with S-211.

ITPCO, the consortium consisting of a wide range of stakeholders, has been working to establish standards for port call optimisation that improves collaboration during port calls. These efforts have resulted in functional definitions (common semantics) for terms used in the Mariner's Handbook (the comprehensive guide to seamanship and key aspects of navigation published by the UK Hydrographic Office and used worldwide by seafarers), agreed process descriptions and guidelines to help ports and port process stakeholders to coordinate and synchronise their activities through the availability of reliable master data for vessels and port infrastructure. The ITPCO published its first guidance document in 2020 (ITPCO, 2019).

These activities all show that the development of PortCDM and data sharing more generally is not only driven by authorities or research institutes but by a fast-growing community of industry players as well.

Work is also proceeding to optimise cargo flow from ports to the hinterland. Initiatives such as the EU rules on electronic freight transport information (eFTI), eCMR (electronic waybills) and the Digital Transport Logistic Forum (DTLF) subgroup on "paperless transport", will establish uniform, predictable and trusted environments for the electronic exchange of information on goods transported within the EU.

---

[16]NCSR 6/8/2, IMO 2018

[17]www.ipcdmc.org

[18]http://cirm.org/

4.3   Roles Are Likely to Change and Evolve Under Digitalisation

Digitalisation is changing the way actors associate with port operations.[19] For example, the traditional role of a ship's master has already begun to change with an increase in remote monitoring of a ships position leading to others providing advice or instructions on what speed to use or what route to take to avoid such things as weather or traffic congestion or to make an optimal arrival time at a port.

Digitalisation will change some roles more than others. Overall, many activities should become easier and be more efficient which could reduce the roles for some actors. At the same time, digitalisation will provide opportunities for providing new or enhanced services. The future role of the ship agent is one example.

Ship agents provide two major types of capital (Watson, 2019) to their clients. First, because they typically have personnel physically located in the ports of call, they provide social capital in the form of a network of connections with the port's service providers. Their specialised local social capital means they know whom to contact for routine and special services. Second, they have developed routines and procedures (organisational capital) to deal with the local laws and regulations and atypical features of their port and its environment. They have created efficient procedures to weave together the various local requirements and services needed for a successful port visit in their territory.[20]

Traditionally, a ship agent, as a representative of the owner, the charterer or both, of a visiting ship, ensures that the essential requirements for a ship's visit are arranged and met. They also guarantee that involved port actors are paid. In the absence of other information, port actors also rely heavily on the information about the port call (arrival time, planned operations, etc.) provided by a ship agent. People increasingly realise that in the future when digitalisation will generate multiple, accessible data feeds that can enable all actors to have a shared and common situational awareness, they will not need to rely on a single source of agent information. Nevertheless, the value of the ship agent will likely remain and could actually be enhanced by their access to those multiple, up-to-date data streams because it will enable them to be even better on-the-spot coordinators than they are today.

Digital data sharing and greater visibility of plans and their modification could enhance this role for ship agents willing to embrace digitalisation. They could go beyond organising the delivery of local services to ensuring that they are delivered with full satisfaction and predictably as well as validating invoices against real time data. The local agent can take on the important role of helping to ensure the fastest possible turnaround where everything is aligned instead of simply sending

---

[19] Digitalization in Maritime Transport: Ensuring Opportunities for Development, UNCTAD Policy Brief No. 75, Geneva, 2019. https://unctad.org/en/pages/PublicationWebflyer.aspx?publicationid=2479

[20] https://hansa-online.de/2019/11/schifffahrt/140080/

intermittent progress reports to its client that may be inaccurate no sooner than they have been sent.

In the redefinition of the ship agent business model, the ship agent could also be the provider of information and optimisation services to transport buyers and cargo owners by becoming the physical and informational integrator of maritime operations in the global transport chain. With the growing ability of the ship agents to collect and analyse incoming data streams, their value proposition, for both the ships and a port's actors, opens new opportunities to change and enhance their business model.

Enhanced digitalisation and collaboration in the maritime transportation sector will change the capital creation recipe for many in the ecosystem. The ship agent is but one example. Those who want to continue to participate profitably in the ecosystem will need to reblend their social and organisational capital to match the digital connectivity and standardised digital data exchange that will dominate the execution of the future port call. Their social capital will decline in value if they do not accommodate digital data sharing for establishing the phasing of a port call and managing its execution. A phone call or email will be a costly alternative to a digital data exchange with service providers to establish when, where and what services that will be provided for the given port call. It also addresses the need for updating these as circumstances require.

5   Current Digitalisation Initiatives in the Maritime Sector

5.1   *Community-Driven Standardisations and Digital Tools Emerging*

The uptake of digitalisation in the maritime sector has been increasing steadily. In 2017, the theme for the IMO's World Maritime Day was … *connecting ships, ports and people*. The IMO's e-navigation initiative is ongoing, as is its work on digital ship reporting. At the same time, Maersk and IBM have been working on a significant collaboration to bring blockchain technology into the maritime sector to massively reduce the reliance on paper documents. In ships and ashore, increasing amounts of relevant data are being transmitted digitally, including a ship's position and details via AIS transponders every 6 seconds, remote engine and machinery monitoring and data describing the loading and details for ship's cargo.

Digitalisation is increasingly playing a pivotal role in ESG (environmental, social and governance) topics by accelerating sustainable initiatives and helping to monitor and mitigate emerging risks and pressures, for example, in tackling environmental pollution and climate change. Digitalisation and the ability to connect different maritime transport actors to enable greater efficiency and to reduce their collective carbon footprint are an obvious example of the benefits for the maritime sector.

In addition to the work being led by the IMO, there are numerous "community" initiatives surfacing within the maritime industry, such as the chainPORT, the Digital Container Shipping Association (DCSA), the Global Industry Alliance (GIA), the IPCDMC, the International Port Community Systems Association (IPCSA), the Maritime Connectivity Platform Consortium, the ITPCO and the Smart Maritime Network.

In parallel with these initiatives, there are numerous digital tool providers emerging to enable data sharing along the supply chain. However, many of these are or have been developed for a single port with the notion of then engaging others along their particular transportation chain. This can lead to non-standardised or proprietary solutions emerging—which is not desirable nor in keeping with the aims of the major intergovernmental and international organisations such as IMO, EU, IHO or IALA. Nonetheless, and fortunately, the tools all strive to embrace a number of common assumptions and principles and in particular that:

- Nothing substantially related to addressing environmental concerns will happen without engaging a multitude of maritime transport producers.
- There will unlikely be a single party providing a tool to the entire maritime transport industry.
- It must be possible for clusters of actors (such as a port) to choose among different solutions meeting their needs.
- The different solutions need to be based on the established standard message formats (such as the use of the S-211 data exchange format) and communication protocols that enable seamless, interoperable data sharing among the various different tools.

A future with greater access to a variety of data streams capable of being combined to provide more predictable and sustainable transport services can be expected by having various tools available and using standardised messaging systems, independent of the domain that they are addressing and connected to. This will require common definitions of data sets used for the exchange of static and dynamic information (e.g. International Taskforce on Port Call Optimization, 2019). This will cater for both enhanced collaboration and interoperability throughout the maritime supply chain and also make connected maritime operations part of the larger supply chain. Establishing and using logistic communication platforms means that information can be entered once and used by many—thereby avoiding the need for actors operating in more than one port or those dealing with multiple actors to rely on a number of dedicated single point-to-point connections.

5.2 The Use of Diverse Digital Technologies Enabling Enhanced Efficiencies

Enabling Collaboration by the Use of Timely Data Sharing

One clear development trend is an enhanced degree of collaboration to glue the different actors of the maritime transport ecosystem together. Some effects have been identified by Lind and Simha (2020) coming out of different development trends enabled by new technologies, such as:

- Port operators expanding their planning horizons
- Ship and port operations becoming seamlessly integrated
- Regions being empowered by digital collaboration among, for example, a port and its operators
- Elastic timing of operations enabling just-in-time arrivals
- Cargo owner and maritime transport providers becoming more integrated

Such initiatives that enable collaboration and digital data sharing around plans and progress improve transport chain visibility as well as create foundations for enhanced utilisation of infrastructure and capacities. This integrated performance approach would also provide foundations for optimising the use of energy, which is in line with goals of the United Nations 2030 Agenda for Sustainable Development.

6 The Importance of International Standards

The IMO and other relevant intergovernmental organisations wish to see global standards prevail for key digital information in the maritime sector. As a contemporary example, the IMO is pursuing the so-called *single-window* concept for the digital reporting via a single portal, without duplication, of all information required by public authorities in connection with the arrival, stay and departure of ships, people and cargo. The single-window concept joins other standardised processes already in place covering such things as obligatory navigation routes, nautical charting and safety-related information.

However, the use of universal digital data standards is much less common in the other aspects of maritime activities that are not under the jurisdiction of the IMO or other relevant authorities, such as detailed port call or cargo information. Naturally, in single window's efforts, the national trade and customs organisations are highly involved.

As part of developing a standardised approach to digital data sharing in those areas not previously addressed at the intergovernmental level, several associations are seeking roles as leaders to establish new practices for collaboration and data sharing. One of them is the ITPCO; others include the IPCSA (Morton & De Cauwer, 2019) and the IPCDMC.

Other groups have also established themselves, such as the DCSA, which covers 9 out of the 11 largest container shipping lines in the world. This alliance is acting on behalf of its members to develop information systems and security standards that address the common challenges related to transmitting, receiving and exchanging data across the industry.

6.1 Important New Standards for the Maritime Transportation Chain

Several standards related to the transport of goods have been developed or enhanced recently for application in maritime contexts. One example, the GS1 standard EPCIS (also registered as ISO/IEC 19987), was developed many years ago for the purpose of communicating the status of goods throughout the supply chain, in other words, by providing the answers to what, where, when and why on the actual status of goods in transit. EPCIS has been implemented widely in the supply chain and is continuously maintained and updated based on industry input. However, EPCIS does not currently support exchanging information about intentions (things that have not actually occurred yet), which is necessary for the distributed coordination of movements and operations (Lind et al., 2018c).

The port call message format standard S-211 is a fundamentally important standard that provides the ability to communicate intentions in a standardised way. S-211 is ISO 19100 compatible and has also been aligned with GS1 EPCIS so as to enable communicating when particular goods items will arrive at particular locations, which may be done by combining data streams from both standards.

6.2 Resistance to Standards

A legacy of the relatively uncoordinated adoption of digitalisation and common data standards within the maritime sector means that there are several different existing and successful electronic data interchange (EDI) connections being used by the larger shipping lines and their partners. Thus, there is some reluctance to make any dramatic changes towards a standardised approach if there is a significant organisational or financial reinvestment cost involved.

The larger shipping companies have historically dominated the adoption of digital technologies by others in the industry. The leading ports would like to set the agenda for the smart and digitalised port, and at the moment, it seems that some of the larger ports are trying to sit in the front seat of the development. In this respect, care needs to be taken to maintain standardisation and the wide adoption of the principles of collaboration and data sharing in accordance with PortCDM

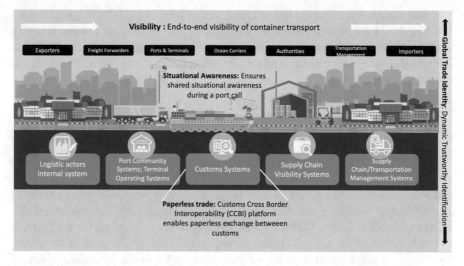

Fig. 3 Enabling end-to-end visibility through a Global Trade Identity (Hvid Jensen, 2019)

and port call optimisation that provide guidelines for the ports of tomorrow without being bound to any particular port.

7 Connected Maritime Operations: Smart Ports and Smart Ships

7.1 Connected Maritime Operations: A Must for an Efficient Global Transport Chain

Connected maritime operations are seen as the way to optimise the maritime transportation chain and thereby provide better services for both the cargo owner and the transport buyer. This connectivity, achieved through digitalisation, enables improved collaboration between the actors and better synchronisation of their individual contributing activities. Port call coordination is one example, which has been highlighted by the World Economic Forum.

Using the container trade as an example, Fig. 3 depicts the need for an integrated view on both the movements of goods between different transport hubs using different means of transport.

Another initiative in support of digitalisation and improved connectivity is the Maritime Connectivity Platform (MCP),[21] formerly known as the Maritime Cloud. The MCP is a framework for enabling efficient, secure, reliable and seamless elec-

---

[21] https://maritimeconnectivity.net

tronic information exchange between all authorised maritime stakeholders across available communication systems. The MCP has been created to enable maritime actors to use digital services to exchange public as well as private information. It brings common Internet standards to maritime navigation and transportation systems by applying open and vendor-neutral technologies. The MCP was created initially to address the goals of the e-navigation initiative of the IMO but now has the potential to support digitalisation across a much wider maritime domain because it is an open-source solution that relies on the Internet concept of Web Services for identity management and service management and, as such, can support more than just the IMO's Maritime Services in the context of e-navigation.

The importance of improved and up-to-date situational awareness within transportation hubs, which PortCDM has enabled, has been recognised in other industries, such as in aviation with Airport CDM and StationCDM for the railway sector.

Further, the European Commission, through the efforts of the Digital Transport and Logistics Forum (DTLF), stresses integrated corridor information systems and has recently launched two projects to demonstrate a concept for a federated network of platforms called FEDERATED and FENIX.

The integration between different modes of transport across borders is an important concern for tomorrow's transport of people and goods.

7.2   Smart Ports

The use of up-to-date information technology in ships and in ports, including real-time data transmission and collection, big-data calculations, digital modelling and remote control, is expected to better guarantee navigational safety and improve operational efficiency. Ships will become more reliable, more efficient and more closely integrated into global supply chains generating cost savings and improving revenue generation.

Enhanced digital collaboration will overcome the legacy of disconnectivity in shipping. The Internet of Things (IoT) is set to play a key role in creating transparency and enhancing efficiency of the global supply chain. Players within the supply chain that can use data to improve their operations and are able to create partnerships can gain significant competitive advantage.

In this context, an increasing number of ports are now aiming at becoming *smart ports*. Expectations include being:

- The driver for sustainability by enabling just-in-time operations
- An information hub advising the use of the transport network of which the port is a hub
- Providing enhanced predictability of operations and the timing of the port visit

It is essential for the port of tomorrow to be connected to the global supply chain, in particular, by being informed about upstream progress to ensure its ability to plan its operations successfully and optimally. Through the introduction of digitalisation and enhanced procedures of collaboration and data sharing, this can be enabled. PortCDM and port call optimisation promote the necessary cultural development of collaboration necessary to achieve environmental and efficiency gains in port call operations and to establish ports as an integrated hub in the global transport chain.

In 2018, Inmarsat carried out a research program to understand how IoT is being adopted within the supply chain.[22] An independent market research firm, Vanson Bourne, interviewed 750 respondents across global transportation companies. The research reports:

- $2.5 million is the average shipowner investment in IoT solutions over the next 3 years. 24% are planning on investing more than $3 million and 14% less than $100,000.
- 100% of shipowners/managers surveyed will be using IoT solutions to meet emission regulations.
- 51% of the respondents said the biggest obstacle in adopting IoT is the lack of timely data. There is a time lag between obtaining the data from the ship and analysing it on the shore side.

7.3   Smart Ships

Integrated information systems capable of autonomously monitoring, recording and analysing the conditions and operations of major equipment such as engines and other shipborne systems are increasingly commonplace in new ships. The data helps to reduce the crew's workload, improve efficiency, and avoid misjudgements.

The digital enhancement of existing ships is more complicated, but not impossible. In the current situation, the shipowner can opt to install particular aspects of digitalisation in the form of specific applications—for example, one for voyage optimisation, another for emission monitoring and another for ballast water monitoring. Then, data from these systems is sent from ship to shore. However, as a result, the shipowner will have several different IoT systems and equipment on board, which can result in some common data perhaps being sent several times from ship to shore. On the shore side, the data from each system might also be stored in different clouds and may not be interoperable if it is locked into different application providers or relies on proprietary data formats.

A truly smart ship will have an integrated IoT platform that is, in effect, one agnostic "box" on board that collects serial, analogue and digital data. Data is transferred from ship to shore through dedicated bandwidth. Data are stored in a centralised, cloud-based database providing an API and a dashboard for the shipowner, so that they can use and analyse the data. In addition, other application providers can tap into the cloud and data can be shared.

---

[22]https://research.inmarsat.com/. Accessed 4 March 2020

At present, shipborne digital transformation has not resulted in significantly smaller crew sizes because the number of sailors for each class is stipulated by regulations, but further technological and regulatory developments are likely to lead to future reductions. In particular, the development of autonomous and semi-autonomous ships, which rely heavily on digitalisation as well as some level of remote monitoring, will minimise or remove the need for permanent manning of some types of ship. This digitalisation will include autonomous route optimisation and collision avoidance. What is clear is that the large-scale application of smart technologies will enable shipowners to save costs in ship maintenance and fleet operations.

8   Concluding Remarks

Shipping companies are strongly driven by the pursuit of enhanced efficiency, and ports are driven to satisfy the needs of their clients of which the shipping companies are the most important. At the same time, emphasis is placed upon ports to deliver services of high quality and enable engaged port call actors to generate revenue. All of this requires enhanced situational awareness empowered by greater digital collaboration and data sharing.

Digitalisation of navigation and international security arrangements is reasonably well covered by internationally agreed global standards and directives under the auspices of the IMO, the EU and other organisations. However, one of the dilemmas with digitalisation, standardisation and data sharing in the port operations environment is the absence of overarching bodies, like the IMO, that can strongly influence standardisation. There is also the tension between catering for local requirements and sensitivities including existing infrastructure to overcome and at the same time enabling those involved to connect.

The challenge is for current stakeholders in the maritime sector to implement digitalisation and to adopt common, interoperable data standards or to risk losing control of the logistic chain. A question for those currently involved is whether progress in standardised digitalisation will be fast enough or whether some of the major suppliers of goods or services, and others, or even some countries will impose their own arrangements, including, in effect, the control of shipping companies and ports at strategic places in the world, by using and imposing their own systems and procedures.

References

BIMCO. (2019). Input paper to IMO Expert Group on Data Harmonization: EGDH 1/7 – IMO Data Set Related to "Port Logistic Operational Data Related to Just In Time Concept".

Hvid Jensen, H. (2019). *Global Trade Identity can be the cornerstone of paperless trade.* World Economic Forum. Retrieved from https://www.weforum.org/agenda/2019/05/global-trade-identity-can-be-the-cornerstone-of-paperless-trade/

IMO. (2018). *Initial IMO strategy on reduction of GHG emissions from ships.* Resolution MEPC.304(72), Adopted on April 13, 2018.

ITPCO. (2019). *Port information manual, version 1.4.5.* International Taskforce Port Call Optimization.

Lind, M., Haraldson, S., Ward, R., Bergmann, M., Andersen, N.-B., Karlsson, M., Zerem, A., Olsson, E., Watson, R. T., Holm, H., Michaelides, M., Evmides, N., Gerosavva, N., Andersen, T., Rygh, T., Arjona Arcona, J., Ferrus Clari, G., Gimenez Maldonado, J., Marquez, M., & Gonzalez, A. (2018a). *Final PortCDM concept description incl. generic specification of identified services – Improving port operations using PortCDM.* STMVal_D1.3. Retrieved from www.stmvalidation.eu/documents

Lind, M., Andersen, T., Bergmann, M., Watson, R. T., Haraldson, S., Rygh, T., Karlsson, M., & Kinn, M. (2018b). *Coordinated value creation in cruise call operations – The case of the Port of Stavanger.* Concept Note #10, STM Validation Project. Retrieved from https://www.ipcdmc.org/galerie

Lind, M., Bergmann, M., Watson, R. T., Haraldson, S., Park, J., Gimenez, J., Andersen, T., & Voorspuij, J. (2018c). *Towards Unified Port Communications – From a project format to a global standard.* Concept Note #9, STM Validation Project. Retrieved from https://www.ipcdmc.org/galerie

Lind, M., Haraldson, S., Karlsson, M., & Watson, R. T. (2016). *Overcoming the inability to predict – A PortCDM future.* 10th IHMA Congress – Global Port & Marine Operations, Vancouver, Canada, April 30–May 2, 2016.

Lind, M., Michaelides, M., Ward, R., Herodotou, H., & Watson, R. T. (2019a). *Boosting data-sharing to improve Short Sea Shipping Performance: Evidence from Limassol port calls analysis.* Article No. 35 [UNCTAD Transport and Trade Facilitation Newsletter N°82 – Second Quarter 2019]. Retrieved from https://unctad.org/en/pages/newsdetails.aspx?OriginalVersionID=2102

Lind, M., Ward, R., Bergmann, M., Haraldson, S., & Zerem, A. (2019b). *Digitalizing the port call process.* UNCTAD Transport and Trade Facilitation Series No. 13, UNCTAD.

Lind, M., & Simha, A. (2020). *Don't miss out on joining the World's Digital Collaboration.* The Maritime Executive, 13/2-2020. Retrieved from https://maritime-executive.com/editorials/dont-miss-out-on-joining-the-world-s-digital-collaboration-1

Michaelides, M., Herodotou, H., Lind, M., & Watson, R. T. (2019). Port-2-Port communication enhancing short sea shipping performance: The case study of Cyprus and the Eastern Mediterranean. *Sustainability Journal, 11*(7), 1912–1934.

Morton, R., & De Cauwer, N. (2019). *Why standards matter* (85th ed.). Port Technology International.

Watson, R. T. (2019). *Capital, systems and objects: The foundation and future of organizations.* Athens, GA: eGreen Press.

The Future of Shipping: Collaboration Through Digital Data Sharing

Mikael Lind ⓘ, Robert Ward ⓘ, Henrik Hvid Jensen ⓘ, Chye Poh Chua ⓘ,
André Simha ⓘ, Jörgen Karlsson ⓘ, Lena Göthberg ⓘ, Toni Penttinen ⓘ,
and Despina Panayiotou Theodosiou ⓘ

1 Society Calls for Action

The UN 2030 Agenda for Sustainable Development, a forecast increase in the use
of maritime transport, and the need to reduce the environmental footprint are all
calls for maritime transport to be more efficient and accountable (see, e.g., DNV
GL, 2018). In this context, Maritime Informatics is an important enabler. Maritime
Informatics covers many domains related to these calls (Fig. 1).

M. Lind (✉)
Research Institutes of Sweden (RISE) and Chalmers University of Technology, Gothenburg,
Sweden
e-mail: mikael@realsearchers.com

R. Ward
Pymble, NSW, Australia
e-mail: robert.ward1@gmail.com

H. H. Jensen
Henrik Hvid Consult, Copenhagen, Denmark
e-mail: henrikhvidjensen@gmail.com

C. P. Chua
ShipsFocus Group, Singapore, Singapore
e-mail: ccp@shipsfocus.com

A. Simha
MSC Mediterranean Shipping Company, Geneva, Switzerland
e-mail: andre.simha@msc.com

J. Karlsson
ABB Marine & Ports, Gothenburg, Sweden
e-mail: jorgen.x.karlsson@se.abb.com

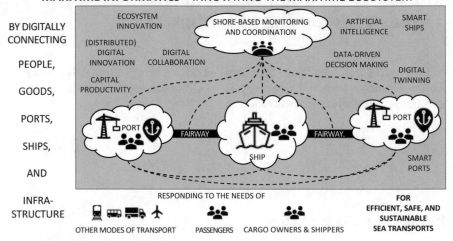

MARITIME INFORMATICS – INNOVATING THE MARITIME ECOSYSTEM

BY DIGITALLY CONNECTING

PEOPLE,

GOODS,

PORTS,

SHIPS,

AND

INFRA-STRUCTURE

Fig. 1 The concerns of Maritime Informatics

Maritime Informatics can enable efficient, safe, and sustainable sea transport through digital connectivity between people, goods, ports, ships, and natural and physical infrastructure. It has a role to play for passengers and cargo owners and shippers. A number of emerging digitally based developments rely heavily on Maritime Informatics, smart ships and smart ports digital twinning, artificial intelligence and machine learning, big data analytics, digital collaboration, and different types of innovation processes, all enabling enhanced capital productivity and data-driven decision-making. These topics are covered in various chapters in this book. Maritime Informatics is a means of addressing some of the key challenges facing the maritime sector.

Building upon industry commentaries [e.g., Maritime 2050 (UK, 2019)], we see a larger involvement of the crowd in the provision of digital services, such as innovation hubs closely associated with diverse maritime operations, a stronger focus upon a new generation of digital navigation and communication technologies, issues covering blockchain-based distributed ledgers to digital documentation for

L. Göthberg
GIGS by Lena G, Gothenburg, Sweden
e-mail: lena@abgigs.se

T. Penttinen
Attracs/Ahola Transport, Kokkola, Finland
e-mail: toni.penttinen@attracs.com

D. P. Theodosiou
Tototheo Maritime and WISTA International, Limassol, Cyprus
e-mail: Despina.t@tototheo.com

seafarers, frameworks for autonomous vessels, approaches to cyber security, and new digital and automated process for smart ships and smart ports to maximise the throughput of goods with seamless onward connections (Lo, 2019). Also, the larger shipping lines see opportunities for enhanced visibility (e.g., Simha, 2019a) and the value of data in machinery and fleet management, port and cargo operations, capacity management, customer experience, and dynamic pricing (e.g., Simha, 2019b). Hansa (2019) and Lind, Simha, and Becha (2020a) have highlighted the changing role of ship agents due to digitalisation.

2   Transitions Being Empowered by Maritime Informatics

Recently, the concept of the five logistic Internets was raised in a World-Economic Forum article extending the "current Internet with foundational, logistics-specific features. It is commercially, politically and competitively neutral. The purpose is to replace the current one-to-one connection with an Internet-like paradigm of 'connect once, then share with everyone, everywhere'" (Hvid Jensen, 2020). These five pillars of a logistic Internet may not capture all necessary movements but is an indication of where we are heading, by putting emphasis on the need for a global trade identity (GTD), shared visibility (SV), Port call optimisation, financial flows (FF), and customs cross-border interoperability (CCBI).

As maritime transport is part of the global supply chain, such a viewpoint requires that operations associated with maritime transport are integrated with other modes of transport. Sames (2019) declares that "to advance into the future, the industry should also consider working seamlessly with ports, cargo owners and other industries to optimise logistics and apply its ocean space expertise to access the resources required to support the world's growing population". The focus put upon port call optimisation covers both the external synchronisation and collaboration activities as well as the internal coordination and collaboration activities (see Lind et al., 2018, 2020b).

Maritime Informatics supports the integration of (maritime) (sub) practices and the supporting processes, procedures, and methods for the coordination within and among those enabled by digital collaboration and data sharing. This also means that Maritime Informatics can realise the integration goals addressed by Hvid Jensen (2020), Sames (2019), and Simha (2019a, 2019b) (see Fig. 2).

2.1   From Data Sharing to Data Verification

Even if we had effective capabilities in place to ensure that data are shared, a key capability is to ensure that these data are reliable. At the moment, there are numerous initiatives to ensure that data quality standards are established by different standardisation bodies. At the same time, it is forecast that there will be

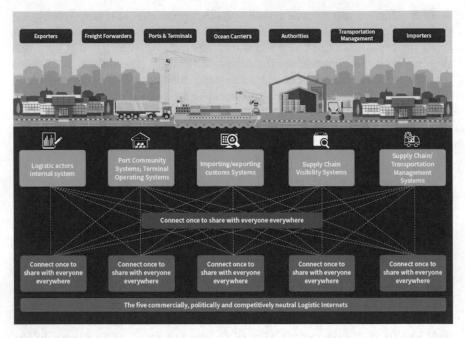

Fig. 2 Logistic Internet extends the current Internet with foundational logistic-specific features (Hvid Jensen, 2020)

an exponential growth in digital data streams (DDSs) (Pigni, Piccoli, & Watson, 2016) exposed both publicly and privately (e.g., European Commission, 2020). However, we may find that the quality of the shared data is not sufficient for sound decision-making. In order for ports, ships, and other transport operators to coordinate precisely, they must be confident that they can rely on a third party's shared data. High-quality data are also essential for associated activities, such as billing for services delivered.

DDSs provide business opportunities for service providers to support the verification of the data generated by transport producers. It is thus most likely that services will emerge where you will verify data by cross-referencing numerous data sources (Fig. 3). An open approach to public and private data source verification should mean that innovations, such as single windows systems, where users can get sufficient on-line information from a single point of entry will gain in reliability.

For industry incumbents, it is important to acknowledge the risks that introducing digital intermediaries could place on an established industry. Using digital data exchange platforms shifts the economy from industry optimisation to ecosystem optimisation. In other industries, we have seen how the emergence of trusted third-parties' platforms has changed the competitive landscape, and in many cases these digital platforms have impacted the incumbents' profits. The digital platforms behind hotels.com, *Uber*, and *Amazon*, for example, are typical of operating models of the largest Internet-based companies. Their role as a go-between or intermediary

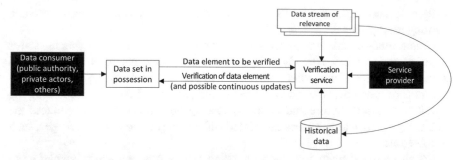

Fig. 3 Setup of a verification service of data elements possibly provided by a third party

piggybacks on the incumbents' investment in assets and services. In doing so, the intermediary service provider between the consumers and the suppliers is in an incredibly valuable and powerful position. It carries few of the costs of providing a service and takes a small cut from the many consumers, which quickly adds up to be a significant income. Controlling the go-between interface is where the power and the profit then lies. The best digital commerce platforms can end up controlling the industry that they engaged to serve, creating new market leaders, and draining some of the profits and revenues of the incumbent companies. In a few years, many traditional industries, including shipping, might have a new set of market leaders who have leveraged their own digital platform model to achieve that position.

Within the maritime sector, incumbents must therefore prepare themselves by deciding how they wish to work with trusted third parties in a digital business ecosystem. The five logistic Internets is a concept that incumbents can use to protect against centralised digital platforms harvesting substantial shares of the shipping industry's profits (Hvid Jensen, 2020).

2.2 From Disconnected to Connected

The volume of data streams generated by connected natural and physical infrastructure, goods, checkpoints, and carriers is continually growing and requiring additional bandwidth. The introduction of 5G wireless communications capability in terminal environments and satellite communication capabilities in regions where land-based communication technologies do not provide adequate services will alleviate some of this need, especially as costs are also declining. These developments foster an unstoppable movement towards connecting the disconnected, which is highly welcomed by maritime transport clients. There is a keenness for supply chain visibility and a higher degree of predictability of the different key events along the transport chain.

Initially, some organisations might resist data sharing, but even with a few contributors, as the connectivity and the availability of diverse data sources grows, there will be increasing amounts of situational awareness data to improve decision quality. Decades of captured AIS data now being used in data analytics and machine learning exemplifies the potential.[1]

Connectivity based on digitally connected objects allows for detecting the status of goods and carriers. Already today, we see automated check-in and check-out solutions for identifying road-bound carriers entering and exiting a port. These solutions can also provide video images of the carrier and its load. Recording the condition of goods before and after any loading operations in a port reduces the ambiguity of any claim process associated with damaged goods and packages, such as containers.

We also see that smart containers are gaining more attention which enables more precise applications of track-and-trace (See Becha, Schroeder, Voorspuij, Frazier, & Lind, 2020; UNECE 2019).

All these connectivity opportunities provide the wherewithal for the digital twinning of maritime resources (such as ships) and sociotechnical systems (such as ports and transport chains) (see Haraldson et al., 2020). Digital twinning is the mapping of the operational characteristics of a physical asset to a set of mathematical equations and is one of the latest technologies to emerge from Industry 4.0—the trend towards automation and data exchange in manufacturing technologies and processes, which include cyber-physical systems (CPS), the Internet of Things (IoT), Industrial Internet of Things (IIOT), cloud computing, cognitive computing, and artificial intelligence. It uses data from sensors on the physical asset to calibrate mathematical equations describing in fine detail the operation of an asset. "Digital twins are more powerful than models and simulations because they leverage DDSs to bridge the barrier between the physical entity and its representation" (Pigni, Watson, & Piccoli, 2020). In larger ports and in other efforts associated with ship technologies, there are opportunities for developing digital twins based on real-time digital data streams and historical data of previous behaviour.[2,3] Digital twinning can be used to determine the most efficient designs, setups, or forecast the lifespan of individual components and determine when predictive maintenance is needed.

2.3   From Shrouded to Transparent Visibility

Due to the distributed and self-organising characteristics of maritime transport, the sector lags other transport sectors in its level of coordination. Too often, the actors have to act and take their decisions independently, unaware of the impact on others because of a lack of situational awareness. Initiatives such as port call optimisation and Port Collaborative Decision Making (PortCDM), discussed more

---

[1] c.f. e.g. www.marinetraffic.com and www.marinebenchmark.com

[2] https://www.hafen-hamburg.de/en/news/maritime-future-summit-evolution-not-revolution%2D%2D-35979

[3] https://www.maritimeinstitute.sg/Events-Activities?tabs=news&year=2018&modal=70

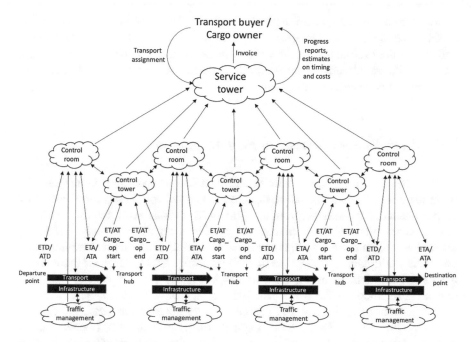

Fig. 4 Supply chain visibility through digital integration throughout the end-to-end transport chain

fully elsewhere in this book, are examples of ways to move from fragmented situational awareness to common situational awareness and therefore improved coordination.

Consequently, maritime delivery times have a higher uncertainty compared to the other sectors. Initiatives such as the IBM-Maersk block-chain effort and the Tradelens environment have been developed to improve transparency and progress awareness for all the relevant stakeholders. Other developments to increase such situational awareness include digitalisation in fleet operating centres, control rooms, port control towers, traffic management for different modes of transport, and service towers (see Fig. 4). The predictable flow of incoming goods and end-to-end visibility are important means for optimising manufacturing processes and for reducing warehouse needs. Cost control reports emerging from the chain of activities, particularly if associated with things like weight and dimensions, also serve as an important means for the transport buyer to optimise the cost per ton for shipments and capacity utilisation.

Using digitalisation enables several independent actors in an ecosystem to work together dynamically and to make the ecosystem more efficient. However, it is important for the incumbents to consider how much power they might relinquish to a trusted central digital platform. Alternatively, they must search for solutions that mitigate the threat from central digital platforms. Another option is a decentralised solution, like blockchain, where the platform is not controlled by a single entity but is governed by the ecosystem using the platform. The shipping industry wants to avoid the emergence of an intermediary that has the potential to control the industry and reduce the profitability of the various parties dependent on it. The challenge is how to build an attractive business model based on a distributed or decentralised platform that is collectively managed.

2.4   From Semi-automatic to Full Automation

Inspired by autonomous land vehicles and autonomous operations more generally, there are now moves to introduce autonomous shipping. These actions are being driven primarily by several prominent maritime nations such as Norway, South Korea, and China, who are placing an emphasis on using already developing technology for autonomous ships based on AI algorithms, machine learning, cloud computing, big data, and augmented reality (Bajpai, 2020). Like for autonomous trucks and autonomous trains, we would expect to see developments in legislation and a clarification on the roles that different actors will take. Maybe shipyards would become operationally responsible for fully autonomous vessel movements with shipping companies chartering capacity from those shipyard operators in the same way that car and truck makers aim to enable the provision of fully automated cars and trucks sold on a transport-as-a-service basis.

"A fully autonomous ship would be considered a vessel that can operate on its own without a crew. Remote-controlled ships are those that are operated by a human from shore, and an automated ship moves according to predefined actions. As the technology matures, more types of ships will likely transition from being manned to having some remote-controlled and possibly even autonomous capabilities. Autonomous ships might be used for some applications, but it is quite possible that there will still be crew onboard some ships even if all hurdles to acquiring a fully autonomous fleet are crossed" (Marr, 2019).

There are also initiatives for full automation for port cargo operations that are monitored by personnel from a control room (Henriksson, 2020). In this context, it is no longer unrealistic to picture a self-driving car motoring from its factory of manufacture on to an autonomous ship in the local port and then driving of at the port of destination and onward to its new owner.

Fully autonomous shipping and associated services will, of course, be independent and not require a constant data feed or link; however, for many ships we could see a combination of remote control and autonomy where high bandwidth is required for a remote operator to take control (Vartdal, Skjong, & St.Clair, 2018).

2.5   From Onboard to Remote Operations

Another clear trend is in remotely controlled operation. Examples include remote surgery in the health sector and platooning or flocking in road-bound transport, where a group of vehicles are driven together as one group. Trials are also underway with shore-based navigational assistance which in the long run will change the role of the pilot supporting ships navigating in areas which today require assistance.

The efforts on autonomous vessels, the digital control room within fleet operation centres, the next generation of VTS, automated cargo operations, and transport service towers are all examples of the movement towards more remote support, monitoring, and interaction. Statements such as "owners need systems that can remotely connect bridge system data with communications infrastructure to give them access to a vessel data dashboard on a per vessel basis" (Rowles, 2020) are now common.

2.6   From Static Electrical Grid Demand to a Flexible Demand/Supply Microgrid

A lot of contemporary efforts are now being put into electrification as a means for more sustainable and environmentally friendly operations. Electrically powered ship and port operations are a focus for many as a means for sustainable shipping. When more ships are going electric and society demands less emissions during a port stay, digitalisation becomes an important enabler for smart microgrid applications and speed up the implementation to make the needed power available at the quay.

Balancing energy supply locally based on current demand/supply will be needed to avoid heavy investment that most likely will be slowing down the shipping industry going electrical. Having a digital application to predict high peaks of energy demand and secure available capacity in the local grid will be crucial. Solutions are already implemented in large electrical grids and proven to play an important role to maximise utilisation of renewable energy like solar, wind, hydro, etc.

There will be a need of a local grid strong enough to provide the power needed and able to predict and manage large as well as fast changes on demand side. One scenario would be to implement a local grid, called Microgrid, with a digital application for controlling the grid to manage the power fluctuations, called smart grid. The Microgrid Control System is responsible for coordinating the operation of different generation sources and loads. A microgrid solution is an attractive alternative compared to invest in new cables connected in the major electrical grid. The Microgrid will be connected to the Point of Common Couplings (PCC), shown in Fig. 5.

To strengthen the local grid, an energy storage must be considered. The energy storage can supplement peak power demands and can possibly in many cases also be used for energy trading back to the major grid. Having an energy storage provides

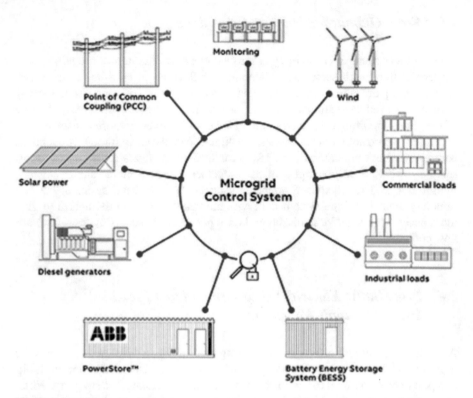

Fig. 5 Smart Microgrid with local energy production, energy storage and connection to main grid (https://new.abb.com/distributed-energy-microgrids/our-offering/microgrid-plus-system)

opportunity for implementing local renewable energy production like solar, wind, etc. Periodically energy overproduction not needed can produce electro fuels like hydrogen that can be used for fuel cells that will be connected to the Microgrid as the Diesel generators shown in Fig. 5.

A Microgrid would also increase the availability of local power supply if there is a blackout in the main grid.

It is possible to imagine a connected ship sharing data with the port by informing the quay grid of the ETA, port stay time, and the power needed during the stay will allow the local grid to better predict demand and secure enough power during the stay. As more ships go electrical while alongside, an implementation of a fleet management concept based on energy demand and priority will be needed. Similar solutions are already implemented for the electric vehicles (EV) market and are proven in use.

3 Concluding Remarks

The future of shipping is digitalisation, automation, and electrification empowered by maritime informatics. We should, however, not forget that maritime transport operations are conducted primarily to fulfil the needs of those that are buying maritime transportation services. We must therefore carefully ensure that any digital innovations provide value for those who pay for the services.

Maritime commerce is driven from several markets, such as the new building market, the freight market, the cruise and passenger market, the demolition market, and of course the stock market. Shipping is a derived-demand business depending on trade, which explains its reactive and temporal-spatial nature. Maritime Informatics cannot detach itself from the business practice that defines it and provides the data to feed it. Maritime commerce is one of the key drivers for the industry's need for development and innovation within maritime informatics. Maritime commerce participants need to time the market in each of their domain. Their need for information to successfully navigate these markets creates a need for many infomediaries and drives the emergence of Maritime Informatics.

At the operational level, particularly in the freight market, ship operators have to keep costs down on board and in port. Another operational pressure is to significantly reduce shipping's carbon footprint. This requires collaborative action across the maritime supply chain by adopting appropriate innovations and digitalisation to minimise carbon emissions and costs. Maritime informatics is key to enabling electrically powered ship and port operations, which is a key step towards reducing emissions.

New digital intermediaries will likely emerge. Current incumbents must consider how to avoid being exploited by these new players yet take advantage of the services they offer.

Standards will become increasingly aligned and initiatives will be taken to continuously provide evidence of the value of digital collaboration in shipping environments. An efficient, safe, and environmentally sustainable sector needs to be developed harmoniously, in order to transform the maritime sector to compete in a digital future. It must move away from:

- Fragmented situational awareness *to* common situational awareness
- Low information quality *to* high and reliable information quality
- Vague planning horizons *to* predictable operations
- Unstructured information exchange *to* standardised data exchange
- Sub-optimised operations *to* a mature collaboration culture
- Unnecessary waiting times *to* just-in-time operations
- Low information systems maturity *to* enhanced information systems maturity

These are exciting times for those willing to create the future of shipping.

References

Bajpai, P. (2020). *Autonomous shipping: Trends and innovators in a growing industry*. Nasdaq. Retrieved from https://www.nasdaq.com/articles/autonomous-shipping%3A-trends-and-innovators-in-a-growing-industry-2020-02-18

Becha, H., Schroeder, M., Voorspuij, J., Frazier, T., & Lind, M. (2020). Global data exchange standards: The basis for future smart container digital services. In M. Lind, M. P. Michaelides, R. Ward, & R. T. Watson (Eds.), *Maritime informatics*. Heidelberg: Springer.

DNV GL. (2018). *Maritime forecast to 2050 – Energy transition outlook 2018*. DNV GL Maritime.

European Commission. (2020). *A European Strategy on data*. Communication from the Commission to the European Parliament, The Council, The European Economic and Social Committee and the Committee of the regions, Brussel, February 19, 2020.

HANSA International Maritime Journal. (2019). *In this industry, change is constant*. Interview with Jonathan C. Williams, General Manager of FONASBA. Retrieved from https://hansa-online.de/2019/11/schifffahrt/140080/

Haraldson, S., Lind, M., Breitenbach, S., Croston, J. C., Karlsson, M., & Hirt, G. (2020). The port as a set of socio-technical systems: A multi-organisational view. In M. Lind, M. P. Michaelides, R. Ward, & R. T. Watson (Eds.), *Maritime informatics*. Heidelberg: Springer.

Henriksson, B. (2020). *Automated container terminals are taking off*. ABB. Retrieved from https://new.abb.com/marine/generations/technology/automated-container-terminals-are-taking-off

Hvid Jensen, H. (2020). *5 Ways to digitalize logistics and boost trade*. World Economic Forum. Retrieved from https://www.weforum.org/agenda/2020/02/how-the-global-logistics-industry-can-collaborate-to-increase-trade-and-reduce-poverty/

Lind, M., Bergmann, M., Haraldson, S., Watson, R. T., Park, J., Gimenez, J., & Andersen, T. (2018). *Port Collaborative Decision Making (PortCDM)*. An enabler for Port Call Optimization empowered by international harmonization, Concept Note #1, STM Validation Project https://www.ipcdmc.org/galerie

Lind, M., Simha, A., & Becha, H. (2020a). *Creating value for the transport buyer with Digital Data Streams*. 9/3-2020, Maritime executive. Retrieved from https://www.maritime-executive.com/editorials/creating-value-for-the-transport-buyer-with-digital-data-streams

Lind, M., Ward, R., Watson, R. T., Haraldson, S., Zerem, A., & Paulsen, S. (2020b). Decision support for port visits. In M. Lind, M. P. Michaelides, R. Ward, & R. T. Watson (Eds.), *Maritime informatics*. Heidelberg: Springer.

Lo, C. (2019). *Maritime 2050: Five talking points from the UK's vision for shipping*. Ship Technology. Retrieved from https://www.ship-technology.com/features/future-shipping-industry-maritime-2050/

Marr, B. (2019). The incredible autonomous ships of the future: Run by artificial intelligence rather than a crew. *Forbes*. Retrieved from https://www.forbes.com/sites/bernardmarr/2019/06/05/the-incredible-autonomous-ships-of-the-future-run-by-artificial-intelligence-rather-than-a-crew/#5f0b7bb86fbf

Pigni, F., Piccoli, G., & Watson, R. T. (2016). Digital data streams: Creating value from the real-time flow of big data. *California Management Review, 58*(3), 5–25.

Pigni, F., Watson, R. T., & Piccoli, G. (2020). *Digital twins: Representing the future*. Working paper. University of Georgia.

Rowles, G. (2020). Optimisation to drive technology advancement in 2020. *Splash247*. Retrieved from https://splash247.com/optimisation-to-drive-technology-advancement-in-2020/?suid=SU00042&medium=li&cmp=340

Sames, P. (2019). *The tipping points: Digital acceleration and climate change*. Maritime Impact, DNV-GL. Retrieved from https://www.dnvgl.com/expert-story/maritime-impact/The-tipping-points-Digital-acceleration-and-climate-change.html

Simha, A. (2019a). *Can improved visibility take shipping to the next level?* Retrieved from https://www.linkedin.com/pulse/can-improved-visibility-take-shipping-next-level-andre-simha/

Simha, A. (2019b). *Are we reaping the full value of our data in shipping?* Retrieved from https://www.linkedin.com/pulse/we-reaping-full-value-our-data-shipping-andre-simha/

UK. (2019). *Maritime 2050 – Navigating the future.* Department for Transport, Great Minister House. Retrieved from https://assets.publishing.service.gov.uk/government/uploads/system/uploads/attachment_data/file/773178/maritime-2050.pdf

UNECE. (2019). *Smart Containers: Real-time Smart Container data for supply chain excellence.* White paper, version 1. UN/CFACT, UNECE. Retrieved from http://www.unece.org/fileamin/DAM/cefact/GuidanceMaterials/WhitePapers/WP-SmartContainers_Eng.pdf

Vartdal, B. J., Skjong, R., & St.Clair, A. L. (2018). *Remote-controlled and autonomous ships.* DNV GL Maritime.

Part II
Maritime Informatics and Decision-Making

Mikael Lind

Informed by system sciences, informatics takes a holistic view to changing human practices, usually for the better. It applies digital technology to enable people to collect, process, and distribute information. From an organisational point of view, it seeks to empower decision-making through the use of information systems. As one of the founders of informatics claims, information system is to serve the object system, where the object system is the practice in focus (Langefors, 1973). In the 1960s, when informatics was introduced as an enabler for efficiency, the organization was conceived as the object system, which then later through the introduction of e-Commerce was expanded to focus on the customer. More recently, the inter-organizational aspects of multi-organisational collaboration have been embraced by informatics.

The maritime industry is a self-organising ecosystem that has been loosely held together by information for centuries. Information enables traders and shippers to overcome national differences and the myriad actors in the world-wide maritime system to request and receive the necessary services to transit oceans, rivers, and lakes and handle cargo in a multitude of ports of varying size and resources (Watson et al., 2020). The time has now come for ecosystems within the maritime sector to be empowered by connectivity and data sharing to deliver integrated performance in the ecosystem.

In this section of the book, we visit a number of applicational areas where Maritime Informatics has and could empower decision-making in the shipping sector. For each of the areas, the focus is on how information can raise the quality of decision-making and thus improve capital productivity.

Chapter "Digital Data Sharing for Enhanced Decision-Making" covers how Maritime Informatics provides a foundation for the maritime aspects of the so-called fourth industrial revolution (Maritime 4.0). Building upon the notion of digital data

M. Lind
Research Institutes of Sweden (RISE) and Chalmers University of Technology, Gothenburg, Sweden

streams (DDSs) attention is paid to the need for the maritime domain to define and standardise the *When*, *Where*, *Who*, *What*, *Why*, and *How* dimensions when capturing the circumstances of an event. Through standardised digital data sharing, affected actors can gain the necessary situational awareness to make coordinated decisions to enhance resource utilisation and increase the safety and efficiency of operations to create value for individuals and society.

Chapter "Digital Data Sharing for Enhanced Decision-Making" is followed by two chapters on how Maritime Informatics provides decision support for port visits and voyaging. **Chapter "Decision Support for Port Visits"** considers the important role that ports have in global trade as transhipment hubs and inter-modal connection points between sea-based and land-based transportation. In order to function efficiently, a well-coordinated port needs to be informed about when ships and hinterland carriers, as episodic tightly coupled actors, will use the port, which can consequently make sound decisions about reserving appropriate resources and infrastructure to serve visiting ships. This chapter also elaborates on how data from systems of production channelise data to systems of record to permit distributed coordination of port call operations among the various involved actors. Such systems of record also form the foundation for an elastic approach to time slot allocation allowing a slot reservation system to enhance the timely interaction of episodic tightly coupled actors.

In **Chapter "Decision Support for Voyaging"**, the authors describe a ship as an information hub, which is both a consumer and provider of data. Furthermore, the chapter examines decision support for navigation and voyage monitoring and recognizes that rapid technological development impacts information systems for decision-making on-board and ashore.

Chapter "A Smart Grid in Container Terminals" explores the shift from conventional fuel-powered vehicles to electric vehicles as one possible step for a sustainable transformation in the logistics sector, such as at container terminals, where heavy-duty vehicles are essential when moving containers around the terminal. Empowered by Maritime Informatics, this field is a promising area for a smart grid application, where the batteries of idle vehicles can be used during less busy times to provide capacity for the energy grid. The need for energy reserves has increased with the integration of intermittent renewable energy sources, which need to be carefully managed to provide a stable power supply. The chapter provides an overview of the cost drivers for a smart electrified container terminal.

In **Chapter "Decision Support in Short Sea Shipping"**, the application of Maritime Informatics for enhanced performance in short sea shipping (SSS) is explored. SSS is commercial waterborne transport that does not transit an ocean. SSS can be a cleaner, safer, and efficient transport system well-suited for areas such as the Mediterranean. The authors identify reliability, quality and safety, and reducing costs and delays in ports as some main challenges and look upon how Maritime Informatics, through digital data sharing and proactive collaboration between nearby ports, can improve the efficiency of SSS within a region.

Chapter "Maritime Informatics for Recreational and Fishing Vessels" illustrates how information and communications technology can support recreational and fishing vessels in their operations and communication with their environment. As these ships use the same water infrastructure as merchant ships, they should all have access to the same digital infrastructure and services to enable complete situational awareness and thus improve safety, environmental sustainability, and efficiency for all at sea.

Chapter **"Support for Financial Decision-Making"** explores key financial processes where Maritime Informatics could make a difference by enhancing existing practices. The chapter acknowledges different types of costs associated with maritime transport, such as capital expenditure (CapEx); operational expenses (OpEx); and those related to environmental, social, and governance (ESG); and finally voyage outlays. Building upon the role of Maritime Informatics to achieve control, mitigate risks, and reduce the costs within each of these cost segments, different opportunities are identified. The economic advantages and resilience emerging from transparency in financial processes through data sharing are considered.

Chapter **"Green Supply Chain Management and Environmental Control and Regulation"** examines the importance of green supply chain management (GSCM) and its relationship to the shipping industry, making reference to the regulatory framework and the enforcement mechanisms and how they impact and enhance green shipping. GSCM adds value through socially responsible management of logistics processes by connecting stakeholders within a corporate structure to promote collaboration and the preservation of the environment. The chapter considers briefly a number of green regulations touching upon the areas under the umbrella of environmental preservation. The chapter acknowledges the key role of Maritime Informatics in supporting to GSCM to comply with the high level of environmental regulations and controls that are in place or proposed.

The final chapter in this section, **"Global Data Exchange Standards: The Basis for Future Smart Container Digital Services"**, acknowledges the importance of global international standards to support the future of global trade. Particular focus is placed on the United Nations Centre for Trade Facilitation and Electronic Business (UN/CEFACT), which is promoting the deployment of smart container solutions. Physical supply chains for shifting goods need a parallel digital supply chain that moves data describing the goods and their progress through the supply chain. As data are the raw material of Maritime Informatics, smart container data flows are key to ensuring that the physical flow is well synchronised with the required documentation flow.

High-quality decision-making starts with relevant, reliable, and timely data, which is then converted into information for decision-making. This section of the book illustrates how Maritime Informatics, through its focus on data standards and data analytics tools, can enhance the maritime sector's decision-making and thus its capital productivity.

References

Langefors, B. (1973). *Theoretical analysis of information systems* (4th ed.). Lund: Studentlitteratur.

Watson, R. T., Lind, M., Delmeire, N., & Liesa, F. (2020). Shipping: A self-organizing ecosystem. In M. Lind, M. Michaelides, R. Ward, & R. T. Watson (Eds.), *Maritime informatics*. Heidelberg: Springer.

Digital Data Sharing for Enhanced Decision-Making

Michael Bergmann (iD), **Omer Primor** (iD), **and Andreas Chrysostomou** (iD)

1 Introduction

Digitalisation is the key process of what is now termed "the fourth industrial revolution" or "Industry 4.0". It is about developing an environment utilising new and disruptive technologies like artificial intelligence (AI), robotics, virtual reality and the Internet of Things (IoT) and is changing how we work and live (Schwab, 2017).

To some, the maritime industry has been lagging, but the pace of adoption of digitalisation has grown in recent years, focused around the term "Maritime 4.0", sometimes also called "Shipping 4.0". In their invitation to a conference on the topic in 2018, the German research organisation Fraunhofer stated: "Maritime 4.0 is the current buzzword in the shipbuilding industry and refers to the digitisation of all processes from planning through design to maintenance" (Fraunhofer, 2018). Similarly, the LINCOLN research project, in an invitation for its Maritime 4.0 event on September 2019, was even more specific on the definition: "The Industry 4.0 becomes Maritime 4.0 to reinforce the research focus to specific blue challenges, to develop innovative digitally connected vessels concepts, to improve the market competitiveness, overall of SMEs, to plan the appropriate skills developments

M. Bergmann (✉)
BM Bergmann-Marine, Grosskrotzenburg, Germany
e-mail: Michael.bergmann@bergmann-marine.com

O. Primor
Windward, Tel-Aviv, Israel
e-mail: omer@wnwd.com

A. Chrysostomou
MarineFields Holding Ltd., Limassol, Cyprus
e-mail: ac@marine-fields.com

M. Lind et al. (eds.), *Maritime Informatics*, Progress in IS,
https://doi.org/10.1007/978-3-030-50892-0_10

and last, but not least to include the environmental sustainability of vessels and shipbuilding" (The LINCOLN project, 2019).

While describing the same idea, these definitions of Maritime 4.0 handle the word *digital* differently. As such, it seems there is an important distinction to be made in Maritime 4.0 when it comes to *Digitisation* and *Digitalisation*. While the word digitisation is used for the conversion of information into a digital form, in essence the conversion from analogue to digital, the term digitalisation is used to describe the use of digital technology to improve business processes and value creation through data analysis.

In this arena, Maritime Informatics plays an important role as it brings maritime digitalisation into the broader maritime technology space, as well as maritime biology and other related maritime aspects of computer science. Maritime Informatics is an enabler for Maritime 4.0 but at the same time benefits greatly from the development towards and within Maritime 4.0. Maritime Informatics is also enabled by Maritime 4.0 because a large-scale digital transformation generates the data necessary for a shift to data-driven decision-making and, with it, operational excellence.

While much information in the maritime ecosystem had been available in digital form for some time, the availability of data for analysis and further digitalisation is very limited. The International Hydrographic Organization (IHO) had a very early start on digitising maritime data with its S-57 Electronic Nautical Charts (ENCs) in the Electronic Chart Display and Information System (ECDIS). The IHO also realised very early that the digitisation needed to be enhanced and as such started the S-100 initiative for full integration of various hydrographic and related information. This was a leading step towards Maritime 4.0. The International Maritime Organization (IMO) soon followed and started its e-navigation initiative. Besides adopting a strategic implementation plan (SIP) for e-navigation, the IMO also agreed to use the IHO's geospatial information (GI) registry, home of the IHO S-100 series of data transfer standards, as the basis for the IMO's Common Maritime Data Structure (CMDS).

Today, the CMDS accommodates numerous compatible standards from different organisations and enables data sharing and interoperability of different data sets across the maritime ecosystem. In addition, the IMO Facilitation Committee (FAL) is working on facilitating digitalisation in shipping, including electronic ship reports with its IMO Compendium (IMO, 2019).

Besides the work on ship-centric Maritime 4.0 digitalisation, the shoreside has also adopted this concept: IALA has spearheaded such work for Vessel Traffic Services (VTS), various shipping lines have set up their fleet operation centres, and collaborations like the Digital Container Shipping Association (DCSA) and organisations like the International PortCDM Council (IPCDMC) have focused their efforts to develop various aspects of Maritime 4.0 both on shore and in collaboration with ships and port operations.

2 Standardisation and Digitisation

In the advent of the age of digitalisation, data standardisation has become paramount in support of the tremendous changes along the whole chain of information processing. In fact, digital standardisation has emerged as a fundamental requirement for all modern data applications. By generating consistency and structure in data, standardisation is key to enabling various subsequent uses of these data—such as sharing, aggregating, benchmarking and modelling—while reducing the overhead costs of pre-processing the data.

Data standardisation has two levels: semantic and technical. The semantic level answers "what exists" and accordingly creates consistent abstraction about entities, their attributes and their relationships. This is known as "data modelling", and by standardising data models across an industry, it enables interoperability. The resulting artefacts are known as semantic standards.

Once such a universal data model exists, the digital encoding of this semantic standard can be developed to enable the creation of machine-readable data sets describing a situation generically. The broad use of these standards eases the processing of the shared data sets enormously. Popular examples of these standards are based on the data exchange language XML (Extensible Markup Language) and its derivation for geospatial information GML (Geography Markup Language). This second set of standards is known as technical standards.

With both semantic and technical standardisation, a good foundation is available to create consistent and interchangeable data sets. In order to reach the broadest use and create interoperability across knowledge domains, authoritative standardisation and standards endorsed by rule-setting organisations like the IMO are required for consistent data sets across the same theme from different producers.

3 Data Versus Information

Watson, Lind, Delmeire, and Liesa (2020) of this book explains that Digitalisation and Maritime Informatics create opportunities for new structures for capital creation and how data sharing enables new opportunities.

Along those lines, sharing data increases the availability of new perspectives for situational awareness and as such can strengthen the foundations for decision-making. However, gathering more data by itself does not necessarily lead to superior decision-making, and its value is often generated once it is analysed and presented to the mariner in a way that enhances situational awareness and knowledge building. The "Pyramid of Competence" (Fig. 1), introduced in 2012, illustrates this need.

It is important to differentiate between "data" and "information". Data, derived from the Latin word "datum", meaning "given", is the uninterpreted fact. Information, again derived from Latin "informare", means "shape" or "give form".

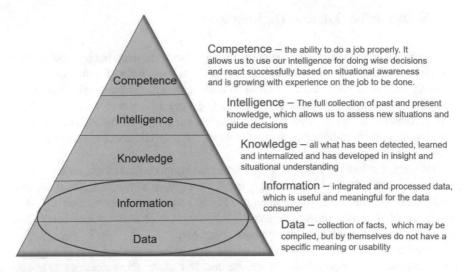

Fig. 1 The pyramid of competence (Bergmann, 2012)

Table 1 Elements of a digital data stream segment (Pigni et al., 2016) with our examples

Element	Description	Example
When	The time when the data segment was created	A timestamp with date, time and time zone
Where	The location of the entity when the segment was created	Latitude, longitude, elevation
Who	The unique identifier of the entity that caused the data segment to be created	Unique identifier (e.g. MRN)
What	The activity that caused the segment to be created	Arrival of a ship in a port, commencing of cargo operation
How	The means by which the event was initiated, authorised or completed	Reporting method
Why	Motivation for the action related to data segment creation	For the purpose of discharging cargo

In order to be useful, digital data sharing therefore needs to aim towards increasing competence by providing meaning and context and contributing to the knowledge of the interpreter. This requires that data streams capture up to six basic elements, being *primitives* that provide a semantic description for an event. A primitive is an expression for "that which cannot be described in terms of other elements or inferred from them". The primitives capture what are commonly known as the 5W+H of narrative (who, what, when, where, why and how) (Table 1) (Pigni, Piccoli, & Watson, 2016).

Capturing these primitives in the data is essential not only for generating meaning and transforming data into information but also to enable further consolidation of shared data arriving from different streams. In particular, data integration is reliant on the "who" primitive, using identifiers for fusion of different data points relating to the same entity.

In recent years, various decision support applications are increasingly making use of big data analytics methods. Generating more knowledge by integrating, analysing and visualising huge data sets into digestible information, these applications support specific decision points by creating a common and more reliable understanding of a situation. This common knowledge, achieved through data sharing, leads to harmonised decisions and as such to decisions of the individual actors which support better the activities of the others involved (Lind et al., 2020; Lind, Bergmann, Ward, & Carson-Jackson, 2018).

4   Enhancing Decision-Making Through Data Sharing

A prominent initiative, supporting enhanced decision-making through data sharing, is the IMO's e-navigation concept (IMO, 2013), which has been worked on by various stakeholders during the last several years. The e-navigation initiative has been the nucleus of starting digitalisation in shipping as it relates to regulations and international requirements.

e-Navigation is the " . . . harmonized collection, integration, exchange, presentation and analysis of marine information on board and ashore by electronic means to enhance berth to berth navigation and related services for safety and security at sea and protection of the marine environment" (IMO, 2013).

The IMO understands that harmonising information and creating a common understanding between players on ships and on shore are essential to improving the safety and efficiency of sea trade. This core mission of IMO will not be sufficiently covered in our rapidly changing, technologically enabled world by the current regulatory instruments, like the International Convention for the Safety of Life at Sea (SOLAS) (IMO, 2014). New or revised protocols need to be developed that continue to ensure global trade is governed by appropriate standards and regulations but at the same time allows the necessary freedom to quickly introduce innovations around maritime safety and efficiency.

Safety of navigation remains a strong focus for the shipping industry. At the same time, growing economic pressures force shipping to look at increasing efficiency in multiple ways:

- The shipping industry needs to reduce costs for sustainable and improved profitability.
- Ports needs to increase efficiency of ship handling to optimise the limited assets available.
- Coastal states hinterland and multimodal transport capabilities are often close to capacity, and limited financial and natural resources are forcing authorities to increase the efficiency of the complete supply chain.

- Environmental agencies and society are requesting reductions in ecological damage, be it through tighter emission control, limiting pollution by ship casualties or oil spills.

e-Navigation is intended to support these preceding needs for the shipping industry by consolidating efforts through modern technology and updated rules and regulatory frameworks.

In the 1960s, the standardised container revolutionised shipping (Watson, Lind, & Haraldson, 2017). Today, the shipping industry expects the next revolution to be the containerisation of information—creating a safer, more efficient and environmentally friendly maritime sector.

Inspired by Airport Collaborative Decision Making (A-CDM), the International PortCDM Council (IPCDMC) aims to establish the necessary overarching guidelines, processes and procedures to make Port Collaborative Decision Making (PortCDM) a successful international concept to improve maritime transport as it relates to port operations and ports' interaction with ships (IPCDMC, 2019). The IPCDMC is working towards data exchange and collaboration between ships and ports, between hinterland operators and ports and within ports.

On an international level, the IPCDMC is governing the PortCDM concept, a concept to support those engaged in, or associated with, port call operations. It aims to improve the efficiency and effectiveness of activities in any port by providing a framework for data sharing, enhanced collaboration and common situational awareness (Lind et al., 2019).

Aimed at enabling more predictable timings and operations in sea transport, PortCDM is building unified and standardised data exchange protocols, addressing the need to ensure a continuous flow of data about intentions, outcomes and possible disruptions related to movements and service provision among all those involved in the berth-to-berth maritime transport process. It also aims at contributing to the operational aspects of a well-coordinated port as a transport hub in the larger transportation ecosystem. This results in a high degree of predictability in the planning and execution of all associated operations and activities contributing to just-in-time (JIT) operations.

The PortCDM process is intended to be dynamic and transparent using standardised messaging and interfaces that trigger and prompt the various actors to review exception alerts and take actions based upon their physical capabilities, preferences and requirements. Provided everyone is kept informed, multiple revisions or iterations to plans can take place during a single port call while at the same time minimising the overall disruption to the final outcomes.

PortCDM focuses on a more dynamic and effective delivery of the existing processes through greater collaboration and the availability of high quality, near real-time data to all the relevant and authorised actors in the maritime transportation ecosystem, underpinned by appropriate protocols to ensure robust data integrity and access control. PortCDM comes with a framework for maturity levels supporting ports and their actors to successively advance PortCDM maturity (Fig. 2). The

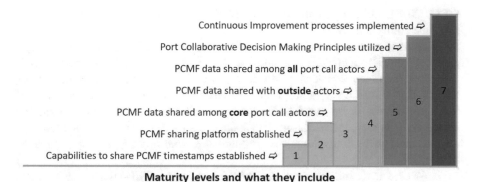

Continuous Improvement processes implemented ⇨
Port Collaborative Decision Making Principles utilized ⇨
PCMF data shared among **all** port call actors ⇨
PCMF data shared with **outside** actors ⇨
PCMF data shared among **core** port call actors ⇨
PCMF sharing platform established ⇨
Capabilities to share PCMF timestamps established ⇨

Maturity levels and what they include

Fig. 2 PortCDM maturity levels (IPCDMC, 2019)

maturity model allows the categorisation of implementation levels of PortCDM in a port based on clearly defined criteria.

On the technical level, the IPCDMC has developed the S-211 standard, a Port Call Message Format within the CMDS. S-211 is used for port call messages by allowing standardised sharing of data on intentions and outcomes of movements, services and administrative events on a given port call (IALA, 2019).

Building upon the foundational logic of the port call process, conceived as different interrelated events, the S-211 port call message format is a response to the lack of standards for sharing data on port call timing between involved actors. S 211 further captures several aligned standards used in maritime transport, as a means for realising the IMO's e-navigation strategy (IMO, 2013). In that sense, the port call message format is kept thin, focused on delivering critical operational data while leaving sensitive business essential (competitive) data aside. Also, it is not part of a larger standardisation monolith, such as the standards maintained by UN/CEFACT or WCO. The S-211 standard allows participants to share data about intentions (plans, estimations, actuals, requests and recommendations) associated with movements or services. S-211 also covers the opportunities for sharing data about the process of reaching agreement on required services by capturing the interrelated communicative acts, such as request and confirm.

S-211 is unique in reflecting high precision in the details communicated, such as the location and timing of arrival and departure, allowing for standardised and precise ship-to-port, port-to-ship, port-to-port, port-to-hinterland as well as port actor-to-port actor data exchange, thereby contributing to efficient coordination.

While the data stream standardised as S-211 is an important data source for Maritime 4.0, others are essential as well. The principal international association for marine electronics companies, Comité International Radio-Maritime (CIRM), is a prominent industry association supporting the development of e-navigation services. CIRM members are engaged in the work of the International Electrotechnical Commission (IEC), supporting the development of S-421 for route plan exchange

(IEC, 2018), build upon the existing RTZ format (IEC, 2014), and enabling interoperability with S-211.

S-421 is in essence focusing on a ship's route, while S-211 focuses on the ship's port call. With both standards within the IMO CMDS, they follow the same data definition template, which is based on the ISO 19xxx series of standards (IHO, 2012). This allows the synchronisation of those data streams, converting the data into information which can then be analysed and accessed through data sharing concepts. This way, the necessary data exchanges for JIT arrivals, associated with an integrated port call performance, are enabled, a topic which is high on the agenda of the IMO.

A focused IMO initiative called GloMEEP "... is a GEF-UNDP-IMO project aimed at supporting the uptake and implementation of energy efficiency measures for shipping, thereby reducing greenhouse gas emissions from shipping" (IMO, 2020). The Global Industry Alliance (GIA), which is behind this initiative, is developing a "Just-in-Time Arrival Guide", which aims "... to provide information to ports on how to facilitate JIT Arrival of ships—with a view to reduce GHG emissions by optimising the port call process and provide a sustainable solution to its customers as a critical node in the end-to-end supply chain" (GIA, 2020).

These two examples, S-211 and S-421, part of a broad range of compatible data streams under development or already available, illustrate how the use of data describing maritime transport from different perspectives can enhance situational awareness, as the shared data streams are merged and information is extracted by the individual actors using data analysis tools. Furthermore, they illustrate the need to develop Maritime Informatics as a distinctive field at the intersection of the maritime industry and information systems.

5 Increasing Reliability and Value of Information Through Fusion of Data Streams

Every organisation seeks to enhance demand for its services, overcoming inefficiencies and boosting innovation in such a way that it is not falling behind its competitors (Pigni et al., 2016). The European Commission recently launched a European strategy for data (European Commission, 2020) in which it claims that "... Today 80% of the processing and analysis of data takes place in data centres and centralised computing facilities, and 20% in smart connected objects, such as cars, home appliances or manufacturing robots, and in computing facilities close to the user ("edge computing"). By 2025 these proportions are likely to be inverted".

From the Maritime 4.0 perspective, the data streams coming out of systems of records, such as PortCDM compliant tools (see Lind et al., 2020), are growing in diversity, scope and scale—such as digital twins, ship movements captured via the automatic identification system (AIS), container status and movements captured by smart container devices or video gate control systems capturing carriers moving in and out of ports from the hinterland point of view. It is thus reasonable to think that a vast number of digital data streams will be available to players across the maritime ecosystem. Nonetheless, the providers of these data streams might want to control access, by regulation or fees, as in the case of commercial data providers. It is therefore likely that there will be a mixture of public and private digital data streams available for the data consumer.

Value creation is dependent on an organisation's capacity to retrieve those relevant data sets that are important to its operations. The organisation needs the ability to identify relevant data streams and access them in real time (Pigni et al., 2016). As the scope and scale of data grows, organisations will increasingly need to develop a data sciences capacity in order to effectively handle data and unlock the information needed for decision-making.

Dedicated ship reporting is one such standardised data stream which is currently used. The traditional "noon report" contains a vessel's position and other relevant data to assess the progress of a ship based on its speed and environmental forces, including weather conditions. But as this is manually compiled data, it may contain errors. Fusing data from noon reports with AIS data [see Regulation 19 of SOLAS Chapter V (IMO, 2014)], for example, can validate a ship position and other data which is contained in both data streams. This allows data analysis to identify suspicious data points and initiate action to resolve any discrepancies.

The development of data streams from different sources using the same technical definitions, such as those of the CMDS, enables the validation and extension of data assets and as such creates additional value. The important GS1 EPCIS data standard (GS1, 2014) is, however, a stand-alone standard for the logistics industry. After consolidation with IPCDMC and others, GS1 is now looking at adding "Maritime Resource Name (MRN)" (IALA, 2020) as an identifier. This will then allow it to interlink its logistical standard with other shipping-related standards under the CMDS, such as S-211.

Besides the increase of quality and reliability of data streams as they are fused, there is an increase in value proposition when joining different data streams. This value creation is underpinned by the fact that different streams may have complementary data, which creates new information. The value proposition for a single data provider is limited, as potential clients might get access to data free of charge and therefore may not be willing to pay for services. Therefore, if data streams are fused and made available in a synchronised way, new value may be created that can be translated into costs for services and build the basis for the business case of service providers. Companies like "JAKOTA Cruise Systems GmbH" with its FleetMon product or "MarineTraffic" are two examples of industry actors combining data streams to generate business. Once data streams are fused, dedicated algorithms can be developed to further analyse the data and create new, enriched data sets. This newly created information goes up the value chain towards building knowledge to support decision-making by factoring millions and billions of data points. One example of such technology is developed by "Windward", an analytics and AI company specialising in maritime applications.

6 Static and Dynamic Data Streams to Support Collaborative Decision-Making

In the digital era, data streams are often identified as static or dynamic data streams. Static data is characterised as data which is compiled and then used over a long period of time. In maritime, ENCs would fall into this category. Here a National Hydrographic Office takes hydrographic surveys and other relevant information and consolidates the results in nautical charts, which are updated from time to time but in between are used unmodified. (Hecht, Berking, Jonas, & Alexander, 2011).

Dynamic data is frequently changing data. Data about the tidal height (UKHO, 2016) or weather data are examples. Within the category of dynamic data exists both real-time data coming directly from sensors, like speed indications, and semi-real-time data, which is collected and then transmitted, like the tidal data in online portals such as the BSH Tide Data portal (BSH, 2020).

The integration of both static and dynamic data, be it real time or semi-real time, can provide additional situational awareness as it provides both knowledge about less volatile baseline data and data with high volatility. The benefit of gaining knowledge about the real situation increases the chance of making good decisions. In Watson et al. (2020), explanation of the "episodic tight-coupled aspect" indicates the value of combining dynamic and static data on operational aspects and explains how collaborative decision-making can improve operational results.

7 Conclusion

Digitalisation is an essential element in growing the economy in the twenty-first century. The maritime sector will need to fill the gap between the digitalisation already achieved in other sectors through Industry 4.0 and what has really only just begun in Maritime 4.0.

With more and more data streams becoming available, both static and dynamic, and the growing importance of IoT to the maritime industry, the need for harmonisation and standardisation is recognised by many to be critical. The maritime domain, however, due to its global character, needs to ensure worldwide adoption of the necessary standards and needs to foster open data streams so all can benefit from the data explosion fed by Maritime 4.0 and enabled by Maritime Informatics.

References

Bergmann, M. (2012). *Public-private-cooperation models*. e-Maritime Conference, Brussels, November 22–23, 2012.
BSH. (2020). *BSH tide data*. Retrieved from https://www.bsh.de/EN/DATA/Tides/tides_node.html

European Commission. (2020). *A European strategy on data*. Communication from the Commission to the European Parliament, The Council, The European Economic and Social Committee and the Committee of the regions, Brussels, February 19, 2020.

Fraunhofer. (2018, August 28). PRESS RELEASE – Maritime 4.0: The digital ship as an information hub. *Fraunhofer*.

GIA. (2020). *Draft just in time arrival guide*. London: Global Industry Alliance.

GS1. (2014). *EPC Information Services (EPCIS) version 1.1 specification – GS1 standard*. Brussels: GS1 AISBL.

Hecht, H., Berking, B., Jonas, M., & Alexander, L. (2011). *The electronic chart* (3rd, revised ed.). Lemmer: Geomares Publishing.

IALA. (2019). *IALA S-211 product specification – 1.1.0 – IALA port call message product specification*. International Association of Marine Aids to Navigation and Lighthouse Authorities.

IALA. (2020). *Maritime resource name*. International Association of Marine Aids to Navigation and Lighthouse Authorities. Retrieved from https://www.iala-aism.org/technical/data-modelling/mrn/

IEC. (2014). *61174 Ed.4 CDV – Annex S (normative), Route plan format for export and import – RTX/Z*. International Electrotechnical Commission.

IEC. (2018). *IEC CD 63173 – MARITIME NAVIGATION AND RADIOCOMMUNICATION EQUIPMENT AND SYSTEMS – DATA INTERFACES – Part 1: S-421 Route Plan based on S-100*. International Electrotechnical Commission.

IHO. (2012). *IHO Publication S-99 – Operational Procedures for the Organization and Management of the S-100 Geospatial Information Registry – Edition 1.1.0*. Monaco: International Hydrographic Bureau.

IMO. (2013). *NCSR 1/28 Annex 7 – DRAFT E-NAVIGATION STRATEGY IMPLEMENTATION PLAN*. London: International Maritime Organization.

IMO. (2014). *SOLAS Consolidated Edition 2014*. London: International Maritime Organization.

IMO. (2019). *FAL 43/7/1 – REVIEW AND REVISION OF THE IMO COMPENDIUM ON FACILITATION AND ELECTRONIC BUSINESS, INCLUDING ADDITIONAL E-BUSINESS SOLUTIONS*. London: International Maritime Organization.

IMO. (2020). *GloMEEP*. Retrieved from https://glomeep.imo.org/

IPCDMC. (2019). *Terms of reference*. International PortCDM Council.

Lind, M., Bergmann, M., Andersen, T., Haraldson, S., Ward, R., Bjørn-Andersen, N., Michaelides, M., Watson, R. T., Ferrus Clari, G., Zerem, A., Rylander, R., Gimenez, J., & Karlsson, M. (2019). *Achieving compliance in collaboration and data sharing with PortCDM*. International PortCDM Council (IPCDMC).

Lind, M., Bergmann, M., Ward, R., & Carson-Jackson, J. (2018, December). *Port collaborative decision making*. London: Seaways. Retrieved from www.nautinst.org/seaways

Lind, M., Ward, R., Watson, R. T., Haraldson, S., Zerem, A., & Paulsen, S. (2020). Decision support for port visits (Chapter 11). In M. Lind, M. Michaelides, R. Ward, & R. T. Watson (Eds.), *Maritime informatics*. Heidelberg: Springer.

Pigni, F., Piccoli, G., & Watson, R. T. (2016). Digital data streams: Creating value from the real-time flow of big data. *California Management Review, 58*(3), 5–25.

Schwab, K. (2017). *The fourth industrial revolution*. World Economic Forum.

The LINCOLN project. (2019). Retrieved from http://www.lincolnproject.eu/maritime-4-0-the-digital-innovation-disruption/

UKHO. (2016). *Admiralty Tide Table – NP201*. Taunton: United Kingdom Hydrographic Office.

Watson, R. T., Lind, M., Delmeire, N., & Liesa, F. (2020). Shipping: A self-organising ecosystem (chapter 2). In M. Lind, M. Michaelides, R. Ward, & R. T. Watson (Eds.), *Maritime informatics*. Heidelberg: Springer.

Watson, R. T., Lind, M., & Haraldson, S. (2017). *Physical and digital innovation in shipping: Seeding, standardizing, and sequencing*. Proceedings of the 50th Hawaii International Conference on System Sciences.

Decision Support for Port Visits

Mikael Lind ⓘ, **Robert Ward** ⓘ, **Richard T. Watson** ⓘ, **Sandra Haraldson** ⓘ, **Almir Zerem** ⓘ, **and Svend Paulsen** ⓘ

1 Introduction

The maritime sector seeks increased efficiency in moving goods and passengers from berth to berth, because of the intense competition between the various players, such as shipping companies, ports, global port operators, and hinterland operators. As global concern over climate change intensifies, opportunities are now being sought to reduce the environmental footprint of all forms of transport including sea transport. As a transport sector, the short sea shipping sector of the maritime industry also competes with options such as road and railway. However, because it is a self-organising ecosystem of many players, the maritime sector lacks the overall ability to optimise its operation. The risk of system detrimental suboptimisation is ever present when each independent player acts in its self-interest. Thus, there needs to

M. Lind (✉)
Research Institutes of Sweden (RISE) and Chalmers University of Technology, Gothenburg, Sweden
e-mail: mikael@realsearchers.com

R. Ward
Pymble, NSW, Australia
e-mail: robert.ward1@gmail.com

R. T. Watson
University of Georgia, Athens, GA, USA
e-mail: rwatson@terry.uga.edu

S. Haraldson · A. Zerem
Research Institutes of Sweden (RISE), Gothenburg, Sweden
e-mail: sandra@realsearchers.com; Almir.Zerem@ri.se

S. Paulsen
Pragmatique Denmark, Copenhagen, Denmark
e-mail: svend.paulsen@pragmatique.dk

M. Lind et al. (eds.), *Maritime Informatics*, Progress in IS,
https://doi.org/10.1007/978-3-030-50892-0_11

be agreement that some actors occasionally might have less than optimal operations in order to ensure that the port ecosystem as an entity is operating optimally.

In most of the world's busiest ports, the principle of first come first served is the standard practice, causing unnecessary inefficiencies and creating unnecessary externalities like high levels of pollution and greenhouse gas emissions. This is often the result of poor integration between contractual issues, legal constraints, and local practices resulting from decades of legacy customs and culture. Digitalisation of the maritime sector, e-Navigation efforts, and integration of sea transport into a holistic transport system call for enhanced harmonisation on a global scale so that the sum of the inherent issues of a self-organising ecosystem is resolved to improve sector efficiency.

Port visits, independent of the type of carrier, are of an episodic nature. Different types of trade are built upon different types of operational logic. The infrastructure and resources provided by the port will thus be co-utilised to serve the many episodic visits made by external actors for their distinct purpose of visiting the port.

This co-utilisation together with the distributed nature of port operations puts high demand on providing a solid foundation for making well-founded decisions. Even though the dominant logic for serving the port's clients has been on a first come first served basis, the port of tomorrow (See Lind et al., 2020) needs to build upon a foundation that assures port call actors of a timely service at the same time enabling a high utilisation of available infrastructure.

This chapter firstly elaborates on the fundamentals of coordinated port operations. This is followed by a framework for how foundations may be established for involved actors' common situational awareness of forthcoming and ongoing port calls used for each of the actors to align their plans in relation to others. This is done by sharing important data from each actor's systems of production with a system of record for a port visit. One of the key foundations for establishing such system of record is to share and aggregate spatial-temporal data as the foundation for making reliable decisions on the timing of the different events related to each other. This is also the foundation for the necessary time slot allocation approach that is elaborated in the closing section of this chapter. Before considering the next steps in maritime digitalisation for more harmonised operations, the role of standardised data sharing and digitalisation is discussed to illustrate how such a shared system of record can be established through initiatives like Port Collaborative Decision Making (PortCDM).

2 Fundamentals of Coordinated Port Operations and the Potential Role of Data Sharing

Lately, a lot of attention has been paid to port call optimisation as an expression of the need to integrate sea and port operations. Consequently, this also means that port call optimisation needs to be integrated with inbound and outbound logistics. Ports are complex operations as they are hubs, though often regarded as a single

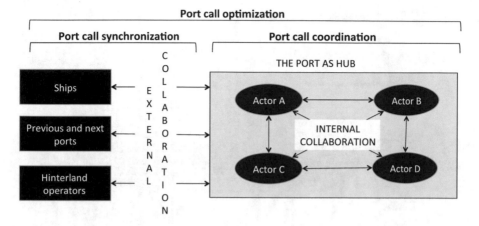

Fig. 1 Two related collaborative processes in port call optimisation (Lind et al., 2018a)

actor serving sea and land transport. Nevertheless, they consist of multiple actors who must act cooperatively to be an effective hub.

When visiting a port, shipping companies and hinterland operators are episodically Tightly Coupled with a range of port facilities. They must participate in closely coordinating with both external and internal processes. In Fig. 1, the integration of internal and external collaborative processes associated with the various episodes of tight coupling of port call optimisation is depicted.

Port call and other turnaround processes are constituted by a series of events and associated actors who need to coordinate their actions with others, maybe for the same event, and preceding and succeeding events. Digitalisation enables the sharing of standardised time stamps in real time among different port actors and episodic Tightly Coupled actors. Time stamps should reflect the progress of different events associated with a turnaround process. In the *metro map* depicted in Fig. 2, key states and core actors associated with a port call are captured. As revealed by this metro map, the services provided by port call actors come together at different coordination points and require the different services and infrastructure to be sequentially synchronised in time and space, for example, at various specified times and location:

- Pilotage requires a vessel and a pilot.
- Arrival and departure from berth requires a vessel and linesmen/moorers and tugs.
- Cargo operations need a vessel, stevedores, loading/unloading equipment, and terminal.
- Departure berthing requires the readiness of the vessel, linesmen/moorers, tugs, and pilots.

The sharing of time stamps for planned and actual events enables actors to achieve enhanced situational awareness, which provides port call actors with

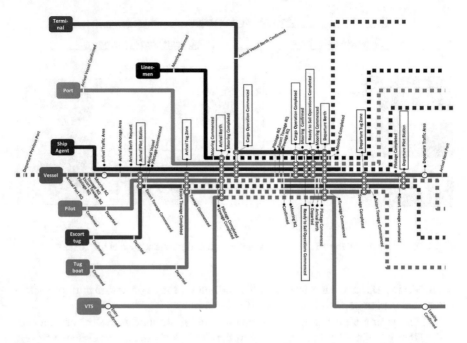

Fig. 2 Different states associated with the port call process (Lind, Haraldson, Karlsson, & Watson, 2016)

enhanced capabilities to coordinate their operations just in time, thereby raising their efficiency and that of the entire system.

Within a port, there will be a number of simultaneous ongoing instances of port call processes, with multiple types of trade operating under different business logics. As the actor network within the port is highly complex and that a port in itself is not an organisational entity, it is unlikely that there will be one party that is able to talk on behalf of the whole port. Port operations therefore rely on collaboration.

Collaboration requires episodic tight coupling between two or more parties to fulfil agreements. The parties interact in patterns of initiatives and responses, such as executing an agreement between a ship and a terminal on the time and location of berthing and the availability of cranage for loading and unloading. This agreement will regulate temporal (when) and spatial (where) dimensions among other characteristics. The fulfilment of this agreement is initiated by someone acting as a representative of the ship and the ship operator ensuring that the ship is at the specified location at the specified time and that the tug operator must match the location and time and be ready to commence towing.

However, this collaboration process is also of interest to others involved in the sequence of activities that need to happen during a port visit. For example, if the terminal operator could get insights of a towage's progress, it could adjust its plans accordingly. Because there are many actors in port call operations, there is a need to establish a schema of how collaborations can be facilitated by a real-time system of record of a port visit and be shared among involved actors. One of today's challenges is that the industry has not arranged its installed base, in all its different parts, to share data to enhance collaboration. There is a need for message formats for capturing spatial-temporal data for essential actions emerging from collaboration revealing the status of a production system and by that enabling enhanced interoperability between systems, within the port, and to other systems along the maritime transport chain.

The industry thus needs to establish capabilities for collaborative dynamics enabled by digitalisation as a basis for everyone to be more informed. Collaboration releases data captured in a system of record to be shared among many and used for making well-informed decisions. The means for generating reliable and relevant data for such decisions is through collaboration and the use of multiple data sources.

3 Systems of Record Provide a Basis for Decision-Making

At its simplest, a system of record is a mechanism for recording and recalling details of obligations and events. Systems of record would have emerged at least with the beginning of agriculture, when farmers and traders needed to record transactions and obligations. The agricultural economy created a need for a long-lasting and unique record of transaction of activity. There was a parallel need for an information system to make sense of these recordings (reading) and teach others how to make them (writing). In the shipping industry, a system of record might store an obligation, for example, to provide a tug service and a certain date, time, and location for, say, 3 hours. It should also record how long the actual tug service event took.

Digitalisation has replaced early society's manuscript records, and current systems of record are based on database and distributed file technology. Today's organisation has many systems of record for areas such as production, sales, accounting, customers, and so on. A business cannot operate without systems of record, which ideally are based on a shareable, high integrity, and secure data management technology. While widely used, spreadsheets are a poor choice for a system of record, because, among other limitations, they are not readily shareable. Ideally, data from the various functional areas are integrated in a single database or data warehouse, but this is a difficult challenge, and often data are siloed in functional databases.

The first key task of a system of record, such as for the movement of ships within a port and their use of resources, is to provide a record of plans and actions. For example, a ship receives certain services during a particular time period and owes specific fees. In this role, a system of record supports the operations of a port, ship, terminal, etc. A second key purpose is to support a system of inquiry, such as data analytics, to learn from operational data to plan future port visits and the future of a port. For instance, a terminal operator might run predictive analytics on an appropriate system of record to forecast how long it will take to unload a ship given the location of every container to be offloaded from the ship when in the port. It can only undertake such an estimate if, over a period of time, it collects precise unloading data that includes the original positions of every unloaded containers on a ship and how long it took to move each one to the dock.

Every system of production should produce a system of record that collects and stores data that records intentions and actuals in sufficient detail to support operational actions and tactical and strategic planning. These records can then be shared among all involved participants, thereby reducing the risk of suboptimisation.

3.1 Systems of Production Create Systems of Record

Sea transport is a self-organising ecosystem (Watson, Lind, Delmeire, & Liesa, 2020), and we reiterate some key aspect of its nature:

- All organisations and ecosystems are in the business of capital creation (Watson, 2019). Typically, they pursue economic capital creation, but some pay prime attention to other forms, such as universities which deal primarily in human capital. A shipping company creates economic capital by using its ships (economic capital) to move products from export to importer. A port creates economic capital by using its location and harbour (natural capital) and infrastructure (economic capital) to serve Tightly Coupled episodes among actors, such as sea-based and land-based carriers, in their efforts of enabling passengers and/or goods to be moved to another carrier.
- Organisations can employ multiple combinations of systems of engagement, framing, inquiry, production, and record in their capital conversion repertoire. Shipping is a system of production because it follows routine practices in transporting goods. It also creates a system of record, as do all actors in the ecosystem.
- The goal of an organisation or ecosystem is to create a competitive bundle of complementary capitals and capital conversion processes. *Digitalisation is an opportunity to change the competitiveness of a capital bundle.*

In Table 1, these system types are depicted with examples from the shipping sector (Haraldson et al., 2020; Watson, 2019).

Every organisation or ecosystem is thus built around systems of engagement to attract customers and around systems of production to meet customer's needs. Both types of systems create systems of record, such as a customer database and records of business processes involving the different production facilities. A further system of record is needed to record details of events related to producing a good or service.

As the ecosystem of shipping is characterised as being self-organised, it becomes crucial for involved actors to be informed of what others have agreed upon and progressed. Standardised data sharing of which systems of record, reflect the content of systems of production, provides a scope that stretches beyond the port actors' areas of operations and provides port actors with all the necessary contextual

Table 1 Types of systems

Type	Intended focus	Example
Engagement	Collaboration and coordination	Port call coordination/synchronisation/optimisation
Framing	The reason for behaving in particular ways	Shipping culture, mission statement
Inquiry	Knowledge production	Data analytics
Production	Products and services	Movement of goods
Record	Data	AIS, time stamps, situational awareness

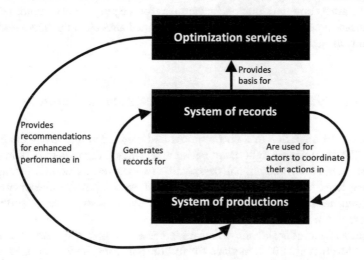

Fig. 3 The interplay between system of productions and systems of record as a mean for distributed coordination and optimisation (Haraldson et al., 2020; Lind et al., 2018b)

information. In Fig. 3, the relationships between the two types of systems are depicted.

Digitalisation is becoming more apparent to support maritime transport and thereby providing great opportunities for actors to supporting their distributed coordination. Among other things, the era of digitalisation can feed data of planned and conducted transactions into systems of record to be shared among involved stakeholders and analysed to support production system optimisation. To gain maximal value from production system data, it should record spatial-temporal digital data for each activity, such as ship movement capture by AIS (the ship automatic identification system), and spatial-temporal data on plans and progress. Thus, for each event the location and time as well as its characteristics should be recorded.

Fundamentally, there is a need to enable the sharing of data from the core events constituting the port call process. One of the approaches that has surfaced for such purpose is PortCDM (Lind et al., 2018a) building its logic upon supporting the establishment of systems of record, based upon collaborative foundations, being used for the involved actors to coordinate their actions. In this way, PortCDM is not intended to be the planning tool for activities in a port call. PortCDM is intended to provide all actors within and around the port call process with common situational awareness emerging from a system of record (Lind et al., 2018b). These systems of record can assist in fine-tuning existing port call plans, once they have been established. Records captured in the system of record are used in a system of inquiry (Watson, 2019) providing foundations for analytics used for making well-informed decisions as well as evaluating the performance of the ecosystem. Through the establishment of the system of record, authorised participating actors will thus be able to obtain a common situational awareness for the purpose of enhanced planning and in that way, at an early stage, become informed about any upstream disruptions potentially affecting their operations.

3.2   The Value of Systems of Record in Actor's Planning

The successful operation of a port requires its independent parties to share data to ensure efficient episodic tight coupling, such as when a tug aids in berthing a ship. To move beyond an operational perspective to long-term resource management, a greater level of data exchange is required to legitimise investments being made. Long-term resource management both provides a structure for forthcoming operations and provides the basis for flexibility.

A port and its independent parties are expected to have a system of production (c.f. Haraldson et al., 2020) in place for fulfilling its most important tasks, where a system of production *is a repetitive sequence of coordinated actions that might be divided among actors to achieve a goal.* We can think of a ship's visit as a system of production with each of the actors performing their specific task, but we also need to recognise that each of the parties has a separate system of production (e.g. the terminal operator) and an associated separate system of record. Two aspects thus become important:

1. The sharing of accurate and detailed real-time data associated with plans and progress
2. Alignment of each actor's intention to enable effective and efficient episodic tight coupling in a timely manner

These two ingredients would create a "system" of data sharing, giving rise to well-coordinated port call processes based on high degrees of predictability and situational awareness (c.f. Lind et al., 2018c).

However, it must be acknowledged that many of the thousands of ports in the world already have some form of installed base of digital infrastructure, each of them supporting the system of production that enables port calls to meet an expected level of quality. Ports might also have a digital infrastructure in place for capturing systems of record, but most often those have been installed for other reasons than long-term and short-term port call coordination efforts, for example, port community systems put in place to support administrative processes. To allow for an emerging systems of record to be effective enough to support decision-making, it needs be connected to the different systems of production that concern the utilisation of the port infrastructure to:

- Ensure that enough data is captured enabling as comprehensive common situational awareness as possible
- Ensure that those involved have aligned foundations to enable them to share their recorded time stamps and thereby allow those time stamps to be matched with others, of the same type or other types

As ports are, in their planning processes, dependent on what happens outside the port, connectivity to outside systems also becomes a necessity. The reasonable way forward is to establish standardised interfaces between different systems to enable standardised sharing of spatial and temporal data associated with the visits being, or about to be, conducted by episodic Tightly Coupled actors.

Since event changes in the system of production are instantly captured and then can be shared in the system of record, it is possible for an individual actor to be notified of desired event changes, such as a ship arriving to the pilot boarding area, and also be informed of possible deficiencies in the overall plan of the port call process. In this way engaged actors may get alerts and indications for:

- *Missing data*, which directs attention towards possible missing data in the system of record based on when they should have occurred in a system of production. One example is a pilotage need requested and confirmed some predefined hours before arrival.
- *Conflicting data*, which directs attention towards actor's different conceptions of time stamps. An example is when a port authority, the terminal operator, and the captain report different estimated times of arrival to berth.
- *Unreasonable relationships*, which directs attention towards the relationships between different time stamps. An example is when the time between estimated times of pilotage commenced and arrival at berth differ outside a defined range.

3.3 Decision-Making in Ports: It Is Not Just About Serving Ships

Port call processes build upon patterns of activities conducted by diverse actors that provide services. There are at least four simultaneous ecosystem-oriented systems of production processes that need to be interlined:

- Sailing ships berth to berth
- Serving ships according to their needs
- Loading and discharging cargo/passengers
- Bringing goods from a hinterland hub to the terminal, or vice versa

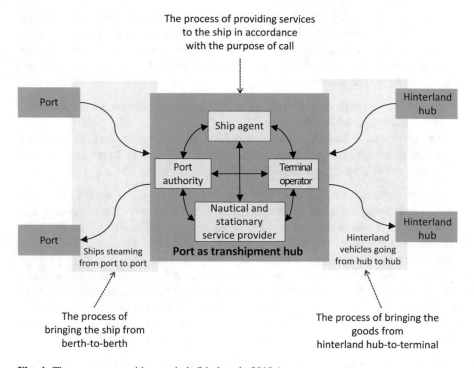

Fig. 4 The port as a transhipment hub (Lind et al., 2018c)

In Fig. 4, these systems of production are depicted. The system of record revealing the progress of actions in those systems of production is thus a complementary product of the actions pursued in the systems of production.

A port's operations rely on insights from all of these four production processes since each production process is dependent on consuming data from all three systems of record and about the progress in other production processes. To support each actor's individual decision-making, it is therefore important that the systems of record are built upon a commonly agreed logic of data sharing needs for each situation by:

- Providing situational awareness
- Aligning different actors by revealing diversities and unrealities in their timing of episodic tight coupling and ensuring that essential data for the coordination of a port call are shared in a timely manner

4 Foundational Building Blocks of the PortCDM Concept

PortCDM records data about relevant actions completed by the production system, resulting in a system of record that can be analysed to enhance the quality of the production system as well as informing ecosystem members of their plans and performances.

During the last decade, the PortCDM concept has been defined and validated within the European Union (EU)-sponsored MONALISA 2.0 and the Sea Traffic Management (STM) Validation projects. The PortCDM concept is an important enabler for the efficient, safe, and environmentally sustainable sea voyage berth to berth. The PortCDM concept comes with operational and technical guidelines for enhanced collaboration and data sharing. At the core of the PortCDM concept is to facilitate the establishment of a system of record building upon being connected to systems of production associated with four arenas of collaboration:

- Internal collaboration within the port
- External collaboration with ships
- Other ports
- Hinterland operators and end customers

PortCDM builds upon sharing time stamps between different port call actors as the basis for:

- Providing enhanced accuracy of essential time stamps in the port call process
- Providing a basis for each port call actor to align the plans of their operations
- Establishing a continually emerging common situational awareness among involved actors.

Common situational awareness is a reflection of the content of the current systems of record concerning a particular port call at a particular time. This also means that when the system of record captures plans, or their realisation, of events in the systems of production, situational awareness will be updated. By establishing a communication channel for updating each other in real time, port actors can maintain an accurate situational awareness (see Fig. 5).

PortCDM provides a system of record for a ship's port visit and other visits of episodic Tightly Coupled actors, such as hinterland carriers (Lind et al., 2018c). Through advanced analytics, it helps to optimise and synchronise the series of events associated with the visit of a particular to a port.

As shown in Fig. 6, PortCDM's unified message format (S-211) supports the digital exchange of data related to a port call, elements of its system of record, to promote coordination among port actors and situational awareness by enabling actors to benefit from the time stamps provided by other actors. Its flexible design supports the recording of planned and completed events. Its extensible nature means it could also include agreements on the provision of services. As a port call occurs across space and time, PortCDM records spatial-temporal attributes and other data for each event planned or executed during a port call.

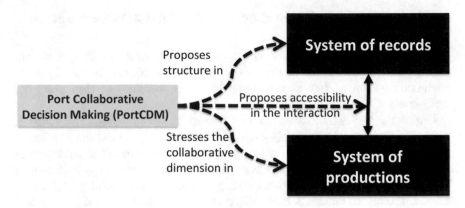

Fig. 5 The role of PortCDM (Lind et al., 2018c)

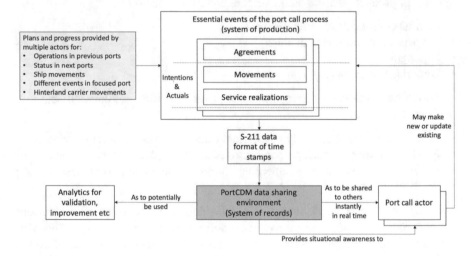

Fig. 6 PortCDM framework

Because maritime operations are conducted in a highly distributed and diverse environment, it is essential for those involved to know the plans and progress of complementary actors in a port visit.

It can also be described in the following way that PortCDM's system of record is a digital intermediary between "those who know" and "those who need to know" about port call process. PortCDM derives its effectiveness from:

- Being a system of record for all port visits
- Use of standardised message format for capturing and sharing event data
- Enabling real-time sharing of planned and executed event data
- Use of a unique identifier for each ship's port call

Finally, a system of record is the input to a system of inquiry, such as machine or data analytics. As such PortCDM is both a system for managing the present, a ship's visit (and other episodic Tightly Coupled actors); and the input to a system for planning the future, a port's capacities.

The goal of PortCDM of minimising ship turnaround times and improving the predictability of the key events in the port call process is limited by insufficient data resources. It is therefore necessary that PortCDM works in alignment with integrating additional types of data from systems of production to ensure a port has the right long-term mix of resources to minimise ship turnaround. For example, data analytics might reveal that the presence of an additional pilot would over a year reduce ship turnaround by, say, 10% due to the ability to conduct more parallel assignments of pilotage and thereby avoid unnecessary waiting times.

Planning for one visit can improve efficiency, as PortCDM has shown, and planning for hundreds of visits will give efficiency another major boost.

PortCDM thus brings collaborative dimensions into port call coordination (port internal collaboration) and port call synchronisation (port external collaboration) into focus. This does not mean that the port call process is optimised, but it does mean that some, though incomplete, data are available for others to start an optimisation process for port calls and other operational services. PortCDM creates a system of record, based on a port's actors' systems of production, which can fuel data analytics, artificial intelligence, and machine learning.

PortCDM is positioned as a concept that through its recommended message format stresses the importance of running the production system without any misunderstandings on key episodes (such as the estimated time of arrival), but also as a creator of a system of record.

For example, planning a port call cannot solely rely on the situation in the port. It builds upon insights on the status of related actors, such as events and progress in the previous port, and movement of ships, and hinterland transport. Today, the system of record is often incomplete and thus not well-suited for learning through data analytics.

An implemented system building upon PortCDM according to its objectives can address this issue. It will require standardised message formats and interfaces for a port's systems of production. In this way, the system building upon PortCDM would enable each actor to plan what resources need to be available in different future coupling episodes contributing to an optimised port. The concept of PortCDM's current system of record reveals what operations were planned for and conducted during a visit, but it has no details of what resources in total were available at the time of the visit or the pattern of resource usage over an extended period. This requires additional details of resource utilisation to be aligned with PortCDM.

5 Shared Situational Awareness Enabling Time Slot Allocation

5.1 Time Slot Allocation Can Improve Maritime Operations

In an ideal world, a ship sails at an economical speed that minimises its environmental footprint and arrives at its destination in accordance with its passage plan, enters port, and begins unloading/loading operations without delay. After a smooth and uninterrupted loading and any necessary maintenance and other administrative matters, the ship then leaves as planned and makes passage to its next port, where the same pattern of events is repeated. Regrettably, this happens all too rarely. The PortCDM concept and port call optimisation initiatives are seeking to change this by avoiding the traditional "hurry up and wait" and "first come first served" principles that predominate the port call process today.

PortCDM relies on data sharing using standardised digital data exchange that allows all actors in the port call process to access the same, up-to-date information about plans and progress related to a ship's port call. This means that all the actors share the same situational awareness and can coordinate their activities and adjust and adapt their individual contributing plans and timings according to the most up-to-date forecasts for key events.

A key element in making an efficient port call is the determination and allocation of the times when certain key events will begin and end, such as port arrival, berthing, commencement, and completion of unloading/loading and departure. If all the involved port call actors meet those times, then a port visit is perfectly synchronised.

Initiatives, such as PortCDM and port call optimisation, have been developed specifically to increase the efficiency and predictability of maritime transport, especially port operations, by looking at how to synchronise activities for ship arrivals, port call operations, and ship departures to ensure a continuous flow of activity with a minimum of waiting time for any of the involved actors. Agreeing on timing ensures an uninterrupted flow of productive activity. It is the foundation for the parties involved in a port call to align their respective actions to enable coordinated and synchronised events, such as just-in-time arrival, just-in-time service provision, and just-in-time departure. This is, in effect, time slot allocation at work.

5.2 Time Slot Allocation: A Common Approach for Synchronisation in Human Practices

The commercial aviation sector has particularly effective arrangements that control the movement of aircraft by assigning slot times for key events. This ensures that the multitude of facilities on the ground are synchronised to minimise delays to the aircraft schedule. Slot allocations are also used to control and maintain safe airspace for aircraft both when moving around an airport and when flying from destination to destination. The larger commercial airports require airlines to secure an arrival slot before taking off from their origin airport.

Within aviation, allocating slot times contributes to:

- More reliable schedules for arrival and departure
- Better and more efficient use of airport resources
- Improved fleet utilisation by airlines
- Safe and efficient transit—especially in congested areas

These gains would be most welcome if they occurred in the maritime sector, which is now being driven by public pressure for less environmental pollution and more reliable, timely, and cost-effective deliveries, together with meeting the enduring need of all those involved to minimise their costs.

The concept of using time slots to synchronise activities is neither unique nor new. For example, physicians and hospitals use slot management. Universities break the day into slots when professors and students meet for class. The booking system for hotel rooms is, in effect, slot allocation, where each room is a slot for a particular day. Once the room slot is allocated as a "confirmed booking", then the various support services such as the room preparation and perhaps breakfast preparation can be arranged and synchronised to ensure a complete service for the customer.

Returning to the aviation industry as one model, while there are obvious benefits from using time slots to synchronise Tightly Coupled events, there are some factors in maritime transport that need special attention. In particular, slot allocation in the maritime domain must be inherently more flexible than aviation to cater for the longer lead times and inevitable unpredictable delays that occur in ship operations. In addition to the obvious need to include a limited amount of buffer time in critical event slots, there must also be a process in place that alerts all those involved as soon as possible when any of the contributors to a slot event cannot meet the previously agreed slot time. This could be caused by such things as the late arrival of a ship, a breakdown of equipment in the port, or the late departure of another vessel that is using the same resources needed for an arriving ship. A major difference between seaports and airports is that seaports are more self-organised and depend upon the capabilities of a multitude of actors to coordinate their respective actions for the better good of a shared common object of interest—the port call. Overall, the ports of the world distribute the responsibility of coordination differently to airports, and there is also variation among ports.

Obviously, it is in the interests of a ship, as well as the other actors involved, to meet an original time slot whenever possible, thereby maximising efficiency and the allocation of their resources. When circumstances change, however, the originally designated time slot must be rescheduled, with inevitably some delays and disruptions to some or all of the involved actors—as is the case today. However, under an efficient data sharing and coordination environment such as can be established under the PortCDM concept, efficient rescheduling should be easier to achieve. This is because, under PortCDM, all those involved can be alerted at the earliest opportunity when any actor is unable to meet an allocated time slot. In addition, the common situational awareness that PortCDM and data sharing provides means that actors can more easily determine when the next opportunity arises for them to meet the particular port call requirements assigned to the slot and to identify what impact, if any, this may have on the other involved actors.

5.3 Synchronising Tightly Coupled Events During a Port Visit

A port call involves numerous different actors—each with a particular activity or role to fulfil. For example, the pilot and tugs must act together before a vessel can berth. Stevedores must prepare the dockside before a ship can come alongside, and line handlers must be ready to secure the ship as it approaches its berth. In any port call, there are numerous similar episodes of tight coupling where one activity cannot proceed without another taking place either beforehand or at the same time. Optimising the allocation of these resources has always been a challenge, particularly when the notice or request for the resources is made late, which is often the case.

The challenges in managing, scheduling, and synchronising a port's resources also vary according to port size. Large ports may have more flexibility because they have more resources (such as the number of pilots and tugs and berths), whereas small ports often have particularly constrained resources—perhaps only one pilot and few berths. At the same time, large ports service more ships and can be subject to consistent excess demand, whereas a small port might face major variations in demand for its services. Considering all these different factors, it is likely that a small number of them could actually limit the overall capacity of a port and, as such, the number or cumulative total of slots available on any day. It might be the total number of berths in the port or the number of hours of access to the port due to tides. Knowing what the critical limiting factors are will influence how and by whom slots are initially allocated. It could be the terminal operator, the harbour authority, or others, according to the circumstances of the port.

5.4 Improved Capital Productivity

Specifically allocating slots by time and place can enable ports to better coordinate the planning and utilisation of the available resources for all the planned episodes of tight coupling.

Under a slot allocation regime, a port's service providers offer their resource as sets of slots that enable a required service to be completed during the booked slot period. Slot allocation forces each service provider to determine their available resources and manage them to meet their obligations.

As an example, the pilotage activity in a port might occupy slots of say, 2 hours, based on the time for a pilot to meet an incoming ship, guide it to its berth, and return to meet another incoming ship. Slots might need to include an element of slack time (buffer time) to cater for unforeseen delays, but this should be limited. In effect a slot is a window with an expected start and finish time. Knowing the time, duration, and location that a slot refers to means that all involved parties can then commit to providing the necessary resources. As a result, a port call can be coordinated by relating a series of multiple connected time slots.

Fixed slot allocation already happens in some ports and terminals, particularly for regular services such as container liners requiring dependable berthing windows and berths week after week so as to meet their scheduled service. Allocating such fixed slots means that containers and cargo can be stacked in a timely manner close to the designated berth resulting in the shortest transit distance to the vessel during loading.

5.5 Time Slot Allocation Requires Standardised Data Sharing and Common Situational Awareness

The key to effective time slot allocation is data sharing between all the involved actors using a standardised data exchange format. Using digital data sharing then enables all the actors to share the same situational awareness picture. Importantly, when an event that is included in the situational awareness picture changes, such as a delay or a required rescheduling of a slot, all actors can be alerted immediately, and an iterative process can begin to find an optimal adjustment.

The longer the time horizon available for committing to a time slot, the more easily contributing parties can manage their resources. It also follows that as soon as any actor finds that they are unable to meet a particular time slot, then this should be declared so that the maximum amount of time remains for other actors to make adjustments and thereby minimise ripple effects.

5.6 Towards a Common Approach for Time Slot Allocation Empowered by PortCDM

To illustrate the principle of time slot allocation in shipping, Fig. 7 shows how slots might be arranged and confirmed. Once a slot is identified by the key actors, then the various other service providers can be invited to confirm that they can meet the relevant requirements for that slot. If they cannot, then a process of iteration can begin so that a number of sequential slots can be mutually determined and reserved that will together meet the full requirements of the port call with a minimum of waiting for all involved.

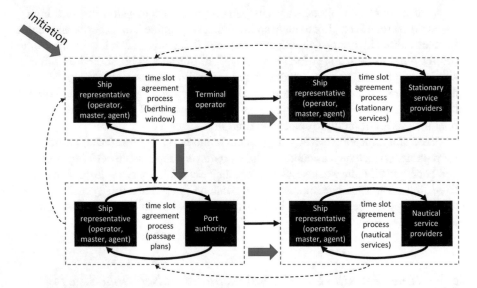

Fig. 7 Time slot allocation throughout the series of events that constitutes a port call of which different port actors are involved

The dotted arrows in the figure indicate that there will be occasions when there is a need to reschedule a previously agreed slot due to disruptions which could be caused by delays at the previous port or because the current port call might not be proceeding according to plan (delayed or finished earlier). In the case of such a delay, or even an early arrival, the same process would be initiated for managing the process of reallocation starting with confirming the capability of the terminal operator to berth the ship at a different time.

This process shown in Fig. 7 is not markedly different from how port calls are currently arranged. However, a key difference is that the coordination and synchronisation process is done primarily through digital data sharing as an iterative, on-line process rather than through individual one-to-one interactions and negotiations between the various actors.

As shown in Fig. 7, negotiation might start between the representative of a ship and a terminal operator to identify an appropriate time slot, often as a part of the contractual arrangement. As the date or time for the slot gets closer, other port call actors would become involved using the initial negotiation between the ship representative and the terminal operator as their point of departure. Depending on the type of trade, this might take place a long time before the actual port call, such as is the case for cruise ship visits, or may be framed within a larger agreement, such as within container scheduling or recurrent ferry visits capturing multiple port calls within the same agreement, or it may concern one visit as might happen in the bulk and general cargo trade.

The initial agreement between the ship representative and the terminal operator will form the foundation for other actors within the port to agree with the ship representative for activities related to passage to/from berth and for services. Other actors will negotiate agreement around this foundational time slot allocation.

Digital data sharing of a ship's progress will enable a time slot allocation to be revised, if necessary, and thus there is greater opportunity to maintain the desired synchronisation between the client's (the shipping company) requirements and the service providers.

By collecting performance times for each slot in a port, predictive analytics can be used to provide guidance on improving timings including buffer times for each service in each port. Of course, the long-term goal is to minimise buffer times since they lower resource utilisation.

6 Outlook: What Will Happen Next?

The establishment of message formats, communication channels, and interaction procedures are just foundational capabilities. The real benefits come when data derived from different areas of operations and related systems of production in the ecosystem are used in optimising the overall ecosystem's performance. The winners are not the ones that are in possession of data, but the ones who can optimise for the good of the whole ecosystem. This is also a call for innovators to enter and enrich the maritime sector by offering new digital value-adding services.

By increasing its information richness through digital data sharing, the maritime transportation sector can improve resource management and its overall efficiency. Ship movements can be conducted with a reduced carbon footprint and a port's resources more fully utilised.

Every industry needs to continually adapt its practices to take advantage of technology that raises its capital productivity. Time slot allocation, a mechanism to synchronise joint actions, is a concept that works well in other sectors. With the support of digital technology, it should therefore also be considered for shipping.

References

Haraldson, S., Lind, M., Breitenbach, S., Croston, J. C., Karlsson, M., & Hirt, G. (2020). The port as a set of socio-technical systems: A multi-organisational view (Chapter 4). In M. Lind, M. Michaelides, R. Ward, & R. T. Watson (Eds.), *Maritime informatics*. Heidelberg: Springer.

Lind, M., Bergmann, M., Haraldson, S., Watson, R. T., Park, J., Gimenez, J., & Andersen, T. (2018a). *Port Collaborative Decision Making (PortCDM): An enabler for Port Call Optimization empowered by international harmonization*. Concept Note #1, STM Validation Project. Retrieved from https://www.ipcdmc.org/galerie

Lind, M., Bergmann, M., Haraldson, S., Watson, R. T., Park, J., Gimenez, J., & Andersen, T. (2018b). *The skilled collaborators – The winners in a digitized maritime sector*. Concept Note #2, STM Validation Project. Retrieved from https://www.ipcdmc.org/galerie

Lind, M., Bergmann, M., Haraldson, S., Watson, R. T., Park, J., Gimenez, J., & Andersen, T. (2018c). *Enabling effective port resource management: Integrating systems of production data streams*. Concept Note #3, STM Validation Project. Retrieved from https://www.ipcdmc.org/galerie

Lind, M., Haraldson, S., Karlsson, M., Watson, R. T. (2016). *Overcoming the inability to predict – A PortCDM future*. 10th IHMA Congress – Global Port & Marine Operations, Vancouver, Canada, April 30–May 2, 2016.

Lind, M., Ward, R., Bergmann, M., Haraldson, S., Zerem, A., Hoffman, J., & Eklund, E. (2020). Maritime informatics for increased collaboration (Chapter 8). In M. Lind, M. Michaelides, R. Ward, & R. T. Watson (Eds.), *Maritime informatics*. Heidelberg: Springer.

Watson, R. T. (2019). *Capital, systems and objects: The foundation and future of organizations*. Athens, GA: eGreen Press.

Watson, R. T., Lind, M., Delmeire, N., & Liesa, F. (2020). Shipping: A self-organising ecosystem (Chapter 2). In M. Lind, M. Michaelides, R. Ward, & R. T. Watson (Eds.), *Maritime informatics*. Heidelberg: Springer.

Decision Support for Voyaging

Robert Ward (iD), **Johan Gahnström** (iD), **Mikael Hägg** (iD),
Fredrik Olindersson (iD), **Mikael Lind** (iD), and **Suzanne Green** (iD)

1 Introduction

The shipping industry, like all other modes of transport, needs to be as safe and as environmentally friendly as possible.[1] The avoidance of marine incidents and the reduction in greenhouse gas (GHG) emissions are particularly important.

During the last 20 years, advances in ships' systems have been significant for increasing the safety of ship operations. This advancement has to a large extent

---

[1] www.imo.org

R. Ward (✉)
Pymble, NSW, Australia
e-mail: robert.ward1@gmail.com

J. Gahnström
CompetenSEA AB, Gothenburg, Sweden
e-mail: johan@competensea.com

M. Hägg
Research Institutes of Sweden (RISE), Gothenburg, Sweden
e-mail: Mikael.Hagg@ri.se

F. Olindersson
Chalmers University of Technology, Gothenburg, Sweden
e-mail: fredrik.olindersson@chalmers.se

M. Lind
Research Institutes of Sweden (RISE) and Chalmers University of Technology, Gothenburg, Sweden
e-mail: mikael@realsearchers.com

S. Green
Swedish Shipowners' Association, Gothenburg, Sweden
e-mail: Suzanne.green@sweship.se

© The Editor(s) (if applicable) and The Author(s), under exclusive licence
to Springer Nature Switzerland AG 2021
M. Lind et al. (eds.), *Maritime Informatics*, Progress in IS,
https://doi.org/10.1007/978-3-030-50892-0_12

been business driven, especially the container shipping industry has been at the forefront. In recent years, on modern ships, a lot of information from ships has been made available in ship managers' offices. More recently this development has been driven by the regulations of the IMO and its increasing requirements concerning safety of navigation, monitoring of ships' position and movements, and anti-pollution measures—many elements of which are addressed in the IMO's e-navigation strategy. All rely increasingly on digitalisation and maritime informatics.

2   The Ship as a Digital Information Source

In the digital era, a ship is both a consumer of data originating from different sources and a provider of data, both associated with its operations and with safe and efficient navigation, but potentially also for providing data associated with what can be detected and reported by a mobile platform; for example, observing the weather and sea conditions at the ship's location at any particular time and submitting it to the Voluntary Observation Ship (VOS) scheme.[2]

Most ships are now sources of some level of information that can be remotely monitored, collected, analysed and acted upon. Data recorded at sea can also be distributed upon return to port, if not previously communicated in real time.

Remotely monitoring ship movements and activities has gained in importance over the last 20 years. It is now an essential part of most shipping companies' operations, where fleet operation centres can monitor the operation of their ships and optimise the utilisation of them globally. It is also a vital part of the safety, security, and environmental protection regimes put in place by government authorities around the world.

The remote monitoring of engines and equipment is another development that relies on digitalisation and informatics. Information from sensors fitted to various equipment in a ship can be read remotely, sometimes continuously or otherwise at intervals depending upon the nature or criticality of the measurements being taken. Remote monitoring of ships' systems now occurs in about one in ten ships. It is said to deliver savings in service costs of anything from 10% to 30%, when measured against traditional preventive maintenance (Latharche, 2017). These figures are only likely to increase in the coming years.

Remote container management of reefer containers is becoming increasingly popular. A shipper can now monitor their container and cargo remotely to ensure that the conditions inside a container are always satisfactory. Bananas and pineapples are examples of delicate fruits where this technology can be used to ensure that they arrive in peak condition.

---

[2]https://www.wmo.int/pages/prog/amp/mmop/JCOMM/OPA/SOT/vos.html

3 Automatic Identification System and Long-Range Identification

An important example of the ship as a source of information is the automatic identification system (AIS)—the automatic tracking system that uses transponders on ships. AIS is now a mandatory carriage requirement for all vessels exceeding 300 gross tonnage (GT) that are subject to the International Convention for the Safety of Life at Sea (SOLAS) (IMO, 1974). AIS was designed to be used by ships to identify other ships in their vicinity and for shore-based stations like a Vessel Traffic Services (VTS) centre to identify ships within or entering their area.

AIS improves navigation safety and environmental protection by assisting in the effective navigation of ships and aids in situational awareness (AIS, 2015). Ship-borne AIS units broadcast ship information to surrounding ships and to shore actors. Messages include "dynamic data" such as position, position accuracy, course, speed, and navigation status and both static and voyage data, including the ships name, type, draft, destination, and estimated time of arrival (ETA) at the next port of call. Position reports are sent frequently depending on the vessel's speed. Static- and voyage-related reports are sent every 6 min. This information is commonly displayed in real time in ships on electronic chart display and information systems (ECDIS) or chart plotters, other computer displays, or compatible navigation radar.

AIS information from ships, together with radar information and other type of surveillance methods, underpins the modern operation of vessel traffic services (VTS), where government and harbour authorities monitor and occasionally control the movement of shipping in confined or congested waters. AIS in any given area can handle a large number of reports. By installing an AIS transponder on static objects, AIS can also be used as an aid to navigation by providing location and additional information on buoys and lights, and real-time environmental parameters such as wind speed and wave height. Further, numerous service providers now offer sophisticated digital services building upon the analysis of big data derived from historical AIS records.

Additional remote monitoring of position was introduced by the IMO in 2006 with the introduction of the long-range identification and tracking (LRIT) of ships. The LRIT regulations apply to all passenger ships, cargo ships of 300 GT and above, and mobile offshore drilling units, whenever they are engaged on international voyages. Under the LRIT regulations, these ships must report their position to their flag administration at least four times a day. Most vessels set their existing satellite communications systems to automatically make these reports (LRIT, 2006).

Special arrangements requiring fishing vessels to regularly and automatically report their location, and movements are now also commonplace requirements placed upon them by governments around the world.

4 Standardised Presentation of Information in Ships

An important aspect of the recent and rapid increase in information available to mariners at sea is how information is presented, because both ships and their crews often rely on information received in languages they might not master. To assist, information should, as much as possible, be presented in such a way that its meaning can be determined without oral or written language or the language skills of either the reader or the sender being a barrier.

On board there are times of both high and low workloads. Modern information systems and display must take these extremes into account. This also means that the presentation of information should be as intuitive as possible, avoid unnecessary clutter, and present personnel with what they need to know, rather than all the information that might be available. Situation-dependent displays of information should be the aim—presenting the mariner with only what they need to know, when they need to know it.

A particularly successful example is the standardisation of the nautical chart and supporting information publications that has been achieved by the International Hydrographic Organization (IHO) such that any mariner in the world can recognise and use a nautical chart produced by any country in the world. It is perhaps only matched by the achievement of the World Meteorological Organization (WMO), which has managed to do the same for the global exchange of meteorological observations and the production and distribution of weather and climate forecasts.

While much progress has been made in the last 100 years on standardising the presentation of one of the most fundamental sources of navigation data—the nautical chart, this has not been the same for other data finding its way to the bridge of a ship. AIS was made a carriage requirement for ships from 2004 onwards with a minimum requirement for the display of AIS data being no more than a teletype display of at least three lines of 16 alphanumeric characters, enough to obtain the target vessel's identity and position. This very basic arrangement does not provide the mariner with an easy way to determine the position and associated information about other ships from AIS messages, other than by hand plotting the geographic coordinates either on a chart or on a radar display. However, most electronic chart systems today allow for a Global Navigation Satellite System (GNSS)-derived position of a ship and AIS information from surrounding ships to be displayed and queried as an overlay to the electronic charts.

Both the IMO and marine equipment manufacturers have grown increasingly aware of the issues described previously and their impact on safety at sea. The IMO now requires the human element,[3] fatigue management,[4,5] and harmonised

---

[3]IMO Assembly resolution A.850(20).

[4]IMO guidelines on Fatigue, MSC.1/Circ.1598.

[5]IMO Assembly resolution A.772(18).

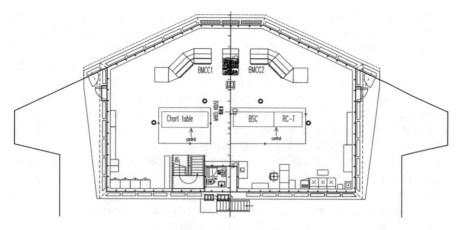

Fig. 1 Modern bridge layout (Source: Courtesy Stena Bulk AB)

displays[6] to be taken into account for most developments associated with a ship's bridge equipment and navigation arrangements. The IMO has finalised some parts of an e-navigation strategy and will continue to work on e-navigation concepts and plans to complete these by 2024–2025. In 2019, the IMO adopted the "Guidelines for the Standardization of User Interface Design for Navigation Equipment" (MSC.1/Circ.1609), which should be applied to Integrated Navigation Systems (INS), ECDIS, and radar equipment, in order to promote standardisation of interfaces to help meet the needs on a ship's bridge.

5   Navigation

5.1   Ships and Supporting Information Technologies for Safe and Efficient Navigation

Most ships voyage across the seas and oceans of the world to move cargo between ports. Ships are designed for different purposes, such as carrying containers, oil and gas, bulk goods (grain, iron ore, coal, etc.), passengers, or project cargo. Over the years, ships have generally become ever larger, especially in the container ship segment, putting additional requirements on navigation and ship manoeuvring and on port infrastructure (see Fig. 1 as an example of a modern bridge layout).

For ships engaged on international voyages, the IMO sets the minimum requirements for the conduct and equipping of ships in relation to safety and protection of

---

[6]IMO Interim guidelines for the harmonized display of navigation information received via communication equipment, MSC.1/Circ.1593.

the marine environment. This is done under the terms of the SOLAS convention and the International Convention for the Prevention of Pollution from Ships (MARPOL). Among other things, chapter V of SOLAS stipulates the equipment that ships must carry and operate in order to navigate safely between ports. While many of the functional requirements have remained the same, for example, the carriage of a nautical chart for navigation, over the years the equipment required has become increasingly more sophisticated and capable. In many cases, this involves the use of digital technology. For navigation, most ships are now required to use an ECDIS together with an appropriate Electronic Navigational Chart (ENC), rather than a paper chart. Both the traditional paper chart and the ENC must also be published under the authority of a government. Like most of the equipment that is required to be carried under SOLAS chapter V,[7,8] both the ECDIS and ENC are governed by comprehensive international standards and equipment approval processes. In addition, there are several applicable existing guidelines.[9,10]

Environmental considerations have now assumed an important place alongside navigation safety in the operation of ships at sea. This ranges from avoiding marine mammals, such as whales and dolphins,[11] to optimising a ship's route to minimise fuel consumption and the emission of GHGs (Watson, Holm, & Lind, 2015). Access to relevant digital information streams is increasingly the way these issues are addressed.

In addition to the active broadcasting of operational data from ships, as described previously, SOLAS requires ships to have an operational Voyage Data Recorder (VDR) that collects data from various on-board sensors. VDR is comparable to the "black box" data recorder carried on aircraft. Although the primary purpose of the VDR is for accident investigation after the fact, its inputs can also provide data for preventive maintenance, performance efficiency monitoring, heavy weather damage analysis, accident avoidance, and training purposes to improve safety and reduce running costs.

---

[7] SOLAS Ch V/15 on Principles relating to bridge design, design and arrangement of navigational systems and equipment and bridge procedures.

[8] MSC.1/Circ.1350/Rev.1 – Unified Interpretations of SOLAS Chapter V.

[9] SN.1/Circ.288 – Guidelines for Bridge equipment and systems, their arrangements and integration (June 2010).

[10] MSC.1/Circ.982 – Guidelines on ergonomic criteria for bridge equipment and lay-out, (December 2000).

[11] https://www.fisheries.noaa.gov/national/endangered-species-conservation/reducing-ship-strikes-north-atlantic-right-whales

5.2   The Four Stages of Safe Passage Between Ports

The IMO[12] has identified four essential navigation undertakings required to achieve a safe passage between ports:

- Appraisal
- Planning
- Execution
- Monitoring

The navigation of a ship is the overall process of taking a ship safely from one port to another. It begins with a planning and preparation stage, when the navigator selects a route and identifies all the constraining factors including the length of the intended voyage, which will affect such things as the time to be taken and fuel and provisions requirements; the expected weather and sea conditions, which may affect the maximum loading or even the ability of the ship to sail in certain conditions; and the maximum draft acceptable along the chosen route, which may affect the maximum load that can be carried. A search must also be made to identify all the applicable rules and regulations along the intended route. These may differ from country to country. Increasingly, most information is available in digital form. In the emerging digital data environment, larger ship operators may undertake the bulk of the passage planning ashore, leaving only the final checking and adjustments to the ship's crew—who are ultimately responsible for the safety of the ship. Commercial services are now available that provide customised and dedicated weather routing services and route optimisation.

A ship's voyage can comprise several different stages:

- Manoeuvring within a port
- Fairway navigation
- Coastal navigation, which is close to and in sight of the shoreline
- Open sea, which is out of sight of land

The different stages of a voyage have different characteristics and introduce different types of hazards, challenges, and information needs. A passage close to the shore always includes the danger of running aground. The ship's draft may be critical in shallower waters and will vary depending on the loading of the ship. The height of the tide must be known to maintain a safe margin below the keel and avoid grounding the ship.

---

[12]IMO Resolution A.893(21), Guidelines for Voyage Planning.

5.3 Appraisal

Appraisal is carried out by the Navigation Officer, who identifies all the necessary information in order to plan a safe voyage. Some of the points the navigation officer should identify include:

- ENCs check: The navigation officer ensures that the entire voyage is covered by official and corrected (up to date) ENC data.
- Quality of data (CATZOC): The navigation officer checks the quality of the data in the ENCs about to be used for navigation. The quality is determined by a combination of the age, thoroughness, and scale of the source data used in the ENCs.
- Navigational warnings: The navigation officer ensures that all relevant NAVTEX, INM-C, and Notice to Mariners (NTM) warnings are indicated on the ENCs.
- Safety depth: The navigation officer sets the safety depth as defined by the captain and company's procedures.
- No-go areas: The navigation officer sets the no-go areas as defined by the captain and the company's procedures, such as non-navigable shallow water.
- Weather routeing: Weather routeing advice obtained from publications or applicable software, and any restrictions are plotted on the ENCs.
- Under keel clearance (UKC) calculations are completed, and any restrictions are plotted on the ENC.
- Air draft: The air draft is calculated, and any restrictions are noted.
- Tide: Height of the tide is considered.
- Trim optimisation elements as per the Ship Energy Efficiency Management Plan (SEEMP) is considered (trim upon sailing (static), targeted trim (static), decision base, max bending moments and shear forces, re-adjustment frequency).
- Environmentally sensitive sea areas noted.
- Load line zones: The load line zones are checked, and any restrictions are considered.
- IMO routeing information: The navigation officer checks whether the traffic separation schemes for the intended voyage are approved by the IMO.
- Security restrictions: Carry out a thorough risk assessment regarding piracy or other security risks along the intended route.
- Sailing directions: Navigation officers check the applicable sailing directions (also known as pilot books) for the peculiarities of the area of sailing.

As can be seen from the bullet points above, there are numerous checks and information gathering activities required for a voyage to be performed safely. Some of the checks can be done using digital sources, while others still require manual handling with the digital/manual mix dependent on the shipping companies' policies, age of the specific ship and therefore the equipment and systems available, and the charterer's requirements.

5.4   Passage Planning of a Ship Voyage

As described in Bowditch's *The American Practical Navigator*, "the passage plan is a comprehensive, step by step description of how the voyage is to proceed from berth to berth, including undocking, departure, sailing, approach and mooring at the destination" (Bowditch, 1802).

When all information is collected and considered, the navigation officer can begin the process of laying out the voyage in the ECDIS. This includes projecting various future events, narrow passages, and course changes expected during the voyage. This is usually done manually or using software where some of the tasks can be automated.

5.5   Ship Navigation Execution and Monitoring

During port manoeuvring, and in fairway and coastal navigation, the density of traffic can increase the risk of a collision. Understanding and taking account of the manoeuvres and intentions of other ships becomes very important. Forecasts of adverse weather conditions are important for all stages of a voyage.

The navigator needs continuous access to relevant, reliable, up-to-date information that will ensure the ship's safe passage and highlights those aspects that might endanger the ship, its crew, or its cargo. Traditionally this was provided in advance of a voyage, in the form of paper nautical charts and supporting nautical publications. Urgent additional information was then provided by radio messages. When in confined waters, navigation is often supported by a pilot providing local knowledge and expertise; often pilotage is regulated by maritime and port authorities.

To perform the execution and monitoring of safe navigation, the navigation officer uses several information systems on the ship's bridge, particularly, ECDIS for anti-grounding, radar systems for anti-collision, AIS for the identification of other ships in the vicinity, and GMDSS equipment for communications.

The digital exchange of information between actors in near or real time enables an enhanced and shared common situational awareness that was not previously possible. However, adoption of digital information technology and the availability of the Internet on board ships still varies widely by company and ship.

5.6   The IMO e-Navigation Concept

As part of its push towards a digitalised maritime environment, the IMO has developed and adopted the e-navigation concept. E-navigation is defined as "the harmonized collection, integration, exchange, presentation and analysis of marine information on board and ashore by electronic means to enhance berth to berth navigation and related services for safety and security at sea and protection of the marine environment" (IMO, 2018). Its purpose is to enhance navigational safety (with all the positive repercussions this will have on maritime safety overall and environmental protection) while simultaneously reducing the burden on the navigator. E-navigation is currently entering its implementation phase, with several supporting services already available or starting to become available—such as electronic chart updating, on-line weather services, and VTS.

E-navigation envisages the provision of information required for safe and efficient navigation being provided digitally as streamed services. The various data and information requirements are grouped under 16 Maritime Services.[13]

MS 1 VTS Information Service	MS 9 Telemedical
MS 2 Navigational Assistance Service	MS 10 Maritime Assistance Service
MS 3 Traffic Organization Service	MS 11 Nautical Chart Service
MS 4 Local Port Service	MS 12 Nautical Publication Service
MS 5 Maritime Safety Information Service	MS 13 Ice Navigation Service
MS 6 Pilotage Service	MS 14 Meteorological Service
MS 7 Tug Service	MS 15 Real-Time Hydrographic and Environmental Information Service
MS 8 Vessel Shore Reporting	MS 16 Search and Rescue service

E-navigation establishes, in effect, a web-based information environment where relevant data streams are shared and made available. Fundamental to making this work is the adoption of common, interoperable data standards such that the need for conversion, recompilation, or re-mapping of data to other file formats is avoided. Currently, the infrastructure to share data is yet to be provided and will have to be built. The current e-navigation strategy plan that was recently updated has outputs ongoing or planned up until 2021. There are currently no declared outputs for the completion of the full IMO e-navigation strategy beyond 2021, but these may be determined by the IMO in the coming years.

5.7 Other e-Navigation Implementations

For electronic navigation, the IHO S-100 data exchange format has been designated as the baseline data exchange format. The IHO developed the S-100 Universal Hydrographic Data Model to cater for future demands for digital products and services and to replace the current models (such as S-52, S-57, and S-63) for

---

[13]MSC.1/CIRC.1610 – INITIAL DESCRIPTIONS OF MARITIME SERVICES IN THE CONTEXT OF E-NAVIGATION.

ENC and ECDIS on board ships. S-100 is aligned with the ISO 19100 series of geographic data standards. Other data exchange standards should, wherever possible, be interoperable/compatible with S100/ISO 19100-based data.

Several other data sharing initiatives are underway to enable data collection, recording, and sharing between ships and shore and vice versa. One such implementation is PortCDM,[14] a concept to support those engaged in, or associated with, port call operations. PortCDM aims to improve the efficiency and effectiveness of activities in any port by providing a framework for data sharing, enhanced collaboration, and common situational awareness. From a ship's perspective, getting access to timely port information is invaluable for planning a journey. For the port and its service providers, getting timely information from a ship is equally important. PortCDM advocates the use of the S-100-based S-211 port call message format that allows the standardised sharing of data on intentions and outcomes of movements, services, and administrative events for a given port call. Another is the exchange of voyage plans between the ship- and shore-based organisations as proposed in the MONALISA and STM Validation Projects.[15]

In all these initiatives, priority is placed on adopting or developing open, internationally recognised, interoperable data exchange standards, particularly S-100 and the business communications standards GS1.

6   Hubs for Information Consumers and Utilisers

As part of any voyage at sea, there are times or places ("events") when the operations of various groups or entities engaged in sea transportation highly influence the performance of the ecosystem as a whole (Lind et al., 2014a). Each of these events involves bringing actors together to coordinate and synchronise their activities for the event to take place successfully. Examples of events related to a voyage are encounters with other vessels, passage through VTS areas, entry and exit to a port, and loading and discharging cargo or passengers.

The voyage events usually involve several, sometimes many, actors who provide and utilise information to perform their tasks. Ideally, each of the involved actors engages in data sharing. An ecosystem, where the performance of an individual party relies on the integrated performance of different entities, requires that data are exchanged between entities efficiently and seamlessly (see Fig. 2; Lind, Fagerhus, Hägg, & Svedberg, 2014b). For any voyage event, the data sharing point is the information hub for that event.

As a voyage proceeds, the outcome of one event may impact the execution of a subsequent event—for example, a change in the completion time could affect the timing or location for the next or subsequent events. For this reason, it is

---

[14]https://www.ipcdmc.org/

[15]www.stmvalidation.eu

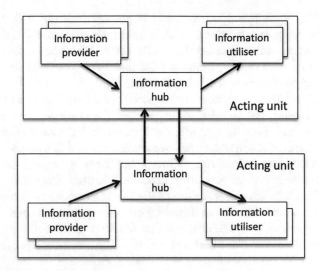

Fig. 2 Distribution of information within and between acting units (Lind, Brödje, et al., 2014a)

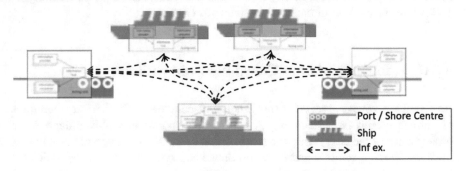

Fig. 3 Ship-to-ship, ship-to-shore, and shore-to-shore information exchange in the context of the sea voyage (inspired from Lind, Brödje, et al., 2014a)

important that the dependent information hubs are interconnected and share relevant information among them. This relationship has been substantially investigated in EU-sponsored initiatives, such as the STM Validation Projects.[16] This ecosystem of interconnected information hubs is depicted in Fig. 3.

One practical implementation of the hub philosophy is the Maritime Connectivity Platform (MCP),[17] a communication framework enabling efficient, secure, reliable, and seamless electronic information exchange between all authorised maritime stakeholders across available communication systems. The MCP is governed by a consortium of not-for-profit organisations and will provide:

---

[16] www.stmvalidation.eu

[17] https://maritimeconnectivity.net/

- *A Maritime Identity Registry*, for secure and reliable identity information. It provides a single login to all services, using identity information provided by trusted stakeholders.
- *A Maritime Service Registry*, for registering, discovering and using all relevant e-Navigation and e-Maritime services, commercial and non-commercial, authorised and non-authorised, for free and against payment. It could be like a sophisticated "yellow pages" phone book or the equivalent of an App Store.
- *A Maritime Messaging Service*, an information broker that intelligently exchanges information between communication systems connected to the cloud, considering the current geographical position and communication links available to the recipient.

7 Voyage Monitoring

In addition to a ship's crew monitoring the progress and execution of a voyage, as part of their navigation task, there are an increasing number of other parties that are vitally interested in knowing the progress and the plans associated with any voyage. This includes ports and associated services wishing to know and prepare for the arrival of ships; governments and related agencies concerned with such things as security, customs, immigration and bio-security; and the owners of goods wishing to know when their goods will be available for collection or delivery.

7.1 Foundational Processes in Voyage Monitoring

The different phases of a voyage form the basis for planning when and how to reach defined states. The execution of a voyage follows has various stages from pre-departure (at port of origin) to arrival (at port of destination). Taking the scope of the voyage as the point of departure, the execution of the sea voyage can be broken into nine possible phases (see the middle part of Fig. 4) (c.f. Lind, Fagerhus, et al., 2014b). The delimitation of each phase is based on spatial and time dimensions related to the voyage between ports. A voyage may include some or all possible phases. The "turn-around process" in ports is covered by the phases of arrival, pre-departure, as well as the inbound and the outbound port manoeuvring.

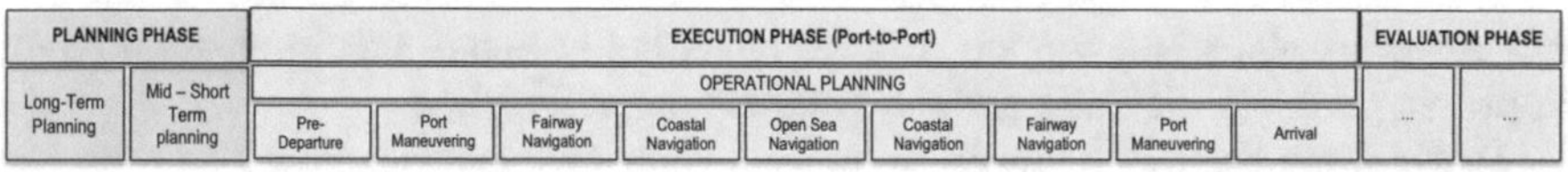

PLANNING PHASE		EXECUTION PHASE (Port-to-Port)										EVALUATION PHASE	
Long-Term Planning	Mid – Short Term planning	OPERATIONAL PLANNING											
		Pre-Departure	Port Maneuvering	Fairway Navigation	Coastal Navigation	Open Sea Navigation	Coastal Navigation	Fairway Navigation	Port Maneuvering	Arrival		...	...

Fig. 4 The different phases of sea voyages (inspired by the work of SESAR) (Lind, Fagerhus, et al., 2014b)

In order to ensure that processes within the execution phases are realised in a safe, environmentally sound, and operationally efficient way, they need to be preceded by long-, mid-, and short-term planning. The probability of reaching performance targets increases substantially when an integrated approach to the planning, execution, and evaluation of each phase occurs.

Ecosystems of this kind cover many co-producing value creating actors. One essential driver for such an integrated approach is that these actors inform each other when different states are expected to occur and are reached in order to enable each actor to optimise their performance. In order to ensure flexibility, since it is difficult or impossible to predict all situations that may occur, it is important to enable re-planning and/or adjustments during execution through real-time data sharing. In Fig. 4 these different stages of voyage execution are depicted and positioned in relation to the planning and evaluation as discussed previously.

7.2 From Sharing Information on Movements Already Made to also Sharing Information About Intended Moves

To provide ship operators with vital and necessary information to determine the most cost-efficient and environmentally friendly passage at sea, it is important to create a dynamic flow of data that can be updated in real time, immediately after any changes of state, wherever in the transport chain such changes occur. The passage plan is the carrier of the latest up-to-date intended route that the ship will take. As demonstrated in the STM Validation Project, a route and route monitoring are useful points of focus for enabling involved actors to share intended plans and progress with each other in a timely and efficient manner. This contrasts with traditional practices where most actors usually only learn of changes to the timing of events outside their control after they have occurred and rarely in advance or in real time.

The STM Validation Project indicated a number of beneficial possibilities from the sharing of up-to-date passage plans (Lind, Fagerhus, et al., 2014b), including:

- Integrated planning and route validation in the interaction between ship masters and ship operators
- Distribution of suggested routes, such as pilotage routes
- Provision of optimisation services associated with routes taking, for example, forecasted weather into account
- Provision of navigational assistance and situational awareness

The sharing of passage plan information between involved parties in real time can result in plans and support arrangements being better synchronised, thereby improving safety, efficiency, and environmental performance.

To facilitate these and similar initiatives such as single-window reporting and PortCDM, the S-421 route exchange format has been developed under the auspices of the International Electrotechnical Commission (IEC) and recognised internationally.

7.3   Supporting Services Related to Voyage Monitoring

The exchange of ship's routes in standardised formats between ships and shore actors has exposed new harmonised and standardised service opportunities, including:

- Route Optimisation

Shore-based services providing route optimisation support to a bridge team in the planning or in the execution phase, including accounting for weather, ice conditions, Maritime Safety Information (MSI), Particularly Sensitive Sea Areas (PSSA), distance, speed, traffic congestion, and bathymetric conditions. Route optimisation is an iterative process and can be performed both pre-departure and continuously en route as needs and conditions change. All plans can and must be changeable at short notice, and as soon as new orders and optimisations are completed, a new agreement must be established and distributed.

- Route monitoring

In addition to monitoring, providing passive and automatic surveillance for detecting deviations from agreed routes; sometimes part of the operations of fleet operating centres, but more usually part of a VTS.

7.4   More Sources of Digital Data from Ships

The European Marine Casualty Information Platform (EMCIP) hosts and stores casualty data and investigation reports notified and submitted to the member states according to Directive 2009/18/EC. The system is connected to the IMO Global Integrated Shipping Information System GISIS to avoid data duplication. It is a tool first intended for use by coastguard services.

There are several initiatives that support maritime operations and safety regionally, including the Maritime Single window concept mentioned earlier, the Mediterranean AIS regional system (MARE), the Marylin project, and the Spationav project.[18]

8   Communication Technologies

Another example of a largely automatic system that broadcasts ship information is the Global Maritime Distress and Safety System (GMDSS) that has been fitted in most ships since the late 1990s. GMDSS provides for sending and receiving distress alerts and maritime safety information, as well as for general communications.

---

[18]https://www.porttechnology.org/technical-papers/providing_full_maritime_domain_awareness_on_the_french_coastline_sofrelog_w/

While satellite Internet connectivity is becoming cheaper and increasingly available in ships around the globe, it is not mandatory. For ships navigating near a coastline, 3G and 4G wireless communication is increasingly being used as an option, but with the short range of these technologies, it is not yet a viable solution for most ships that require continuous connectivity throughout a voyage.

The VHF Data Exchange System (VDES) is a new radio communication solution that operates between ships, shore stations, and satellites using AIS in the marine mobile VHF frequency band. Using dedicated satellite channels, every ship with a VHF antenna is able to communicate globally. With VDES it will be possible to establish a broadband data link, making it more economical for ships to maintain a data connection at sea by eliminating the need to use satellites in coastal waters, while not compromising future global satellite connectivity. VDES is expected to cover up to 50 km from the nearest land-based equipment, which will allow ships to benefit from modern communication and navigation methods without increasing costs. Services envisaged for delivery via VDES include "Ice charts", "Engine monitoring", and "Environmental monitoring" using smart buoys.

Internally ships are increasingly being connected; normal wired ethernet is the most common, but there are a range of bus and serial technology standards now on board some ships to transfer data. One of the most common is the NMEA 0183 protocol layer. The NMEA specification requires a physical-level protocol compatible with RS422 at 4800 bps. It is RS422 rather than RS232 because NMEA expects many navigational devices to feed a common serial bus.

IEC has developed two standards that are intended to replace NMEA 0183 in the longer term. IEC 61162-450:2018 specifies interface requirements and methods of test for high speed communication between shipboard navigation and radio communication equipment as well as between such systems and other ship systems that need to communicate with navigation and radio-communication equipment. The specification describes the transport of NMEA sentences over IPv4. IEC 61162-460:2018 and is an add-on to IEC 61162-450 where higher safety and security standards are needed, for example, due to higher exposure to external threats or to improve network integrity.

In addition, technologies like Wi-Fi are also used commonly on-board ships, but seldom in safety related applications.

9 Concluding Remarks

The rapid technological developments in the world generally and shipping and ports specifically will continue to affect the development of information systems for decision making both on board and ashore. Each voyage creates data that can be used to improve decision-making for a ship's next voyage and those of other ships. The data that ships and service providers generate and stream will create new opportunities for Maritime Informatics practitioners and researchers to improve decision-making for voyage planning and execution.

References

AIS. (2015). Resolution A.1106(29). Adopted on 2 December 2015 (Agenda item 10). Revised guidelines for the onboard operational use of shipborne automatic identification systems (AIS).

Bowditch, N. (1802). *The American practical navigator*. Defense Mapping Agency Hydrographic Topographic Center.

IMO. (1974). *International Convention for the Safety of Life at Sea (SOLAS)*. IMO.

IMO. (2018). *E-navigation strategy implementation plan, update 1, MSC.1/Circ.1595 25*. IMO.

Latharche, M. (2017). *Condition based maintenance (CBM) for engines*. 19/9-2017. ShipInsight.

Lind, M., Brödje, A., Watson, R. T., Haraldson, S., Holmberg, P.-E., & Hägg, M. (2014a). *Digital infrastructures for enabling sea traffic management*. The 10th International Symposium ISIS 2014 "Integrated Ship's Information Systems".

Lind, M., Fagerhus, G., Hägg, M., Svedberg, U. (2014b). *Sea Traffic Management in MonaLisa 2.0*. Preliminary findings within the MONALISA 2.0 project, MONALISA 2.0.

LRIT. (2006). Resolution MSC.202(81) (adopted on 19 May 2006). Adoption of amendments to the international Convention for the Safety of Life at Sea, 1974, as amended.

Watson, R. T., Holm, H., & Lind, M. (2015). *Green steaming: A methodology for estimating carbon emissions avoided*, Thirty Sixth International Conference on Information Systems, Fort Worth.

A Smart Grid in Container Terminals: Cost Drivers for Using the Energy Storage of Electric Transport Vehicles for Grid Stability

Christine Harnischmacher ⓘ, Maike Greve ⓘ, Alfred Benedikt Brendel ⓘ, Boris Wulff ⓘ, and Lutz M. Kolbe ⓘ

1 Introduction

Port electrification has recently gained momentum largely because of environmental concerns. Cities do not want ships burning fossil fuels in their harbours or trucks idling while waiting for a ferry. As well as creating a physical infrastructure for enabling ships and trucks to plug in, there is also a need for an informational infrastructure to enable a port to predict its electricity needs and collaborate with its local utility company to ensure these are met. The plugging in of a large cruise ship, for example, is similar to suddenly adding several hundred households to the grid. Thus, another role for Maritime Informatics is to support such predictions and provide analyses for determining plug-in requirements. There is also pressure on container terminal operators to move to electric vehicles for moving containers within a port. This conversion from traditional to electric vehicles also offers the opportunity to integrate these vehicles into the smart grid so their batteries can be a source of electricity.

The logistics sector is considered the second largest source of greenhouse gas emissions in the European Union as well as in the United States (REN21, 2019). The governments of many countries are working on means to combat the anthropogenic climate change (Harmelink, Voogt, & Cremer, 2006). The shift from conventional vehicles to electric vehicles is a promising change for a more sustainable mobility

C. Harnischmacher (✉) · M. Greve · A. B. Brendel · L. M. Kolbe
University of Göttingen, Göttingen, Germany
e-mail: christine.harnischmacher@uni-goettingen.de; maike.greve@uni-goettingen.de;
abrendel@uni-goettingen.de; lkolbe@uni-goettingen.de

B. Wulff
HHLA Container Terminal Altenwerder GmbH, Hamburg, Germany
e-mail: wulff@hhla.de

M. Lind et al. (eds.), *Maritime Informatics*, Progress in IS,
https://doi.org/10.1007/978-3-030-50892-0_13

sector (Valentine-Urbschat & Bernhart, 2009). Information systems (IS) play a vital role in this change by, for instance, providing the means for implementing smart grid concepts to support the integration of renewable energy sources (Watson, Boudreau, & Chen, 2010). In the context of the transportation sector, container logistics offers a promising field for smart grid application as it is a big energy consumer; however, it has gained little attention from researchers so far.

To exploit the potential of renewable energy in container logistics, the electrification of heavy-duty container vehicles provides an important and impactful first step (BESIC-Konsortium, 2016). Because automated guided container transport vehicles (AGVs) are not on duty every hour of the day (Steenken, Voß, & Stahlbock, 2005), in idle times their batteries can be used as primary control reserves (PCRs) for the energy grid. PCRs are important for the stability of the electrical grid as the integration of renewable energy sources leads to fluctuations in supply (e.g. more energy is available on sunny days via solar plants) (Kahlen, Ketter, & van Dalen, 2014). The unused battery capacities can be used to store and provide PCR, depending on the current status of grid supply and demand. Overall, this secondary use of the battery could promote the sustainability of all container logistics and opens up a new source of revenue. Energy grid operators could reimburse providers of PCRs; however, the provision of PCRs also produces new costs, such as development and implementation of specialist IS, battery and infrastructure degradation, among others. This makes the decision for or against the provision of PCRs for container logistics operators ambiguous.

To view the economic efficiency of such secondary use from the point of view of the operators, it is necessary to establish and calculate the costs in a clear manner. Hence, this chapter strives to answer the following question with two sub-questions:

- *What are the cost drivers that arise when providing primary control reserves by batteries in an electrified system?*

   – *To what extent has the current literature explored and systemised the cost drivers that derive through PCRs in electrified systems?*
   – *How do experts evaluate the cost drivers connected to this specific case?*

To answer these questions, a three-phase research approach was applied to develop a model that evaluates the costs of the secondary use of AGV batteries. The first phase answers the first sub-question by reviewing the current literature with regard to systemisation of costs and cost drivers for PCR as well as the use of electrified systems. In the second phase, experts from port and energy industries were contacted to gain further insights. Lastly, the information gained through the two sub-questions was connected to develop a general cost model for the use of PCRs. This research is an important component in assessing the resources required to implement the concept piloted in the Port of Hamburg. The scientific analysis of a specific use case in cooperation with partners from the port and the energy industry provides a far-reaching consideration of the practice-relevant economic aspects.

2 Background

As Watson et al. (2010) define the term "Energy Informatics", they underline the importance of a subfield in IS research that focuses on information systems that improve the efficiency of energy demand and supply systems. Driven by the desire to behave environmentally sustainable and by the increase of renewable energy sources, the energy sector is undergoing a major transformation. Smart grids integrate all players in the electricity market into one overall system through the interaction of generation, storage, grid management and consumption and can, therefore, incorporate demand response and demand-side integration (Schmidt, Eisel, Hildebrandt, & Kolbe, 2015). Thus, smart grid research had been, for example, conducted in the area of ecological economics, environmental psychology and energy engineering (Corbett, 2011).

Against this background, container terminal logistics provides a promising area to reduce greenhouse gas emission during port operations (BESIC-Konsortium, 2016). Hence electrification and the use of smart grids can be applied to achieve sustainability. As a container terminal is an extensive and complex setting, it often presents a barrier of implementation. Therefore, to facilitate novel IS implementations, IS research should engage in the removal of this barrier and investigate the individual information needed for decision-making, e.g. analysing the strength, weaknesses, opportunities and threats (Johnson, Scholes, & Sexty, 1989) of smart grid applications. Most importantly, cost driver analysis is an essential first aspect for the operator's decision process to ensure economic benefits and prevent unprofitable outcomes.

In order to make economically beneficial decisions, the operator has to gain insight into total costs that arise in the context of implementation, usage and constructions that have to be weighed against the benefits and revenues. Commonly, analyses that include considerations like these are referred to as life cycle cost analysis (LCCA) models (Rapaccini, Porcelli, Saccani, Cinquini, & Lugarà, 2013). In the IT industry, the specific LCCA approach of the total cost of ownership (TCO) method is used as a suitable tool for this purpose (Ferrin & Plank, 2002). It is defined as "a purchasing tool and philosophy which is aimed at understanding the true cost of buying a particular good or service from a particular supplier" (Ellram, 1993). The term "true costs" not only refer to the purchasing and actual costs in the accounting sense but also to qualitative factors that are integrated into various interpretations of the concept (Ellram, 1994). In the framework of the total cost of ownership model one essential step, outlined by (Ellram, 1993) is the identification of these costs.

Research utilising the TCO method in the context of electric vehicles has been conducted with diverse focuses. Several studies compare the TCO of electric vehicles to those of conventional vehicles (Lebeau, Macharis, Van Mierlo, & Lebeau, 2013; Wu, Inderbitzin, & Bening, 2015) in order to evaluate the different composition of the TCO. Other research strictly focuses on electric vehicles (Babin et al., 2018; Taefi, Stütz, & Fink, 2017) with the goal of identifying the main factors that influence the TCO of electric vehicles.

This chapter pinpoints approaches leading to a reduction in the TCO of electric vehicles in order to make them more competitive in the automotive market. Babin et al. (2018) focus their study on the reduction of TCO of commercial electric vehicles through optimisation of battery size and charging strategy, while Taefi et al. (2017) assess the cost-optimal mileage.

3 Setting

In this study, the publicly funded electric mobility project FRESH (Flexibilitäts-management und Regelenergiebereitstellung von Schwerlastfahrzeugen im Hafen) serves as a business case to integrate the battery capacities of AGVs into the energy network as flexible storage units for a contribution to grid stability and power supply. Currently, renewable energy accounts for around 40% of public net electricity in Germany (Frauenhofer ISE, 2019). In comparison with fossil sources, renewables cannot match energy supply to demand. This results in deviations in net frequency. In the German energy grid, these deviations are compensated for with power from the balancing power market, namely, PCRs, secondary control reserves (SCRs) and minute reserves (MRs). In a day-ahead auction, energy producers can enter the capacities that they want to provide during a certain period of time. If their tender is accepted, they will have to deliver the specified energy at their bid price. In the case of frequency fluctuations, the capacities are claimed, and providers will be provided additional compensation. Virtual power plants (VPPs) are intended to compensate for fluctuations by digitally linking various energy producers and consumers by bundling the offers and needs of the participants (Kahlen et al., 2014). This can be implemented in the setting of container terminals. All container terminals include the transportation of the containers from the cranes that move them to the shore to the storage area (Kemme, 2013). This is generally done by the AGVs that transport one or two containers per vehicle depending on the size and weight of the containers. Electrification of these vehicles massively reduces the greenhouse gas emission of the terminal.

Traditional AGVs are generally diesel-powered and consume large amounts of fossil fuels (see Fig. 1—Basic case). Alternatively, battery-powered vehicles with lithium-ion batteries can be used to reduce emissions (see Fig. 2—Electric case). Furthermore, due to the implementation of a VPP, a vehicle's battery can be connected to charging stations during idle times to provide PRCs for the energy market (see Fig. 3—Smart electric case).

At the container port of Hamburg, Germany, it is planned to use 100 AGVs with lithium-ion batteries for transportation. During less busy times, the port does not need all AGVs. Therefore, as a secondary exploitation, the AGVs can be connected to 1 of the 18 electric charging stations, to provide or store energy via a virtual

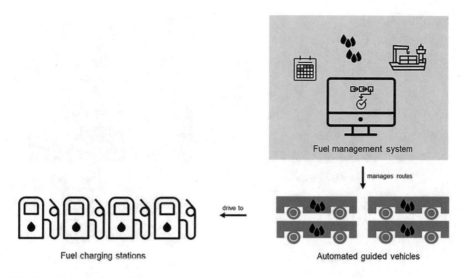

Fig. 1   Basic case: fuel vehicles

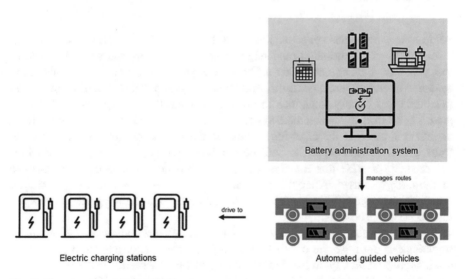

Fig. 2   Electric case: electric vehicles

power plant when the power grid requires it. Figure 3 demonstrates this interplay of the components.

The battery administration system is a component of the AGV management system that coordinates the AGVs with its primary focus on the fulfilment of the logistical demands of the container terminal, namely, the transportation of containers between vessels and the storage area. As this IS is specifically designed to simulate and instantiate the logistical processes using battery-powered AGVs,

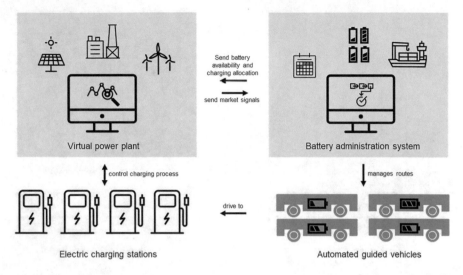

Fig. 3 Smart electric case: electric vehicles and VPP

vehicle charging times are scheduled to fit the logistical demands of the container terminal. Through the additional requirements imposed by the secondary use of the vehicles' battery capacities as balancing power, the battery administration system will extend into a flexibility management system that will predict day-ahead availability of battery capacities in order to provide their energy as PCRs to the grid. The flexibility management system will signal available capacities in the form of AGVs located at the charging stations to the remote control unit of the VPP. Subsequently, these capacities will be combined with further external capacities to constitute a VPP that matches the pre-qualifications necessary to participate in the energy market. After the rendering of a PCR is concluded, the flexibility management system will regain control over the AGVs and reintegrate the vehicles into logistical processes.

The project demonstrates how digitisation and electrification of this aspect of logistics can optimise the power system and pioneer reaching a "zero-emissions" goal. More specifically, in the final stage of the project with all AGVs in operation and usage of power generated from renewable energy sources, CO_2 emissions can be reduced by around 15,500 T/year.

4   Research Approach

In order to determine all relevant costs that occur in the context of providing PCR through AGV batteries in an electrified container transportation system, a three-phase research approach was considered. Firstly, we reviewed existing work on cost

Table 1 Systemisation of cost drivers

	Pre-transaction	Transaction	Post-transaction
Management	For example, personnel management including training, coordination, procedure changes		
Delivery	For example, accept delivery, expedite late orders, arrange incorrect orders, purchasing prices		
Service	For example, installation of equipment, oversee maintenance, order spare parts		
Communication	For example, communication with suppliers, maintenance of purchasing information system, inventory records and invoice adjustments		
Price	For example, negotiate terms of contract with respect to quality, quantity, delivery, purchase discount, etc. This category was not addressed by literature and experts in this context and is therefore omitted in further analysis		
Quality	For example, selection of suppliers, maintain supplier relation, inspect the quality of incoming products		
Miscellaneous	All cost drivers that do not belong to any of the other categories. For example, taxes, insurance, etc.		

Adapted in parts from Ellram and Siferd (1993)

analysis in electrified systems to find a systemised scheme for the cost analysis and to identify relevant costs that were addressed in similar settings. Secondly, experts from different relevant fields evaluated the cost of the described project setting. For this evaluation, we report on expert interviews with project partners experienced in the port and electric industries. Finally, we aggregated the results to identify a cost model that is based on a systemised scheme and holds for this specific use case. The approach is summarised in Table 1 and is described in the following subsections.

4.1 Phase 1: Literature Review

For defining a basic model of the costs, the relevant literature was identified and analysed. This was done in two steps.

First step: seminal works on cost analysis, especially total cost of ownership, were reviewed to gain insights into the general structure of cost drivers to guide our model development process. Our research is based on the systemisation of the TCO method (Ellram, 1993, 1994), which is the foundation for many following studies (Ferrin & Plank, 2002; Lebeau et al., 2013).

Second step: a structured literature analysis was conducted to find and evaluate the current status quo of cost drivers in settings that include the electrification of logistic systems, which is similar to this study's setting of container terminal logistic and grid stability through PCR.

4.2 Phase 2: Expert Evaluation

To expand the results of the literature review, experts from various relevant disciplines were asked about cost drivers connected to their setting. The experts, who came from the port logistics industry, were questioned with regard to the cost of general AGV acquisition and usage, while the experts from the energy industry were asked about the investment cost of the virtual power plant as well as the cost and earnings through PCRs. The qualitative interviews included eight partners, all of whom were familiar with the project setting. The six partners, who work for the port, came from different departments and included technical as well as operational expertise. All of them were also involved in similar projects (e.g. BESIC). Two partners are experts in the field of electric industry and were involved in several projects that involved using a virtual power plant to balance supply and demand through PCRs. Each interview was moderated by two of the authors and directed by open questions regarding

- The actual costs through AGV use for container transportation
- The potential time to use AGVs that are not needed for transportation
- The actual cost of the electric charging stations
- The costs of modifying the charging stations and connecting the virtual power plant
- The potential earnings and cost through active attendance at the electricity market

    In the end, all answers were summarised and aggregated.

4.3 Phase 3: Aggregation

The resulting scheme of phase 1 was applied to the cost drivers identified by the literature and also to systemise the identified cost drivers by experts. As a result, there is a common structure for all relevant factors. Identical factors were omitted. The resulting model was analysed with regard to the chosen categories as well as the origins of the costs. This is connected to the electrification process described previously. The systemised result can help to improve the decision quality of the implementation process of a smart electrified container terminal.

5 Results and Findings

In the following, we present the identified costs for the provision of PCRs via a secondary usage of AGV battery capacities. The identified costs come from relevant literature and were supplemented by experts. We then connected the results to identify a relevant cost model.

5.1 Literature-Based Model

To develop a system of potential cost drivers in this context, a systematic categorisation of costs is needed. Two major classifications are suggested in the literature: firstly, Ellram and Siferd (1993) suggest that all cost associated with the acquisition, use and maintenance should be evaluated. Furthermore, the costs can be separated into six categories: management, delivery, service, communication, price and quality. The different categories are illustrated through examples in Table 1.

Secondly, Ellram (1993) extends this result by categorising the costs of ownership in the order of incurrence: pre-transaction, transaction and post-transaction. Ferrin and Plank (2002) conclude that a categorisation scheme is likely to be elusive, but the latter three categories are a valuable first systematisation; however, a more complex scheme could be needed. For this reason, we combined both approaches and add a further category "Miscellaneous" to extend the scheme, if none of the suggested categories fit the costs. Table 1 shows the combined categorisation. This scheme for categorising cost drivers was used for further analysis of costs through literature and expert evaluation.

The literature mainly addresses costs that arise through the electrification of vehicles. Most cost drivers are connected to the battery and its life expectancy. In this area, long-term research is missing. At the moment, the number of life cycles is estimated, and therefore major costs that would arise through battery degradation or the need of replacement can only be estimated (Kahlen et al., 2014; Smith, Neubauer, Wood, Jun, & Pesaran, 2013). The cost drivers of the implementation of a VPP were evaluated only by Kahlen ct al. (2014). Therefore, the results from literature with respect to the secondary use of the batteries for the trade of PCR via a VPP are limited. An exhaustive overview of the cost drivers deduced through the literature review is provided by Greve, Harnischmacher, Lichtenberg, and Kolbe (2019).

5.2 Case-Specific Model

To extend the results from the literature, expert evaluation with focus on the additional costs that arise through the secondary use of the batteries within the AGV transportation system was assessed. During the group discussion, the main cost categories (acquisition costs, operating costs, logistics costs, control reserve marketing, insurance, maintenance costs, personnel costs, miscellaneous) were split into single cost factors (Greve et al., 2019).

In addition to the ten cost drivers identified by experts that are identical to the results of the literature research, the experts included more specific costs of the project setting like the cost related to the battery administration system or the information system of the VPP. Also, the aspect of insurance and additional personnel was not mentioned in the literature but arose during the group discussion.

To be able to match the results of the two sources, the identified cost drivers of the experts were sorted in the systemised scheme of the literature.

5.3 Applied Model

In the final phase, all cost drivers identified by literature and experts were summed up in one scheme (see Table 2).

The tabular form of presentation shows that the costs that derive before the transaction, in this case, the generation and trade of PCR, mainly belong to the delivery category and contain the acquisition of all relevant supplements. The greatest variation of cost factors occurs during the transaction phase. In this phase especially, operating and maintenance costs are the key factors. In the case of termination, reselling and disposal costs matter. The derived cost factors can be used to gain insights about the implementation process. The transition from a container terminal with fuel-powered AGV through electrification of the vehicles up to the generation and trade of PCR by a smart electrified system was demonstrated. Figure 4 shows the number of cost drivers that are consistent over the process and the number of cost drivers that are added or no longer relevant. The results show that there are general cost drivers that also hold for a non-electrified container terminal that uses fuel-powered AGV. These cost drivers are shown in bold in Table 2 and include, for example, the purchasing cost of AGVs and the maintenance of software and hardware. Due to the change from fuel-powered to electrified vehicles, the following cost drivers arise: purchasing of batteries and conversion of AGVs, the cost to change software from fuelling management to electric charging management, costs connected to the disposal of fuelling stations and the purchase of electric charging stations, installation and investment costs and maintenance costs of for the new charging stations. Furthermore, the costs regarding battery lifetime and degradation are difficult to estimate. Besides, fuel costs are eliminated, and environmental costs are reduced. When using the batteries to generate PCR during idle times by connecting the AGVs with the charging stations to energy reserves in the market via a VPP, the following cost drivers (underlined in Table 2) need to be considered: cost to change the battery administration system, so the AGVs drive to charging station when not used for transportation; purchasing costs VPP (hardware and software); maintenance of VPP; and VPP costs to interact with market and get exact estimates and costs for the prequalification necessary to participate in the PCR market.

Table 2 Overall cost drivers based on literature review and expert evaluation

	Pre-transaction	Transaction	Post-transaction
Management	**Commercial and technical management** Administration (purchasing contracts) *Prequalification*	Administration of post-purchase agreements **Commercial and technical management** **Operating costs** – Electricity – *Server* – Battery administration system *Training costs of deep learning software*	Reselling **Commercial and technical management**
Delivery	**Purchase price software** (battery administration system *and VPP system*) *Cost for software training—deep learning* **Purchase price hardware AGVs** – With battery – Electric charging stations – *Virtual power plant* **Initial capital costs** Installation Investment **Cost for the land use**	**Capital cost** Energy consumption costs **Annual operating costs** **Labour costs**	**Disposal costs**
Service	Service by supplier **Maintenance of software** (battery administration system) *Maintenance of software VPP*	**Maintenance of hardware (downtime, spare parts)** **Maintenance of software (material and personnel costs)** Service by supplier Sparse battery holding costs Charge point maintenance **Spare part storage**	
Communication	*Adjustments battery administration system* Supplier communication	**Maintenance management** *VPP costs to get accurate estimates*	
Quality		**Replacement** **Repair** Supplier ability to change technology *Battery degradation* Battery replacement Energy conversion efficiency	
Miscellaneous	**Taxes** **Environmental issues**	**Taxes** **Environmental issues** **Depreciation** Lifetime of battery **Insurance**	**Taxes** **Environmental issues** **Reserves for disposal/re-instatement obligation**

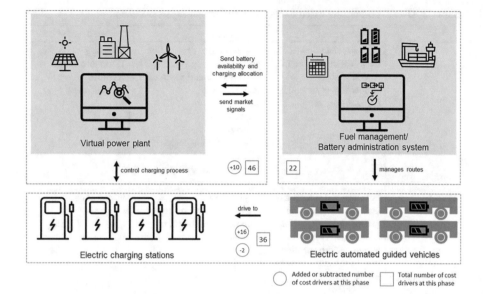

Fig. 4 Cost drivers for the transition to smart electrification

6   Discussion

Based on the three-phase approach, this chapter identifies relevant cost drivers for a smart electrified container terminal. The cost drivers can be analysed with regard to the transformation of a terminal from the use of fuel-powered AGVs, through the electrification of the AGV up to the smart use of their batteries for trading on PCR via a VPP. All identified cost drivers are based on the relevant literature and expert evaluations.

This chapter contributes to Maritime Informatics and smart grid research, as it helps to understand the specific economics of a sustainable transformation towards electrification and use of energy reserves, which is especially applicable for container terminals with electric AGVs. This research helps companies to evaluate changes and risks in implementing a more sustainable ecosystem with electric AGVs and offering PCR. Therefore, the chasm between companies that have already implemented this innovative approach and companies that are more likely to rely on known solutions and convenience can be bridged by available information on emerging cost factors (Moore, 2001).

Secondly, the analysis of virtual power plants to provide and trade PCR through the use of AGV battery capacities is a contribution to the logistic management sector. This means that unused energy can be exploited and additional revenues can be generated for the operator through the secondary use of the batteries. This study reports the cost drivers for such a scenario and addresses the process of changeover and implementation so that the barrier of actual implementation for operators is

reduced and the transformation to lower greenhouse gas emissions in the logistics sector is achievable. The results promote implementation and thus serve as a pioneer for other industries with mobile energy sources and access to the electricity market. Examples include logistics warehouses with electric forklift trucks.

This chapter discusses only the cost drivers, not the actual costs. While the trade of PCR generates revenues, these are not discussed in this chapter. Furthermore, the possibility of generating additional revenues from a secondary use of the AGVs as flexibility reserves for grid stability depends greatly on the power market structure of a specific country or region. Lastly, the research is based on one specific container terminal. Further research should address the similarities and differences among container terminals to adjust the results to a general manner, which will simplify transfer to other similar settings.

7 Conclusion

Effective evaluation of the financial consequences of a proposed change requires a well-defined process that identifies all capital investments and ongoing operational costs and estimates their parameters. Maritime Informatics can contribute to shipping industry change management by developing open process models for common major changes by identifying the key elements, major cost components and a method for financial analysis. It can build tools and identify data sources for enabling execution of these process models. This chapter is a start towards such a contribution.

This research provides a systemised overview of the cost drivers that arise in the process of electrifying a container terminal and using an AGVs battery capacity to generate PCR for the electricity market when there is a supply shortage. Detailed insight is given to enhance the implementation of such systems and provide a practical example that can be used for transfer to other domains that contain electrified components.

Acknowledgements The research and development project "Flexibilitätsmanagement und Rege-lenergiebereitstellung von Schwerlastfahrzeugen im Hafen" (FRESH) is funded by the German Federal Ministry of Economic Affairs and Energy (01ME8002D) in the context of the funding program "IKT für Elektromobilität II".

References

Babin, A., Rizoug, N., Mesbahi, T., Boscher, D., Hamdoun, Z., & Larouci, C. (2018). Total cost of ownership improvement of commercial electric vehicles using battery sizing and intelligent charge method. *IEEE Transactions on Industry Applications, 54*(2), 1691–1700.

BESIC-Konsortium. (2016). *Batterie-Elektrische Schwerlastfahrzeuge Im Intelligenten Containerterminalbetrieb (BESIC).* Abschlussbericht Im Rahmen Des Förderprogramms IKT Für Elekromobilität II, Hamburg.

Corbett, J. (2011). Demand management in the smart grid: An information processing perspective. In *17th AMCIS Proceedings* (pp. 1–8).

Ellram, L. (1993). Total cost of ownership: Elements and implementation. *International Journal of Purchasing and Materials Management, 4*(9), 3–11.

Ellram, L. (1994). A taxonomy of total cost of ownership models. *Journal of Business Logistics, 15*(1), 171.

Ellram, L., & Siferd, S. P. (1993). Purchasing: The cornerstone of the total cost of ownership concept. *Journal of Business Logistics, 14*(1), 163.

Ferrin, B. G., & Plank, R. E. (2002). Total cost of ownership models: An exploratory study. *Journal of Supply Chain Management, 38*(2), 18–29. https://doi.org/10.1111/j.1745-493X.2002.tb00132.x.

Frauenhofer ISE. (2019). Renewable sources contribute more than 40 percent to Germany's public net electricity generation in 2018. *Frauenhofer ISE* (pp. 4–8).

Greve, M., Harnischmacher, C., Lichtenberg, S., & Kolbe, L. M. (2019). *Smart grid in container terminals – Systematization of cost drivers for using battery capacities of electric transport vehicles for grid stability.* 25th Americas Conference on Information Systems, AMCIS 2019, July 8. Retrieved from https://aisel.aisnet.org/amcis2019/green_is_sustain/green_is_sustain/3

Harmelink, M., Voogt, M., & Cremer, C. (2006). Analysing the effectiveness of renewable energy supporting policies in the European Union. *Energy Policy, 34*(3), 343–351.

Johnson, G., Scholes, K., & Sexty, R. W. (1989). *Exploring strategic management.* Canada: Prentice-Hall.

Kahlen, M., Ketter, W., & van Dalen, J. (2014). Balancing with electric vehicles: A profitable business model. In *Twenty Second European Conference on Information Systems* (pp. 1–15). Retrieved from http://ecis2014.eu/E-poster/files/0653-file1.pdf

Kemme, N. (2013). Design and operation of automated container storage systems. In *Contributions to management science* (pp. 1–456). Heidelberg: Physica-Verlag HD.

Lebeau, P., Macharis, C., Van Mierlo, J., & Lebeau, K. (2013). Electric vehicles for logistics: A total cost of ownership analysis. In *2013 World Electric Vehicle Symposium and Exhibition (EVS27)* (Vol. 6, pp. 307–318). IEEE.

Moore, G. A. (2001). Crossing the chasm – Marketing and selling high-tech products to mainstream customers. *Control (Chicago, IL).*

Rapaccini, M., Porcelli, I., Saccani, N., Cinquini, L., & Lugarà, A. (2013). LCCA and TCO: A how-to approach to assess the costs in the customer's eye. In *The philosopher's stone for sustainability* (pp. 405–410). Berlin: Springer.

REN21. (2019). *Renewables 2019 Gloabl Status Report.*

Schmidt, J., Eisel, M., Hildebrandt, B., & Kolbe, L. (2015). Applying demand response programs for electric vehicle fleets. In *21st ACMIS Proceedings* (pp. 1–13).

Smith, K., Neubauer, J., Wood, E., Jun, M., & Pesaran, A. (2013). *Models for battery reliability and lifetime: Applications in design and health management (presentation).* NREL (National Renewable Energy Laboratory).

Steenken, D., Voß, S., & Stahlbock, R. (2005). Container terminal operation and operations research – A classification and literature review. In *Container terminals and automated transport systems: Logistics control issues and quantitative decision support* (pp. 3–49). https://doi.org/10.1007/3-540-26686-0_1

Taefi, T. T., Stütz, S., & Fink, A. (2017). Assessing the cost-optimal mileage of medium-duty electric vehicles with a numeric simulation approach. *Transportation Research Part D: Transport and Environment, 56,* 271–285.

Valentine-Urbschat, M., & Bernhart, W. (2009). Powertrain 2020 – The future drives electric. Roland Berger Strategy Consultants Report. In *Roland Berger Strategy Consultants* (Vol. 9).

Watson, R. T., Boudreau, M.-C., & Chen, A. J. (2010). Information Systems and environmentally sustainable development: Energy informatics and new directions for the IS community. *MIS Quarterly, 34*(1), 23–38.

Wu, G., Inderbitzin, A., & Bening, C. (2015). Total cost of ownership of electric vehicles compared to conventional vehicles: A probabilistic analysis and projection across market segments. *Energy Policy, 80,* 196–214.

Decision Support in Short Sea Shipping

Michalis Michaelides (ID), **Mikael Lind** (ID), **Lars Green** (ID), **Jørn Askvik** (ID), **and Zacharias Siokouros** (ID)

1 Introduction

Shipping of today is arranged in patterns of Short Sea Shipping and Deep-Sea Shipping, having the consequence that different ports have specialised in different ways (such as feeder ports and larger gateway ports into different regions of the world). This chapter is concerned with how maritime informatics may contribute to enhanced sustainability in short sea shipping. Building upon Chapter 2 (Watson, Lind, Delmeire, & Liesa, 2020) in this book, short sea shipping is concerned with glueing together port nodes, as self-organised entities, by the movements of episodic tight coupled actors made between those nodes. As the name "short" sea shipping implies that the relative distance between the nodes is small, downstream

M. Michaelides (✉)
Department of Electrical Engineering, Computer Engineering and Informatics, Cyprus University of Technology, Limassol, Cyprus
e-mail: michalis.michaelides@cut.ac.cy

M. Lind
Research Institutes of Sweden (RISE) and Chalmers University of Technology, Gothenburg, Sweden
e-mail: mikael@realsearchers.com

L. Green
ShortSea Promotion Centre Sweden, Gothenburg, Sweden
e-mail: lars.green@greenconsultinggroup.se

J. Askvik
ShortSea Promotion Centre Norway, Oslo, Norway
e-mail: shortsea@shortseashipping.no

Z. Siokouros
Cyprus Marine and Maritime Institute (CMMI), Larnaca, Cyprus
e-mail: zacharias.siokouros@marinem.org

© The Editor(s) (if applicable) and The Author(s), under exclusive licence to Springer Nature Switzerland AG 2021
M. Lind et al. (eds.), *Maritime Informatics*, Progress in IS,
https://doi.org/10.1007/978-3-030-50892-0_14

221

ports need to be updated on the progress made for serving the arriving ship in the upstream ports, in order to secure that foundational basis for planning is established in the downstream port. Achieving connectivity between ports through means of standardised digital data sharing, therefore, becomes crucial.

There is no standard, unequivocal definition of Short Sea Shipping (SSS). The European Union (EU) defines SSS as the movement of cargo and passengers by sea between ports situated in geographical Europe or between those ports situated in non-European countries having a coastline on the enclosed seas bordering Europe (Commission, 2001). However, in the case of the USA, the Maritime Administration defines SSS as commercial waterborne transportation that does not transit an ocean and utilises inland and coastal waterways to move commercial freight. SSS is also considered by some as a competitor to road transport (Suárez-Alemán, Trujillo, & Cullinane, 2014), and hence they only refer to those corridors that have a land alternative. Moreover, in the case of Sweden, SSS is defined as "an intra-European intermodal transport in one transport unit with one of the modes of transport being ShortSea". For the purposes of this chapter, we will use the EU's geographical definition of SSS.

Considering the current worldwide SSS situation, many governments support the economic and ecological analysis, which states that SSS outperforms all other comparable transport modes from an environmental perspective. Thus, different policies have been implemented to promote SSS corridors on a worldwide basis (Bendall & Brooks, 2011; Brooks & Frost, 2004; Perakis & Denisis, 2008; Sánchez & Wilmsmeier, 2005).

In Europe, according to the goals set by the European Commission, SSS should constitute an alternative to road transport, either as part of an intermodal transport chain or as a fully substitutable mode, depending on the type of corridor. Problems such as congestion, pollution, and other environmental aspects have encouraged the development of emission reduction transport policies. Furthermore, competition issues have arisen with respect to the unbalanced modal split in the freight transport market, where road transport absorbs around half of the total market. The main goal is that by 2030 at least 30% of what is currently carried as road freight traffic over a distance of 300+ kilometres will be shifted to other modes, such as rail or SSS and that this figure will be 50% by 2050 (Commission, 2011).

The European Commission asserts that SSS offers a set of advantages that no other mode can provide within the EU, especially in relation to the environment, an observation supported by the previously cited literature. In Paixão and Marlow (2002), the strengths and weaknesses of SSS are presented and analysed. Strengths include geographical advantages (the EU has a coastline in excess of 67,000 km and 60–70% of its industrial and production centres are located within 150–200 km of the coast), financial advantages, human resources, energy advantages, environmental advantages, underused capacity for expansion and employment opportunities. SSS disadvantages lie in the areas of port operations, corporate culture and structure, innovation, information systems, marketing and customer service approaches. In Medda and Trujillo (2010), the main determinants of SSS success and the limits to its development are discussed by focusing primarily on the European case. These are grouped in three categories: (1) environmental (external costs of road freight transport associated with air pollution, infrastructure, noise and congestion), (2) operational (distance, product and type of ship) and (3) infrastructure (administrative and port characteristics). Sea transport is one of the most sustainable and economically competitive modes of transport compared to road and rail transport. By including the private and external costs into the total transport cost, SSS has a genuine economic advantage in relation to the road transport system. SSS can alleviate traffic congestion and enhance economic development by maintaining freight flow efficiency; however, it first needs to show a clear advantage for the carrier, either in terms of cost or time saving.

Considering the advantages of SSS and its potential role in intermodal worldwide freight, the EU has developed a number of different policies in recent years with the aim of promoting intermodal competition through different measures and tools. These include various EU communications, such as two white papers: "European transport policy for 2010: time to decide" in 2001, and "Roadmap to a Single European Transport Area: Towards a Competitive and Resource Efficient Transport System" in 2011, as well as the programme for the promotion of SSS in 2003, through which SSS Promotion Centres were founded in 13 European countries. Furthermore, these include EU programs such as the Pilot Action for Combined Transport (PACT), Marco Polo I and II, Galileo and Trans-European Transport Network (TEN-T), which have been designed (with slight differences among them, in terms of time and specific objectives), to promote different (and socially preferred) modes of transport and intermodality (Suárez-Alemán, Trujillo, & Medda, 2015). Within this framework, Motorways of the Sea (MoS) is one of the TEN-T initiatives that aim at introducing new intermodal maritime-based logistics chains in Europe in order to bring forward SSS as "a real competitive alternative to land transport". All three programs have been promoting SSS by giving support to companies with a project to transfer freight from road to rail or SSS routes or inland waterways.

Nevertheless, with a total budget of Euro 895 million (considering the three aforementioned programs), the EU measures have not yet attained the proposed goals (Suárez-Alemán et al., 2015). It seems that the EU policy has not stimulated major observable differences with regard to the modal split. A possible explanation is provided in Douet and Cappuccilli (2011), which raises the hypothesis that SSS has not been well defined in the EU, and the market potential for the modal shift from land to sea has been overestimated. According to the authors, the EU geographical definition may be accepted, but it does not correspond to the purposes of its programmes orientated to the modal shift from road to sea. More specifically, while the performance of SSS has been in line with that of road transport, a deeper analysis of cargo flows reveals that this corresponds mainly to captive cargo that could not be shipped otherwise. Seaborne traffic in direct competition with road transport is very limited, especially for containers and Ro-Ro traffic held in captive traffic where there is no direct road competition.

2 Environmental Sustainability of Short Sea Shipping

CO_2 emissions from maritime transport currently represent around 3% of the total annual anthropogenic greenhouse gas (GHG) emissions, which are expected to increase by 150–250% until 2050, in business-as-usual scenarios, due to an estimated tripling of world trade (Bouman, Lindstad, Rialland, & Strømman, 2017). Achieving the 1.5–2 °C climate target, as set by the Paris Agreement, requires net zero GHG emissions across all economic sectors, including shipping. Consequently, the maritime sector is facing the challenge to significantly reduce its GHG emissions, as a contribution to the international ambition to limit the effects of climate change. As a result, much recent literature focuses on measures and policies for attaining these reductions.

The technical possibility of achieving the 1.5 °C goal of the Paris Agreement is examined in Halim, Kirstein, Merk, and Martinez (2018) through a model-based impact assessment. The authors consider three possible measures to achieve decarbonisation of international shipping by 2035: (1) technological (ship material and design), (2) operational (lower speeds, ship size and ship–port interface) and (3) alternative fuels/energy (biofuels, synthetic, LNG, fuel cells, electric, wind). Using a combination of the available measures, they then present four different decarbonisation pathways that can create a possible 82–95% reduction in CO_2 emissions by 2035. The study in Eide, Longva, Hoffmann, Endresen, and Dalsøren (2011), also shows there is a significant potential for cost-effective CO_2 emission reduction for the shipping industry, both in the current fleet, and towards 2030. The study uses a new integrated modelling approach, combining activity-based emission modelling, which includes 25 emission reduction measures with a future fleet development model. In Bouman et al. (2017), a comprehensive overview of the CO_2 emissions reduction potentials and measures is presented based on a review of around 150 studies published in the literature following the Second IMO GHG Study from 2009 (Buhaug et al., 2009). According to the reviewed literature, emissions can be reduced by more than 75%, based on current technologies and by 2050, through a combination of measures (both technical and operational), if policies and regulations are focused on achieving these reductions. An example of such a regulation is the IMO's Energy Efficiency Design Index (EEDI), which is now applicable for all vessels built after 2013, and puts thresholds on the CO_2 emitted per ton of goods transported for a fully loaded vessel as a function of its size and its type. In the case of Northern Europe, the reference of SSS being sustainably superior to any other mode of transport is tricky at best. Under certain given circumstances, SSS can be superior in terms of CO_2 reduction, but the result can be presented very differently if you include *all* emissions and take into account the distinct relationship between emission levels and the vessel utilisation.

The effect of environmental aspects relevant to SSS and MoS, in particular with respect to modal choice, is examined by the study in López-Navarro (2014). The author proceeds to estimate the environmental costs of several routes of the Spanish MoS, using the values the EU provides to calculate the external costs for the Marco Polo freight transport proposals (2013). The results indicate that in two thirds of the cases (48 out of 72) the maritime intermodal option involves lower environmental costs; but, importantly there are also 24 routes where the road option is environmentally preferable due to greater distances in some cases and faster speeds in others, mainly for passenger transport, to keep transit times down to an acceptable level. As the author points out, one of the theoretical advantages the literature attributes to SSS over road freight transport is lower fuel consumption, which depends on relatively low speed; these benefits might be erased, however, when high-speed vessels are used. Therefore, from the shipping industry's perspective, it is necessary to enhance energy efficiency (lower fuel consumption, use of cleaner fuels, etc.) in order to retain this advantage.

The importance of achieving energy efficiency for vessels in SSS is also highlighted in Johnson, Johansson, and Andersson (2014), as energy costs are on the rise in this sector, not only due to increasing costs of crude oil, but because of more strict requirements on sulphur content in marine fuel in designated Sulphur Emission Control Areas (SECAs). Compared to deep-sea shipping, SSS is also exposed to competition from other means of transport, such as rail or truck transport. There is thus a risk that increased energy costs could cause a modal shift of cargo to land-based transportation, effectively increasing the total environmental impact. In Grosso, Lynce, Silla, and Vaggelas (2010), the aim is to identify factors influencing SSS operators pricing policies for both the sea and the inland part of the intermodal chains. Interest is concentrated in the Mediterranean area, which is experiencing extensive use of SSS (not feeder) for cargo and passenger transport. Based on interviews with 15 SSS operators (mostly Italian), fuel cost is the most important element influencing the variation in both costs incurred and pricing policy. Other factors involve port costs and market drivers. Finally, the origin and destination of the goods influence the choice of provided service (door-to-door or port-to-port) for the majority of the operators.

Fuel consumption is exponential in relation to the vessel speed steaming through the water. This, combined with the fact that ships are usually served on a first-come-first-served basis, further increases the environmental concerns coming out of shipping. There is a need to enhance the planning horizon for ports that are involved in short sea shipping and by that slowly settle a situation where time slot allocation is used to a wider extent (Lind et al., 2020, Chapter 11), building upon a high degree of predictability of when events are commenced and completed, thus allowing for optimising the capacity used for steaming and serving the ships.

3   Port Efficiency and Time in Ports

As nodes within maritime transport networks, ports are crucial to the success of many of the available intermodal options (Suárez-Alemán et al., 2014). Frequently, however, they either constitute or are perceived as constituting bottlenecks that reduce the competitiveness of maritime corridors (Wilmsmeier, Hoffmann, &

Sanchez, 2006). According to Medda and Trujillo (2010), this can be attributed to the frequent lack of good road and rail links to ports, the low adaptability of port capacity to SSS, a low level of reliability and the non-coordinated administrative formalities. The authors discuss desired characteristics of an SSS port and pose the question of whether SSS services should share port facilities with conventional shipping or have separate ones. In any case, a port must avoid bottlenecks in the transport chain and give priority to SSS types of traffic for SSS to thrive. In order to become a hub, a port needs to be elected as port of call by a large shipping company or mega-alliance and be able to offer large capacities of container handling and storage, lower cost, high reliability and efficient connections with other transport systems.

Aggressive pricing of port services and efficient vessel and berth scheduling (see for example Dulebenets (2018), Dulebenets, Kavoosi, Abioye, and Pasha (2018), Dadashi, Dulebenets, Golias, and Sheikholeslami (2017)) can raise the competitiveness of intermodal transport that includes a sea leg, and this is line with the European policy for promoting SSS. According to (Strandenes, 2004), port charges make-up 40–60% of overall transit costs in SSS, whereas port charges in deep-sea transport are only 5–10% of the costs, thus increasing port efficiency by reducing waiting and turnaround times is important for reaching the goal set by the EU. Within this context, the appropriate analysis of port efficiency, therefore becomes an absolutely necessary prerequisite to identifying the port-centric factors that crucially influence the success or failure of policies to promote more sustainable freight transport and to inform future policy on such matters. Thus, maritime transportation policy needs to focus on port efficiency when attempting to promote SSS. An efficient port has the scope to charge higher prices if it provides faster and more reliable services or if it allows the shipper to save elsewhere in a supply chain (Wilmsmeier et al., 2006).

Port efficiency studies have traditionally focused on factors such as size, or value of the labour force, or the number or value of capital items, as inputs into the port production process, with quantities (typically couched in terms of Twenty-foot Equivalent Units (TEUs) containers or tons) as the product of the production process. A survey of port efficiency studies (González & Trujillo, 2009) divides the findings into two main approaches: non-parametric Data Envelopment Analysis (DEA) and parametric Stochastic Frontier Analysis (SFA). The emphasis is on the measurement methodologies, the variables used and the results in terms of various port activities as well as on relevant dimensions such as port size, ownership and location. A main conclusion is the need to better describe the port activity for which the efficiency assessment is conducted and to collect more data from the relevant authorities. In Cullinane, Wang, Song, and Ji (2006), the authors apply both DEA and SFA approaches to study the efficiency of the container port industry for the world's largest container ports (ranked in the top 30 in 2001). For the efficiency analysis, the inputs used include the total quay length, the terminal area, the number of quayside cranes, the number of yard gantry cranes and the number of straddle carriers, while information on labour inputs is determined from a pre-determined relationship to terminal facilities. The output used is the container throughput.

In the aforementioned analyses of port efficiency, the *time in port* has not been explicitly considered, quantified or linked to the output of the port production process. Even though it is generally accepted that the time a ship spends in a port can be a significant determinant of that port's competitiveness and, therefore, of maritime transport itself, particularly in the case of intermodal freight movements and SSS, we found only a few attempts in the literature where the time in ports is actually investigated. In Suárez-Alemán et al. (2014), through the development of a conceptual and theoretical model, the direct utilisation of the time in ports as a suitable measure for port efficiency analysis is proposed, and a methodology is described for evaluating the efficiency of SSS ports or terminals on this basis. In Johnson and Styhre (2015), it is shown that even with a conservative reduction of the time in port between 1–4 h and with a corresponding speed reduction at sea the potential for increased energy efficiency was between 2 and 8%. The paper analyses a case study using both qualitative and quantitative data of a short sea dry bulk shipping company that mainly operates in the North and Baltic Seas. A port's time efficiency is identified in Sánchez et al. (2003) as one of the most important determinants of water-borne transport costs. The study uses Principal Component Analysis (PCA) from a survey conducted at 41 port terminals in Latin American ports mainly handling general containerised cargoes. In Strandenes (2004), port pricing structures that enhance ship efficiency (i.e. cargo carried per deadweight ton per period) are discussed by providing incentives for reducing the turnaround time in port and the time waiting for port access. A theoretical intermodal competition model is used in Suárez-Alemán et al. (2015) to compare alternative modes— road transport vs. SSS. The model includes a parameter related to various port inefficiencies that comprise port access time, ship waiting time in port (due to, for example congestion), customs and other documentation and administrative procedures, as well as hourly container load and unload rates.

The validation of PortCDM (Lind, Watson, et al., 2018) shows that standardised digital data sharing and enhanced collaboration can reduce unnecessary waiting times during port visits and inform about the expected time of the port visit with a high degree of predictability. As the focus has been placed upon just-in-time shipping lately, it is to be expected that ports informing about when operations are to be finished with a high predictability, would become a part of the value proposition.

SSS offers a set of advantages that no other mode can provide, especially in relation to the environment. The ecological sustainability of SSS, however, relies on port efficiency and the time spent in ports for realising its advantages as compared to other modes of transport. In the related literature on port efficiency, there is a gap in quantifying the different waiting and idle times during a port call process, as well as identifying their root causes. In Michaelides, Herodotou, Lind, and Watson (2019), the effect of time in port is considered by investigating the factors influencing the various waiting times at the Port of Limassol, both from a quantitative and a qualitative perspective. The qualitative results are based on the views of key people involved in the port call process. The quantitative analysis relies on data from over 8000 port calls during 2017–2018, which are analysed with respect to ship type, port of origin and shipping agent. The calculated Key Performance Indicators

(KPIs) include arrival punctuality, berth waiting and berth utilisation. The analysis clearly reveals considerable variation in agent performance with regard to the KPIs, suggesting a lack of attention to the social aspect of a port's socio-technical system.

For shipping, and particularly for SSS, there are obvious and immediate benefits from improving efficiency by assisting all those involved in the port call process to engage more easily to give shipping companies, port service providers and ships' agents better information and decision support systems to boost their efficiency and that of their port (Lind, Michaelides, Ward, Herodotou, & Watson, 2019). In particular, the analysis of recent port call statistics for the Port of Limassol, Cyprus (Michaelides et al., 2019), which was one of the Port Collaborative Decision-Making (PortCDM) testbeds participating in the Sea Traffic Management (STM) Validation project, indicates that there is an opportunity to improve port call data sharing through applying the PortCDM concept. Better data are essential for better decision-making.

4   PortCDM for Increased Efficiency in Short Sea Shipping

Port operators need a sound framework and accurate data for planning their operations. To realise a port call that meets expectations, such as fast turn-around, just-in-time operations and minimal waiting times for all involved, port operators need to ensure that all involved parties have access to the necessary data for their planning in a timely fashion. This includes both data related to a port's internal capabilities, such as the availability of resources and infrastructure required to serve a ship, as well as data on external conditions, such as the progress of a ship travelling towards a specific port. This means, for example, the ability to forecast with high precision the time of departure of a ship from a specific berth location, especially when another ship is planning on using the same berth in the near future. The same goes for ship movements in that a port should be able to forecast with high precision the estimated time of arrival of a particular ship to its service area.

The weakest link in a port call's chain of operations often determines its success. Therefore, all actions associated with a port call need to be considered. For example, a port may have streamlined coordination of all its internal operators (pilots, tug-boats, linesmen, terminals), but a wrong estimate of the time of arrival can easily disrupt the entire process. In order to both manage and avoid unforeseen disruptions, the Sea Traffic Management concept includes PortCDM (Lind, Watson, et al., 2018), (Lind, Bergmann, Haraldson, Watson, Park, et al., 2018) for expanding the planning horizons of port call processes, and the alignment of all actors in port call operations. Coordination is based on standardised data sharing that reflects the spatial and temporal nature of a port call. These shared data can also constitute a valuable system of records for efficiency analysis and port planning.

PortCDM builds upon the idea that the timing of intentions and time when actions are completed are shared via a standardised message format for time stamps. Each message has a timestamp, such as when an event is planned, and the required resources and location, as appropriate. These data are used for planning the use of the systems of production within a port, such as container handling. They are also captured as a system of record for port performance analysis and resource planning. The shared data should cover all the different dimensions of the port call process, from a ship's intended arrival at the port area until it leaves after having been served according to the purpose of call.

In order for the port call process to be realised as efficiently as possible, all involved actors need to be aligned in their operations and thereby, integrated performance throughout the port call process is highly likely to be achieved. By capturing shared data, such as agreements of operations, planned ship movements, outcomes of service deliveries and movements, the involved actors can gain insights into the consecutive progress of a ship's port call and provide a basis for planning. PortCDM promotes real-time data sharing as a means of providing all involved actors a common situational awareness. This enables them to adjust their plans accordingly and to make updates independently as they occur before or during a port visit.

SSS is particularly challenging because of the short horizon for the planning of operations. PortCDM can assist by supporting the exchange of standardised messages between neighbouring ports. As identified within the STM validation project, there is a desire for the downstream port to know the progress in the current port visit and also to know the status of subsequent ports in a sequence of port visits. Special focus is directed towards the provision of data of the estimated and actual time of departure from the previous port (ETD and ATD) and the estimated time of arrival (ETA) to the next port. These data when accurately communicated between ports can form the basis for better coordination of the port call activities at the port of destination, especially when there is only a short distance between the visited ports. Equally important, of course under SSS conditions is to continually track the vessel at sea, either by continuous ship-2-port communication or by other means of tracking, once the voyage begins. Ship-2-port communication within STM is enabled through the exchanging of voyage plans in a standardised format between the ship and the destination port. We emphasise that the various decisions made at the upstream port (e.g., slowing down port operations due to insights of what is happening in the next port) are data elements for establishing situational awareness for everyone, including the destination port, the captain of the ship and the shipping company. The ship captain, ultimately, is the one who decides when to leave berth and other such ship-oriented decisions.

For PortCDM to be a reality, ports and ships must be able to communicate by digital means in a common language and format. P2P communication is enabled by the Port Call Message Format (PCMF), established by IALA in 2019 as the S-211 standard (Lind, Bergmann, Watson, et al., 2018). Facilitated by PortCDM the ultimate objective is to ensure high reliability and accuracy of data for all involved actors based on a shared and common situational awareness. This can be achieved by adopting principles for ensuring a high degree of predictability, such as the combination of multiple data sources providing event timing data in real time and aligned actors with each other in terms of shared data and situational awareness.

5 Shortsea Promotion Centre Norway

Industry development mainly comes from two factors: Simplicity and transparency—both elements lacking in the Shortsea shipping industry.

The goal for the Norwegian government is to transfer at least 30% of all road-cargo over a distance 300+ kilometres to rail or Shortsea by 2030 and 50% by 2050. The latest forecast in the Norwegian transport plan indicates growth in cargo-transport of 290 million tons in 2050—80%, which will be transported by road. The Norwegian national transport plan forecasts growth in freight transport of 290 million tons by 2050. Eighty percent of this cargo is assumed to be transported by road. The increase corresponds to a 100 km long continuous number of trucks every day—a significant set-back to the ambition of transferring goods from the road to the sea.

The challenge is to acknowledge that the customer decision process is not only a decision between different competitors but also an assessment of risk. A customer using road-based logistics with success will evaluate Shortsea as an operational risk, "Why change something that ain't broken?" Time spent identifying and assessing alternative solutions is part of the transaction cost for the customer. Lack of transparent and readily available information will create barriers for change, regardless of operational efficiencies. The "disruptive" player in the Shortsea shipping world will be the one who provides relevant and accessible information allowing for decisions based upon comparisons on relevant criteria.

Decision support systems need to address both operational efficiencies as well as customer need for easily accessible and transparent information—supporting all phases of the customer journey. Shortsea Schedules (Fig. 1) is an online service

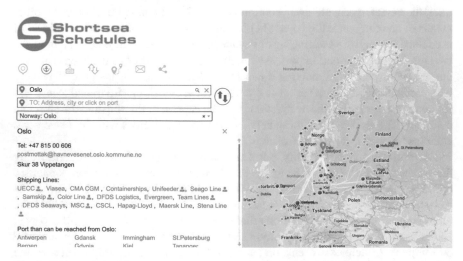

Fig. 1 Shortsea Schedules (https://www.shortseaschedules.com/) is an online service providing the user with an overview of all the different Shortsea alternatives available in various corridors

providing the user with an overview of all the different Shortsea alternatives available in various corridors. The information provides the user with information like shipping line, departure and arrival times, lead-time, direct/indirect routing, type of service (Ro-Ro/Lo-Lo) and contact information. The service allows for quick comparison of the different alternatives and identification of the optimal solution; thus, creating the foundation for an efficient decision process.

In the future road map for Shortsea Schedules will see the introduction of three elements essential for an efficient decision-making process:

- Door-door information (Ship/Rail/Truck)—providing relevant information on the actual demand the cargo owner's is looking to solve.
- Adding an environmental calculator allowing for comparisons based upon sustainability.
- Price-calculator—adding an opportunity to compare prices between the different suppliers, between various corridors and modes of operation.

Reinventing the operational models requires a move from product-orientation to customer-orientation, allowing the industry to become more involved in the value chain and providing an even higher degree of supply chain transparency. Transparency creates competition, and competition creates larger markets.

6   Short Sea Shipping in the Cyprus Context

In this section, we particularly focus on Cyprus, which as an EU member and an island in the Eastern Mediterranean Sea, having an important role to play in improving the efficiency and sustainability of SSS in its vicinity. Especially so, as more than 90% of its seaborne transport is currently SSS. As an accredited transshipment hub, Limassol could be a focal point for large shipments from other countries. Cargoes could be consolidated and sent to Cyprus, from where they could be efficiently distributed to various nearby ports, such as those in Egypt, Israel and other countries in the Middle East, using smaller vessels and SSS operations.

6.1   Cyprus in the International Maritime Sector

Cyprus, established as an international shipping centre about 55 years ago, has managed to attract shipping companies due to its excellent maritime infrastructure, and a high level of expertise, particularly in the fields of ship-surveying, ship-brokering and maritime insurance. Today, the Cyprus Registry is classified as the 22nd largest merchant fleet globally and the 3rd largest fleet in the EU, with approximately 900 ocean going vessels of a gross tonnage exceeding 49 million tons. It is estimated that approximately 4% of the world's fleet and around 20% of global third-party ship management activities are controlled from Cyprus. For companies

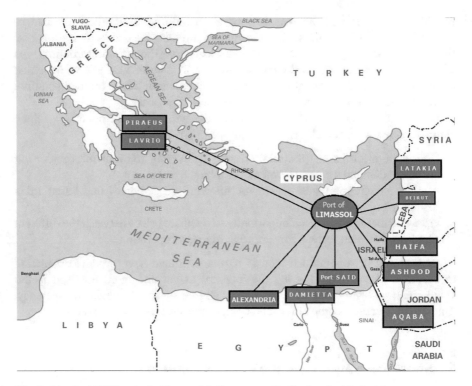

Fig. 2 Limassol EU Port in the Eastern Mediterranean. Credit: Soterios Voskarides

established in Cyprus, around 87% are controlled by Cypriot and EU interests. The island's ports have developed purpose-built container terminals and Cyprus is one of the first countries of the Eastern Mediterranean to use specialised gantry cranes. Moreover, the island is now considered one of the most important cruise centres and transportation hubs in the region. The Cypriot Government's vision is to develop initiatives that will further expand Cyprus's role as a communication bridge between the EU and the countries of Middle East, such as Egypt, Jordan, Lebanon and Israel. In addition, the interest of major shipping organisations in using hub ports in the region has increased the need for upgrading the physical and digital infrastructure for providing more cost-efficient services.

The geographical location of Cyprus encourages the use of its ports as transshipment hubs for SSS (see Fig. 2). Another favouring factor is also the political stability of Cyprus relative to several countries in the region. Cyprus is expected to become a shipping knowledge centre, both exchanging information with steaming ships in the Eastern Mediterranean region for optimising their routes and avoiding possible hazards, and with other ports in the region to enhance the planning horizon among the stakeholders within the port.

6.2   Port of Limassol and the Importance of Port-2-Port Communication

To be a successful transshipment hub, a port should be able to plan its operations precisely and ensure that relevant data are available to visiting ships as well as to neighbouring ports. This is particularly important for Cyprus as the distances between Limassol and its neighbouring ports are quite small.

Port of Limassol has over the last three and a half years, based on its participation within the PortCDM testbeds within the STM Validation project, developed a maturity in data sharing. This journey will continue by enhancing port call operations with PortCDM capabilities, as an important milestone in enabling SSS. The PortCDM platform enables real-time situational awareness to all participants involved in the port's maritime activities for the purpose of increasing operational efficiency within and around the port. The scope of this work extends from coordinating port call operations within the port to collaborative decision-making across ports. New services for port-to-port collaboration will also be explored and developed.

Port-2-Port (P2P) communication is a lubricant of short sea shipping (Lind, Bergmann, Haraldson, Watson, Michaelides, et al., 2018). Such functionality is of particular importance to the various operators at Limassol. Importantly, since January 2017, following privatisation, operations at the port of Limassol are handled by three private operators: DP World (general cargo and cruise terminal), Eurogate (container terminal) and P&O Maritime (pilotage, towage and mooring services). The main problem currently identified by all operators is the inability of ships and shipping agents to provide accurate estimates of a ship's intended arrival (ETA). According to Constantinos Aristidou, the berth planner of P&O Maritime: "Normally the shipping agents announce the incoming vessels on the Port Community System (PCS) about a week before, however, it sometimes happens that this announcement is made only eight hours before arrival!" This, combined with the short routes between Limassol and the surrounding ports creates a serious coordination problem for planning the various operations on the port side in order to promptly receive a ship (just-in-time) without unnecessary delays. As Constantinos adds: "The distance between the port of Limassol and some of the closest surrounding ports in the area is about 150 miles (240 km), which means it would only take about ten hours to reach Limassol from those destinations."

6.3   Benefits of Enhanced Port-2-Port Collaboration

PortCDM is expected to have a lasting impact on the maritime sector at both the national and international level. Towards this end, the ports of Cyprus, and especially the port of Limassol will be upgraded as information hubs, exchanging information with both nearby ports and ships in the Eastern Mediterranean. This is one of the primary goals of the newly approved STEAM (Sea Traffic Management in the Eastern Mediterranean) project (https://steam.cut.ac.cy). Such enhancement will upgrade the capabilities of all port actors involved in the port call process including the shipping agents. Moreover, the P2P communication can help establish the Cyprus ports as transshipment hubs for short sea shipping by improving their competitiveness in the area. Of course, a successful transshipment hub needs a complementary combination of efficient cargo handling equipment and digital data sharing to ensure the maximum utilisation of investments in the hub and to enhance the value of shipping in its catchment area. This is expected to increase the maritime traffic in the Eastern Mediterranean and especially through the Cyprus ports, thus stimulating economic growth of the maritime sector in Cyprus. The proposed solutions will help enhance the political and economic position of Cyprus in the Eastern Mediterranean and will improve communication with other nearby countries and ports, such as Damietta and Alexandria in Egypt, Haifa and Port Said in Israel, and Aqaba in Jordan. Therefore, P2P communication can contribute to the creation of an appropriate environment for the reduction of goods' transport fees, to and from the aforementioned countries. The wider upgrading and optimisation of the port services is expected to have a positive impact on the cost of transporting Cypriot freight, resulting in positive effects for Cypriot traders and consumers. The enhanced SSS operations can help towards upgrading the maritime significance of Cyprus, not just in the Eastern Mediterranean area, but globally.

7   Conclusions

The sustainability of Short Sea Shipping is central to a clean, safe, and efficient transport system. For shipping, and particularly for SSS, there are obvious and immediate benefits from improving efficiency by assisting all those involved in the port call process to engage more easily to give shipping companies, port service providers, and ships' agents better information and decision support systems to boost their efficiency and that of their port. In particular, an analysis of recent port call statistics for the Port of Limassol, Cyprus, indicates that there is an opportunity to improve port call data sharing through applying the Port Collaborative Decision-Making concept. Better data are essential for better decision-making.

The experience of the Cyprus ports is not unique, it is just an example of a phenomena that exists all over the world. It follows that every port should become connected to other ports so as to provide the basis for efficient SSS. Many of the world's ports, large and small, are confronting the same issues with regard to making SSS more efficient—this applies equally in developed and less well-developed countries. Better data sharing based on the PortCDM concept is a key way forward. This, in turn, will make shipping more efficient and sustainable, thereby contributing to meeting the important climate and sustainability goals advocated by the United Nations.

Acknowledgments This work was co-funded by the European Regional Development Fund and the Republic of Cyprus through the Research Promotion Foundation (STEAM Project: INTEGRATED/0916/0063).

References

Bendall, H. B., & Brooks, M. R. (2011). Short sea shipping: Lessons for or from Australia. *International Journal of Shipping and Transport Logistics, 3*(4), 384–405.

Bouman, E. A., Lindstad, E., Rialland, A. I., & Strømman, A. H. (2017). State-of-the-art technologies, measures, and potential for reducing GHG emissions from shipping-a review. *Transportation Research Part D: Transport and Environment, 52*, 408–421.

Brooks, M. R., & Frost, J. D. (2004). Short sea shipping: A Canadian perspective. *Maritime Policy & Management, 31*(4), 393–407.

Buhaug, Ø., Corbett, J., Endresen, Ø., Eyring, V., Faber, J., Hanayama, S., et al. (2009). *Second IMO GHG study* (Vol. 24). Tech. Rep. London: International Maritime Organization (IMO).

Commission, E. (2001). *European transport policy for 2010: Time to decide: White paper*. Office for Official Publications of the European Communities.

Commission, E. (2011). *Roadmap to a single European transport area: Towards a competitive and resource efficient transport system: White paper*. Publications Office of the European Union.

Cullinane, K., Wang, T.-F., Song, D.-W., & Ji, P. (2006). The technical efficiency of container ports: Comparing data envelopment analysis and stochastic frontier analysis. *Transportation Research Part A: Policy and Practice, 40*(4), 354–374.

Dadashi, A., Dulebenets, M. A., Golias, M. M., & Sheikholeslami, A. (2017). A novel continuous berth scheduling model at multiple marine container terminals with tidal considerations. *Maritime Business Review, 2*(2), 142–157.

Douet, M., & Cappuccilli, J. F. (2011). A review of short sea shipping policy in the European union. *Journal of Transport Geography, 19*(4), 968–976.

Dulebenets, M., Kavoosi, M., Abioye, O., & Pasha, J. (2018). A self-adaptive evolutionary algorithm for the berth scheduling problem: Towards efficient parameter control. *Algorithms, 11*(7), 100.

Dulebenets, M. A. (2018). A comprehensive multi-objective optimization model for the vessel scheduling problem in liner shipping. *International Journal of Production Economics, 196*, 293–318.

Eide, M. S., Longva, T., Hoffmann, P., Endresen, Ø., & Dalsøren, S. B. (2011). Future cost scenarios for reduction of ship CO2 emissions. *Maritime Policy & Management, 38*(1), 11–37.

González, M. M., & Trujillo, L. (2009). Efficiency measurement in the port industry: A survey of the empirical evidence. *Journal of Transport Economics and Policy, 43*(2), 157–192.

Grosso, M., Lynce, A.-R., Silla, A., & Vaggelas, G. K. (2010). Short sea shipping, intermodality and parameters influencing pricing policies: The Mediterranean case. *NETNOMICS: Economic Research and Electronic Networking, 11*(1), 47–67.

Halim, R., Kirstein, L., Merk, O., & Martinez, L. (2018). Decarbonization pathways for international maritime transport: A model-based policy impact assessment. *Sustainability, 10*(7), 2243.

Johnson, H., Johansson, M., & Andersson, K. (2014). Barriers to improving energy efficiency in short sea shipping: An action research case study. *Journal of Cleaner Production, 66*, 317–327.

Johnson, H., & Styhre, L. (2015). Increased energy efficiency in short sea shipping through decreased time in port. *Transportation Research Part A: Policy and Practice, 71*, 167–178.

Lind, M., Bergmann, M., Haraldson, S., Watson, R. T., Michaelides, M., Herodotou, H., et al. (2018). *Port-2-port communication enabling short sea shipping: Cyprus and the Eastern Mediterranean, concept note # 5*. Tech. Rep. STM Validation Project. https://www.ipcdmc. org/galerie

Lind, M., Bergmann, M., Haraldson, S., Watson, R. T., Park, J., Gimenez, J., et al. (2018). *Port collaborative decision making (PortCDM): An enabler for port call optimization empowered by international harmonization, concept note # 1*. Tech. Rep. STM Validation Project. https:// www.ipcdmc.org/galerie

Lind, M., Bergmann, M., Watson, R. T., Haraldson, S., Park, J., Gimenez, J., et al. (2018). *Towards unified port communications - From a project format to a global standard, concept note # 9*. Tech. Rep. STM Validation Project. https://www.ipcdmc.org/galerie

Lind, M., Michaelides, M. P., Ward, R., Herodotou, H., & Watson, R. T. (2019). *Boosting data-sharing to improve Short Sea Shipping Performance: Evidence from Limassol port calls analysis*. Tech. Rep. Article No. 35 [UNCTAD Transport and Trade Facilitation Newsletter No. 82 - Second Quarter 2019]. https://unctad.org/en/pages/newsdetails.aspx?OriginalVersionID= 2102

Lind, M., Ward, R., Watson, R. T., Haraldson, S., Zerem, A., & Paulsen, S. (2020). Decision support for port visits. In M. Lind, M. Michaelides, R. Ward, & R. T. Watson (Eds.), *Maritime informatics* (chap. 11). Cham: Springer.

Lind, M., Watson, R. T., Ward, R., Bergmann, M., Bjorn-Andersen, N., Rosemann, M., et al. (2018). *Digital data sharing: The ignored opportunity for making global maritime transport chains more efficient*. Tech. Rep. Article No. 22 [UNCTAD Transport and Trade Facilitation Newsletter No. 79 - Third Quarter 2018]. https://unctad.org/en/pages/newsdetails.aspx? OriginalVersionID=1850

López-Navarro, M. Á. (2014). Environmental factors and intermodal freight transportation: Analysis of the decision bases in the case of Spanish motorways of the sea. *Sustainability, 6*(3), 1544–1566.

Medda, F., & Trujillo, L. (2010). Short-sea shipping: An analysis of its determinants. *Maritime Policy & Management, 37*(3), 285–303.

Michaelides, M. P., Herodotou, H., Lind, M., & Watson, R. T. (2019). Port-2-port communication enhancing short sea shipping performance: The case study of Cyprus and the Eastern Mediterranean. *Sustainability, 11*(7), 1912.

Paixão, A., & Marlow, P. B. (2002). Strengths and weaknesses of short sea shipping. *Marine Policy, 26*(3), 167–178.

Perakis, A. N., & Denisis, A. (2008). A survey of short sea shipping and its prospects in the USA. *Maritime Policy & Management, 35*(6), 591–614.

Sánchez, R. J., Hoffmann, J., Micco, A., Pizzolitto, G. V., Sgut, M., & Wilmsmeier, G. (2003). Port efficiency and international trade: Port efficiency as a determinant of maritime transport costs. *Maritime Economics & Logistics, 5*(2), 199–218.

Sánchez, R. J., & Wilmsmeier, G. (2005). Short-sea shipping potentials in central America to bridge infrastructural gaps. *Maritime Policy & Management, 32*(3), 227–244.

Strandenes, S. P. (2004). Port pricing structures and ship efficiency. *Review of Network Economics, 3*(2), 135–144.

Suárez-Alemán, A., Trujillo, L., & Cullinane, K. P. (2014). Time at ports in short sea shipping: When timing is crucial. *Maritime Economics & Logistics, 16*(4), 399–417.

Suárez-Alemán, A., Trujillo, L., & Medda, F. (2015). Short sea shipping as intermodal competitor: A theoretical analysis of European transport policies. *Maritime Policy & Management, 42*(4), 317–334.

Watson, R. T., Lind, M., Delmeire, N., & Liesa, F. (2020). Shipping: A self-organizing ecosystem. In M. Lind, M. Michaelides, R. Ward, & R. T. Watson (Eds.), *Maritime informatics* (chap. 2). Cham: Springer.

Wilmsmeier, G., Hoffmann, J., & Sanchez, R. J. (2006). The impact of port characteristics on international maritime transport costs. *Research in Transportation Economics, 16*, 117–140.

Maritime Informatics for Recreational and Fishing Vessels

Jin Hyoung Park ⓘ, Mikael Lind ⓘ, Niels Bjørn-Andersen ⓘ,
Thomas Christensen ⓘ, Fredrik von Elern ⓘ, and Fred Pot ⓘ

1 Introduction: Merchant Ships vs. Non-merchant Ships

Merchant ships follow the international regulations of Convention for the Safety of Life at Sea (SOLAS) issued by the International Maritime Organization (IMO) (1974). This Convention is mainly about merchant shipping; however, in this chapter we specifically focus on ships and craft used for recreational and professional fishing purposes, which do not have to comply with most of the SOLAS regulations,

J. H. Park (✉)
KRISO, Daejeon, South Korea
e-mail: jin.h.park@kriso.re.kr

M. Lind
Research Institutes of Sweden (RISE) and Chalmers University of Technology, Gothenburg, Sweden
e-mail: mikael@realsearchers.com

N. Bjørn-Andersen
Copenhagen Business School, Copenhagen, Denmark
e-mail: nba.digi@cbs.dk

T. Christensen
Maritime Connectivity Platform Consortium, Daejeon, South Korea
e-mail: thomas@dmc.international

F. von Elern
Swedish Maritime Technology Forum (SMTF), a part of Research Institutes of Sweden (RISE), Gothenburg, Sweden
e-mail: fredrik.vonelern@ri.se

F. Pot
BM Bergmann-Marine, Seattle, WA, USA
e-mail: fred.pot@bergmann-marine.com

M. Lind et al. (eds.), *Maritime Informatics*, Progress in IS,
https://doi.org/10.1007/978-3-030-50892-0_15

237

because it is only "chapter five (often called 'SOLAS V') ... that applies to all vessels on the sea, including private yachts and small craft on local trips as well as to commercial vessels on international passages".[1]

Another major difference between merchant and non-merchant ships is that while the merchant ship is predominantly regulated based on international/global regulations, regulations for all other non-merchant ships and craft are mainly based on national regulations.

Non-merchant ships include recreational vessels, fishing boats, local tourist boats, military and other government-owned vessels and ships for building marine infrastructure such as harbours, dams, tunnels and canals. They are part of the overall maritime ecosystem. For all non-merchant ships, efficiency, safety and environmental sustainability are nevertheless important performance factors for their owners, crews and society. However, their challenges and digital opportunities are in many ways different from merchant ships. Accordingly, this chapter is devoted to the special situations of the two largest of these types of non-merchant ships, recreational boats and professional fishing vessels.

2 Information Services for Recreational Boats

This section deals with recreational craft from modest dinghies to competitive sailing boats to yachts. These types of vessel constitute by far the largest number of craft at sea.

2.1 The Characteristics of Recreational Boating

The owner of a recreational boat or a private yacht needs information before and during sailing. For example, they might need information services to choose a port to visit, check weather forecasts, plan a route, share a planned route with friends and family, check safety before departure, report departures, receive marine meteorological information, report on dangerous obstacles and report port entry. We use the concept "Maritime Informatics for recreational boating" as a generic term for information services that support a pleasurable and safe sea voyage with respect for environmental sustainability from the preparation of a trip to the end of the journey.

Maritime Informatics for recreational boating aims to provide boaters with better "quality in use" of information. Unlike merchant ships, the dependency among Maritime Informatics service providers for recreational boating is weak. Instead, the focus is on how conveniently and satisfactorily a mariner can use information

---

[1] See https://en.wikipedia.org/wiki/SOLAS_Convention

obtained from many independent sources. Recreational sailors need information at the right place at the right time and in the right form for their level of nautical skills. There are several suppliers and information centres of excellence, but it is fair to say that maritime information available to seafarers, such as MSI,[2] are not always easy to use by non-professionals, because they are designed for professionals.

2.2 Digital Interfaces for Recreational Boats

Today many recreational craft have dedicated navigational instruments, such as chart plotters, GPS and radar. Different standards used for on-board systems are based on IEC 61162-1, IEC 61162-3, OneNet and Wi-Fi.

To avoid cabling complexities and to reduce costs, the boating industry is trending towards using on-board Wi-Fi hotspots. Sensors are equipped with a secure hotspot that any Wi-Fi-enabled computer, tablet or smartphone within Wi-Fi range can connect to if it has connection credentials. Once connected the device can use an app to process the sensor information and display it in a user-friendly manner.

Examples are wireless radars that contain a Wi-Fi hotspot (Fig. 1). Radar installation requires only a 12 V DC power supply cable. The connected tablet uses an app to show a fully functional radar image with range controls, setting up guard zones and forward-looking display of echoes.

Another type of display is an electronic chart system (ECS) app. It displays information from multiple sensors. An example is iSailor from Wärtsilä (Fig. 2). It can be used for voyage planning, conning and collision avoidance (including calculation of the closest point of approach (CPA), estimated time of arrival (ETA) calculations, and replay). It displays satellite-derived position, rate of turn, heading, automatic identification system (AIS) targets, depth trend and (true) wind. ECS chart can typically be updated when the device is connected to the Internet. It is also possible to use it for automatic track control.

iSailor includes the option to subscribe to weather overlays and water current predictions. It has limited functionality when used on an iWatch. iSailor has export and import functionality to exchange routes with others using SMS and e-mail in several formats including KMZ and Route Exchange (RTZ). The KMZ format enables exporting to Google Earth.

---

[2]The Maritime Safety Information (MSI) service is an internationally co-ordinated network of broadcasts of Maritime Safety Information. This information contains navigational warnings, meteorological information (forecasts and warnings) and distress alerts. MSI is part of the Global Maritime Distress and Safety System (GMDSS).

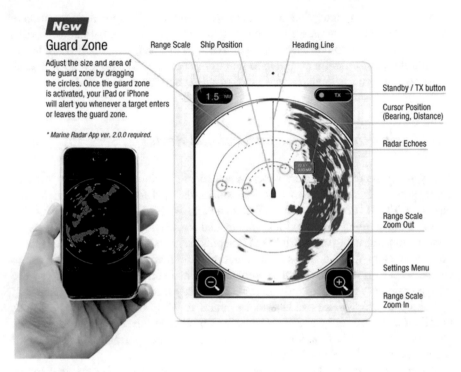

Fig. 1 Wireless radar display (Source: https://www.furuno.com/files/Brochure/215/upload/ DRS4W_E_20151116.pdf)

Wi-Fi-enabled tablets are typically less expensive to purchase, install and maintain than chart plotters but have similar functionality. They have the added advantage of portability.

Current Prediction

In several premier boat cruising areas, water current prediction is vital for voyage planning, and a digital model can assist. An example is the Pacific Northwest Current atlas app published by TinyOctopus (Fig. 3). Some of the narrows in this area experience currents of up to 12 knots with severe turbulence which is more than most sailing boats can handle. For safety, voyage planning in this cruising area must incorporate current predictions.

Boaters can also benefit from knowledge of current and future wind speeds and directions (Figs. 4 and 5).

The organisation or authority responsible for maritime information services varies by country and can be a mix of government and commercial services. For example, in the United States, the US Coast Guard provides boating safety information. They have developed a public boating safety app for the public, with

Fig. 2 A tablet display for navigation (Source: http://isailor.us/faq/i/Transas_iSailor_User_Manual.pdf)

some location-based services for boaters with a smartphone (Fig. 6).[3] The US Customs and Border Protection provides apps that recreational boaters can use to report entry into the US waters (Fig. 7).

Maritime information for recreational boating is typically designed for a single person, who consumes multiple services given by multiple service providers: single-consumer-multiple-providers (SCMP). This makes it important for developers of boating apps to find useful services easily and correctly. Apps or websites can collect, integrate and harmoniously show information relevant for recreational boating. Furthermore, as a boater will access multiple services, sharing their credentials among multiple service providers will lead to better experience that requires only one login for the use of multiple services.

---

[3] https://uscgboating.org/mobile/

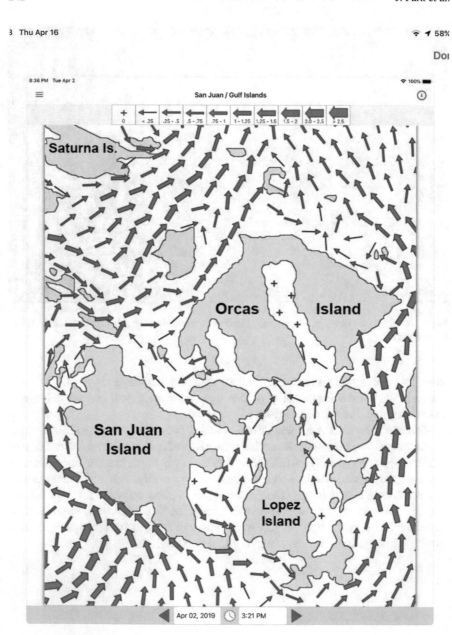

Fig. 3 Digital prediction of currents

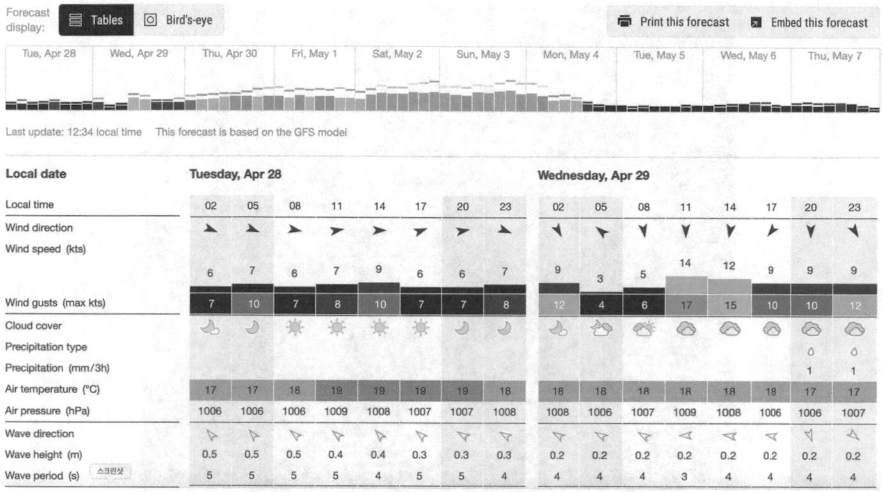

| | Tue, Apr 28 | Wed, Apr 29 | Thu, Apr 30 | Fri, May 1 | Sat, May 2 | Sun, May 3 | Mon, May 4 | Tue, May 5 | Wed, May 6 | Thu, May 7 |

Last update: 12:34 local time   This forecast is based on the GFS model

Local date	Tuesday, Apr 28								Wednesday, Apr 29							
Local time	02	05	08	11	14	17	20	23	02	05	08	11	14	17	20	23
Wind direction																
Wind speed (kts)	6	7	6	7	9	6	6	7	9	3	5	14	12	9	9	9
Wind gusts (max kts)	7	10	7	8	10	7	7	8	12	4	6	17	15	10	10	12
Cloud cover																
Precipitation type															◊	◊
Precipitation (mm/3h)															1	1
Air temperature (°C)	17	17	18	19	19	19	19	18	18	18	18	18	18	18	17	17
Air pressure (hPa)	1006	1006	1006	1009	1008	1007	1007	1008	1008	1006	1007	1009	1008	1006	1006	1007
Wave direction																
Wave height (m)	0.5	0.5	0.5	0.4	0.4	0.3	0.3	0.3	0.2	0.2	0.2	0.2	0.2	0.2	0.2	0.2
Wave period (s)	5	5	5	5	4	5	5	4	4	4	4	3	4	4	4	4

Fig. 4 Wind forecast service from Windfinder.com

There are also digital solutions available today that enable private berth owners and harbours to offer their vacant berths for rent to skippers, such as mooringo.com and dockbooking.com. These digital applications also allow skippers to tailor their experience by getting advice on local events and local business services (Figs. 8 and 9).

There are opportunities for maritime informatics entrepreneurs to integrate other digital data streams to provide expanded information servers to recreational boaters. Also, they can develop machine learning-based tools for improving current and wind predictions to support safer sailing and motoring.

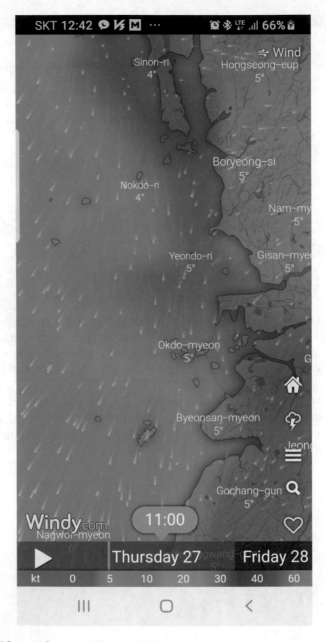

Fig. 5 Wind forecast from a mobile app: Windy.com app

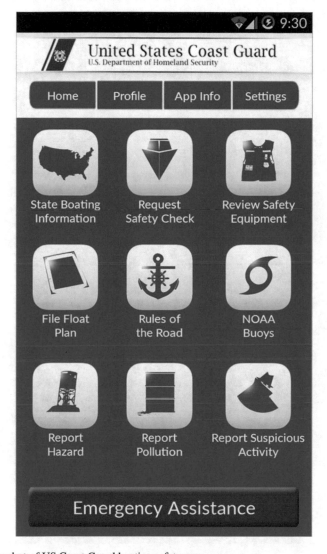

Fig. 6 Screenshot of US Coast Guard boating safety app

3 Information Services for Fishing Vessels

The fishing industry undertakes catching, culturing, processing, preserving, storing, transporting, marketing and selling fish.[4] All coastal countries have exclusive economic zones (EEZ) as prescribed by the 1982 United Nations Convention on the

---

[4]http://www.fao.org/faoterm/collection/fisheries/en/

Fig. 7 Screenshot of US Customs and Border control ROAM app

Law of the Sea (UNCLOS). The EEZ is a zone extending 200 nautical miles from the land zone over which a country-state has special rights regarding the exploration and use of marine resources, including energy production from water and wind. Within these EEZs, there are country-specific rules, such as particular quotas for which fish may be caught.

Fig. 8 Capabilities for mooringo.com (from harbours' perspective)

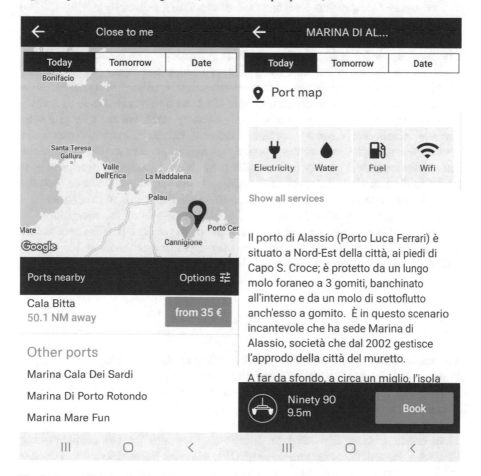

Fig. 9 Capabilities for dockbooking.com (from skippers' perspective)

3.1 The Characteristics of Fishing

Fishing can be broadly divided into sports and commercial fishing. When it comes to sport fishing, there is a huge difference between the parents taking their boy to the beach with a simple fishing pole and the dedicated sport fisher. For the latter, digitalisation has changed sport fishing. Cheaper nautical instruments such as chart plotters, echosounder and the combination of these have changed the methods and fishing grounds for many sport fishers. For instance, combo instruments plotters/echosounders enable a sport fisher to create a map of the seabed for precision fishing on very deep waters.

Commercial fishing has also changed dramatically, especially during the last 30 years to become highly professional, often with huge ships performing highly efficient operations. There is an increasing concern for safety and environmental sustainability, which is introducing a number of restrictions on operations.

When we evaluate efficiency, we typically consider the outputs (value of catch) for given inputs. The resources, which are necessary input for fishing, include fuel costs, depreciation of the ship and time spent that can be expressed as man-hours.

In commercial fishing, the output is measured by sales. Factors affecting sales revenue include the quantity, species, freshness, fish size, market demand and auction winnings. Improving the efficiency of fishing is more important to small-scale fisheries (SSFs) as they have smaller financial margins. They always need to be efficient to survive. However, sustainability is also an important issue, because unconditional efficiency improvements can lead to the depletion of fish stocks.

In this regard, maritime informatics for fishing vessels or fisheries should be developed with all these considerations in mind. In particular, SSFs, which lack the business capabilities and resources of their larger competitors, need to actively utilise maritime informatics services.

3.2 Digital Interfaces for Fishing

The decisive factor in maximising fishing efficiency is identifying fishing opportunities. There are a variety of apps on the market to provide information that helps locate fishing points such as sea surface temperatures (SST), chlorophyll concentration, currents, species of fish, hotspots, fishing bank, artificial reefs, shipwrecks, fishing records and sea weather forecasts.

In addition, there is a need for information services for sustainable fishing. For example, a mobile app suite, ABALOBI, provides traceability of fish caught, sold, transported and cooked (Fig. 10). It provides a sustainable and transparent ecosystem for "hook-to-cook". Information provided by the app suite includes

Fig. 10 Different apps in the ABOLOBI app suite for the fishing industry (Source: http://abalobi. info/app-suite)

electronic catch documentation, traceability information, transaction information, marketplace information for seafood with a story and safety at sea information.[5]

3.3 Digitalisation for Monitoring, Control and Surveillance for Fishing

A large challenge for sustainable fisheries governance is the illegal, unreported and unregulated fishing, which undermines the ability of fishery governors to make sound, informed decisions (Österblom, 2014; Sumaila, Alder, & Keith, 2006), and it threatens the food security and livelihoods of fishing communities (Petrossian, 2015). It is therefore a major concern to find new methods for the monitoring, control and surveillance of fishing (MCS) that historically and most effectively have to be conducted a large distance from shore (Toonen & Bush, 2020).

As both fishing fleets and the fish stocks are mobile, there is a need for collecting spatially referenced data on the location of fishing vessels, their gear and fish catch in order to be able to minimise illegal, unreported and unregulated fishing activity (Toonen & Bush, 2020). Technologies identified for such purpose include drifting fish attraction devices, on-board cameras, drones and satellite vessel-monitoring systems (Fig. 11).

These three spatial dimensions of information gathering from the water, air and space set new standards for enforcing fishing restrictions and create possibilities for new communities of ocean governance. "The focus on transparency and information has de-territorialised the actors and means of control over ocean governance, as well as also re-territorialised existing (legal and illegal) fishing practices" (Toonen & Bush, 2020, pp. 133). This also means that, in the same way as for other segments of maritime activity, different sub-communities of actors need to apply standardised data access and exchange in order to enable trusted and controlled interoperability.

---

[5] www.abalobi.info

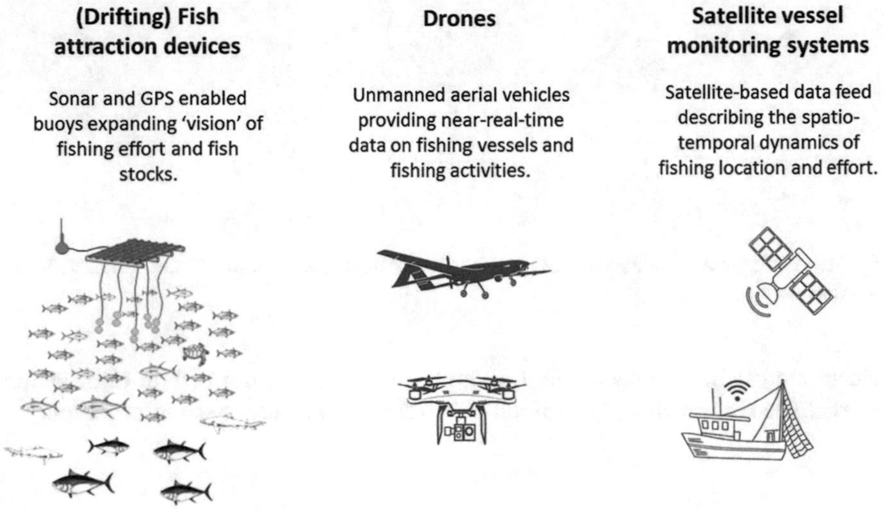

(Drifting) Fish attraction devices
Sonar and GPS enabled buoys expanding 'vision' of fishing effort and fish stocks.
Drones
Unmanned aerial vehicles providing near-real-time data on fishing vessels and fishing activities.
Satellite vessel monitoring systems
Satellite-based data feed describing the spatio-temporal dynamics of fishing location and effort.

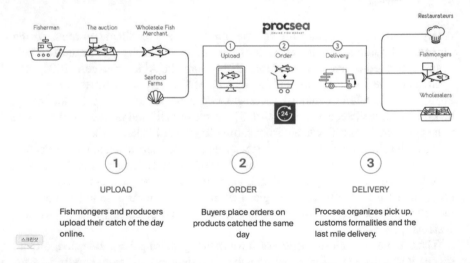

Fig. 11 Three cases of monitoring, control and surveillance technologies (Toonen & Bush, 2020)

Fisherman
The auction
Wholesale Fish Merchant
Seafood Farms
procsea
1 Upload
2 Order
3 Delivery
24
Restaurateurs
Fishmongers
Wholesalers
1
UPLOAD
Fishmongers and producers upload their catch of the day online.
2
ORDER
Buyers place orders on products catched the same day
3
DELIVERY
Procsea organizes pick up, customs formalities and the last mile delivery.
스크린샷

Fig. 12 From sea to table. Procsea reduces the chain ensuring availability, diversity, quality and transparent prices (Fernández-Medrano, 2018)

3.4 Emerging Digital Fish Marketplaces Meeting Demand and Supply

Digitalisation is also enabling a balance of fish supply and demand. For example, Procsea[6] provides a Software-as-a-Service (SaaS)-enabled marketplace for fresh fish and seafood. This marketplace solution matches the needs of all "law-abiding" fisherman, fishmonger, producer, restaurant, fish seller and wholesaler (Fig. 12).

4 Future Digitalisation for Recreational and Fishing Vessels

A digital transformation is well under way both for recreational vessels (primarily to enhance the pleasure of boating) and for fishing vessels (primarily to enhance the efficiency of operations and value of a catch).

One interesting example of what the future might hold can be seen in South Korea. Here e-Navigation services are supported through LTE[7] Maritime, a free service based on an LTE network capable of securing a broadband link between a ship and shore up to 100 km from the coast. The project began in 2016, and it will be completed by the end of 2020 following validation of e-Navigation services for ships sailing in Korean waters. Since a large number of ships sailing in Korean waters are fishing vessels operating offshore, six information services are being developed for the so-called non-SOLAS ships[8] by the SMART-Navigation project, which are planned to be provided officially by the Korean government starting in 2021. The entire set of information services were designed and developed around the Maritime Connectivity Platform (MCP).[9] These services are:

- Navigation Monitoring & Assistance Service (NAMAS), which will monitor the navigation of vulnerable ships and raises an alarm to prevent collisions and groundings.
- Ship-borne System Monitoring Service (SBSMS), which will monitor on-board systems on passenger ships to detect hazardous events, such as flooding, fire and engine failure.
- Safe & Optimal Route Planning Service (SORPS), which will provide safe and optimal route plans (Fig. 13).
- Real-time Electronic Navigational Chart Distribution & Streaming Service (REDSS), which will enable domestic non-SOLAS ships to download electronic

---

[6]https://procsea.com/en/

[7]Long-Term Evolution.

[8]By "non-SOLAS" we mean ships, which do not have to comply with all SOLAS requirements but only the so-called Chapter V of SOLAS. The largest number of these are recreational vessels, fishing vessels and navy vessels, but of obvious reasons, these systems are not for military ships.

[9]https://maritimeconnectivity.net

Fig. 13 Automatic route planning using SORPS architecture of SMART-Navigation service system (https://iho.int/mtg_docs/com_wg/HSSC/HGDM/Meetings/HGDM1/HGDM-1-5-1.pdf)

navigational charts. It supports chart streaming service as well for small ships which do not have an on-board electronic chart system.

- Pilot & Tugs Assistance Service (PITAS), which will provide pilots and tugs with information needed for pilotage.
- Maritime Environment and Safety Information Service (MESIS), which will provide maritime safety information including navigational warning, weather information, hydrographic information and maritime environment information.
- SMART-Navigation service system, which will provide a National Single Service Gateway for information exchange between ship and shore.

5 Concluding Remarks

An examination of today's digital solutions for recreational and fishing vessels identifies opportunities to enhance current technological support. Future digital solutions, which are relevant for both recreational and for fishing vessels, include:

- Systems for following ship movements provided by AIS
- Digital surveillance services for water, air and space
- Digital services for empowering the interaction among multiple parties involved in maritime activity, such as ship and shore interaction
- Digital services for matching demands and needs, such as berth space

For fishing vessels, there are systems particularly relevant to the commercial and sustainable exploitation of the resources of the sea:

- Digital services for matching sellers and buyers of fish are especially relevant in markets where the supply of fish is volatile.
- Systems for policing areas closed for commercial fishing and protected by conservation orders, such as legal size or age limits on fish caught.

These types of digital solutions will provide data for enhanced situational awareness for recreational boats and fishing vessels and thereby contribute substantially to making maritime operations more efficient, safe and environmentally sustainable.

References

Fernández-Medrano, S. (2018). *Our 9th investment: Procsea, the revolution of the B2B fish market*. Retrieved from https://medium.com/samaipata-ventures/our-9th-investment-procsea-the-revolution-of-the-b2b-fish-market-dc98e9747958

IMO. (1974, November 1). *International convention for the safety of life at sea (SOLAS)* (Vol. 1184, p. 278). UN Treaty Series, London.

Österblom, H. (2014). Catching up on fisheries crime. *Conservation Biology, 28*(3), 877–879.

Petrossian, G. A. (2015). Preventing illegal, unreported and unregulated (IUU) fishing: A situational approach. *Biological Conservation, 189*, 39–48.

Sumaila, U. R., Alder, J., & Keith, H. (2006). Global scope and economics of illegal fishing. *Marine Policy, 30*(6), 696–703.

Toonen, H. M., & Bush, S. R. (2020). The digital frontiers of fisheries governance: Fish attraction devices, drones and satellites. *Journal of Environmental Policy & Planning, 22*(1), 125–137.

Support for Financial Decision-Making

Corrado Lillelund Forcellati ⓘ, **Claire Georgeson** ⓘ, **Mikael Lind** ⓘ,
Sukhjit Singh ⓘ, **Carl Sjöberger** ⓘ, **and Johan Woxenius** ⓘ

1 Financial Management in Shipping

Financial management in shipping is a high-risk activity due to the substantial amount of invested capital, the cyclical nature of the industry, and the reputational risks involved—for example, as a result of adverse news related to sanction breaches, code of conducts, and environmental disasters. The complexity around sourcing, validating, and reporting relevant information and dealing with documentation based on archaic and paper-based commercial and legal frameworks adds to the risk. Almost a century ago, Fayle (1933, p. 276) noted that: "The

C. L. Forcellati (✉)
Risk Consulting/Sustainability, Singapore, Singapore
e-mail: corrado.forcellati@hotmail.com

C. Georgeson
Cass Business School at City University of London, London, UK
e-mail: claire.georgeson@cass.city.ac.uk

M. Lind
Research Institutes of Sweden (RISE) and Chalmers University of Technology, Gothenburg, Sweden
e-mail: mikael@realsearchers.com

S. Singh
The University of Trinidad and Tobago, Chaguaramas, Trinidad and Tobago
e-mail: sukhjit.singh@utt.edu.tt

C. Sjöberger
Chalmers University of Technology, Gothenburg, Sweden
e-mail: carl.sjoberger@chalmers.se

J. Woxenius
University of Gothenburg, Gothenburg, Sweden
e-mail: johan.woxenius@gu.se

M. Lind et al. (eds.), *Maritime Informatics*, Progress in IS,
https://doi.org/10.1007/978-3-030-50892-0_16

extreme elasticity of tramp shipping, the ease with which new-comers can establish themselves, and the very wide fluctuations of demand, make ownership of tramp steamers one of the most speculative of all forms of legitimate business".

As a result, if we consider a ship as a legal entity operating in a maritime network of agents, brokers, banks, and suppliers (hereafter "the actors"), we will understand that the costs and risks associated with a maritime voyage are highly distributed, scattered, and often hidden among the multitude of parties. This is also due to the highly secretive nature of the global shipping industry. There is a certain mismatch between what bankers and investors like and what shipping can offer as an industry. To limit risk, bankers like well-defined corporate structures, transparency, and predictable earnings and investors prefer high yields and steady growth. Shipping offers highly volatile asset values and revenues, internationally mobile assets, activities, and corporate structures, and the latter are often less formal with many family owned rather than stock-listed firms. In all this is an interesting business for ship owners, but it easily turns into a nightmare for bankers and investors. In such a setting it becomes clear that the network's attractiveness, resiliency, compliance, and sustainability over time will benefit greatly by promoting transparency and cost visibility.

In an era of maritime informatics, there are substantial gains in achieving higher degrees of transparency associated with planned and conducted operations in the maritime transport chain.

1.1 A Myriad of Actors Defining a Maritime Transport Chain

The maritime transport sector is a connected network of actors forming a complex and complicated value chain (Haraldson et al., 2020). Whereof *complicated* refers to the myriad of actors, as illustrated in Fig. 1, ensuring that cargos reach their destinations on time. *Complexity* refers to the opacity around the network in terms of available, accessible, and accurate data and information.

In theory, the most *valuable* value chain is the one where its network is clearly mapped and roles and responsibilities clearly defined and where monies, goods, and service levels can be tracked, managed, reported, and eventually improved. The value of such a chain is in its transparency and its predictability.

In practice, however, despite an increasing focus and requirements of financiers[1] to perform increasingly due diligences on the value chain, *consistent transparency* can be achieved only by sharing data and information throughout the value chain or by enforcement actions from lawmakers, regulators, and financiers embracing frameworks to mitigate the risks related to environmental, social, and governance

---

[1] Financiers refer to banks, investors, and any other legal entities providing funding and capital to the maritime sector.

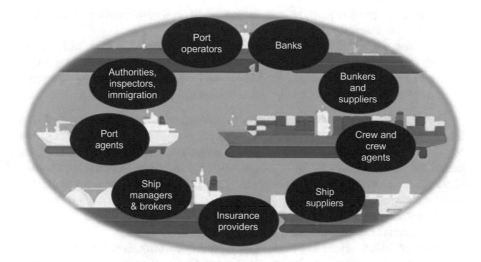

Fig. 1 Various actors involved ensuring ships' safe voyage (from Lind et al., 2018a)

(ESG) in their credit exposures. One example is the Poseidon Principles (2019), which will be covered later in this chapter.

1.2 The Spread of Costs and Risks Throughout the Value Chain

Based on the myriad of actors and the complexity of the maritime network, a discussion on how to fairly and consistently spread the costs and risks of a voyage throughout the value chain in terms of resiliency, compliance, and sustainability becomes highly relevant. We use the following operational definitions:

- *Resiliency* is the ability to withstand events that could affect the cash flow of a ship by taking into account the different charter arrangements (see Sect. 2.1) and its legal validity, hence impact on liquidity in stressed situations. Charter fees are the principal source of repayment in connection with ship financing, impacting liquidity and profitability ratios that financiers use to monitor the performance of a shipping loan.
- *Compliance* is the licence to operate a business in respect to and within a given set of rules and regulations, such as trade sanctions and anti-money laundering.

Compliance can have a significant impact on liquidity and thereby a borrower's repayment capability and hence covenants.[2]

- *Sustainability* is defined as the investment required to decarbonise and operate with respect to environmental, social, and governance requirements and a ship owner's personal criteria. Sustainability can have a potential impact on cash flows and the collateral value of a ship and therefore the value to loan ratio.[3]

For financial management and decision-making, costs are often classified as a capital expense (CapEx) or an operational expense (OpEx). CapEx are "funds used to acquire, upgrade, and maintain physical assets such as property, buildings, an industrial plant, technology, or equipment" (Kenton, 2019). "Capital expenditure should not be confused with OpEx, which are shorter-term expenses required to meet the ongoing operational costs of running a business. Unlike capital expenditures, operating expenses can be fully deducted on the company's taxes in the same year in which the expenses occur" (ibid.).

Maritime informatics can provide substantial opportunities to cost control and risk mitigation associated with both CapEx and OpEx. We also acknowledge that different shipping segments have different business logics and may differ in terms of the impact of CapEx and OpEx.

In terms of risks, there is mounting pressure from financiers to request and perform enhanced due diligences by measuring, mitigating, and reporting financial and non-financial risks, for example, in terms of trade sanctions, environmental and climate performance, and unknown liens tied to the ship.

Increasingly, the maritime network will benefit by promoting connectivity solutions among the actors to secure and share relevant data and information to help mitigate risks and reduce costs throughout the value chain. The industry is familiar with collaboration and sharing. Collaborative arrangements between owners with regard to their tonnage have existed for many years and are referred to as a "pool". The principle is simple; two or more ship owners merge their commercial operations to form a larger offering to their clients. This means that these ships work collectively, enabling the owners to offer more contracts and tonnage options and also share expenses. By sharing costs, and also profits and losses, the pool enhances its ability to secure funding from sources beyond traditional shipping financiers.

The mechanism of ship mortgage and pledge over present and future earnings will likely remain distinctive for the industry. Equally so, the right to enforce financial obligations will remain essentially in their current form, such as repossession, sale, and arrest (eventually followed by sale) of the ship (Girvin, 2019). Events like the COVID-19 pandemic represent triggers for performing material impairment tests of the securities pledged the favour financiers. Depending how well those

---

[2]Provisions required by financiers to ensure adequate mechanism to monitor the performance of a financial transaction.

[3]The value to loan ratio is a covenant ensuring that the value of the mortgaged ship does not fall below a certain percentage (e.g. 110%) of the loan debt provided by the financiers.

events are described in the deed of covenants (ibid.), they can and will be considered as an event of default to be enforced.

The assessments of the performance of a specific financial structure are based on past and present information—mainly financial data around past earnings—supporting the evaluation of present "state of things" as a starting point wherefrom to predict and forecast future market conditions, for example, in terms of stress testing.

The preceding approach is rather "subjective" in terms of assessment models, outlooks and risk statements, and appetite for ship owners, banks, and other relevant actors in the different segments of maritime transport. It relies on scattered data points at best. At worst, those data points are immaterial, inaccurate, or inaccessible. Therefore, they are misleading in terms of financial management and decision-making. Maritime informatics can contribute to achieving control, mitigating risks, and reducing the subjectivity of the assessments and thereby the costs associated with financial assessments.

In order to understand the role that informatics could play, we briefly look at traditional ship financing and characteristics. Traditional ship owning and building were heavily dominated by seafaring nationals and families throughout the 1900s, in particular by Greeks, Germans, Danes, and Norwegians. Traditionally shipping routes were localised, and there was no need for large fleets. Finance was dominated by local banking structures (half equity, half finance) backed by very low interest rates.

As tonne miles increased with the prominence of Chinese industrialisation from the 1950s onwards, so too did financial options. Traditional financing was replaced with modern twenty-first century finance; bonds, debt sharing, and initial public offering (IPOs) began to influence who had the ability to raise funds, and competition was introduced into every element of the shipping chain, from ship construction to ship owning. Today, we are accustomed to large oil majors with A+ grade bonds; however, ship owners are often within the junk bond section. This is a segment in which more transparency could enhance an owner's potential to raise cheaper funds, as we will explore in the next section.

2 The Financing of Maritime Transport Services

Shipping is a transnational, cross-jurisdictional, and cyclical industry with highly leveraged assets. Thus, the ability of a ship owner to understand and time this complex market is a critical dimension for investment decisions, impacting the capability to finance investments throughout the lifetime or possession of a ship. Understanding the market requires insights and investments, and there are high levels of uncertainty and sheer luck. Therefore, it is vital that potential investors, banks, and all lenders have up-to-date and accurate information pertaining industry metrics and not be reliant on rules of thumb or simplistic drivers such as oil prices.

Typically, financers translate uncertainties into risks, which result in a premium to be paid in terms of higher capital costs, mainly interest related. Markets will usually translate uncertainties and luck into higher or lower operational costs. For capital as well as operating costs, the translation can differ widely between shipping segments.

The shipping industry is operated through different types of chartering. This means that the ship may or may not be owned by the shipping company that provides services to its clients. A ship can be chartered at several layers, and operational costs, manning, and technical or nautical management could be outsourced. Chartering contracts (Gorton, Hillenius, Ihre, & Sandevärn, 2009; Tallack, 1996) are divided into three types: voyage charter, time charter, and bareboat charter.

Voyage charter, is an agreement for the transport of goods at sea where the ship is doing for the charterer one or consecutive voyages. Freight is determined depending of area, cargo, distance, passages risk, and overall freight market level. A voyage charter is a contractual agreement between the owner and charterer whereby the owner loads the cargo, undertakes the voyage including all costs and responsibilities, and delivers the cargo to the charterer or its customer. It resembles taking a taxi between two points. The consecutive version of a voyage charter is agreed with a single shipper; freight is usually then calculated in the same way as for a traditional voyage charter. Such trade is usually called tramp shipping. The owner of the ship covers capital, operating, and voyage costs. In certain types of voyage charters, sling for loading and discharging sawn timber in a general cargo open hatch ship is not included. Under a voyage charter, the owner has a larger share of contractual obligations and responsibility, and the masters follow instructions from the ship owner.

Time charter enables the charterer to "rent" a ship for a period of time, or for a specific voyage. Freight is prepaid and covers a certain time, such as 30 days. It is similar to hiring a bus with driver for a vacation or excursion. The charterer is liable for all costs including bunkers, fairway dues, canals, and port fees, but the owner remains responsible for the cost of the crew and the financing of the ship. These types of charters are often paid by the day, 30 days in advance, and are often tied by contractual constraints, such as trading and cargo exclusions, enabling the charterer to only use the ship for its core business and not "to play the market". Under a time charter contract, the owner has less contractual responsibilities than it would have under a voyage charter. The owner covers capital and operating costs, but voyage costs are covered by charterer. The master is instructed by the ship owner regarding the ship and the charterer regarding the cargo.

Bareboat charter is uncommon in the "spot" market and is usually reserved for very long-term charters between an owner and a charterer with a long-standing relationship. Under this agreement, the owner builds a ship, and the charterer is responsible for all cost, including the crewing and management of the ship. It resembles leasing or renting a car. These types of contracts are common between refineries, or state-controlled entities that need control of tonnage, yet do not want the capital expenditure of building the ship appearing in their balance sheet. It is

Table 1 Different charter types associated to different costs

Charter type	Duration	Capital costs	Operating costs	Voyage costs	ESG costs
Voyage charter	Single voyage days to weeks	Ship owner	Ship owner	Ship owner	Ship owner
Time charter	Days to years	Ship owner	Ship owner	Charterer	Ship owner
Bareboat charter	Months to several years	Ship owner	Charterer	Charterer	Ship owner

common that the ship is additionally re-chartered for as a time or voyage charter. The master is both appointed and instructed by the charterer.

These different types of chartering procedures are summarised in Table 1. The ESG costs will always be carried by the ship owner, who owns the asset. The type of charter determines the data to correctly allocate costs and hence contribute to enhance the predictability of present and future cash flows.

In shipping, strategic plans are developed based on a company's vision and goals, bearing in mind competitive advantage and challenges. A practical plan is to establish key performance indicators (KPI) and targets. For example, a KPI from a customer's perspective with direct impact on financial objectives is average running cost per day per ship. Achieving this KPI requires a set of performance measures from each ship, such as the number of overdue planned maintenance tasks. Increasingly, financiers include ESG-related KPIs mainly around decarbonisation in terms of reduction of CO_2 emissions measured as "carbon intensity" (see Sect. 3.4).

Data analysis assists in developing a minimum cost scenario highlighting the potential savings and how they can be realised. This also allows integration of risk management with such scenario developments. Different types of shipping are also used in exemplifying maritime informatics opportunities. For the elaboration of the characteristics on different types of shipping, see Lind et al. (2020).

3   The Different Maritime Transport Costs

Building upon "general cost classification" (Stopford, 2008), OpEx can be distributed over operating cost for operating a ship and voyage costs associated with the actual voyage. The price of a transport needs thus to reflect CapEx, OpEx, voyage costs, and increasingly ESG costs, mainly in terms of preventive measures, both CapEx and OpEx, to mitigate climate and social risks.

Understanding the diversity and nature of operating costs is extremely important. Most business models utilise cost-efficiency to increase shareholder value; however, most costs within the shipping industry are considered as "sunk". They are paid operating and running costs and include:

- Dry-dock (maintenance costs)
- Crewing/management fees

Dry-docking is an inescapable part of ship ownership and a requirement of the regulations set by the International Maritime Organization (IMO, 2017). Appropriate crewing of a ship is also a core part of a ship's regulatory compliance and operational requirements. A crew often includes a mix of seafarers with a variety of nationality, experience in years, and rank required for specific voyages.

The costs associated with operating ships are diverse, non-standard, and involve high levels of complexity. At the macro level, costs can be categorised (Lind, Lillelund Forcellati, et al., 2018a; Stopford, 2008; Wijnolst & Wergeland, 1996), as below and detailed later in Table 2:

- Voyage cost (OpEx)
- Operating cost (OpEx)
- Capital cost (CapEx)
- ESG cost

3.1 Voyage Costs and the Role of Maritime Informatics

A voyage requires many services, each of which generates expenses that need to be tracked, validated, and classified to create a system of record. Subsequently, these data can be analysed to determine, for example, the profitability for each voyage and identify actions for improving performance (Lind et al., 2018b).

Voyage costs vary by locations and jurisdictions and are potentially impacted by the opacity of the value chain because of different rules, regulations, cultures, and codes of conduct throughout the value chain.

Furthermore, the services and goods related to a specific voyage can be difficult to predict due to unplanned and unscheduled events. When a service is required by a ship, usually the service provider cannot provide much transparency if the process remains largely manual, unstructured in its communication, and difficult to reconcile due to language, geographies, and cultures. Digital records can support cost calculation and verification, such as the "Pay-As-You-Sail" (PAYS) licencing model for electronic charts. Another example, very helpful during the Covid-19 pandemic, is the digital loss prevention tool (TELP) introduced by the Swedish Club (TradeWinds, 2020).

3.2 Operational Costs and the Role of Maritime Informatics

Maintenance is an important contributor to achieve the intended lifetime of technical capital assets, such as ships. Maintenance regards all technical and management actions intended to retain an item in, or restore it to, a state in which it can perform as required (ISO, 2016). This captures combinations of all the technical and associated administrative activities required to keep equipment, installations,

Table 2 Different costs associated to maritime transports (building upon Stopford, 2008; Wijnolst & Wergeland, 1996) and digital data streams driving financiers' costs and risks

Costs			Digital data streams driving financiers' costs and risks			
Type	Category	Definition	Resiliency	Compliance	Sustainability	
Voyage cost (OpEx)	Canal costs	Costs associated to the passage of canals	Canal fees and accumulated fees throughout the voyage	Sharing of time slots for passage in standardised formats	Present and future trade patterns	
	Port fees	Costs associated with cargo handling at a port (often includes agency fees as well)	Open, national, international, and offshore and dual flags registers capturing fees Accumulated fees throughout the voyage	Port congestion and regulation (code of conduct)		
	Agency fees	Costs associated with calling a port for cargo handling		Sharing of plans and progress by involved actors		
	Bunker	Costs for ships fuel. Determined by ship machine, size, speed, hull, weather, draft, etc.	Fuel efficiency/smart metres	Country-specific regulations	Possible introduction of green tax regulation Data on used type of bunker	
Operating cost (OpEx)	Crew costs/ management fees	Costs associated to the crewing of the ship and the technical management in some cases	Operating as a pool, stand-alone, in-house, or outsourced ship management	Own vs. third parties' services meeting standardised and agreed requirements	Contingency plans for crew Insurance coverage	

(continued)

Table 2 (continued)

Costs			Digital data streams driving financiers' costs and risks		
Type	Category	Definition	Resiliency	Compliance	Sustainability
	Repairs and maintenance	Costs for repairs when damage occurs, maintenance of ship equipment (hull, cargo handling equipment, engine, auxiliary, superstructure, etc.). This includes costs for spares kept onboard and minor repairs	Employability Equipment/infrastructure condition Access to spare parts	Frequency of expected and conducted repairs	Regular inspections and certifications
	P&I, Kasko	Insurance costs for cargo (third party), machinery, and hull	Laws of a specific flag	Sanction regimes	Standing and reputation
	Dry-dock	Costs for periodic dry-dock when larger maintenance and repairs are carried out. The maximum interval between any two dry-dock inspections should not exceed 60 months; however, this interval is reduced to 36 months for ships over 10 years old	Transhipment	Black-listed	
	Management fee	Costs for commercial and operational activities like technical, nautical, and crew management and administrative tasks like equipment purchase and arranging insurance and claims. Usually called administration cost or overhead. Varies with the size and trading area of a ship and dependent on the business model of the owner but usually sensitive to economics of scale	Size of cargo	Benchmarking with similar companies in the industry	Contractual framework and standards
Capital cost (CapEx)	Interest (own cap)	Expectations or requirements from equity owners usually defined as a discount rate of invested capital. Often referred to as the yield	Ownership (e.g. special purpose vehicle) and injected own funds		

	Interest (loan)	Interest payments to a financial institution Costs for depreciation over a ship's economic life and is largely set by its new (or second-hand market) price. Depending of segment, this cost could vary widely. Lifespan in wet bulk and product tankers is 15 years; passenger ships could have an economic lifespan of 30 years or more. Calculations also must consider residual value as ships could trade in another geographical areas to prolong their economic life. Finally, a ship's rest value is set by its weight and internals as scrap	Financial ratios impacted by freight rates, interest and currency exchange rates fluctuations (Future) earnings capacity	Corporate incorporation (state owned, public or privately listed, etc.) and quality of security package and jurisdictions	Reputation and shareholders Creditworthiness of the charterer or shipper Managerial capacity and integrity
	Depreciation	Interest payments to a financial institution Costs for depreciation over a ship's economic life and is largely set by its new (or second-hand market) price. Depending of segment, this cost could vary widely. Lifespan in wet bulk and product tankers is 15 years; passenger ships could have an economic lifespan of 30 years or more. Calculations also must consider residual value as ships could trade in another geographical areas to prolong their economic life. Finally, a ship's rest value is set by its weight and internals as scrap	Ship values impacted by demand and supply of ships in different segments		Level of governmental subsidies; e.g. tax incentives for investing in greener technology
ESG cost	Taxes	Future carbon taxes on bunker fuel impacting the OpEx	Conducted trade/activity (e.g. oil, bulk, passengers)	Additional security in the form of parent guarantee	Full disclosure of ownership Due diligence of the supply chain (e.g. know your customer's customer) Carbon intensity
	Compliance	Disclosure and reporting requirements to banks, regulators, agencies, etc.			
	Depreciation	Scrubbers, retrofit, and new propulsions impacting the CapEx			

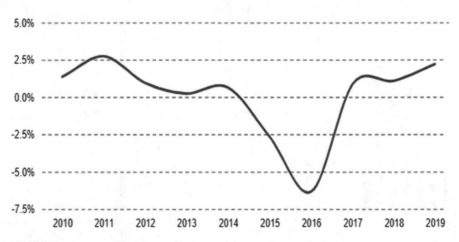

Fig. 2 Ship operating cost index (annual change in percent) (Drewry, 2019)

and other physical assets in the desired operating condition or to restore them to this condition. Maintenance cost is a significant portion of the operational cost, and breakdowns and downtime have an impact on a ship's performance, higher repair costs, and health, safety, and the environment. The cost categories such as spares, stores, lubricants, maintenance, and repair are the expenses that support a ship manager's decisions in terms of effective and efficient technical management. These costs are rapidly increasing, especially with a ship's age. It can be up to 20–30% of total operating expenses. The latest Ship Operating Costs Annual Review and Forecast 2019/2020 by Drewry (2019) (Fig. 2), which includes ships in the container, chemical, dry bulk, oil tanker, LNG, LPG, general cargo, reefer, roro and car carriers sectors, presents an increase in costs on broad-basis across all the main cargo carrying sectors. According to Drewry's estimates, the average daily operating costs on 46 different types of ships and sizes increased by 2.2% in 2019, in comparison to underlying increases of 1.1% and 0.7%, respectively, in the previous 2 years. Costs on stores, spares, and lubricants increased for a third year. Expenses on repair and maintenance and dry-docking fastened to 3.1% in 2019.

Maintenance optimisation models indicate the best decision given a certain problem and available information. The traditional OpEx optimisation approach links to the income and are usually run through cost-cutting programmes in order to meet the income and market challenges. However, smart OpEx management can provide solutions for cost savings in the range of 14–45% (Brattekaas, 2019). The traditional approach lacks investment in digital solutions and optimisation via innovation. Even the Best Practice Ship Management Study (Fraunhofer and Germanischer Lloyd, 2013), which compared snapshots of 200 shipping companies at an interval of 2 years in 2010 and 2012, for each USD1000 CapEx, only USD7 were invested in software technologies. As a comparison, the oil and gas industry invests USD35 in new assets for every USD1000 in CapEx. Nevertheless, the ongoing change and next management generation has lowered the barriers to more widespread use of information systems in all departments. There is scope for maintenance optimisation due to the technological push and economic necessity, which is today possible via digital solutions, data integration, and analysis at a very nominal cost to optimise business processes.

The growing trend towards business intelligence applications is to integrate data and automate reporting. The wide range of compatible modules combined with reliable communication and data management can simplify operations, optimise performance, and save costs. In recent years, companies across multiple industrial sectors have invested in improving their understanding of both historical and real-time data that they possess. The source of the data is specific to the processes, but the objective for all remains the same: to use data analytics techniques to develop a toolset facilitating prediction of performance based on real-time and historical data.

Condition monitoring (CM) has gained traction in recent years, as scheduled overhauls are significantly more cost-effective than unscheduled repairs. In maritime applications, maintenance strategy has evolved from a planned to a predictive maintenance model mainly on the back of CM developments in the sector.

Condition-based maintenance constantly checks the performance of equipment, providing alerts or alarms in advance of potential equipment failures and collects data for evaluation. The data analysis offers a machinery health management system capable of supporting appropriate decisions about maintenance actions based on diagnostics or prognostics information, available resources, and operational demand. An online system connected to a ship's communication network enables exchange of process parameters, such as output, speed, temperature, and start and stop variables. Based on process parameters, online CM systems can independently relate data to operating status and use variable alarm thresholds. Data synchronisation with online monitoring systems uses the variables received to decide whether there has been a significant change (trigger alarm value/initiate event) or additional measurements initiated (smart data) or the data should be saved/discarded.

A combined implementation of offline and online systems offers the most economical approach to reliable CM. Using this combined approach, critical machines can be monitored around the clock using online systems whereas less critical machinery is monitored at suitable frequency, such as with planned maintenance system (PMS),[4] using offline measurements. The result is a reliable and cost-efficient CM programme and a general reduction of the workload for the onboard crew. Any retrofit or addition of equipment arising from the need of regulatory compliance adds to the maintenance cost will result in certain increases to operating costs. These additional costs cannot be ignored, and ship owners and operators must find new and innovative ways to reduce their OpEx.

---

[4]PMS is a software system that allows maintenance teams and operators to plan maintenance tasks. It allows to request and schedule tasks at set intervals based on maker or class requirements.

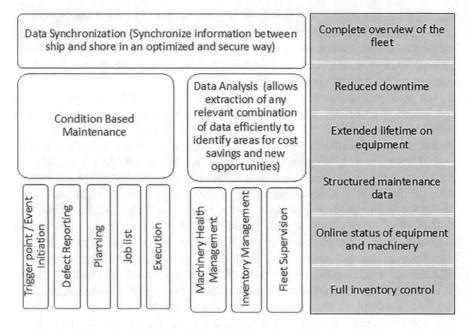

Fig. 3 Benefits of data synchronisation for condition-based maintenance

Adopting maritime informatics principles may be intimidating and be perceived to be a costly add-on without real benefit; however, the best justification of enabling digitalisation is in the data itself. Without measurement, new learning is not possible. Investments are required for onboard sensors, data transmission, and analytics. Data can support investment in a machinery health management system where benefits can far outweigh the risk (See Fig. 3). Maritime informatics for every shipping business will soon be a necessity for continued commercial buoyancy. To achieve financial efficiency in OpEx, ship owners need to monitor and analyse performance more frequently than the traditional use of daily noon reports or weekly maintenance reports.

3.3 Capital Costs and the Role of Maritime Informatics

The decisions on where to incorporate which law to follow and how to operate and manage a ship have an impact on the capital costs. Broadly speaking, capital costs are a function of the profile of the borrower (incorporation, management structure), its ownership, commitment (invested capital, additional securities pledged in favour of financiers, recourse *vs.* non-recourse), the operating risks (present and future cash flow), its financial standings (earnings ability), and the quality of collaterals to offer. The prior decisions are influenced by:

- The economic cycles and the volatility in demand impacting freight rates and ship values for the different segments of maritime transports
- Laws and regulatory requirements
- Risk profile and ownership requirements

It appears clear that the decision-making can be severely weakened when flows of critical data are potentially withheld by vested interests within the value chain. Unclear decision-making is detrimental to the network, and increased capital costs and opaqueness spreads throughout the value chain.

Timely disclosures of relevant and accurate information promote resiliency, compliance, and sustainability resulting in predictability. Trust and confidence are built when assessing, managing, and reporting the present and future costs of capital. In this regard, several indicators can assess the predictability of capital costs:

1. Macro outlook especially in terms of low economic growth
2. Over-capacity within the different segments
3. Falling new or second-hand ship prices
4. Technological obsolescence, either due to the introduction of more efficient ship models, propulsion methods, or changes in regulation

3.4 ESG Costs and the Role of Maritime Informatics

ESG initiatives and investments are opportunity costs impacting the predictability of capital, operational, and voyage costs. They can arise as a consequence of failing to comply with targets and thresholds (e.g. IMO goals for reducing greenhouse gas emissions by at least 50% by 2050) and result in possible fines, higher interest rates, additional capital injections, higher fees to port agents, delays, and rectification of incidents. In many cases, it means no access to borrowing funds.

In this regard, the newly introduced Poseidon Principles (2019) are consistent with the policies and ambitions of the IMO requiring signing banks to align their credit portfolios to responsible environmental targets around carbon emission by reporting the carbon intensity[5] of a ship's financial exposures based on four principles:

1. Decarbonisation trajectories for each ship type and size class. Signing banks will be required to assess whether the carbon intensity of credit exposures is aligned with the IMO's greenhouse gas targets. The assessment is performed based on

---

[5]Carbon intensity represents the total operational emissions generated to satisfy a supply of transport work (grams of CO_2 per tonne-nautical mile [gCO_2/tnm]). Carbon intensity is typically quantified for multiple voyages over a period of time (e.g. a year).

parameters such as fuel consumption and distance travelled in terms of Annual Efficiency Ratio.[6]
2. Accountability for using data and information from classification societies and other organisations recognised by the IMO.
3. Enforcement by including precedent covenants and definitions in new loan facilities.
4. Transparency by way of having signing banks to report annually—first report in mid-2020—on their climate alignment to IMO targets.

While the Poseidon Principles only consider the environmental and climate risk aspect of ESG, increasingly social and governance elements are being introduced to assess the impact on capital costs over time.

Key IMO derivatives, including the exclusion of green energy penalties, hinder emerging countries developing their industrial capacities. If the correct metrics are used when determining risk, then developing countries could have greater access to international funding, which is typically reserved for companies in developed countries with established corporate governance. Maritime informatics should seek to aid these developing countries.

4   Maritime Informatics for Financial Decision-Making

Maritime informatics can enable and enhance the predictability of flows through digital data sharing, collaboration, and connectivity among actors and the capabilities within existing operational systems, such as CM. It can disrupt existing financing practices by adding great value to financial analysis of maritime transport services when assessing risks, calculating ratings, and consequently interest margins for a specific loan transaction.

The ability to secure distribution and access to relevant data for each cost category in terms of resiliency, compliance, and sustainability will enhance the sector's ability to attract new types of financiers, anticipate and mitigate risks, and withstand disruptive events. In the following table, relevant digital data streams[7] for enhancing the financial arm of maritime informatics are identified.

The maritime industry has been traditionally compliance driven. The compliance with upcoming regulations can appreciably drive the CapEx and OpEx. The ESG costs are becoming increasingly important for ship owners, investors, and financiers. Ship owners face a huge variety of ESG risks beginning at the construction phase and continue throughout the trading life of a ship concluding at the end of its

---

[6]Annual Efficiency Ratio is a carbon intensity metric using data from the IMO Data Collection System collecting consumption data for each type of fuel oil used during a voyage (for further reference IMO Ship Fuel Oil Consumption Database).

[7]A digital data stream is a "continuous digital encoding and transmission of data describing a related class of events" (Pigni, Piccoli, & Watson 2016).

lifecycle. Maritime informatics have a huge opportunity to shape the way in which capital providers, banks, investors, funds, and other sources of finance address their direct and indirect responsibility into the future. The big data required for this purpose is voluminous and complex that traditional data-processing applications handle inadequately. Digitalisation can help to address impacts of upcoming regulations and compliance. Compliance is fundamental to valid trading of ship, while additional operational costs are generated. For example, with the recent IMO2020 sulphur cap enforcement, bunker procurement processes have become more complex. A sophisticated bunker plan is critical, as hedging of bunkers has become more competitive, thus impacting the overall operating costs. However, digitalisation can provide innovative solutions to tackle these challenges more efficiently by planning voyages carefully while taking regulations into account during cargo and freight evaluations. It can also provide informed decision-making by integrating any operating cost of emission abatement method and compare future bunker requirements to multiple scenarios and thus simulate different bunker impacts on the financial performance of the ship.

Ship owners collect vast volumes of data associated with various equipment onboard to optimise ship performance. However, much of these data are fragmented as data is collected by multiple applications. Further ship owners, equipment manufacturers, classification societies, and shipyards handle this on a ship-by-ship basis. Maritime informatics offers an opportunity to combine this data and can make this knowledge available for improving financial decision-making. The timing for harvesting the benefit of digital data sharing and enhanced transparency is excellent.

The COVID-19 pandemic is sparking an urgency for digitalising flows and processes, thus building resiliency throughout the value chain. Regulators are enhancing frameworks and introducing guidelines and instruction to secure a compliant operational baseline. Finally, stakeholders—whether it is about investors, financiers, and end-consumers—are signing up to sustainable principles and commitments and increasingly putting pressure on the maritime network to disclose accurate and useful information for the economic advantage of the whole sector.

5 Conclusion

Maritime informatics is digital data sharing and enhanced transparency-empowered decision-making through data analytics. It has direct applicability to financial issues for maritime transport. The ability to analyse data to reduce costs and mitigate risks will improve finance management. Data analytics can support:

- Optimal steaming for just-in-time arrivals
- Reduction of unnecessary waiting times by enhanced coordination
- Efficient utilisation of human resources
- Service providers and service consumers while establishing market-based business deals

- Predictive maintenance based on digital twins of key assets and their components
- Optimised cargo planning

These are some examples on how maritime informatics can play a decisive role in the digital transformation of financial decision-making.

References

Brattekaas, O. (2019, August 30). Why we need new approach to OPEX management? *Shipcosts*. Accessed April 18, 2020, from https://shipcosts.com/blog/why-we-need-new-approach-to-opex-management.html; https://shipcosts.com.

Drewry. (2019). *Drewry's ship operating costs annual review and forecast 2019/20*. London.

Fayle, E. C. (1933). *A short history of the world's shipping industry*. London: George Allen & Unwin.

Fraunhofer, & Germanischer Lloyd. (2013). *Best practice ship management study 2013*. GL Maritime Software and Fraunhofer CML, Hamburg. Accessed April 18, 2020, from https://www.cml.fraunhofer.de/content/dam/cml/de/documents/Studien/Best-practice-Studie-2013.pdf.

Girvin, S. (2019). *Aspects of ship finance: The market, ship mortgages and their enforcement*. National University of Singapore Centre for Maritime Law Working Paper 19/05, Singapore. Accessed April 18, 2020, from https://law.nus.edu.sg/cml/pdfs/wps/CML-WPS-1905.pdf.

Gorton, L., Hillenius, P., Ihre, R., & Sandevärn, A. (2009). *Shipbroking and chartering practice* (7th ed.). Abingdon: Informa Law.

Haraldson, S., Lind, M., Breitenbach, S., Croston, J. C., Karlsson, M., & Hirt, G. (2020). The port as a set of socio-technical systems: A multi-organisational view (Chapter 4). In M. Lind, M. Michaelides, R. Ward, & R. T. Watson (Eds.), *Maritime informatics*. Heidelberg: Springer.

IMO. (2017). *Survey guidelines under the Harmonized System of Survey and Certification (HSSC)*. Accessed April 18, 2020, from http://www.imo.org/en/KnowledgeCentre/IndexofIMOResolutions/Assembly/Documents/A.1120%2830%29.pdf.

ISO. (2016). *ISO 14224:2016 Petroleum, petrochemical and natural gas industries — Collection and exchange of reliability and maintenance data for equipment*. Accessed April 18, 2020, from https://www.iso.org/obp/ui/#iso:std:iso:14224:ed-3:v2:en.

Kenton, W. (2019). *Capital expenditure – CapEx definition*. Accessed April 18, 2020, from https://www.investopedia.com/terms/c/capitalexpenditure.asp.

Lind, M., Lillelund Forcellati, C., Lane, A., Watson, R. T., Andersen, T., Bergmann, M., Sancricca, M., Haraldson, S., Ward, R., Bjorn-Andersen, N., & Theodossiou, S. (2018a). *Using PortCDM data to increase the efficiency of financial transaction processing*. Concept Note #19, STM Validation Project. Accessed April 18, 2020, from https://www.ipcdmc.org/galerie.

Lind, M., Watson, R. T., Ward, R., Bergmann, M., Bjørn-Andersen, N., Rosemann, M., Haraldson, S., & Andersen, T. (2018b). *Digital data sharing: The ignored opportunity for making global maritime transport chains more efficient*. Article No. 22 [UNCTAD Transport and Trade Facilitation Newsletter N°79 – Third Quarter 2018]. Accessed April 18, 2020, from https://unctad.org/en/pages/newsdetails.aspx?OriginalVersionID=1850.

Lind, M., Ward, R., Bergmann, M., Haraldson, S., Zerem, A., Hoffman, J., & Eklund, E. (2020). Maritime informatics for increased collaboration (Chapter 8). In M. Lind, M. Michaelides, R. Ward, & R. T. Watson (Eds.), *Maritime informatics*. Heidelberg: Springer.

Pigni, F., Piccoli, G., & Watson, R. T. (2016). Digital data streams: Creating value from the real-time flow of big data. *California Management Review, 58*(3), 5–25.

Poseidon Principles. (2019). *Poseidon Principles – A global framework for responsible ship finance*. Copenhagen. Accessed April 18, 2020, from https://www.poseidonprinciples.org/download/Poseidon_Principles.pdf

Stopford, M. (2008). *Maritime economics* (3rd ed.). London: Routledge.

Tallack, R. L. (1996). *Commercial management for shipmasters: A practical guide*. London: Nautical Institute.

TradeWinds. (2020, April 2). *Swedish Club's TELP can help owners negotiate coronavirus.* TradeWinds. Accessed April 18, 2020, from https://www.tradewindsnews.com/insurance/swedish-clubs-telp-can-help-owners-negotiate-coronavirus-/2-1-784074.

Wijnolst, N., & Wergeland, T. (1996). *Shipping*. Delft: Delft University Press.

Green Supply Chain Management, Environmental Controls and Regulations in Shipping

Photis M. Panayides ⓘD, **Andria E. Alexandrou** ⓘD, and **Stelios E. Alexandrou** ⓘD

1 Introduction

The environment is an important issue in today's businesses and society. Governments and consumers have higher expectations from organisations and corporations in terms of environmental and social performance. In response, companies embark not only upon initiatives to green their areas of trade and interest but also those of their supply chain partners. Companies are increasingly adopting green practices and also trying to engage their suppliers and purchasers with such initiatives through their production and development processes in order to meet environmental expectations. This form of environmental management is called green supply chain management (GSCM).

GSCM is an interdisciplinary concept that is gaining more popularity in the shipping industry (Yang, Lu, Haider, & Marlow, 2013a) and links to sustainability. Sustainability through green chains is a new discipline for strategic competitiveness. Corporations to remain and encourage sustainability are nowadays faced with increasing challenges to balance business performance and economic gains with environmental issues. There are increasing regulatory pressures, through the introduction of legislation, for areas such as energy conservation and waste management.

The environment is of utmost importance in the shipping industry's context. Lately, there have been increasing concerns about this core pillar of corporate social responsibility. There have been different attempts on several levels to encourage green shipping. Regulatory pressures are crucial to driving organisations to under-

P. M. Panayides (✉) · S. E. Alexandrou
Cyprus University of Technology (CUT), Limassol, Cyprus
e-mail: photis.panayides@cut.ac.cy; stelios.alexandrou@hotmail.com

A. E. Alexandrou
Queen Mary University of London/Jackson Parton Solicitors, London, UK
e-mail: andria.alexandrou@hotmail.com

© The Editor(s) (if applicable) and The Author(s), under exclusive licence to Springer Nature Switzerland AG 2021
M. Lind et al. (eds.), *Maritime Informatics*, Progress in IS, https://doi.org/10.1007/978-3-030-50892-0_17

take sustainability initiatives. National, regional and international regulators, as well as trade associations and certification bodies, have expressed their increasing concern regarding the preservation of the environment. Because of such pressures within recent years, environmental requirements have increased in number, bringing with them new operating challenges.

Uncontrolled business activities can prove detrimental in the quest for environmental preservation and sustainability. Environmental problems can also increase through businesses' activities and through the activities of corporations' employees. Regulatory pressures must remain in place to promote environmental preservation. It is important for corporations to adopt GSCM practices in order to minimise their adverse effects on the environment. Under such considerations, the green supply chain is an essential and important factor for securing an effective, successful and smooth cooperation between the stakeholders and the different corporate layers amongst them, for example, when the shipping industry was required to shift to low-sulphur fuel in January 2015. Making GSCM work depends in no small part from the availability and use of relevant, reliable data and information (maritime informatics), in order to take appropriate decisions and to coordinate activities amongst all the actors along the maritime supply chain.

It is well established that shipping covers around 90% of the global trade and, in so doing also, contributes towards environmental pollution. Indeed, "maritime transport emitted around 796 million tonnes of CO_2 in 2012, which accounts for no more than about 2.2% of the total emission volume for that year" (IMO, 2014), thus contributing to global warming. Studies have shown that the "interaction between global SOx reductions and CO_2 . . . indicate that the higher fuel cost for distillates will motivate shippers to lower speeds, which will offset the increased CO_2 emissions at the refineries. Scrubbers, in contrast, will raise speeds and CO_2 emissions" (Lindstad, Rehn, & Eskeland, 2017).

Other examples include oil-related accidents by ships, such as the tanker Exxon Valdez. Nonetheless, in support of Yang's et al. (2013b), despite its position as a "relatively climate friendly" industry "compared to air and land-based transport, it is a considerable source of pollutants" (Yang et al., 2013b). Marine oil spills can prove disastrous to marine life, as the constituent elements in crude oil are incredibly "difficult to clean up, and last for years in the sediment and marine environment". Cargo residues at ports from different industry stakeholders, like shippers, may still become a significant cause of sea pollution, regardless the number of regulations present that prohibit any such actions. Nevertheless, non-enforcement is a chance that some ships face are prepared to take, even at present; recalling Yang's et al. (2013a) statement, "vessels still intentionally discharge illegal wastes" (Yang et al., 2013a).

Discharge of illegal wastes is not the only way whereby pollution takes place. Ships can cause damage to the environment through other means, including the noise pollution that ships can create, which disturbs natural wildlife. Ballast water from tanks "can spread harmful algae and other invasive species" (Yang et al., 2013a). Ballast water, which is taken up at sea and is then released by ships in port, is "a cause of unwanted exotic marine life". Water pollution from ballast water or oil spills has a direct effect on marine life. Air quality is another component of the environment that has been adversely affected with the development of shipping.

This chapter examines the importance of GSCM and its relation to the shipping industry, making reference to the regulatory framework and the enforcement mechanisms that are in place and how they impact and enhance green shipping. It considers briefly a number of "green" regulations that touch upon the areas that are under the umbrella of environmental preservation, while it also examines the internal and external pressures for environmental performance. On a final note, it considers integrating the internal and external green practices while analysing the important practices for the successful implementation of a GSCM strategy by shipping firms.

2   Laws, Regulations and Stakeholders' Actions

The shipping industry is increasingly being linked with environmental problems and is regularly challenged on the need to combat the adverse environmental outcomes emanating from its operation. Hence, appropriate mechanisms are crucial for monitoring the industry's behaviour and enforcing regulatory compliance which acts as an important driver for the adoption of GSCM.

This section discusses the mechanisms that create laws, regulations and standards that the industry is encouraged and, in some respect, mandated to address. It also touches upon a few of the different ways whereby enforcement is encouraged and the impact of such enforcement on corporations, driven by key stakeholders.

2.1   International Actions and Regulations

Various regulations range from international to national imposed by Governments. In the industry, usually these are based on or influenced by international laws set by the International Maritime Organization (IMO), the United Nations' body responsible for administering the international regulatory regime for shipping and for maintaining shipping standards worldwide. The IMO sets the universal framework for standards that cover international shipping. The IMO guides the industry towards a more sustainable future in several areas, amongst those is ship design and construction, equipment, manning, operation and disposal. IMO *adopts* legislation, which is then *implemented* by Governments (IMO, IMO Instruments) and enforced. Nevertheless, "The enforcement of IMO conventions depends upon the Governments of Member Parties" (IMO, Introduction). There are also laws at a national level that also guide shipping firms in minimising their impact on the environment.

As a result, on a practical perspective, the industry is constantly seeking to overcome and combat behaviour that may detrimentally affect the environment. In an effort to achieve long-term sustainability, the industry is continuously seeking to improve its standards for the environmental performance of its ships. Compliance and enforcement with standards require significant investment of time and money, both for corporations and for regulators.

The IMO has different pillars that govern different areas. The most relevant and directly applicable to this chapter is the International Convention for the Prevention of Pollution from Ships (MARPOL). This Convention covers pollution by oil, chemicals, harmful substances in packaged form, sewage and garbage (Gollasch et al., 2007; Yang, 2018).

The IMO adopted an International Convention Protocol seeking to achieve "sustainable maritime development in 1992" (Lee, Kwon, & Ruan, 2019). Consequently, the IMO has taken a number of proactive measures in an effort to reduce greenhouse gas (GHG) emissions. This chapter identifies several relevant internal and external drivers alongside the regulatory aspects and customs that enhance environmental sustainability within the industry, such as the reduction of ship's speed. Reducing speed by 60–70% from design speed can lower fuel consumption and emissions (Chang & Danao, 2017). As a result, the IMO adopted the Energy Efficiency Design Index (EEDI) and the Ship Energy Efficiency Management Plan (SEEMP) in 2013 as the results of the technical and the operational measures, respectively (Chang & Danao, 2017).

2.2   EU Law

The regulations that are discussed in this section emanate from the European Union (EU). Amongst the sources of EU law are the Directives and Regulations. In the EU, laws are enforced at different levels. A Regulation, which may have a wide application, is "a binding legislative act" (EU, "Regulations, Directives and other acts"). It can be "binding in its entirety and is directly applicable to all Member States" (Article 288 TFEU). In contrast, a Directive is "a legislative act that sets out a goal that all EU countries must achieve" (EU, "Regulations, Directives and other acts"). It is binding as to the "result to be achieved", and it is for national legislators (of the Member States) to choose the "form and methods" to employ to achieve the required outcome (Article 288 TFEU).

It is highly important to understand that there are matters whereby control and, therefore, enforcement lies with the EU. Hence, there are certain activities over which the Member States cannot exercise jurisdiction when the EU has done so, while there are other areas where there is a shared jurisdiction between the EU and the Member States.

The EU encourages environmental protection across its Member States. Further, it "has strived for an active role in tackling maritime emissions more generally, both at home and globally" (European Commission, 2020). For example, setting sulphur emission reduction standards for ships berthing (or anchoring) in EU ports (EMSA, Sulphur Directive; European Commission, 2011). The European Commission amongst other powers has also the power to propose legislation within the EU. The EU has the power to monitor (as also environmental laws), report and verify any non-compliance traced within Member States (EU, 2019; EU "Applying EU law"; EU, Report). An example is the "cap and trade systems" (EU, ETS), which aims by 2030 for emissions' reductions via the proposed emissions and energy policy framework. Another example in an EU Directive that compels ships at berth and at anchor within European ports to use marine fuel with "a sulphur content not exceeding 0.1% by mass." (European Commission 2011). Nevertheless, Port State Control has the ability to monitor compliance with regulations within Member States' territorial waters. A matter discussed in the sections below.

2.3 National Laws and Enforcement

Intergovernmental organisations, such as the IMO, have been successful in facil-itating the negotiation of environmental agreements on an international basis. Nonetheless, implementation of environmental agreements, directives, lies with the State parties who agree to incorporate these as part of their national legislation. Therefore, it is each State's responsibility to enact legislation or implement and enforce the existing ones (depending on the type), in order to adhere to international measures, which in turn will affect not only the industry but also corporations at large.

Pressure from Governments on corporations is sometimes an important mecha-nism in encouraging a compliant or even a proactive culture. A debatable method to achieve this is through enforcing stringent sanctions in circumstances of non-adherence to such measures. Fierce enforcement driven through national laws is a powerful mechanism influencing shipping companies to adopt greener practices.

Ships must comply with the standards imposed by the Flag State (country) in which they are registered in. Ships must also comply with the standards imposed by the country whose territorial waters' a ship has entered, irrespective that enforcement for that specific standard is not required in their Flag State.

Port State Control: Enforcement

Ports "provide an opportunity for verifying if visiting foreign ships comply with certain types of national or international technical standards . . . " (Molenaar, 2007). Port State Control (PSC) is the procedure of inspecting foreign vessels, (IMO, PSC) when entering the jurisdiction of another Flag State. PSC is a mechanism that encourages enforcement. PSC is a State instrument that confirms that ships are meeting the standards and requirements contained in the International Con-ventions and Regulations (including regulations and environmental regulations) and monitoring compliance (Molenaar, 2007). For example, if a ship does not comply with international standards, such as IMO standards, then there is always the risk of the ship being detained (IMO, I.C.C) and, in certain, more specific circumstances being arrested. Therefore, "PSC provides a 'safety net' to catch substandard ships" (IMO, PSC; also see Directive (2009), for EU). While the strictness of enforcing regulations at the PSC level varies with each State, such enforcement mechanisms have maintained their strong application through the introduction of the "no favourable treatment" words/clause found in the various Conventions, such as in MARPOL [Art.5(4)].

Memorandums of Understanding: Enforcement
Further to the discussion on enforcement and Port State Control, regional memorandums of understanding (MoUs)[1] also encourage the enforcement of the relevant requirements. MoUs are multilateral agreements that encourage and improve efficiency and the effectiveness of PSC measures, by recording details of ships' PSC inspections and performance in the various different ports of call. These records (as such in Paris MoU) are then made available to authorised parties to enable the inspection history and performance of ships to be shared to other PSC authorities (EMSA, Thetis).

The increasing number of participating States in the MoUs assists in ensuring compliance with the standards, laws and regulations. The compilation and sharing of records rewards compliant Flag States, by ranking them on their performance in enforcing the standards—using colour labels, viz., white, grey, black[2] (for instance, in Paris MoU see Paris MoU (2017), Tokyo MoU), and also benefits compliant ships, by offering them less frequent and thorough inspections, (Fairplay, 2010) according to how good their previous inspections have been.

2.4 Stakeholders' Actions and Pressures

Actions and Practices
Corporate bodies can form groups that develop standards or adopt cultural norms and/or practices to influence companies to adopt environmentally friendly strategies and to comply with environmental standards. Such actions are often successful because they are driven by the industry, more precisely its stakeholders. The Norwegian Shipowners' Association (Chang & Danao, 2017) is an example of an industry group that promotes green shipping, through the continued reduction of GHG emissions and by launching forums on environmentally friendly shipping. Such initiatives are regarded as constituent elements to incentivise the adoption of environmental initiatives (Walton, Handfield, & Melnyk, 1998; Zhu & Sarkis, 2004) and practices. An example is the adoption of ISO 14001 certification that offers the requirements for an Environmental Management System (EMS).

---

[1]Nine regional agreements on port State control—Memoranda of Understanding or MoUs—have been signed: Europe and the North Atlantic (Paris MoU); Asia and the Pacific (Tokyo MoU); Latin America (Acuerdo de Viña del Mar); Caribbean (Caribbean MoU); West and Central Africa (Abuja MoU); the Black Sea region (Black Sea MoU); the Mediterranean (Mediterranean MoU); the Indian Ocean (Indian Ocean MoU); and the Riyadh MoU. The US Coast Guard maintain the tenth PSC regime.

[2]The colour denotes the extent of enforcement of those standards; White colour describes the most compliant ones, as opposed to the Black ones.

Researchers (Bansal & Roth, 2000) and non-governmental organisations (NGOs) have produced a variety of interesting observations that cover a wider spectrum of factors, such as what motivates firms to adopt corporate ecological responsiveness. Industry initiatives, from organisations and NGOs, also have an important role in encouraging an environmentally friendly culture. For example, the Transport and Environment (T&E) "works together with other members of the Clean Shipping Coalition to reduce *air pollution* and *climate* impacts of shipping globally and in Europe" (Transport and Environment Organisation).

Classification Societies and Protection and Indemnity Clubs
Shipping organisations and societies within the industry encourage environmental compliance. Companies work to conform to the relevant standards in an effort to prevent losses that would incur through non-compliance.

The social responsibility to protect the environment may not be the only driving force in the compliance wave emerging from corporations. Shipping firms and organisations, for instance, encourage environmental compliance and the adoption of "green practices", because they acknowledge the importance that such action may have on a company's image and reputation (Bansal & Roth, 2000; Chang & Danao, 2017). Several studies have been conducted, one of which "assumes that adopting green shipping practices lead to the overall improvement of environmental and production performance of the shipping firm" (Chang & Danao, 2017). Environmental standards compliance can affect the prestige of a corporation and its relationships with key stakeholder. Protection and Indemnity Clubs (P&I Clubs), Classification Societies and industry associations can play a crucial role in the enforcement of environmental standards.

P&I Clubs are regularly updating their policies in light of the regulations that are being created or amended from time to time, while "due attention has been given by underwriters to risk assessment by owners they insure" (Mandaraka-Sheppard, 2009), thus encouraging a best practice in their insured risks. Securing insurance within a P&I Club usually requires compliance with environmental regulations. This dually benefits the Club and the Member, as it minimises exposures to environmental related risks. P&I Clubs provide insurance cover to protect their members against third-party liabilities arising amongst other, and from pollution incidents, they also naturally expect that members follow sound environmental practices, which likely affect their membership status. This encourages members to demonstrate a continuous commitment to environmentally responsible shipping practices that may likely affect maintenance of their membership.

The Classification Societies, being the organisations that establish and maintain technical standards for the construction and operation of ships, also contribute to encouraging good environmental practice. The Classification Societies may also perform certain public functions, when Flag States in some scenarios delegate responsibilities to Classification Societies (Recognised Organizations), for "statutory surveys and related activities, on behalf of flag State administrations" (Cariou & Wolff, 2011). Moreover, the International Association of Classification Societies (IACS) is "a not for profit membership organisation of classification societies that establish minimum technical standards and requirements that address [amongst other the] environmental protection" (IACS, Introduction). Further, it "polices the quality of its members' work", (Mandaraka-Sheppard, 2009). Such actions and measures seek to ensure the industry's compliance with standards and requirements.

3   Environmental Regulations in the Shipping Industry

Significant oil pollution incidents have received major global attention. Amongst these are the *Torrey Canyon* (1967), *Argo Merchant* (1976), *Amoco Cadiz* (1978), *Atlantic Empress* (1979), *Exxon Valdez* (1989), *Nakhodka* (1997), *Erika* (1999) and *Prestige* (2002) disasters. Oil spills may occur through routine ship operations, such as in bunkering and fuel operations. It is unknown the extent and frequency of oil spills that are linked to the industry; nonetheless it is estimated to be reducing (ITOPF, 2019). It has been estimated that there were approximately 358 spills during the 1990s compared to 181 in the 2000s (ITOPF, 2019).

The IMO's regulations are expanding (Lee & Nam, 2017) by setting conditions in place to monitor environmental performance. Examples of these are mainly in the MARPOL 73/78 Convention, the Convention on Oil Pollution Preparedness, Response and Co-operation regarding Hazardous and Noxious Substances (OPRC-HNS), the Anti-fouling Systems (AFS) Convention, the Ballast Water Management (BWM) Convention and the Ship Recycling Convention. According to recent IMO developments, ships are to be constructed with an immediate reduction in GHG emissions by 2050 (IMO, Emissions).

The "initial GHG strategy was adopted by IMO's Marine Environment Protection Committee (MEPC), during its 72nd session" that identifies "different levels of ambition", such as the reduction of "CO2 emissions . . . across international shipping, . . . by 2030" (IMO, 2018). In addition to the MARPOL 73/78 Annex, discussions on ship construction are also persistent, having the prominence of "eco-friendly vessels to shipping companies [that] relies in their role as strategic vessels that can avoid environmental fines, regulations, various other fines, and taxes as well as their energy-efficient capability" (Lee & Nam, 2017).

3.1   Air Emissions/Pollution

Regulation of carbon dioxide (CO_2) and emissions of sulphur oxides (SOx) (MARPOL, Annex VI, Regulation 14) and nitrogen oxides (MARPOL, Annex VI, Regulation 13) by ships have been introduced by the IMO. In an effort to limit the sulphur cap, four Emission Control Areas (ECAs) were introduced in January 2015 through additional requirements in the MARPOL Convention. The ECAs are in the Baltic Sea, the North Sea, North America and the US Caribbean, where the maximum allowable fuel sulphur content within the ECA is 0.10% m/m (IMO, Regulation 14).

In January 2020, the IMO introduced increased limitations on sulphur emissions by ships; the "sulphur content of fuel oil used on board commercial ships trading outside...(ECAs) must not exceed 0.50% m/m" (MARPOL, Annex VI; ICS, 2019). Ensuring compliance with the sulphur cap is crucial, "apart from the significant additional cost of compliant fuel" (ICS, 2019). Nevertheless, due to the increasing concerns and pressures, companies must comply and to even become proactive, in order to sustain their competitive advantage, as this is explained in a later section of this chapter.

The sulphur emission controls as part of MARPOL, "require operators to consider alternatives to the current widespread use of high-sulphur fuel oil (HSFO)" (McKinsey, 2019). Companies can switch to low-sulphur fuels. Amongst the alternatives is "the installation of scrubber systems to remove sulphur from the gas stream or a switch to very-low sulphur fuel oil (VLSFO), marine gasoil (MGO), or the liquefied natural gas (LNG)" (McKinsey, 2019).

LNG has been introduced as an attractive and less polluting option combating the several challenges that industry stakeholders may until now be faced with. By using LNG, ships can limit and mitigate their carbon footprint. Nevertheless, it is early days to identify the impacts of these recent (2020) amendments of MARPOL.

Another set of regulations provide requirements for the different categories of emissions NOx and CO_2, as mentioned above. The MARPOL Convention addresses these by also setting control levels for these emissions.

In another effort to reduce the polluting emissions by ships, an Energy Efficiency Design Index (EEDI) has been established by the IMO. The IMO has "agreed a work plan to continue the work on energy efficiency measures for ships, to include the development of EEDI frameworks for ship types and sizes, and propulsion systems, not covered by the current EEDI requirements and the development of EEDI and SEEMP-related guidelines" (IMO, EEM). The IMO has set standards in reducing the approximately 2.2% (as estimated in 2012) industry share of global CO_2 greenhouse gas emissions (IMO, Emissions). Further to the above, "EEDI requires a minimum energy efficiency level per capacity mile...for different ship type and size segments" (IMO, EEM).

3.2   Ballast Water Management

The International Convention for the Control and Management of Ships' Ballast Water and Sediments is an important Convention that came into force in 2017 and sets a framework in the maritime industry to minimise the harmful environmental impacts of the discharge of ballast water from ships. Under the Convention, ships must have a ballast water management (BWM) plan and keep a certificate on-board, and existing ships must conduct ballast water exchange in accordance with the D-1 standard, or for new ships built after 2017 meet (no later than 2024) the D-2 ("discharge") standard, that is, the ballast water performance standard. Therefore, from September 2017, ships are required to have a *ballast water management plan*, a *ballast water record book* and an *International BWM Certifi*cate (IMO, BWM Document). Ultimately, "most ships will need to install an on-board ballast water treatment system" (IMO, BWM).

The various examples described above illustrate the practical efforts that are aimed towards improving the environmental impact of the maritime industry. Regulatory pressures constitute one of the most important drivers for industry's stakeholders to adopt internal green practices as well as external green collaborative practices, known as green supply chain management. Apart from the regulatory efforts that the industry has embarked upon, corporations have also set goals for achieving environmental sustainability within their practices, in an effort to establish from the managerial level a healthy business. What these practices are is addressed in the following sections.

4 The Need for a GSCM Strategy

Globalisation, along with intense competition, has changed the way shipping companies operate. To serve the world's demand for sea transport and the need for achieving greater scale economies, more and larger ships are being added to the global merchant fleet. Such growth has several environmental impacts, such as GHG, waste, noise pollution and oil spills that largely increase the various stakeholders' concerns for such ship operations.

With the intensified public and governmental focus on ecological problems resulting from pollution and with the various marine accidents that can cause catastrophic effects to the natural environment, various stakeholder groups have increased pressure on shipping firms to adopt necessary practices aiming at preventing pollution and protecting the natural environment. Furthermore, the IMO, and specifically its Marine Environment Protection Committee (MEPC), is developing and ratifying more green regulations under the various conventions, such as MARPOL and BWM, as described in the previous section. Since concerns, pressures and regulations related to the environment are increasing, the adoption of green management practices, internal and external, has become an integral part of strategy formulation for shipping companies, due to the belief that it may ultimately contribute to a competitive advantage (Yang et al., 2013a).

Competition now lies on the basis of the effectiveness and the value of the supply chain. Since environmental performance is a major concern, and the supply chain is an ultimate driver for shipping operations, GSCM practices are now being considered as more crucial within the shipping industry.

GSCM started with shipping firms greening their practices internally while increasingly collaborating and working externally with their supply chain members, to develop a mutual understanding of environmental risks and responsibilities, making plans to resolve green related problems and providing resources skills and knowledge to collectively achieve common environmental goals, in order to reduce their environmental impact and improve the environmental performance of the overall supply chain (Vachon & Klassen, 2008).

5   GSCM Practices

Internal environmental management, green shipping management practices and external green collaborative practices are crucial for the development and successful implementation of GSCM that leads shipping firms to performance and competitive improvements. This is also supported by the study of Yang et al. (2013a) which found that internal green practices and external green collaborative practices positively influence green performance and competitiveness of container shipping firms in Taiwan.

5.1   Internal Environmental Management

Internal green practices constitute the daily green shipping procedures and operations that reflect a shipping firm's strategic decision to perform its services in an environmentally friendly manner. They consist of integrating processes to provide an environmentally friendly service with the aim of pollution prevention. Items such as management support and commitment are important and necessary for the implementation of green practices. Cooperation is an important pillar for the successful implementation of internal integration, where all the participants within an organisation, must work together with the same direction, orientation and cooperative philosophy. Cross-functional cooperation is a significant practice for the successful implementation of GSCM that leads eventually to performance improvements (Zhu & Sarkis, 2004).

5.2   Green Shipping Management Practices

Green shipping practices are those adopted by shipping firms aiming at waste reduction and resource conservation in cargo handling and distribution (Lai, Lun, Wong, & Cheng, 2011). Practices such as company policy and procedures for environmental protection; shipping documentation that focuses on promoting reductions in resource utilisation; the use of environmentally friendly materials and equipment that promotes the eco-design and emphasises on reducing, recycling and reusing shipping materials; and the use of environmentally friendly fuels form proactive green shipping practices aiming at pollution prevention (Lai, Wong, Lun, & Cheng, 2013).

Several studies examine various green management systems and practices regarding the mitigation of the negative and harmful effects of ship operations. Such an example is found in Psaraftis' and Kontovas' (2010) study, which proposes that

- Technical measurements such as efficient hulls and energy efficient engines
- Market-based instruments such as emission trading system
- Operational measurement such as speed optimisation and speed reduction and use of low-sulphur fuels

are three key ways to reduce the greenhouse gas emissions of ships. In addition, Lai et al. (2011) propose that green shipping practices such as company policy and procedures, the use of environmentally friendly shipping equipment and materials and the design of shipping activities and equipment that promotes the reduction of pollution constitute the main green practices that shipping firms need to adopt in order to reduce the negative impact from shipping-related activities and to improve their environmental and productivity performance.

5.3   External Green Collaboration

External green practices include a firm's interaction and collaboration with its supply chain members (Yang et al., 2013a). With inter-organisational relationships, firms will place, structure and monitor their practices, procedures, and strategies with the aim of environmentally friendly services in order to fulfil customer requirements. The main objective of GSCM is to improve the green performance and service value of the overall supply chain. Success at the supply chain level results in success at the firm level (Rao & Holt, 2005).

External green collaborative practice "involves mutual understanding of environmental risk and responsibilities, conducting joint decision-making to resolving environmental problems, sharing resources, skills and knowledge, and achieving environmental common goals collectively among suppliers, partners, and customers in the supply chain" (Yang et al., 2013a). Shipping firms tend to collaborate with their supply chain members by focusing on setting environmental common goals, sharing environmental plans and working together in a cooperating and mutual understanding environment to prevent and reduce pollution (Vachon & Klassen, 2008). An example is the Sustainable Shipping Initiative (SSI)[3] alliance, whose objective is to encourage supply chain collaboration towards a sustainable future.

Supply chain partners collaborate and work together to adopt and implement commercially successful processes and practices that have a positive environmental impact. Sustainable Shipping Initiative's proactive green philosophy is to "tackle some of the shipping sector's greatest opportunities and challenges, a vision of an industry in which sustainability equals success". SSI is a multi-stakeholder

---

[3]For an overview of the SSI alliance, see http://www.ssi2040.org/about-the-ssi/#

initiative that brings together leading organisations such as charterers, ship owners, shipyards, ports and port operators, banks, ship finance, insurance providers, classification societies and technology companies, with shared goals and equal determination in improving the sustainability of the shipping industry in terms of social, environmental and economic impacts (SSI, 2020).

External green collaboration constitutes a crucial practice for a successful implementation of a GSCM strategy, where it helps in the process of integrating the internal with external environmental practices, hence, aiming at working together to reduce and prevent pollution or other environmental impacts. The main focus of external green collaboration is to achieve more proactive environmentally sound processes and operations in order to prevent pollution and improve environmental performance (Vachon & Klassen, 2008). The way that shipping firms respond to environmental problems may be a crucial indicator of its overall competitiveness (Porter & Van der Linde, 1995).

The importance of a firm's green marketing, reputation and image has been enhanced by the increasing stakeholder pressures which companies face to improve their environmental performance. With the adoption of green marketing practices, shipping firms improve their reputation status, and this may lead to superior performance outcomes over time and eventually to competitive and financial improvements (Roberts & Dowling, 2002).

6   The Role of Digitalisation on Environmental Performance in Shipping

Digitalisation has a vital role in the successful implementation of internal and external green collaborative practices aiming at pollution prevention and protection of the environment more generally. The plethora of regulations, monitoring and reporting that is now required demands a digitalised environment both to effectively and accurately gather data, but equally, to enable its storage, analysis and subsequent use in improving and predicting future performance and identifying trends and shortfalls in performance. Digital data also goes hand in hand with the automation of processes and operations, which, in turn, can contribute to better safety and improved commercial and environmental performance.

International shipping can play a crucial role in the transformation towards sustainability, by designing and developing new vessel types with innovative technologies and also by improving the operational performance of the current fleet. For example, corporations adopting new product lifecycle management technologies, such as digital prototyping and design simulation, can significantly improve their management and reduce the time and costs involved. Such developments may also assist corporations to accurately predict the performance of a vessel across a complete set of operating and manoeuvring conditions (HSN, 2018). Environmentally friendly designs of vessels such as innovative propulsion technology that aims at reducing energy consumption and development will improve the green and economic performance of ship-owning companies and the performance and competitiveness of their supply chain members.

The adoption of internal green practices by ports and the design and development of innovative digital platforms are seen in different projects amongst those being "PortCDM" and in the Port of Rotterdam the "Pronto" application and the "Environmental Shipping Index". These innovative digital platforms facilitate the supply chain collaboration improving in that way the operational and environmental performance of vessels and ports.

In contemporary introductions of tools for Port Collaborative Decision Making (PortCDM) and port call optimisation (c.f. Lind, Ward, Bergmann, Haraldson, & Zerem, 2019), software applications are designed for port calls optimisation that benefits just-in-time arrivals and reducing a ship's waiting time in a port. Those software applications provide real-time insight into the available berths and handling capacity. If an incoming ship has to wait until a berth becomes available, it can reduce its navigation speed—effectively shortening its waiting time in the port. This cuts the volume of emissions generated during the voyage and at the berth and saves fuel (Port of Rotterdam, 2019). Therefore, these innovative efforts contribute to the achievement of sustainable common strategies and goals.

The new era of digitalisation and the associated improvements in safety and green performance can significantly reduce the environmental impact generated by shipping operations and at the same time can improve the operational and environmental performance and the competitiveness of the environmentally proactive shipping firms and their members in the supply chain. Therefore, these efforts establish a win-win situation for shipping and the natural environment.

7   Conclusion

The maritime industry is required to comply with many regulations at an international, regional and national level concerning pollution control and its environmental impact. As well as through regulations, pollution control and environmental impacts are also being addressed through the introduction of various standards and practices within the industry.

Shipping firms complying with the ISO 50001 international standard for energy management systems can increase their environmental performance and decrease their costs, by reducing their energy consumption and CO_2 emissions and their fuel costs, by using energy efficient systems and engines. These performance improvements eventually lead those environmentally proactive shipping firms to competitive improvements.

This chapter described a number of key regulatory mechanisms in place that lead those in the maritime industry to adopt ethical and socially responsible practices for protecting the environment and that are crucial for GSCM, for environmental performance and for competitiveness in the shipping industry. For a sustainable society and a profitable industry, shipping companies need to implement GSCM in an effective and cost-expedient manner and to comply to a high degree with environmental regulations, controls and measures. The introduction of digitalisation within the maritime industry should make compliance easier to achieve and to monitor. GSCM, which adds value through the socially responsible management of logistics processes, by connecting stakeholders within a corporate structure to promote collaboration and the preservation of the environment, upholds a crucial role within the industry. Maritime informatics also has an obvious role to play in both the regulatory compliance and monitoring and also in GSCM.

References

Bansal, P., & Roth, K. (2000). Why companies go green: A model of ecological responsiveness. *Academy of Management Journal, 43*, 717–736. https://doi.org/10.5465/1556363.

Cariou, P., & Wolff, F. C. (2011). A longitudinal analysis of piracy in shipping. *Economics Bulletin, 31*(2), 1055–1062.

Chang, Y. T., & Danao, D. (2017). Green shipping practices of shipping firms. *Sustainability, 9*, 829. https://doi.org/10.3390/su9050829.

Directive 2009/16/EC of the European Parliament and of the Council of 23 April 2009 on port State control. Retrieved from https://eur-lex.europa.eu/LexUriServ/LexUriServ.do?uri=OJ:L:2009:131:0057:0100:EN:PDF

EMSA. Port State Control Inspection Database – THETIS. (EMSA, Thetis). Retrieved from http://www.emsa.europa.eu/emsa-homepage/335-implementation-tasks/ship-inspection-support/2951-port-state-control-inspection-database-thetis.html

EMSA. Sulphur Directive. Retrieved from http://www.emsa.europa.eu/main/air-pollution/sulphur-directive.html

EU. (2019). *Monitoring and reporting of environment legislation.* Retrieved from https://ec.europa.eu/environment/legal/reporting/products_en.htm

EU Emissions Trading System (EU ETS). (2020). Retrieved from https://ec.europa.eu/clima/policies/ets_en

EU. Annual report on monitoring the application of EU law. (EU, Report). Retrieved from https://ec.europa.eu/info/publications/annual-reports-monitoring-application-eu-law_en

EU. Applying EU law. Retrieved from https://ec.europa.eu/info/law/law-making-process/applying-eu-law_en

EU. Article 288. Retrieved from https://eur-lex.europa.eu/legal-content/EN/TXT/?uri=celex:12016E288

EU. Regulations, Directives and other acts. Retrieved from https://europa.eu/european-union/eu-law/legal-acts_en

European Commission. (2011). *Proposal for a Directive of the European Parliament and of the Council amending Directive 1999/32/EC as regards the sulphur content of marine fuels* [Internet]. Retrieved from https://www.europarl.europa.eu/registre/docs_autres_institutions/commission_europeenne/sec/2011/0918/COM_SEC(2011)0918_EN.pdf

European Commission. (2020). *Cleaner Air in 2020: 0.5% sulphur cap for ships enters into force worldwide.* Retrieved from https://ec.europa.eu/commission/presscorner/detail/en/IP_19_6837

European Commission. Reducing emissions from the shipping sector. Retrieved from https://ec.europa.eu/clima/policies/transport/shipping_en

Fairplay. (2010). *Paris MoU to reward owner virtue.* Fairplay.

Gollasch, S., David, M., Voigt, M., Dragsund, E., Hewitt, C., & Fukuyo, Y. (2007). Critical review of the IMO international convention on the management of ships' ballast water and sediments. *Harmful Algae, 6*(4), 585–600. https://doi.org/10.1016/j.hal.2006.12.009.

HSN. (2018). *Digitalization is key for sustainable shipping success.* Retrieved from https://www.hellenicshippingnews.com/digitalization-is-key-for-sustainable-shipping-success/

IACS. Introduction. Retrieved from http://www.iacs.org.uk/about/

ICS. (2019). *Compliance with the 2020 'Global Sulphur Cap' for ships' fuel oil in accordance with MARPOL Annex VI.* Retrieved from https://www.ics-shipping.org/docs/default-source/resources/guidance-for-compliance-with-the-2020-global-sulphur-cap-july-2019.pdf?sfvrsn=24

IMO. (2018). *UN body adopts climate change strategy for shipping.* Retrieved from http://www.imo.org/en/MediaCentre/PressBriefings/Pages/06GHGinitialstrategy.aspx

IMO. *Port state control (PSC).* Retrieved from March 2020. http://www.imo.org/en/OurWork/MSAS/Pages/PortStateControl.aspx

IMO, GHG study. (2014). *Third IMO Greenhouse Gas Study 2014.* Retrieved from http://www.imo.org/en/OurWork/Environment/PollutionPrevention/AirPollution/Documents/Third%20Greenhouse%20Gas%20Study/GHG3%20Executive%20Summary%20and%20Report.pdf

IMO. Energy efficiency measures. (IMO EEM). Retrieved from http://www.imo.org/en/OurWork/Environment/PollutionPrevention/AirPollution/Pages/Technical-and-Operational-Measures.aspx

IMO. Frequently asked questions implementing the ballast water management convention. (IMO, BWM Document). Retrieved from http://www.imo.org/en/MediaCentre/HotTopics/Documents/FAQ%20-%20Implementing%20the%20Ballast%20Water%20Management%20Convention.pdf

IMO. Greenhouse gas emissions. (IMO, Emissions). Retrieved from http://www.imo.org/en/OurWork/Environment/PollutionPrevention/AirPollution/Pages/GHG-Emissions.aspx

IMO. Implementation, control and coordination (I.C.C). Retrieved from http://www.imo.org/en/OurWork/MSAS/Pages/ImplementationOfIMOInstruments.aspx

IMO. Implementation of IMO Instruments. Retrieved from http://www.imo.org/en/OurWork/Safety/Implementation/Pages/ImplementationOfIMOInstruments.aspx

IMO. International convention for the control and management of ships' ballast water and sediments (BWM). (IMO, BWM). Retrieved from http://www.imo.org/en/About/Conventions/ListOfConventions/Pages/International-Convention-for-the-Control-and-Management-of-Ships'-Ballast-Water-and-Sediments-(BWM).aspx

IMO. Introduction. Adopting a convention, Entry into force, Accession, Amendment, Enforcement, Tacit acceptance procedure (IMO, Introduction). Retrieved from http://www.imo.org/en/About/Conventions/Pages/Home.aspx

IMO. Sulphur oxides (SOx) and Particulate Matter (PM) – Regulation 14. Retrieved from http://www.imo.org/en/OurWork/Environment/PollutionPrevention/AirPollution/Pages/Sulphur-oxides-(SOx)-%E2%80%93-Regulation-14.aspx

ITOPF. (2019). *Oil tanker spill statistics.* Retrieved from http://www.itopf.org/knowledge-resources/documents-guides/document/oil-tanker-spill-statistics-2019/

Lai, K. H., Lun, V. Y. H., Wong, C. W. Y., & Cheng, T. C. E. (2011). Green shipping practices in the shipping industry: Conceptualization, adoption, and implications. *Resources, Conservation and Recycling, 55*(6), 631–638. https://doi.org/10.1016/j.resconrec.2010.12.004.

Lai, K. H., Wong, C. W. Y., Lun, V. Y. H., & Cheng, T. C. E. (2013). Shipping design for compliance and the performance contingencies for shipping firms. *Transportation Research Part E: Logistics and Transportation Review, 55*, 74–83. https://doi.org/10.1016/j.tre.2013.03.004.

Lee, P. T., Kwon, O. K., & Ruan, X. (2019). Sustainability challenges in maritime transport and logistics industry and its way ahead. *Sustainability, 11*, 1331. https://doi.org/10.3390/su11051331.

Lee, T., & Nam, H. (2017). A study on green shipping in major countries: In the view of shipyards, shipping companies, ports, and policies. *The Asian Journal of Shipping and Logistics, 33*(4), 253–262. https://doi.org/10.1016/j.ajsl.2017.12.009.

Lind, M., Ward, R., Bergmann, M., Haraldson, S., & Zerem, A. (2019). *Digitalizing the port call process.* UNCTAD Transport and Trade Facilitation Series No. 13, UNCTAD.

Lindstad, H. E., Rehn, C. F., & Eskeland, G. S. (2017). Sulphur abatement globally in maritime shipping. *Transportation Research Part D: Transport and Environment, 57*, 303–313. https://doi.org/10.1016/j.trd.2017.09.028.

Mandaraka-Sheppard, A. (2009). Modern maritime law and risk management. *Taylor & Francis.* https://doi.org/10.4324/9781315793207.

McKinsey and Company. (2019). Forced boil-off gas: The future of LNG as a fuel for LNG carriers.

Molenaar, E. J. (2007). Port state jurisdiction: Toward comprehensive, mandatory and global coverage. *Ocean Development & International Law, 38*(1–2), 225–257. https://doi.org/10.1080/00908320601071520.

Paris MoU. (2017). *List of recognized organizations.* Retrieved from https://www.parismou.org/list-recognized-organizations

Port of Rotterdam. (2019). *Digitalisation improves environmental footprint of shipping sector.* Retrieved from https://www.portofrotterdam.com/en/news-and-press-releases/digitalisation-improves-environmental-footprint-of-shipping-sector

Porter, M. E., & Van der Linde, C. (1995). Toward a new conception of the environment-competitiveness relationship. *Journal of Economic Perspectives, 9*(4), 97–118. https://doi.org/10.1257/jep.9.4.97.

Psaraftis, H. N., & Kontovas, C. A. (2010). Balancing the economics and environmental performance of maritime transportation. *Transportation Research Part D: Transport and Environment, 15*(8), 458–462. https://doi.org/10.1016/j.trd.2010.05.001.

Rao, P., & Holt, D. (2005). Do green supply chains lead to competitiveness and economic performance? *International Journal of Operations and Production Management, 25*(9), 898–916. https://doi.org/10.1108/01443570510613956.

Roberts, P. W., & Dowling, G. R. (2002). Corporate reputation and sustained superior financial performance. *Strategic Management Journal, 23*(12), 1077–1093. https://doi.org/10.1002/smj.274.

Sustainable Shipping Initiative (SSI). (2020). *Vision 2040 – Sustainable shipping.* Retrieved from https://www.ssi2040.org/about-the-ssi/our-vision/.

Transport and Environment Organisation (T&E). Retrieved March 2020, from https://www.transportenvironment.org/what-we-do/shipping-and-environment

Vachon, S., & Klassen, R. D. (2008). Environmental management and manufacturing performance: the role of collaboration in the supply chain. *International Journal of Production Economics, 111*(2), 299–315. https://doi.org/10.1016/j.ijpe.2006.11.030.

Walton, S. V., Handfield, R. B., & Melnyk, S. A. (1998). The green supply chain: Integrating suppliers into environmental management processes. *International Journal of Purchasing and Materials Management, 34*(1), 2–11. https://doi.org/10.1111/j.1745-493X.1998.tb00042.x.

Yang, C. S. (2018). An analysis of institutional pressures, green supply chain management, and green performance in the container shipping context. *Transportation Research Part D: Transport and Environment, 61*, 246–260. https://doi.org/10.1016/j.trd.2017.07.005.

Yang, C. S., Lu, C. S., Haider, J. J., & Marlow, P. B. (2013a). The effect of green supply chain management on green performance and firm competitiveness in the context of container shipping in Taiwan. *Transportation Research Part E: Logistics and Transportation Review, 55*, 55–73. https://doi.org/10.1016/j.tre.2013.03.005.

Yang, C. S., Lu, C. S., Xu, J., & Marlow, P. M. (2013b). Evaluating green supply chain management capability, environmental performance, and competitiveness in container shipping context.

Journal of the Eastern Asia Society for Transportation Studies, 10, 2274–2293. https://doi.org/10.11175/easts.10.2274.

Zhu, Q., & Sarkis, J. (2004). Relationships between operational practices and performance among early adopters of green supply chain management practices in Chinese manufacturing enterprises. *Journal of Operations Management, 22*(3), 265–289. https://doi.org/10.1016/j.jom.2004.01.005.

Global Data Exchange Standards: The Basis for Future Smart Container Digital Services

Hanane Becha ⓘ**, Michael Schröder** ⓘ**, Jaco Voorspuij** ⓘ**, Todd Frazier** ⓘ**, and Mikael Lind** ⓘ

1 Importance of International Standards Development

1.1 Introduction to the Smart Container

In this chapter, a "smart container" is generally considered to be a marine shipping container, which is fitted with a permanently installed monitoring device. However, for other modes of transport, such as air or road, a unit load device (ULD) is also

H. Becha (✉)
UN/CEFACT Transport and Logistics Vice Chair, Marseille, France
e-mail: hbecha@gmail.com

M. Schröder
Hapag-Lloyd AG, Hamburg, Germany
e-mail: Michael.Schroeder@hlag.com

J. Voorspuij
GS1 AISBL, Brussel, Belgium
e-mail: jaco.voorspuij@gs1.org

T. Frazier
FedEx Express, Los Angeles, CA, USA
e-mail: tcfrazier@fedex.com

M. Lind
Research Institutes of Sweden (RISE) and Chalmers University of Technology, Gothenburg, Sweden
e-mail: mikael@realsearchers.com

© The Editor(s) (if applicable) and The Author(s), under exclusive licence   293
to Springer Nature Switzerland AG 2021
M. Lind et al. (eds.), *Maritime Informatics*, Progress in IS,
https://doi.org/10.1007/978-3-030-50892-0_18

considered a container, which may be fitted with an attached monitoring device to convert it into a smart container.

The smart container solution could be based on various technical pillars:

- An active smart device fixed on a container or included in the container
- A platform collecting the data, processing it, and sharing with the different stakeholders
- A catalogue of APIs for easy integration of the physical data
- Various communication protocols including those wireless communications technologies enabling multi-hopping and collaboration between devices

A "smart device" has an embedded set of sensors enabling it to send out real-time information on location, door opening and closing, vibrations, temperature, humidity, and any measured physical parameters of the surrounding environment of the asset to a data collection centre. These tracking and monitoring devices can also be used to equip other types of assets such as wagons and trailers. Extra remote sensors could also be added/paired with the main smart device to address the specific needs of a given cargo consignment.

When smart container trip plans, cargo information, and other information are shared with smart container service providers, smart containers can differentiate business-as-usual conditions during the journey versus out-of-bounds conditions when certain measures exceed the configured thresholds, alerting stakeholders to take action (Becha, 2020b). For example, if a container is sealed prior to shipping, the smart container solution would alert the stakeholder if a door was opened during a journey.

The United Nations Economic Commission for Europe (UNECE) Trade Facilitation White Paper on Real-Time Smart Container data for supply chain excellence provides a detailed look into the various benefits of using smart containers as well as the various potential use cases for this technology (UNECE, 2019).

Smart container solutions empower supply chain stakeholders to enhance their operations using reliable physical data to provide door-to-door visibility and AI-based predictive services for deriving such things as estimated time of arrival (ETA) at any point along the route of the container. Smart container solutions increase the efficiency, safety, and ecological sustainability of the whole shipping industry.

1.2 Why Global Multimodal Data Exchange Standards Are Important for Usage of Smart Containers

Adoption of global multimodal data exchange standards is a win-win situation, since these standards guarantee interoperability. In fact, smart container standardisation effort (Becha, 2020a, 2020c) is one of many standardisation initiatives (Lind et al., 2020a) supporting global trade. Standards enable stakeholders in the logistics chain to reap the maximum benefits from smart container solutions, while enabling them to share data and associated costs. Standards-based data exchange usage increases the ability to collaborate, which in turn increases efficiency. Additionally, such standards reduce development and deployment costs and cut time to market for Internet of Things (IoT) solution providers.

Data exchange standards developed in an open process offer a useful aid to all parties interested in the technical applications and implementation of smart container solutions. Additionally, if solution providers find there are new data elements required to accommodate changing business requirements, it is possible to create a backwards-compatible revision of the standard to accommodate their needs.

With the ramp-up of new and emerging technologies, these standards are more necessary than ever. The risks of not developing or not following standards include:

- Proprietary technologies with significant deployment limitations
- Lack of interoperability among systems and devices
- Reduced capability for the international validation of technology deployment
- Costly and time-consuming integration
- Risk of vendor lock-in

Smart containers global, multimodal data exchange standards will accelerate the adoption of smart container solutions by the logistic chain stakeholders.

The United Nations Centre for Trade Facilitation and Electronic Business (UN/CEFACT) Smart Container Business Requirements Specification (BRS) ensures that the various ecosystem actors share a common understanding of smart container benefits by presenting various use cases. It also details the smart container data elements (UN/CEFACT, 2019). Defining the data elements that smart containers can generate accelerates integration and the use of smart container data on different platforms for the enhancement of operations. In addition, utilising standard smart container data enables open communications channels between supply chain actors.

There is a need for smart container data exchange standardisation to avoid the complexity of a multitude of interfaces such as the case of electrical outlets throughout the world (Fig. 1). Service providers may be limited in their ability to provide for all solutions for their customers in the absence of a global standard.

Many supply chain stakeholders are constantly enhancing their processes as they try to reach logistics excellence, and they are reviewing their stance towards their service providers in maritime transportation. More information on who they are, what forces are transforming their industries and what additional requirements they are now placing on maritime transportation is detailed in Voorspuij and Becha (2020). Standard data models and standard APIs would help stakeholders to make the necessary transformation to achieve supply chain excellence (Becha, 2019). Indeed, APIs are key to ensuring simplification and acceleration of the integration of digital services from various sources. Data sharing is particularly important in the logistic supply chain due to the large numbers of diverse players and because container movements are global (see also Voorspuij & Becha, 2020). Easy

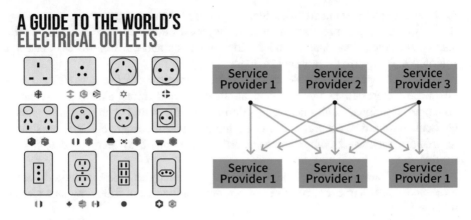

Fig. 1 Complexity with lack of standard interfaces

access to information for all relevant stakeholders enables situational awareness and empowers data-driven risk analysis and decision-making (c.f. Watson, Lind, Delmeire, & Liesa, 2020). Common situational awareness means that involved actors share the same conception of the same phenomenon (e.g. the status, progress and outcome of a particular process) (Lind, Simha, & Becha, 2020c). Smart container data and predictive services enable supply chain efficiency and improve collaboration between all stakeholders.

1.3   Standards Organisations: UN/CEFACT and Other Related Organisations

Standards, be they national, regional or global, are the fruit of collective efforts and guarantee interoperability. They can be revised to meet industry needs and remain relevant over time. Standards organisations, where participants from different segments of the industry gather, are among the few places where competitors work side by side. Standards organisations offer a safe place to do so from an anti-trust perspective. Standards development participants are industry experts, tech companies and customers representing all fields of the industry.

UN/CEFACT: Its Role and Framework
UN/CEFACT is a subsidiary intergovernmental body of the United Nations Economic Commission for Europe (UNECE) and a global standardisation organisation. UN/CEFACT's mission is to improve the ability of business, trade and administrative organisations from developed, developing and transitional economies to exchange products and relevant services effectively. Its principal focus is on facilitating national and international transactions through the simplification and harmonisation of processes, procedures and data flows.

Adoption of UN/CEFACT standards is voluntary. There are no legal requirements to adopt[1] them. However, if no standards are defined and used for smart containers, then smart container solution providers will have to develop different interfaces for each stakeholder, or at least do extra work mapping to and from their data elements. Under this scenario, customers might find themselves locked into a single device provider or needing significant additional effort to integrate smart container data from multiple solution providers.

UN/CEFACT experts have decades of experience in developing global standards. Their continually increasing Core Components Library (CCL) is a comprehensive catalogue of data elements interrelated by business context, which covers buying, shipping and payment processes. CCL is a cornerstone of the Smart Container Project. UN/CEFACT's open process attracts experts from intergovernmental organisations, individual country authorities and the business community to collaborate on standards development. The best-known standards are the UN/EDIFACT electronic data interchange (EDI) message standards used by organisations globally.

Currently, various organisations are working on industry-related standards based on the associated organisation-specific data models. Some are intergovernmental organisations such as the World Customs Organization (WCO) and the International Maritime Organization (IMO). These two organisations have distinct data models. However, efforts are ongoing to ensure that semantics for their data elements are consistent with UN/CEFACT CCL and reference data models.

Other Standards Organisations
In addition to UN/CEFACT, there are other standards development organisations (SDOs) working on standards that impact shipping and the maritime sector:

- Ship-planning Message Development Group (SMDG):[2] Works with UN/CEFACT Transport and Logistics Domain to define electronic data interchange (EDI) messages and will initiate work on APIs soon
- Digital Container Shipping Association (DCSA):[3] Focuses on driving standardisation, digitalisation and interoperability in container shipping to unify the ocean shipping industry and to "create value and to quickly overcome the pain points in the industry"
- International Air Transport Association (IATA);[4] Focuses on creation of global standards for airline safety, security, efficiency and sustainability
- GS1:[5] Focuses on providing a common language that ensures key processes run smoothly in several industries, including maritime

---

[1] Adopt assumes a willingness to implement from within their own processes.
[2] http://www.smdg.org/
[3] https://www.dcsa.org/
[4] https://www.iata.org/Pages/default.aspx
[5] https://www.gs1.org/

- International Standards Organisation (ISO):[6] An international standard-setting body composed of representatives from various national standards organisations, namely, the ISO/TC 104 freight containers committee and ISO/TC 204 Intelligent Transport Systems (ITS)/general fleet management and commercial/freight working groups.

2 UN/CEFACT Smart Container Project

2.1 UN/CEFACT Smart Container Development Methodology for Data Standards' Messaging and Communications

The UN/CEFACT Transport and Logistics Domain is a subgroup of UN/CEFACT, which initiated the Smart Container Project in January 2018. This project aims to promote the usage of multimodal transport using smart containers and to define the deliverables required for integrating smart container data into the different industry processes of stakeholders throughout the end-to-end supply chain (see Voorspuij & Becha, 2020).

The initial task was to define the data elements that would define these processes. The Smart Container Project will evolve to serve the whole ecosystem (Fig. 2). Each new project of the UN/CEFACT domain is based on its CCL or the appropriate subset such as the Multimodal Transport Reference Data Model (MMT). The CCL brings together the data exchange requirements of international multimodal transport processes including related trade, insurance, customs and other regulatory documentary requirements based on the integration of trade facilitation and e-Business best practices.

The UN/CEFACT CCL data model is extensible and can evolve to meet changing needs of buy/ship/pay process stakeholders. Smart container data elements and their associated semantic definitions will be used to enrich the UN/CEFACT CCL and the MMT (see Fig. 2 top right <New data-elements>). The MMT includes transport booking, transport ordering and freight invoicing processes, together with the actual transportation and the required border clearance processes-related data elements. Stakeholders can choose from and reuse data elements, as well as enrich the global reference data models (e.g. MMT) and the CCL as part of the UN/CEFACT standards development processes. The smart container efforts will provide all data elements needed to support messaging for the smart container use cases identified in the Business Requirements Specification (UN/CEFACT, 2019). Once data elements are agreed upon, the Smart Container Project will create contextualised, technology-agnostic notification message structures.

---

[6]https://www.iso.org/home.html

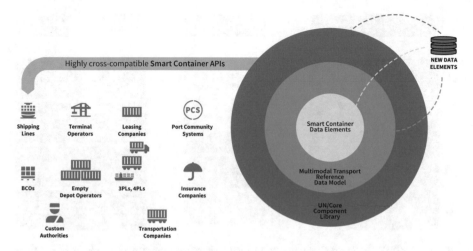

Fig. 2 Standard APIs based on standard UN/CEFACT data elements to better serve the whole ecosystem

The methodology of the UN/CEFACT Smart Container Project is based on four steps (Fig. 3):

1. *Identify stakeholders and the smart container services* that could enhance their business processes. Clear value propositions are described based on using smart container data related to different services. The UN/CEFACT first deliverable was a white paper that promotes the smart container and its use cases. Decision-makers in different organisations will find answers to questions such as "What is in it for me?" and "Why should I care?"
2. *Derive data elements,* to be exchanged by smart container solutions, from the use cases (outputs and inputs of the services). Some of these data elements are already part of the CCL, such as the consignor and the consignee. Other data elements are new, such as different physical parameters that smart containers have measured, and pairing information—the when, where, and by whom the tracking device was installed. Inputs for a smart container service include expected physical values or trip plan descriptions, enabling the smart container solution provider to generate alerts, measurements, and predictive values, such as ETA. The Smart Container Project selects data elements required from the CCL and defines the semantics for all the new smart container data elements (business definitions and data structures) and their relationships. The deliverable will be the UN/CEFACT smart container data model.
3. *Select a subset of data to define a contextualised message structure* to meet the requirements of a given use case. This message structure is technology-agnostic—independent from the technology that will be used to communicate the data.

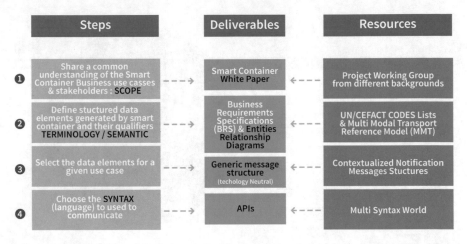

Fig. 3 UN/CEFACT Smart Container Project methodology—from data elements to APIs definition

4. *Define a specific syntax-based information exchange using a chosen technology*, which may result in API definitions or EDI message definitions based on standardised data elements.[7]

2.2 Smart Container Project Current Status

An official UN/CEFACT white paper completed in December 2018 defines the smart container solution ecosystem and the value of this service for each player (e.g. the actors and the various potential use cases for this technology). Subsequently, the Smart Container Business Requirements Specifications (BRS) was developed and published in September 2019. The BRS is an official global UN/CEFACT deliverable that explains the value proposition of different smart container use cases in detail, with the focus on data exchanges, values and formats. The BRS also clearly identifies that the more information a smart container service provider receives about the planned trip and the desired physical parameters values, the more value that can be obtained from the smart container investment (e.g. targeted alerts instead of simply periodic measurements).

---

[7]For the sake of simplification, as shown in Fig. 2, we "limit" the number of data elements from CCL in each step. However, in practice, the Smart Container Reference Data Model (RDM) uses CCL data elements that were not in the MMT. Furthermore, the smart container efforts have contributed a large number of new data elements that will prove valuable all over the buy/ship/pay model of UN/CEFACT.

At this stage, the focus is on finalising the smart container data model to meet the requirements as described in the developed BRS (e.g. developing class diagrams and an XML schema).

In addition to the Smart Container Project, in March 2020 the UN/CEFACT called for participation in a new project called "Cross Industry Supply Chain Track and Trace".[8] The project aims to develop the business cases and electronic messages necessary for tracing (monitoring the history) and tracking (monitoring the present and future movements) of an asset. A traceable asset can be any item (e.g. an object, a product or other traded item or a service) that needs to be tracked along a supply chain. The data exchanged concerns trade, transport and/or their products. The outputs will be the harmonised XML schemas to support business processes.

UN/CEFACT and other standardisation organisations will continue to develop and maintain standards for smart containers to ensure these will support the business requirements of stakeholders now and in future.

2.3   SOA Architecture Development Approach for the Smart Container Solution

In today's complex intermodal transport markets, it is difficult for any single player to gain total visibility of door-to-door cargo transport activity including physical location, condition, documents, processes and the required trade data for answering business questions or making a fully informed operational decision. This means that supply chain stakeholders need to share significant volumes of data from many different sources to be able to conduct their daily business (Haraldson et al., 2020). Stakeholders must integrate these data and feed it directly into their business processes. To enhance international trade and to take advantage of growing volumes of data, digitalisation and data sharing is required.

Application development paradigms are shifting from a traditional style, where applications are developed standalone from scratch to approaches where applications become services used as add-ons to primary programmes. The ability to plug and play different services and data sources is key to ensuring agile, cost-efficient development and continuous adaptation of composite services, using the service-oriented architecture (SOA) paradigm (Fig. 4), to satisfy changing business process requirements. SOA can support a consumer-centric approach (Becha, 2012; Becha & Amyot, 2008, 2015a, 2015b; Sellami & Becha, 2014, 2015a, 2015b) and simplify aligning business goals with IT architecture to provide a business real-time access to needed data.

SOA is not new at all. It captures multiple long-time best practises such as loosely coupling and agility. It seems "suddenly" to be very relevant for flexibility and

---

[8]https://uncefact.unece.org/display/uncefactpublic/Cross+Industry+Supply+Chain+Track+and+Trace+Project

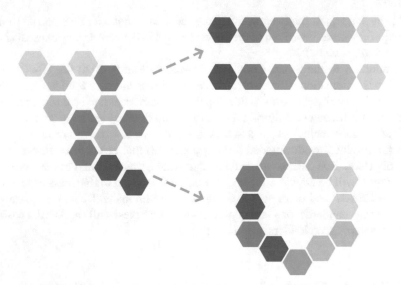

Fig. 4 SOA architecture paradigm—application development facilitating the ability to plug and play different services and data sources

easy integration, namely, with the increasing availability of IoT data and artificial intelligence (AI) based value-added services. SOA is technology agnostic and "will maintain its worth because it is always amenable to use in the newer Web technologies, for both development and integration".[9] Application designers can implement SOA using a wide range of technologies. Standards-based APIs become the perfect "glue" between different services that enable this integration paradigm and help prevent lock-in to single-vendor solutions.

Organisations may combine various component services (individual hexagons on the left of Fig. 4) to deliver composite solutions for various business requirements (the structures on the right of Fig. 4).[10]

Ultimately, technology should be adapted to meet the needs of the stakeholders and business processes and not the other way around.

A service is like a "black box". There is no need to understand or to master the internal logic of the service. The service description should convey what is accomplished when the service is invoked, according to the conditions for using the service. It also defines the service inputs, outputs, and associated semantics. What matters is the input and output data flow.

Semantics deal with the meaning of individual words and data elements, irrespective of the context. Syntax is the use of specific language based on programming

---

[9]https://searchapparchitecture.techtarget.com/feature/Old-SOA-versus-new-SOA-Open-APIs-change-the-game

[10]The same component services can combine in solutions for different business requirements.

or application grammar. API definition is the agreement of the data's syntax and semantics (see Voorspuij & Becha, 2020).

An SOA approach promotes sharing and reusing software components. Software applications are built by composing loosely coupled services, residing in the network and accessible via standardised protocols, into larger composite services, or applications. Hence, adoption of the SOA approach is significantly shifting traditional software development methodology. It often accelerates application development by an order of magnitude compared to the development time in current, long-established and tightly coupled, monolithic environments. In addition, the use of an SOA approach enables new business processes to be implemented quickly from existing services and allows those implementations to be adjusted rapidly to meet changing requirements.

The current state of the art is providing services that can be orchestrated and enriched to meet the business process needs of any actor in the transport and logistics ecosystem. The availability and the provision of these services can accelerate an industry's digital transformation and allow development of new applications and services. This establishes the need for a clear standard and collaboration between stakeholders.

The key is having independent services with defined standards-based APIs that can be called to perform their tasks in a standard way. The service does not need to know the calling application, and the calling application does not need to know how the service actually performs its tasks. An API-based strategy is key for episodic tightly coupled actors within the self-organised ecosystem of maritime transports (Watson et al., 2020) to handle interaction with different information hubs (Ward et al., 2020) along the maritime transport chain.

2.4   The Role of APIs

A service consumer can discover and choose API-based services from a service registry to create a composite service in response to particular business process needs (Fig. 5). The SOA approach allows consumers to perform service composition without having to develop or even understand the underlying service logic and implementation details of each component accessed via an API.

Services must be stripped of custom business logic or usage so they can be reused in different business domains. A service that implements a single company's business logic might be of little use to another. However, a service that implements generic business logic for a specific line of business should be interesting for all companies in that business domain.

A typical five-step process makes services available (Fig. 5). Service providers publish descriptions of their services in registries (Step 1). Once registries are available, service consumers can then query (Step 2) these registries to discover (Step 3) the available published services. They can then choose, invoke, and even

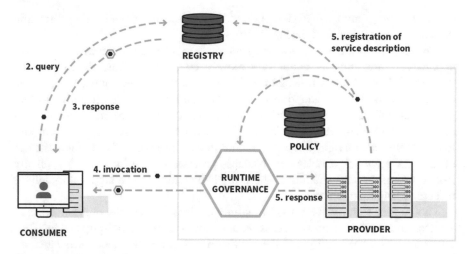

Fig. 5 Services and typical actions

compose services to meet their business process needs (Step 4). Once invoked, the service will perform its functionality and send a response, if required (Step 5).

SOA Principles:

- *Orchestration:* Your application becomes a composition of multiple third-party services (service consumer and a service provider) (Fig. 6).
- *Black boxes*: Third-party services provide specific functionalities (data set) when they are invoked.
- *Explicit boundaries*: Interfaces are key to exchanging data (input/output). APIs are the only way to communicate with an SOA service. This ensures loose coupling.
- *Standards interfaces:* APIs enable services to plug and play, avoiding vendor lock-in.[11]

Service providers may collect, monitor and manage smart container data, as well as commercialise required Internet of Things (IoT) devices and data transmission technologies (right half of Fig. 7). IoT devices are physical objects with embedded technology that sense, interact or communicate with their internal states or the external environment. Service providers also have the responsibility to expose smart container APIs that could be used by all stakeholders who have the right to access these data. Stakeholders may incorporate value-added services from several service providers into their supply chain solution (left side of Fig. 7).

---

[11] Vendor lock-in is a situation in which a customer using a product or service cannot easily transition to a competitor's product or service. Vendor lock-in is usually the result of proprietary technologies that are incompatible with those of its competitors.

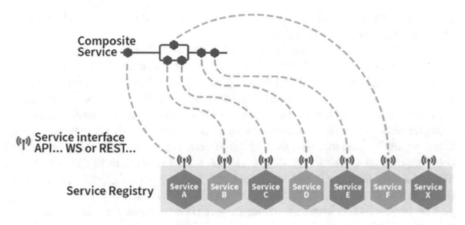

Fig. 6 SOA-based applications are composite services—to invoke a service or services, consumers need the API description(s)

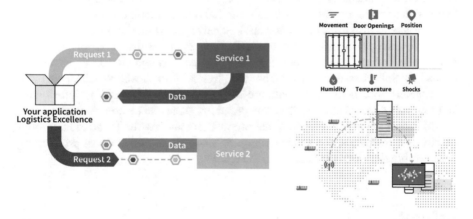

Fig. 7 Invoking value-added services using standard APIs

In the case of proprietary, rather than standardised API development, consumers are generally restricted to one solution provider. However, if we agree on API specifications standards, service(s) consumers have the option to select their desired service provider and to change relatively quickly and easily to another provider.

3 Conclusion

Smart containers will revolutionise the capture and timely reporting of data throughout the supply chains. Such containers are an essential building block to meet the emerging requirements for end-to-end supply chains (e.g. Lind et al., 2020b; Lind, Ward, Watson, et al., 2020a; Voorspuij & Becha, 2020). As leading carriers adopt smart container solutions, they gain valuable data that can be shared with shippers and other supply chain stakeholders.

However, generating and collecting data is not enough to make smart container solutions or supply chains "smart". Stakeholders already manage huge amounts of data and struggle with multiple technologies that take time away from their core businesses. A smart container solution must deliver data that matters, in a standard format for easy integration into different systems. It must enable unambiguous data interpretation and empower all involved stakeholders with actionable information. Clear semantic standards are essential for effective smart container data exchange ensuring that all stakeholders understand the same information in the same way. Then and only then can smart containers truly become part of digital data streams (Lind, Ward, Watson, et al., 2020a; Pigni, Piccoli, & Watson, 2016).

The UN/CEFACT Smart Container Project aims to create multimodal communications standards that can facilitate a state-of-the-art solution in providing and exposing services. Any intermodal ecosystem stakeholder may then orchestrate and enrich these services to meet their business process needs. The availability and exposition of these services can boost the digital transformation of the transportation and logistics industry, fuelling innovation in new applications and services.

Physical supply chains that move goods need a parallel digital supply chain that moves data describing the goods and their progress through the supply chain. The smart container data flows ensure that the physical flow is well synchronised with the required documents flow. Data are the raw material of Maritime Informatics. Without data streams emanating from operations, there can be no data analytics. As we digitalise, we improve operational productivity and lay the foundation, through Maritime Informatics, for another round of strategic and operational productivity based on big data analytics and machine learning.

References

Becha, H. (2012). *Exposing and aggregating non-functional properties in SOA from the perspective of the service consumer*. PhD Thesis, University of Ottawa Ottawa, ON, Canada. Retrieved from https://www.semanticscholar.org/paper/Exposing-and-aggregating-non-functional-properties-Amyot-Boukerche/2df699b1425526d4027d7ee8f4c5e197bad52b0b.

Becha, H. (2019). *How standard APIs open the door to powerful digital services*. Retrieved from https://hananebecha.home.blog/2019/11/28/the-un-cefact-smart-container-project/.

Becha, H. (2020a). *Standardization supporting global trade*. Port Technology International, Ed. 91. Retrieved from https://www.porttechnology.org/editions/shipping-2020-a-vision-for-tomorrow/.

Becha, H. (2020b). *The power of parameters in smart container solutions: Delivering data that matters, from periodic events to context-based alerts*. Retrieved from https://hananebecha.home.blog/2020/01/29/the-power-of-parameters-in-smart-container-solutions/.

Becha, H. (2020c, March). The UN/CEFACT Smart Container Project. *The magazine of international Institute of Marine Surveying*, Issue 91. Retrieved from https://www.iims.org.uk/wp-content/uploads/2020/02/The-Report-March-2020.pdf.

Becha, H., & Amyot, D. (2008). *Next generation service engineering* (pp. 195–202). IEEE Computer Society.

Becha, H., & Amyot, D. (2015a). Consented consumer-centric non-functional property description and composition for SOA-based applications. *International Journal of Web Engineering and Technology, 10*(4), 355. https://doi.org/10.1504/IJWET.2015.073949.

Becha, H., & Amyot, D. (2015b). *Consumer-centric non-functional properties of SOA-based services* (pp. 18–27). 6th International Workshop on Principles of Engineering Service-Oriented and Cloud Systems (PESOS 2014), Hyderabad, India, May 2014. ACM.

Haraldson, S., Lind, M., Breitenbach, S., Croston, J. C., Karlsson, M., & Hirt, G. (2020). The port as a set of socio-technical systems: A multi-organisational view (Chapter 4). In M. Lind, M. Michaelides, R. Ward, & R. T. Watson (Eds.), *Maritime informatics*. Heidelberg: Springer.

Lind, M., Ward, R., Watson, R. T., Haraldson, S., Zerem, A., & Paulsen, S. (2020a). Decision support for port visits (Chapter 11). In M. Lind, M. Michaelides, R. Ward, & R. T. Watson (Eds.), *Maritime informatics*. Heidelberg: Springer.

Lind, M., Ward, R., Hvid, J. H., Chua, C. P., Simha, A., Karlsson, J., Göthberg, L., & Penttinen, T. (2020b). The future of shipping – collaboration through digital data sharing (Chapter 9). In M. Lind, M. Michaelides, R. Ward, & R. T. Watson (Eds.), *Maritime informatics*. Heidelberg: Springer.

Lind, M., Simha, S., & Becha, H. (2020c). *Creating value for the transport buyer with Digital Data Streams*. The Maritime Executive. Retrieved from https://maritime-executive.com/editorials/creating-value-for-the-transport-buyer-with-digital-data-streams.

Pigni, F., Piccoli, G., & Watson, R. T. (2016). Digital data streams: Creating value from the real-time flow of big data. *California Management Review, 58*(3), 5–25.

Sellami, S., & Becha, H. (2014). *Prioritizing consumer-centric NFPs in service selection* (pp. 283–292). Advances in Conceptual Modeling, Proceedings (WISM 2014), Demos, Atlanta, GA, October 27–29, 2014.

Sellami, S., & Becha, H. (2015a). *Web services discovery based on semantic tag* (pp. 465–472). On the Move to Meaningful Internet Systems, Proceedings (ODBASE 2015), Confederated International Conferences: CoopIS, ODBASE, and C&TC 2015, Rhodes, Greece.

Sellami, S., & Becha, H. (2015b). *WSTP: Web Services Tagging Platform* (pp. 486–490). Service-Oriented Computing – 13th International Conference, Proceedings (ICSOC 2015), Goa, India. Retrieved from https://link.springer.com/chapter/10.1007%2F978-3-662-48616-0_35.

UN/CEFACT. (2019). *The UN/CEFACT Smart Container Business Specifications (BRS)*. Retrieved from https://www.unece.org/fileadmin/DAM/cefact/brs/BRS-SmartContainer_v1.0.pdf.

UNECE. (2019). *The UNECE Trade Facilitation White Paper on Real-time Smart Container data for supply chain excellence*. ECE/Trade/446. Retrieved from https://www.unece.org/index.php?id=53347.

Voorspuij, J., & Becha, H. (2020). Digitalisation in maritime regional and global supply chains (Chapter 5). In M. Lind, M. Michaelides, R. Ward, & R. T. Watson (Eds.), *Maritime informatics*. Heidelberg: Springer.

Ward, R., Gahnström, J., Hägg, M., Olindersson, F., Lind, M., & Green, S. (2020). Decision support for voyaging (Chapter 12). In M. Lind, M. Michaelides, R. Ward, & R. T. Watson (Eds.), *Maritime informatics*. Heidelberg: Springer.

Watson, R. T., Lind, M., Delmeire, N., & Liesa, F. (2020). Shipping: A self-organising ecosystem (Chapter 2). In M. Lind, M. Michaelides, R. Ward, & R. T. Watson (Eds.), *Maritime informatics*. Heidelberg: Springer.

Part III
Maritime Informatics Technology

Michalis Michaelides

Smart sensor technologies and the digitalisation of data are transforming today's world including the maritime sector (Aslam et al., 2020). Ships are currently becoming equipped with hundreds of sensors for monitoring various parameters of interest related to the physical environment in which a vessel is operating (weather, temperature, sea conditions, etc.), as well as the characteristics and state of the vessel, while wearable devices that can indicate the physiological and mental condition of the crew are possibilities, too. Ports are also becoming equipped with advanced monitoring systems and tracking technologies which allow port authorities to provide essential services in a faster and more efficient manner using various sensors, such as inertial sensors, ultrasonic sensors, eddy current sensors, radar, LiDAR, imaging sensors and RFID readers and tags. The "Ocean of Things" project at the US Defence Advanced Research Projects Agency (DARPA) aims to likewise wire up the high seas with swarms of floating, connected sensors (Anderson, 2020). The collected data from these various sensors includes both spatial and temporal information, as they can be linked both with a geographical location and the time of occurrence of a specific event. To extract useful information from the data, we need to have in place appropriate techniques for *data acquisition*, *management*, *analysis* and *visualisation*. Such intelligent algorithms will empower human users to "*make sense*" of the *spatial-temporal*[1] data and provide enhanced decision support.

In this section of the book, more details are provided on each of these important dimensions of dealing with spatial-temporal data. The chapters outline what is

---

[1] In the following, the terms "spatial-temporal" and "spatiotemporal" will be used interchangeably.

M. Michaelides
Department of Electrical Engineering, Computer Engineering and Informatics, Cyprus University of Technology, Limassol, Cyprus

considered state of the art in each of these areas with respect to the underlying technology and how it can be tailored to the needs of the maritime world.

Chapter "Big Maritime Data Management" provides an extensive overview of the maritime data value chain and discusses state-of-the-art technological solutions for managing and processing maritime data in efficient and effective ways. The maritime data value chain defines the series of activities needed to appropriately manage data during the entire lifecycle of data as well as to extract value and useful insights from maritime data. The four key activities identified are (1) data acquisition for collecting data across different and geographically dispersed data sources; (2) data pre-processing for transforming, integrating and assessing the quality of the data; (3) data storage for storing data in a persistent and scalable way; and (4) data usage for processing the data and extracting value.

Chapter "Spatiotemporal Data Analytics for the Maritime Industry" presents the state of the art in spatiotemporal analytics and provides an overview of its practical applications in the maritime industry. Having the right information at the right time is a key ingredient to creating value for any business, and the maritime industry is no different. From optimising vessels routes and preparing ports for efficient operations to reducing pollution and saving the environment, data analytics makes a difference for various maritime industry stakeholders. The described scenarios are (1) long-term route planning, (2) environment preservation, (3) collision avoidance, (4) cargo tracking and (5) port call optimization.

Chapter "Data Visualisation Tools for Enhanced Situational Awareness in Maritime Operations" elaborates on how to create meaningful data visualisations providing decision support to enable distributed coordination in self-organised ecosystems involving multiple actors. Much of the data benefits from being visualised for specific needs, such as in the coordination of port call operations where the multitude of actors, constituting a self-organised ecosystem, sharing data amongst themselves to create situational awareness based on secure digital data streams. This means presenting shared data in real-time in a standardised format to generate value for the maritime industry. As port call operations are complex and engage multiple actors, different visualisation tools are useful to address the many concerns raised by the different actors.

Chapter "Intelligent Maritime Information Acquisition and Representation for Decision Support" reviews technological advancements in intelligent information acquisition and representation to aid human users and organisations make sense of the complex maritime environment. Human and environmental processes in the maritime environment are becoming increasingly complex due to the intensification of human activity and its impact on the natural environment. Adequately representing these complex and changing processes requires novel agile methods of data collection and interpretation. Data acquisition and representation methods need to adapt to specific purposes by identifying mission-specific information while operating under resource constraints with the goal to provide meaningful representations of requested information to humans for effective decision support.

Chapter "AIS Data Analytics for Intelligent Maritime Surveillance Systems" first reviews maritime traffic surveillance systems for spatial-temporal data collection. Then a computational framework is presented to efficiently compress, transfer and acquire necessary information for the further analysis of large-scale AIS data composed of two parts: (1) a lossless compression algorithm that compresses AIS data into binary form and (2) an aggregation algorithm which derives movement and activity information of vessels grouped by grid or time window from the compressed binary files. Finally, a use case of maritime big data intelligent surveillance is described briefly.

References

Aslam, S., Michaelides, M., & Herodotou, H (2020, May 8). Internet of ships: A survey on architectures, emerging applications, and challenges. *IEEE Internet of Things Journal (Special Issue on IoT for Smart Ocean)*. https://doi.org/10.1109/JIOT.2020.2993411.

Anderson, C. (2020, March 14). American researchers want to fill the oceans with sensors. *The Economist*. https://www.economist.com/science-and-technology/2020/03/14/american-researchers-want-to-fill-the-oceans-with-sensors.

Big Maritime Data Management

Herodotos Herodotou ⓘ, **Sheraz Aslam** ⓘ, **Henrik Holm** ⓘ,
and Socrates Theodossiou ⓘ

1 Maritime Data Value Chain

Modern maritime equipment constructors, ship owners and agents, transport and logistics companies, and port authorities are collecting enormous amounts of heterogeneous data at an unprecedented scale and pace. Almost all kinds of vessels are now equipped not only with satellite positioning sensors for collecting positioning information, but also sensor devices recording ship performance, condition, temperature, and humidity (Lytra, Vidal, Orlandi, & Attard, 2017). AIS (Automatic Identification System) data involving the position, course, and speed of vessels travelling on the ocean is openly available and mandatory for ships of over 300 gross tonnage and all passenger vessels. MarineTraffic, an AIS vessel tracking web site, reports collecting 520 million AIS messages daily involving 180 thousand distinct vessels from 3000 active AIS stations worldwide (Perobelli, 2016). Port authorities and various port actors (e.g., cargo terminals, tug operators) are also collecting port call data related to the activities of arrival, berthing, loading/unloading, shifting, anchorage, and departure of ships from ports (Michaelides, Herodotou, Lind, & Watson, 2019). From an environmental perspective, various sensors are also being deployed at sea, recording data related to various oceanographic, environmental,

H. Herodotou (✉) · S. Aslam
Cyprus University of Technology, Limassol, Cyprus
e-mail: herodotos.herodotou@cut.ac.cy; sheraz.aslam@cut.ac.cy

H. Holm
Svenska Beräkningsbyrån AB, Torslanda, Gothenburg, Sweden
e-mail: henrik@berakningsbyran.se

S. Theodossiou
Tototheo Maritime, Limassol, Cyprus
e-mail: Socrates@tototheo.com

M. Lind et al. (eds.), *Maritime Informatics*, Progress in IS,
https://doi.org/10.1007/978-3-030-50892-0_19

and meteorological parameters of interest, with data volumes reaching up to 5 GB per day (Lytra et al., 2017).

As more data is acquired, stored, and analysed, all maritime stakeholders are focusing on performing timely and cost-effective analytical processing for generating value and deep insights to automate various decision-making processes. Analytical processing is already driving several new application scenarios with significant impact across the maritime industry such as optimising marine transport and preventing accidents (Zhao, Li, Feng, Ochieng, & Schuster, 2014), improving fuel consumption (Beşikçi, Arslan, Turan, & Ölçer, 2016), optimising port operational efficiency (Yang et al., 2018), environment preservation and monitoring (Akyuz, Ilbahar, Cebi, & Celik, 2017), and real-time cargo tracking (Yeoh et al., 2011).

The **maritime data value chain** defines the series of activities needed to appropriately manage data during the entire data life-cycle as well as to extract value and useful insights from maritime data (Cavanillas, Curry, & Wahlster, 2016; Ferreira et al., 2017). The European Commission considers the data value chain to be 'the centre of the future knowledge economy, bringing the opportunities of the digital developments to the more traditional sectors (e.g., transport, financial services, health, manufacturing, retail)' (DGConnect, 2013). In the maritime domain, four key activities are identified: (1) *Data Acquisition* for collecting the data across different and geographically-dispersed data sources; (2) *Data Pre-processing* for transforming, integrating, and assessing the quality of the data; (3) *Data Storage* for storing data in a persistent and scalable way; and (4) *Data Usage* for processing the data and extracting value. Figure 1 outlines the main activities that comprise the maritime data value chain.

Data Acquisition is the process of collecting data from several sources before it is stored in a data warehouse or some other storage system (Curry, 2016). The maritime data sources generate structured, semi-structured, and unstructured data about ships, routes and trajectories, port operations, fishing and maritime biodiversity, oceans, and environmental conditions (Ferreira et al., 2017). This data is often spatiotemporal in nature, including both a geographical position and a time component, while it is reported in various formats such as GeoJSON, KML, CSV,

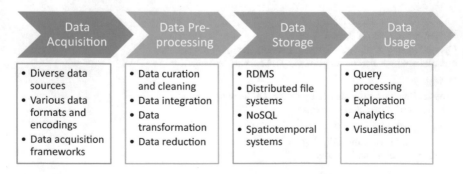

Fig. 1 The maritime data value chain

or RDF. The new data generated by each source is collected using a data acquisition framework following the message queuing, publish/subscribe, or event processing paradigms (Curry, 2016). The data acquisition process is described in Sect. 2.

Data Pre-processing consists of a set of methods for transforming, linking, and cleaning the data to make certain that it meets the desired data quality requirements for its effective usage (Yablonsky, 2018). Data, depending on the source and communication link characteristics, can suffer from a variety of faults including noise, outliers, and bias. Furthermore, certain parts of the data may be entirely missing due to a faulty communication link or sensor. Various data cleaning and reconstruction techniques are used for removing faulty data as well as replacing missing data. After cleaning the data from each source individually, data integration techniques are used for combining data based on a common timeline and frame of reference in order to identify and exclude inconsistent data. This involves dealing with cases of delayed data, or an out-of-order sequence, or having different sampling rates. Finally, data integration also aims at increasing data interoperability via linking existing repositories of relevant scientific open data with raw maritime data coming from the various sources (Lytra et al., 2017). The data pre-processing methods are categorised and detailed in Sect. 3.

Data Storage refers to technological solutions for storing data in a way to ensure data persistence, consistency, availability, and scalability (Ferreira et al., 2017). These solutions often rely on partitioning, distribution, compression, and indexing of data for ensuring applications have fast and easy access to the data. While relational database management systems (RDBMS) are widely used for storing maritime data, the semi- or unstructured nature of data as well as the prominent spatiotemporal component of data are challenging the status quo. NoSQL technologies (e.g., MongoDB, HBase, Cassandra) have been designed for supporting more flexible data models while storing the data in more scalable ways. At the same time, specialised spatial or spatiotemporal systems such as PostGIS and GeoMesa have emerged for dealing with such type of data efficiently and effectively. Data storage solutions are presented in Sect. 4.

Data Usage involves query processing, analytics, and visualisation techniques and tools for accessing the underlying maritime data and generating value for various data-driven business activities. Query processing may involve browsing, searching, reporting, finding correlations, identifying patterns, and predicting relations across maritime data (Curry, 2016). Several query processing engines offer declarative or scripting languages and different execution methods for managing and processing data over different infrastructures and data models. Section 5 discusses query processing while the next two chapters cover data analytics and visualisation.

2   Data Acquisition

Data acquisition is the first fundamental phase of the maritime data value chain (recall Fig. 1) and involves the processes of (1) identifying the relevant data sources such as port calls, AIS stations, Internet of Things (IoT) devices, and weather stations (Sect. 2.1), (2) collecting the structured, semi-structured, and/or unstructured data in various formats and encodings (Sect. 2.2), and (3) employing a data acquisition framework for gathering and delivering information (Sect. 2.3).

2.1   Data Sources

The maritime domain includes a wide variety of heterogeneous data sources that complement each other and generate data about port visits, vessel routes and trajectories, sensory information about equipment, as well as oceans and environmental conditions (Lytra et al., 2017).

Port Operations Systems Port community, transport, and logistics systems are considered an important source of maritime data related to the activities of arrival, berthing, loading/unloading, shifting, anchorage, and departure of ships from ports. Examples of such data include arrival/departure timestamps, cargo information, crew lists, customs declarations, and much more. The data tend to be structured or semi-structured in nature and fairly accurate as it is often used to calculate port fees and other commercial operations (Rødseth, Perera, & Mo, 2016).

AIS Stations AIS is an automatic tracking system installed on vessels and used primarily by vessel traffic services (VTS). AIS allows maritime stakeholders to monitor and track vessel movements in real time within the range of very high frequency (VHF) radios on base stations located along coastlines or satellites. An AIS module typically contains a standardised VHF transceiver, a positioning system (e.g., global navigation satellite system (GNSS) receiver), and other navigation sensors (e.g., gyrocompass). AIS data is transmitted by ships every 3–10 s encoded in a specialised format and contains information about the vessel (e.g., unique identification, name, flag, type, dimension), the current status (e.g., longitude, latitude, speed, heading), and its voyage (e.g., destination, estimated time of arrival, draught). It is estimated that over 520 million vessel positions are recorded and processed daily (Perobelli, 2016).

Sensing Devices In the current maritime era, most of the ships and ports are connected with IoT devices containing an array of sensors that generate a huge amount of data in real time. For instance, modern vessels use built-in sensors, advanced dynamic position systems, control systems, navigational sensor systems, etc., to enable automatic fault detection and preemptive maintenance, cargo tracking, and energy-efficient operations. IoT-based sensors are also used in containers for monitoring and maintaining temperature and humidity to ensure the viability of perishable goods.

Oceanic and Weather Stations Various decisions in the shipping sector, such as route planning and voyage optimisation, are directly impacted by oceanic and weather data as discussed in Chapter 22 (Kyriakides, Hayes, & Tsiantis, 2020). Such data typically includes temperature, humidity, wind speed, rainfall, sea currents, tidal variations, and wave characteristics. Usually, the maritime industry forecasts weather information using ensemble models, historical data, and current measurements. Historical weather data is available online and comes in various formats and resolutions. However, this data is less beneficial in areas where weather phenomena are affected by small-scale geographic features such as being near the coast or within narrow ocean currents (Rødseth et al., 2016).

2.2 Data Formats and Encodings

Various data formats and encodings are used for both storing and exchanging maritime data. The various formats have been developed targeting different objectives and are often used for specific applications. Some of the most common formats are:

- **Network Common Data Form (NetCDF)** is a set of machine-independent data formats employed to create, share, and access array-oriented scientific data. One of its key features is that the underlying data structure, the variable names, and necessary metadata are embedded with the actual data. NetCDF is commonly used in various oceanography and GIS applications, including weather forecasting and climate change.
- **Geospatial data interchange format based on JSON (GeoJSON)** is an open standard format based on the popular JSON format and it is used to describe simple geographical features, along with non-spatial attributes (Gelernter & Maheshwari, 2019). GeoJSON is a widely used format, especially for map visualisations and other map-related functionalities.
- **Geography Markup Language (GML)** is an XML-based modelling language for representing geographical features in a standard fashion, including their properties and interrelationships. In addition to geometric properties, GML can represent physical entities (e.g., ships, rivers) and sensor data that may or may not have geometric aspects. Finally, GML also serves as an open interchange format for online geographic transactions.
- **Keyhole Markup Language (KML)** is another XML-based language used primarily for the visualisation of geographic information on two or three dimensional maps. It was made popular by its use on Google Earth. Even though the KML grammar has several similarities with the GML grammar, the two formats are not compatible with each other.

- **Parquet**, **RCFile**, and **ORC** are open-source column-oriented data formats that are widely used within the Apache Hadoop ecosystem. These formats are optimised for large streaming reads of specific data columns, but also support finding required rows quickly. In addition, these formats typically offer very efficient compression and enable fast query processing.

2.3   Data Acquisition Frameworks

Most data acquisition frameworks follow the message queuing, publish/subscribe, or event processing paradigms for collecting new data generated by the data sources and sending it to the data storage system (Lyko, Nitzschke, & Ngomo, 2016). Internally, the data acquisition frameworks typically implement a predefined protocol. While several organisations have devised their own proprietary, enterprise-specific protocols, a few open protocols have been widely adopted over the last few years.

The **Advanced Message Queuing Protocol (AMQP)** (Kramer, 2009) was the result of a collaboration among 23 companies aiming to compile a protocol that (1) is easily extensible and simple to implement; (2) allows message encryption; (3) has reliable failure semantics; (4) can support different messaging patterns (e.g., direct messaging, publish/subscribe); (5) is independent of specific implementations or vendors. To enable these features, AMQP relies on four key layers, namely the transport, messaging, transaction, and security layers. According to the transport layer, messages originate from sender nodes, are forwarded by relay nodes, and consumed by receiver nodes. The messaging layer is responsible for ensuring the structure of valid messages, while the transaction one controls the transfers between senders and receivers. Finally, the security layer enables the encryption of messages.

There are several data acquisition frameworks that are employed to collect, access, and share data in the maritime industry. **Apache Kafka** (Apache Kafka, 2019) is a distributed publish-subscribe messaging system designed to transfer data from various sources to downstream storage systems for batch processing or real-time processing with stream engines. Hence, Kafka enables using a single data pipeline for both offline and online data consumers. Kafka also provides mechanisms for data partitioning as well as parallel load into Hadoop-compatible systems. **Apache Flume** (Apache Flume, 2019) is another open-source system specialised in collecting, aggregating, and moving large amounts of log data from multiple sources into a single (often distributed) data storage system. Flume has a flexible architecture based on streaming data flows and supports a variety of failover and recovery mechanisms (Cavanillas et al., 2016).

3 Data Pre-processing

Data pre-processing is an essential step in the maritime big data value chain in order to enable effective data exploration and data analysis. The data pre-processing pipeline, illustrated in Fig. 2, consists of (1) data curation and cleaning to ensure the quality of the data (Sect. 3.1); (2) data integration to efficiently link heterogeneous data (Sect. 3.2); (3) data transformation to simplify or speedup further analysis (Sect. 3.3); (4) data reduction to reduce the amount of data needed for analysis (Sect. 3.4).

3.1 Data Curation and Cleaning

The potential impact of data analysis depends heavily on the quality of the underlying data used for the analysis. For instance, if dirty data (i.e., data polluted with misspellings, truncations, corruptions, unexpected notations, and other irregularities) is not properly cleaned before analysis, then the quality of the data analysis will suffer. Hence, data quality issues can have a major impact on data management operations, particularly on the decision-making phase of any organisation (Curry, Freitas, & O'Riáin, 2010). In order to maximise data utilisation, data curation provides technological and methodological data management support by enhancing the quality of the data. Data curation is defined as 'the active and on-going management of data through its life-cycle of interest and usefulness; curation activities enable data discovery and retrieval, maintain quality, add value, and provide for reuse over time' (Cragin, Heidorn, Palmer, & Smith, 2007). In

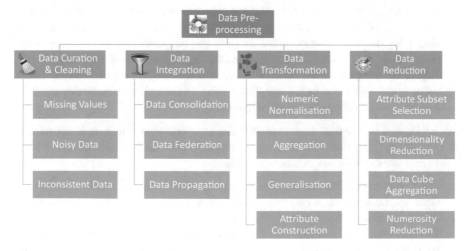

Fig. 2 Taxonomy for data pre-processing techniques

simple terms, curation is a key activity for managing and promoting the data usage from its point of creation and for ensuring the quality of the data for future purposes or reuse.

With reference to the maritime industry, several data management methods focus on AIS data cleaning tasks. There are several issues with AIS data related to the fact that it is a 30-year old technology that was not designed for large-scale acquisition (Holm & Mellegård, 2018; Svanberg, Santén, Hörteborn, Holm, & Finnsgård, 2019). Firstly, AIS messages may get lost or become corrupt during the unsecured VHF transmission. Secondly, some message fields, such as the next port destination and estimated time of arrival, are manually entered by officers on the bridge and thus frequently contain inconsistent or non-standardised values. In addition, the timestamps associated with AIS messages are recorded by AIS stations and, unless they are in the same time zone and time-synced, can often lead to time discrepancies that cause a ship's record to skip in time. Finally, AIS contains a lot of special cases that need to be handled carefully, such as the 'UTC second' field allowing the values 0–59 (as expected) and the value 61 to indicate that there is something wrong with the GNSS.

In general, data cleaning is the process of managing and maintaining accurate, clean, and consistent data through identification and removal of duplicate or inaccurate data. There are three key tasks in data cleaning: (1) fill missing values, (2) smooth out noisy data, and (3) correct inconsistent data (Han, Pei, & Kamber, 2011).

Missing Values Sometimes, data values are missed during recording due to, for example, faulty equipment, power outages, or unreliable network transfers. There exist several data cleaning techniques used to handle missing values, including:

- Manually entering missing values, which can be time-consuming and not scalable for large datasets with too many missing values;
- Replacing missing values with the same predefined constant, which represents either a real default value or a special value to indicate that it is unknown;
- Replacing missing values with the mean value computed from all the other values observed so far or from values observed during a specific time interval;
- Replacing missing values with the most probable one, which can be determined using some inference-based technique such as Bayesian inference or machine learning (e.g., regression, neural networks).

Noisy Data Distorted or corrupted data that may contain meaningless information is considered noisy data. The three main methods that can be used to remove noise from data are the following (Han et al., 2011):

- **Binning:** This method sorts and distributes the data into equi-width buckets/bins. Data smoothing is then performed by replacing the values in each bin by either the bin's median, mean, or boundary value.
- **Regression:** This method smooths noisy data by fitting it into a regression function. Linear regression and multiple regression are often used for fitting the data and smoothing out the noise.

- **Clustering:** This method groups similar values into clusters and marks the values that fall outside the clusters as outliers.

Inconsistent Data Inconsistencies in the recorded data for some entries can be rectified manually by external references. For example, inconsistencies or mistakes in textual entries such as the manually entered port destination field in AIS signals can be rectified using natural language processing techniques or matching against known data sources (e.g., the list of ports worldwide) (Abdallah, Iphar, Arcieri, & Jousselme, 2019). Moreover, knowledge engineering tools (i.e., software applications defined by domain experts for a specific purpose) can be used to find inconsistencies in known data constraints. For instance, known functional dependencies among attributes can be exploited to find values that contradict the functional constraints (Malik, Goyal, & Sharma, 2010).

3.2   Data Integration

The process of data integration involves combining and merging data originating from several sources into a single, organised, and coherent view, often in a data warehouse. Data integration is considered a key component of various mission-critical projects of data management, such as building an enterprise data warehouse for a maritime organisation, migrating data from single or multiple databases to a new destination in order to organise data in a coherent way, and synchronising data among several applications (Wang et al., 2016). Consequently, there exists a variety of data integration techniques exploited by the maritime industry to merge data from different sources (e.g., AIS data, port call data) to create a single unified view. This section provides an overview of three key data integration techniques, namely data consolidation, data federation, and data propagation. Furthermore, data integration techniques are adapted based on the complexity, heterogeneity, and volume of involved data sources.

1. **Data consolidation** refers to the process of consolidating/combining data from various sources into a centralised and single destination data repository. This unified data repository is then utilised for different purposes like data analysis. Moreover, it can also serve as a data source for downstream applications. There are two operational paradigms for data consolidation: batch and inline (Loshin, 2010). The batch paradigm gathers snapshots of datasets into a single location (e.g., a temporary location or the unified database), and then performs on them a variety of consolidation tasks such as parsing, standardisation, blocking, and matching. The inline paradigm employs some of the consolidation tasks as soon as new data enters the system within the operational services of the system. For example, new data instances are parsed and standardised on the fly before being compared and/or consolidated with existing data instances already stored in the centralised repository. Overall, data consolidation methods minimise inefficiencies in data management systems, like duplication of data, cost related

to reliance on several databases, and maintaining multiple data management points.

2. **Data federation** is another technique of data integration, which is employed to consolidate data and simplify access for end-users and front-end applications. In this technique, distributed data with different data models is integrated into a virtual database that features a unified data model. This means that there is no physical data integration involved behind the virtual database. Rather, a uniform user interface is created by data abstraction for accessing and retrieving data. Consequently, when an application and/or database users query the federated virtual database, the query is decomposed and sent to the relevant underlying data source. Hence, unlike a centralised data repository, data federation provides on-demand data access to users and applications for data stored in various repositories.

3. **Data propagation** is opted for data integration when data is distributed from one or multiple enterprise data sources to one or several local access databases. Data warehouses need to organise a huge amount of data on a daily basis. They may start with a small amount of data and start growing day by day via continuously receiving and sharing data from/to different data sources. Data warehouses, data stores, and operational databases are becoming indispensable tools in today's organisations. These data sources need to be continuously updated and the update process often involves shifting data from one system to another. To make the shifting process more efficient, the moves need to be performed in batches within a brief period without affecting the performance, i.e., the availability of data from the warehouse. To tackle the above-mentioned issues, there exist several technologies used for data propagation such as enterprise data replication (EDR), enterprise application integration (EAI), and bulk extract (Alguliyev, Aliguliyev, & Hajirahimova, 2016). Furthermore, big data integration solutions are remarkably efficient compared to traditional methods of data integration in the maritime industry and offer multiple features to support large volume, huge data diversity, and high speed of data retrieval (Dong & Srivastava, 2013).

3.3   Data Transformation

Data transformation is the process of converting data formats and structures into other forms that are more appropriate for data storage or data mining. The plurality of data formats that appear in the maritime industry has culminated the use of a variety of data transformation techniques, including the following:

1. **Numeric normalisation** involves scaling attribute data to fall within a predefined range, such as between 0 and 1. Two common forms of normalisation are min-max normalisation, which uses the minimum and maximum values to perform the transformation, and z-score normalisation, which uses the mean and standard deviation to transform the values.

2. **Aggregation** applies various operations on data in order to present information in summary form, and it is particularly useful for performing statistical analysis. For instance, the data from daily ship arrivals at a specific port can be aggregated to calculate weekly or monthly statistics. Aggregation is often employed to construct a data cube for analysing the data at multiple granularities (Han et al., 2011).
3. **Generalisation** refers to the process of replacing the low-level or primitive data with higher-level concepts by using concept hierarchies (Narang, Kumar, & Verma, 2017). For instance, numerical attributes describing the size of vessels can be generalised to the higher-level concepts, like small, medium, and large vessels.
4. **Attribute construction** is utilised to construct new attributes from a given set of values in order to enhance accuracy and to assist the data mining procedure (Malik et al., 2010). For instance, we can add the attribute *'area'* for any maritime object, like the waiting area at a port terminal, based on the attributes *'length'* and *'width'*. By combining various attributes, new information can be discovered and analysed.

3.4   Data Reduction

A data warehouse may store terabytes or sometimes petabytes of data and, hence, it can be very time-consuming to perform data analysis operations on the raw data. Data reduction methods can be applied to attain a reduced form of data, which is smaller than the original data but still maintain the key properties of the dataset. In this way, mining on the reduced data offers more efficiency and produces the same or very similar statistical results (Narang et al., 2017). There exist various data reduction strategies, the most common of which are explained below:

1. **Attribute subset selection:** Sometimes, data contains hundreds of attributes, some of which may be irrelevant to the data analysis or mining task. For instance, suppose the task is to classify or compute statistics for the arrived vessels at a port based on the country or region of origin. In this case, some attributes are irrelevant, such as the ship name, ship type, etc. Hence, the key objective of attribute subset selection is to select the relevant attributes to make the data mining process more efficient. Heuristic and meta-heuristic algorithms are often employed for attribute selection because of their lower time complexity (Min & Xu, 2016).
2. **Dimensionality reduction:** In dimensionality reduction, data encoding is applied in order to achieve a reduced size of the original data. If the original dataset can be reconstructed from a compressed dataset without losing any information, it is called lossless data reduction. On the contrary, if some information is lost during reconstructing the original dataset, then it is called lossy data reduction. Principal components analysis and discrete wavelet

transform are common procedures that can lead to lossy data reduction (Cunningham & Ghahramani, 2015).
3. **Data cube aggregation:** Data aggregation operations to construct multi-dimensional data cubes can also lead to data reduction. For instance, consider a dataset that contains a daily report of arriving and departing vessels at a port. However, suppose the task at hand involves generating reports of monthly and annual vessel traffic at the port. Aggregation operations can be performed to get a dataset that is smaller in volume but still contains the necessary information to complete the task (Narang et al., 2017). Data cubes store data in multi-dimensional arrays, making it efficient to access specific values with fixed offsets instead of moving across tables, and thus can greatly assist the data analysis tasks.
4. **Numerosity reduction:** The volume of data can also be reduced by exploiting alternative, more condensed data representations. These representations can be either parametric (where a model is employed to capture the data characteristics and thus only the model parameters are needed) or non-parametric (e.g., samples, clusters, sketches, histograms).

4 Data Storage

Storage of large-scale data is a flourishing area that has gained a lot of attention in the last decade, both commercially and from academia (Kokkinakos et al., 2017). Especially in the maritime domain, where a lot of sensors are used on board ships and generate vast volumes, efficient and reliable storage methods are needed to ensure data quality, scalability, and availability (Ferreira et al., 2017). Usually, data is stored in various formats that are feasible for fast sequential-logging, without any indexing or other analytics capabilities (Wang et al., 2016). For instance, due to small storage requirements and fast loading times, CSV (comma separated values), Matlab data files, or custom binary files are typically used to store the data. However, linear algorithms are required for every basic operation while using these data formats. Basic operations include the selection of data during a specific time window, column selection, finding specific values, etc. Apart from the traditional data warehouses, in the current technology era, distributed file systems (Sect. 4.1), NoSQL data stores (Sect. 4.2), and spatiotemporal systems (Sect. 4.3) are considered the latest storage technologies and are explained in detail below. Table 1 offers a comparison between the different data storage technologies.

4.1 Distributed File Systems

A distributed file system (DFS) is employed to build a hierarchical view of multiple file servers and to persistently store files on a set of nodes, which are connected

Table 1 Comparison of different data storage technologies

System category	Example systems	Description	Benefits	Limitations
Distributed file systems	HDFS, NFS, AFS, NetWare	Clients and storage resources are dispersed in the network and the goal is to provide a common view of a unified file system, even though it has a distributed implementation. Data are stored in files of various formats	Data availability and reliability; load balancing and scalability; flexibility in storing unstructured data in any format	No efficient access to particular parts of the data; no indexes
NoSQL key-value stores	Dynamo, Voldemort, Redis, Riak	Data is represented as a collection of key-value pairs. Create, read, update, and delete operations are supported based only on user-defined keys	Operational simplicity for lowest total cost of ownership; great scalability; low access latency	Only simple operations supported; no complex queries or data joins; a value can be updated only as a whole
NoSQL document stores	SimpleDB, CouchDB, MongoDB, DynamoDB	Data are organised in documents based on user-defined keys. The system is aware of the (arbitrary) document structure and supports indexing on multiple fields. Works best with semi-structured data	Support for lists, nested documents, and searches based on multiple fields; efficient and scale-out architectures	Data consumption is bit-high because of de-normalisation; no support for data joins
NoSQL wide-columnar stores	BigTable, HBase, Cassandra	Data is organised into tables and attributes are organised into column families. A column family resembles a document, so the system has knowledge of its underlying structure	Improved cache locality; efficient at data compression; good performance on aggregation queries; good scalability	No transactions; increased tuple reconstruction costs; increased cost of inserts
NoSQL graph stores	Neo4j, ArangoDB, TitanDB	Specialised in the efficient management of graph data, which contains nodes connected by edges. Graph representation shows not only useful information about entities but also how each entity connects with or is related to others	Efficient handling of highly connected data; fast searching based on relationships	Optimised only for graph-like data; not efficient in handling queries that span the entire database
Spatiotemporal systems	PostGIS, PostGIS-T, TerraLib, GeoMesa	Database management systems adapted to manage entities/objects containing space and time information. Spatiotemporal objects can dynamically update their spatial location and/or extents along with time	Optimised for receiving intensive updates; efficient access methods to store and retrieve spatiotemporal objects	Most existing systems are centralised and offer limited scalability; distributed systems lack support for advanced operations

through a network (Thanh, Mohan, Choi, Kim, & Kim, 2008). In a DFS, the data is stored on storage media located on multiple (perhaps remote) servers; however, the stored data is accessed as if it was stored locally. A DFS allows users to organise, manipulate, and share data seamlessly, regardless of the actual data location on the network. However, file availability and location are considered key issues in DFS, which are solved using the replication of files (Thanh et al., 2008). Replication methods are categorised into two types, namely pessimistic replication and optimistic replication (Toader & Toader, 2017). There exist several distributed file systems, such as the Hadoop Distributed File System (HDFS), Network File System (NFS), NetWare, and CIFS/SMB.

HDFS (Shvachko, Kuang, Radia, & Chansler, 2010) is the main storage system utilised in the Apache ecosystem and it is widely used by popular big data analytics platforms such as Hadoop and Spark. The files stored on HDFS are broken down into relatively large blocks (64–128 MB), which are then replicated and distributed over the cluster nodes. HDFS implements a distributed file system using a master/worker architecture, which provides fault tolerance and high-performance access to data over highly-scalable clusters with commodity hardware. The master node, called NameNode, is responsible for maintaining the file system namespace and executing the typical file system operations (e.g., create directory, open file). The worker nodes, called DataNodes, are responsible for storing the actual data on locally-attached storage media as well as performing read/write operations and other various tasks such as block creation, replication, and deletion.

4.2 NoSQL Data Stores

NoSQL data stores have emerged to address horizontal scalability and high availability requirements of data management in the Cloud, which are hard to achieve with traditional relational database management systems. NoSQL stores follow a shared-nothing architecture and work by replicating and partitioning data over large clusters of network-connected servers. The data storage models do not rely on the relational data model. In addition, they distribute workloads of simple operations such as key-based searches, while they support reads and writes of one or a small number of records. There is no or very little support for complex queries or joins. NoSQL databases are particularly useful in two cases: (1) to store data without a predefined schema; and (2) to analyse streams of live data in real time, where pre-processing and indexing of records is not possible (Wang et al., 2016).

There are four key types of NoSQL stores and multiple systems for each type (Davoudian, Chen, & Liu, 2018). In particular, there are key-value stores, document stores, extensible record or wide-columnar stores, and graph stores. Below we outline the key features of each type.

Key-Value Stores Key-value stores (e.g., Dynamo, Voldemort, Riak) offer a basic key-value interface. The values are stored based on user-defined keys, while the system is unaware of the structure of the value. In a distributed setting, data is typically replicated and partitioned so that each server contains a subset of the total data. Moreover, several existing stores, such as Voldemort (Sumbaly et al., 2012), provide tunable consistency (i.e., strong or eventual consistency), which offers tradeoffs between availability, latency, and consistency. Key-value stores can be used with simple applications that are mainly developed for storing and finding data based on a single attribute. For example, a web interface can visualise aggregate information for AIS or maritime sensor data that are precomputed and stored in a key-value store.

Document Stores Document-oriented NoSQL systems (e.g., SimpleDB, CouchDB, MongoDB) store data in JSON or JSON-like format and support queries using specific APIs. The primary unit of data is a document, which is a JSON object comprising named fields. Field values may be strings, numbers, dates, or even ordered lists and associative maps. Documents are stored based on user-defined keys but, unlike key-value stores, the system has knowledge of the document structure. Document stores are useful for applications that store multiple different kinds of objects and need to search data based on multiple fields. For example, a document store can be used for storing position and voyage AIS vessel information to support computational maritime situational awareness applications (Cazzanti, Millefiori, & Arcieri, 2015).

Wide-Columnar Stores Wide-columnar NoSQL databases such as BigTable, HBase, and Cassandra follow a sparse data model that resembles a three-dimensional sorted map from the triplet ⟨row key, column key, timestamp⟩ to a value. The row key identifies a full record, while a column key comprises a column family and a column name (i.e., a named field). A column family resembles a document, so the system has knowledge of its underlying structure. The column family information is then used to replicate and distribute data both horizontally and vertically. Overall, wide-columnar databases are optimised for storing large amounts of semi-structured data such as AIS data and ship routes, which can then be efficiently analysed by higher-level data processing systems such as Spark (Qin, Ma, & Niu, 2018).

Graph Stores Graph database systems (e.g., Neo4j, ArangoDB, TitanDB) are optimised for storing graph data, i.e., data consisting of nodes (vertices) connected by edges (links). This representation shows not only useful information about entities but also how each individual entity connects with or is related to others. Internally, the data is stored as nodes and edges, both of which can have multiple attributes. Secondary indexes for both nodes and edges are also supported, enabling the fast retrieval of nodes by attributes and edges by type. For example, a graph can be built consisting of vessel voyages between ports based on the arrivals and departures of vessels from ports, which can then be used for analysing vessel movement patterns (Carlini et al., 2020).

4.3 Spatiotemporal Systems

A spatiotemporal or spatial-temporal system is a database management system that is adapted to manage entities/objects containing space and time information. A spatiotemporal object is a special type of object that dynamically updates its spatial location and/or extents along with time. Some typical examples from the maritime domain are a moving vessel whose location continuously changes over time, or oceanic measurements collected by sensors on-board a drifting buoy. Spatiotemporal systems have a lot of key applications in various domains, especially in the maritime industry, and are used with Environmental Information Systems (EIS), Traffic Control Systems (TCS), Location-Aware Systems (LAS), and Geographic Information Systems (GIS). Unlike conventional data storage systems, spatiotemporal ones are able to manage dynamic properties of objects in an efficient way. In particular, they are optimised for receiving intensive updates due to the constantly changing properties of spatiotemporal objects. Furthermore, sampling-based or velocity-based updating methods are adapted to minimise the objects' updates (Xiong, Mokbel, & Aref, 2017). Besides the updating methods, spatiotemporal systems also adopt new access methods to efficiently store and retrieve spatiotemporal objects (Nguyen-Dinh, Aref, & Mokbel, 2010).

PostGIS (Corti, Kraft, Mather, & Park, 2014) is a spatial database extension for the popular PostgreSQL database system. PostGIS provides new spatial-specific data types to PostgreSQL such as support for points, lines, polygons, and other geometric objects. In addition, it offers specialised features for geometric and geographic processing, topogeometry functions and topologies, as well as raster processing and analysis. Finally, it implements several standards such as GML, KML, and GeoJSON (recall Sect. 2.2). **PostGIS-T** (Simoes, Queiroz, Ferreira, Vinhas, & Camara, 2016) is a recent extension of PostGIS that focuses on the temporal dimension of spatial data. It implements a formal spatiotemporal algebra and adds supports for three types of spatiotemporal data, namely time series, trajectories, and coverages. Unlike PostGIS-T that builds on top of PostgreSQL, **TerraLib** (Câmara et al., 2008) extends object-relational database techniques to support spatiotemporal data types, while supporting multiple underlying DBMSs, including PostgreSQL, MySQL, and Oracle. Furthermore, TerraLib enables spatial, temporal, and attribute queries on the stored data. Storing maritime data in such systems has been used in the past for performing various AIS-based route analysis as well as help visualise ship routes from raw AIS data (Fiorini, Capata, & Bloisi, 2016).

In the distributed systems arena, **GeoMesa** (GeoMesa, 2019) is an open-source suite of tools that can be used for storing, transforming, indexing, and querying spatiotemporal data on top of other distributed computing systems. Specifically, GeoMesa offers spatiotemporal indexing capabilities for point, line, and polygon data stored in Accumulo, HBase, Google BigTable, and Cassandra. In addition, GeoMesa provides stream processing in near real time for spatiotemporal data streamed through Apache Kafka. GeoMesa is currently used by *exactEarth*, an

AIS vessel tracking data service company, for storing more than 25 million AIS messages per day (exactEarth, 2020). Recently, several approaches have extended Apache Spark for supporting spatial and spatiotemporal data. **LocationSpark** and **SpatialSpark** directly extend Spark's core data model to provide users with granular control over spatial operation execution plan, while **GeoSpark** builds specialised indexes over spatiotemporal data (Yu & Sarwat, 2019).

5 Data Usage

Data usage involves query processing, analytics, and visualisation methods and tools for accessing the underlying maritime data and generating value for different data-driven business activities. The proper data usage in the decision-making of a growing industry like the maritime industry can improve competitiveness by reducing operational costs, providing better services to end-users, or any other parameters, which can be measured against existing performance criteria (Cavanillas et al., 2016). Query processing may involve browsing, searching, reporting, finding correlations, identifying patterns, and predicting relations across maritime data (Curry, 2016). A plethora of query processing systems have been developed over the years, the most popular of which are described in this section.

5.1 Query Processing Systems

Query processing systems provide query facades on top of storage or file systems. They usually offer an SQL-like query interface to access the data; however, they follow different approaches and exhibit difference performance compared to traditional DBMSs. For example, Hive and SparkSQL provide SQL-like functionality over large-scale distributed data, Presto and Impala specialise in interactive data processing, and GeoMesa and GeoSpark provide spatiotemporal querying and analytics.

Apache Hive Apache Hive (Apache Hive, 2019) is built on top of HDFS to offer query and analysis over large-scale structured data. It provides an SQL-like interface, termed HiveQL, to query data stored in different storage systems and databases, which integrate with HDFS. Hive runs queries by translating them in either Tez or MapReduce jobs. Hence, Hive queries often suffer from high latencies, even for a smaller dataset. In addition, Hive has the flexibility to develop schemas efficiently as schemas are stored independently and data is validated only at query time. This is known as schema-on-read compared to the schema-on-write approach of traditional relational DBMSs. Hive works best for analysing and generating reports for structured data such as port management, transport, and logistics data.

SparkSQL SparkSQL offers a programming abstraction called Data Frames and acts as a distributed SQL query engine. In contrast to Apache Hive, SparkSQL provides query processing with lower latency due to the in-memory processing capabilities of Spark. SparkSQL supports the HiveQL interface and enables HiveQL queries to run faster than Hive, even without any modifications in data and queries (Xin et al., 2013). Moreover, it allows strong integration with other Spark ecosystems such as integrating SQL query processing with machine learning applications. SparkSQL has recently been extended with several geospatial functions, which enable the execution of complex geospatial analytics tasks in the maritime domain (Hezbor & Hughes, 2017).

Apache Impala Apache Impala (Apache Impala, 2019) also provides query processing with low latency. It employs massively parallel processing database techniques to enable users to issue low latency SQL queries on data stored in Apache HBase and HDFS without requiring data transformation or movement. Impala employs an SQL-like interface similar to Apache Hive; however, in order to achieve low latency, it adapts its own distributed query engine. Impala has been employed in the past for mass spatiotemporal trajectory data sharing (Zhou, Chen, Yuan, & Chen, 2016).

Presto Presto (Presto SQL, 2019) is an open-source, distributed SQL query engine optimised for executing interactive analytical queries over large-scale datasets. It allows querying data from various sources, e.g., relational DBMSs, Cassandra, Hive, or even proprietary data stores. A Presto query combines data from several sources and allows analytics across the entire software stack. Additionally, unlike other Hadoop-based tools (e.g., Impala), Presto is able to work with any flavour of Hadoop or without it.

GeoSpark GeoSpark (Yu, Zhang, & Sarwat, 2019) is a cluster computing framework that is developed to process large-scale spatial and spatiotemporal data (e.g., ships location data, weather maps, etc.). It extents SparkSQL and Apache Spark with SpatialSQL to efficiently load, process, and analyse a huge amount of spatial data. In addition, GeoSpark has introduced a novel interface that follows the MM-Part-3 standard, an international standard specifying the storage, retrieval, and processing of spatial data using SQL. Overall, GeoSpark is able to produce optimised spatial query plans and to run spatial queries on large datasets efficiently (Yu et al., 2019).

6   Conclusion

Maritime stakeholders are continuously collecting large volumes of heterogeneous spatiotemporal data from various sources, for example, sensor data, AIS data, traffic data, port call data, and environmental monitoring data. The maritime data value chain defines the series of the four key activities needed to appropriately manage this data, namely data acquisition, pre-processing, storage, and usage. As described in this chapter, a large arsenal of technological tools and frameworks are currently available for efficiently collecting, cleaning, integrating, storing, and analysing the data in order to extract value and useful insights that will satisfy several critical applications in the maritime industry (e.g., optimising port operations, planning optimised routes, performing predictive maintenance).

Nevertheless, the large volume and variety of data in combination with the unique characteristics of spatiotemporal data, are turning data mining, big data analytics, and data visualisation into significantly challenging issues in the maritime domain due to high computation and communication complexities. In addition, the integration of data management technologies that span multiple ships and ports is still an open challenge mainly because of unreliable and slow transmissions as well as incompatible application programming interfaces. With regard to spatiotemporal systems, current distributed ones (e.g., GeoMesa, SpatialSpark, GeoSpark) are capable of handling large volumes but lack support for advanced operations for geometric, geographic, and topogeometric processing and analysis. Hence, a multi-discipline, coordinated effort is still needed to advance the features and functionalities provided by the most relevant prior research projects and large-scale data processing systems used by the maritime industry today.

Acknowledgments This work was co-funded by the European Regional Development Fund and the Republic of Cyprus through the Research and Innovation Foundation (STEAM Project: INTEGRATED/0916/0063).

References

Abdallah, N. B., Iphar, C., Arcieri, G., & Jousselme, A.-L. (2019). Fixing errors in the AIS destination field. In *Oceans 2019-Marseille* (pp. 1–5).

Akyuz, E., Ilbahar, E., Cebi, S., & Celik, M. (2017). Maritime environmental disaster management using intelligent techniques. In *Intelligence systems in environmental management: Theory and applications* (pp. 135–155). Berlin: Springer.

Alguliyev, R. M., Aliguliyev, R. M., & Hajirahimova, M. S. (2016). Big data integration architectural concepts for oil and gas industry. In *Proceedings of the IEEE 10th International Conference on Application of Information and Communication Technologies (AICT)* (pp. 1–5).

Apache Flume. (2019). Last accessed: November 22, 2019. https://flume.apache.org/

Apache Hive. (2019). Last accessed: November 22, 2019. https://hive.apache.org/

Apache Impala. (2019). Last accessed: November 22, 2019. https://impala.apache.org/

Apache Kafka. (2019). Last accessed: November 22, 2019. https://kafka.apache.org/

Beşikçi, E. B., Arslan, O., Turan, O., & Ölçer, A. (2016). An artificial neural network based decision support system for energy efficient ship operations. *Computers & Operations Research, 66*, 393–401.

Câmara, G., Vinhas, L., Ferreira, K. R., De Queiroz, G. R., De Souza, R. C. M., Monteiro, et al. (2008). TerraLib: An open source GIS library for large-scale environmental and socio-economic applications. In *Open source approaches in spatial data handling* (pp. 247–270). Berlin: Springer.

Carlini, E., de Lira, V. M., Soares, A., Etemad, M., Machado, B. B., & Matwin, S. (2020). Uncovering vessel movement patterns from AIS data with graph evolution analysis. In

Proceedings of the 23rd International Conference on Extending Database Technology (EDBT) (p. 7).

Cavanillas, J. M., Curry, E., & Wahlster, W. (2016). *New horizons for a data-driven economy: A roadmap for usage and exploitation of big data in Europe*. Berlin: Springer.

Cazzanti, L., Millefiori, L. M., & Arcieri, G. (2015). A document-based data model for large scale computational maritime situational awareness. In *Proceedings of the 2015 IEEE International Conference on Big Data (Big Data)* (pp. 1350–1356).

Corti, P., Kraft, T. J., Mather, S. V., & Park, B. (2014). *PostGIS cookbook*. Birmingham: Packt Publishing Ltd.

Cragin, M. H., Heidorn, P. B., Palmer, C. L., & Smith, L. C. (2007). An educational program on data curation. In *Science and Technology Section of the Annual American Library Association Conference*.

Cunningham, J. P., & Ghahramani, Z. (2015). Linear dimensionality reduction: Survey, insights, and generalizations. *The Journal of Machine Learning Research, 16*(1), 2859–2900.

Curry, E. (2016). The big data value chain: Definitions, concepts, and theoretical approaches. In J. M. Cavanillas, E. Curry, & W. Wahlster (Eds.), *New horizons for a data-driven economy: A roadmap for usage and exploitation of big data in Europe* (pp. 29–37). Cham: Springer International Publishing.

Curry, E., Freitas, A., & O'Riáin, S. (2010). The role of community-driven data curation for enterprises. In *Linking enterprise data* (pp. 25–47). Berlin: Springer.

Davoudian, A., Chen, L., & Liu, M. (2018). A survey on NoSQL stores. *ACM Computing Surveys, 51*(2), 40.

DGConnect. (2013). *A European Strategy on the Data Value Chain*. Tech. Rep. Brussels: European Commission. http://ec.europa.eu/information_society/newsroom/cf/dae/document.cfm?doc_id=3488

Dong, X. L., & Srivastava, D. (2013). Big data integration. In *Proceedings of the IEEE 29th International Conference on Data Engineering (ICDE)* (pp. 1245–1248).

exactEarth AIS Vessel Tracking. (2020). Last accessed: March 30, 2020. https://www.exactearth.com/

Ferreira, J., Agostinho, C., Lopes, R., Chatzikokolakis, K., Zissis, D.,Vidal, M.-E., et al. (2017). Maritime data technology landscape and value chain exploiting oceans of data for maritime applications. In *Proceedings of the 2017 International Conference on Engineering, Technology and Innovation (ICE/ITMC)* (pp. 1113–1122).

Fiorini, M., Capata, A., & Bloisi, D. D. (2016). AIS data visualization for maritime spatial planning (MSP). *International Journal of e-Navigation and Maritime Economy, 5*, 45–60.

Gelernter, J., & Maheshwari, N. (2019). Qualitative study of the incompatibility of indoor map file formats with location software applications. *Open Geospatial Data, Software and Standards, 4*(1), 7.

GeoMesa. (2019). Last accessed: November 22, 2019. https://www.geomesa.org/

Han, J., Pei, J., & Kamber, M. (2011). *Data mining: Concepts and techniques*. Amsterdam: Elsevier.

Hezbor, A., & Hughes, J. (2017, November). *Maritime Location Intelligence with exactEarth data and GeoMesa*. Last accessed: March 30, 2020. https://www.eclipse.org/community/eclipse_newsletter/2017/november/article3.php

Holm, H., & Mellegård, N. (2018). Fast decoding of automatic identification systems (AIS) data. In *Proceedings of the International Conference on Computer Applications and Information Technology in the Maritime Industries (COMPIT)*.

Kokkinakos, P., Michalitsi-Psarrou, A., Mouzakitis, S., Alvertis, I., Askounis, D., & Koussouris, S. (2017). Big data exploitation for maritime applications: A multi-segment platform to enable maritime big data scenarios. In *Proceedings of the 2017 International Conference on Engineering, Technology and Innovation (ICE/ITMC)* (pp. 1131–1136).

Kramer, J. (2009). Advanced message queuing protocol (AMQP). *Linux Journal, 2009*(187), 3.

Kyriakides, I., Hayes, D., & Tsiantis, P. (2020). Intelligent maritime information acquisition and representation for decision support. In M. Lind, M. Michaelides, R. Ward, & R. T. Watson (Eds.), *Maritime informatics* (chap. 22). Cham: Springer. https://doi.org/10.1007/978-3-030-50892-0

Loshin, D. (2010). *Master data management.* Burlington: Morgan Kaufmann.

Lyko, K., Nitzschke, M., & Ngomo, A.-C. N. (2016). Big data acquisition. In J. M. Cavanillas, E. Curry, & W. Wahlster (Eds.), *New horizons for a datadriven economy: A roadmap for usage and exploitation of big data in Europe* (pp. 39–62). Cham: Springer International Publishing.

Lytra, I., Vidal, M.-E., Orlandi, F., & Attard, J. (2017). A big data architecture for managing oceans of data and maritime applications. In *Proceedings of the 2017 International Conference on Engineering, Technology and Innovation (ICE/ITMC)* (pp. 1216–1226).

Malik, J. S., Goyal, P., & Sharma, A. K. (2010). A comprehensive approach towards data preprocessing techniques & association rules. In *Proceedings of the 4th National Conference.*

Michaelides, M. P., Herodotou, H., Lind, M., & Watson, R. T. (2019). Port-2-port communication enhancing short sea shipping performance: The case study of Cyprus and the Eastern Mediterranean. *Sustainability, 11*(7), 1912.

Min, F., & Xu, J. (2016). Semi-greedy heuristics for feature selection with test cost constraints. *Granular Computing, 1*(3), 199–211.

Narang, S. K., Kumar, S., & Verma, V. (2017). Knowledge discovery from massive data streams. In *Web semantics for textual and visual information retrieval* (pp. 109–143). Hershey: IGI Global.

Nguyen-Dinh, L.-V., Aref, W. G., & Mokbel, M. (2010). Spatio-temporal access methods (Part 2). *IEEE Data Engineering Bulletin, 33*(2), 46–55.

Perobelli, N. (2016, June). *MarineTraffic - A Day in Numbers.* Last accessed: March 22, 2019. https://www.marinetraffic.com/blog/a-day-in-numbers/

Presto SQL. (2019). Last accessed: November 22, 2019. https://prestosql.io/

Qin, J., Ma, L., & Niu, J. (2018). Massive AIS data management based on HBase and Spark. In *Proceedings of the 3rd Asia-Pacific Conference on Intelligent Robot Systems (ACIRS)* (pp. 112–117).

Rødseth, Ø. J., Perera, L. P., & Mo, B. (2016). Big data in shipping - Challenges and opportunities. In *Proceedings of the 15th International Conference on Computer and IT Applications in the Maritime Industries (COMPIT).*

Shvachko, K., Kuang, H., Radia, S., & Chansler, R. (2010). The Hadoop distributed file system. In *Proceedings of the IEEE 26th Symposium on Mass Storage Systems and Technologies (MSST)* (Vol. 10, pp. 1–10).

Simoes, R. E., de Queiroz, G. R., Ferreira, K. R., Vinhas, L., & Camara, G. (2016). PostGIS-T: Towards a spatiotemporal PostgreSQL database extension. In *Proceedings of the XVII Brazilian Symposium on Geoinformatics (GeoInfo)* (pp. 252–262).

Sumbaly, R., Kreps, J., Gao, L., Feinberg, A., Soman, C., & Shah, S. (2012). Serving large-scale batch computed data with project Voldemort. In *Proceedings of the 10th USENIX Conference on File and Storage Technologies* (pp. 18–30).

Svanberg, M., Santén, V., Hörteborn, A., Holm, H., & Finnsgård, C. (2019). AIS in maritime research. *Marine Policy, 106*, 103520.

Thanh, T. D., Mohan, S., Choi, E., Kim, S., & Kim, P. (2008). A taxonomy and survey on distributed file systems. In *Proceedings of the Fourth International Conference on Networked Computing and Advanced Information Management* (Vol. 1, pp. 144–149).

Toader, C., & Toader, D. C. (2017). Modelling a reliable distributed system based on the management of replication processes. *North Economic Review, 1*(1), 312–320.

Wang, H., Zhuge, X., Strazdins, G., Wei, Z., Li, G., & Zhang, H. (2016). Data integration and visualisation for demanding marine operations. In *Proceedings of the MTS/IEEE OCEANS 2016 Conference* (pp. 1–7).

Xin, R. S., Rosen, J., Zaharia, M., Franklin, M. J., Shenker, S., & Stoica, I. (2013). Shark: SQL and rich analytics at scale. In *Proceedings of the 2013 ACM SIGMOD International Conference on Management of Data* (pp. 13–24).

Xiong, X., Mokbel, M. F., & Aref, W. G. (2017). Spatiotemporal database. In *Encyclopedia of GIS* (pp. 2150–2151). Berlin: Springer.

Yablonsky, S. (2018). Innovation platforms: Data and analytics platforms. In *Multi-Sided Platforms (MSPs) and sharing strategies in the digital economy: Emerging research and opportunities* (pp. 72–95). Hershey: IGI Global.

Yang, Y., Zhong, M., Yao, H., Yu, F., Fu, X., & Postolache, O. (2018). Internet of things for smart ports: Technologies and challenges. *IEEE Instrumentation & Measurement Magazine, 21*(1), 34–43.

Yeoh, C.-M., Chai, B.-L., Lim, H., Kwon, T.-H., Yi, K.-O., Kim, T.-H., et al. (2011). Ubiquitous containerized cargo monitoring system development based on wireless sensor network technology. *International Journal of Computers Communications & Control, 6*(4), 779–793.

Yu, J., & Sarwat, M. (2019). Geospatial data management in apache spark: A tutorial. In *Proceedings of the IEEE 35th International Conference on Data Engineering (ICDE)* (pp. 2060–2063).

Yu, J., Zhang, Z., & Sarwat, M. (2019). Spatial data management in apache spark: The GeoSpark perspective and beyond. *Geoinformatica, 23*(1), 37–78.

Zhao, Y.-x., Li, W., Feng, S., Ochieng, W. Y., & Schuster, W. (2014). An improved differential evolution algorithm for maritime collision avoidance route planning. *Abstract and Applied Analysis, 2014*, 10 pp.

Zhou, L., Chen, N., Yuan, S., & Chen, Z. (2016). An efficient method of sharing mass spatiotemporal trajectory data based on Cloudera Impala. *Sensors, 16*(11), 1813.

Spatiotemporal Data Analytics for the Maritime Industry

Patrick Schmitt ⓘ, Marcin Lukasz Bartosiak ⓘ, and Torbjörn Rydbergh ⓘ

1 Introduction to Spatiotemporal Data Analytics

One of the most distinctive features of the modern world is the ubiquitous character of data and digital data streams. The first decades of the twenty-first century are characterised by the importance of just-in-time information and the power of information organisations (Watson, 2013). Having the right information at the right time is key to efficient and effective decision-making, which results in creating value for the organisations. With the pervasive digital data streams being produced by a growing number of devices (Pigni, Piccoli, & Watson, 2016), one can get insights into almost every human activity. These data, when placed in the right context, can become an unmatched source of valuable and useful knowledge for business decision-makers on various levels of the organisational hierarchy. For this reason, the last decade witnessed a growing interest in the use of data analytics in a wide variety of fields. It became a well-accepted business rule that making strategic decisions based on data means making better strategic decisions (McAfee & Brynjolfsson, 2012).

The maritime industry is no different in this sense—timely managed and analysed data creates value for all stakeholders. However, the maritime industry is a

P. Schmitt
BearingPoint GmbH, München, Germany
e-mail: patrick.schmitt@bearingpoint.com

M. L. Bartosiak (✉)
Università di Pavia, Pavia, Italy
e-mail: marcin.bartosiak@unipv.it

T. Rydbergh
Marine Benchmark, Västra Frölunda, Sweden
e-mail: torbjorn.rydbergh@marinebenchmark.com

M. Lind et al. (eds.), *Maritime Informatics*, Progress in IS,
https://doi.org/10.1007/978-3-030-50892-0_20

335

special case as it deals with dynamically changing conditions of the environment (Duck, 2012) and sea traffic (Merrick, van Dorp, Mazzuchi, & Harrald, 2001). To face these challenges, initiatives like Sea Traffic Management[1] have been trying to improve communication and information sharing among actors of the maritime transport industry. By utilising modern information infrastructure across the supply chain, they address the needs of shipping companies, cargo owners and port authorities (Sea Traffic Management, n.d.). The aim of such initiatives is to draw a clear picture of the overall maritime transportation industry and involve all relevant stakeholders in collaborative decision-making processes (Lind, Haraldson, Karlsson, & Watson, 2015). From optimising vessels' routes and preparing ports for efficient operations to reducing pollution and saving the environment, data analytics can help in achieving these goals. However, given the complex and dynamic nature of the maritime industry (see Watson, Lind, Delmeire, & Liesa, 2020), the traditional methods of analytics may not be accurate enough (Harrald, Mazzuchi, & Stone, 1992). Spatiotemporal data—data sets composed of spatial coordinates and timestamps, are particularly well-suited for analyses of complex and dynamically changing environments, as it is the case for the maritime industry (Andrienko & Andrienko, 2006). Spatiotemporal data analytics provides information on variable interactions between events in space and time, supporting situational awareness of the past, the present and the likely future.

Thus, in this chapter, we present a brief introduction to spatiotemporal data analytics. After a general introduction of data analytics, we explain the specificities of spatiotemporal data—presenting their properties and particular structure that differentiates it from other types of data. Finally, we present application examples of spatiotemporal data analysis in the maritime industry along the voyage process.

2 Data Analytics

Data are raw, unorganised facts that must be processed to become meaningful to humans. Data are usually presented as sets of numbers, strings, images, etc. By itself, a dataset does not carry much value. Only after being processed into a meaningful form, data becomes useful—data becomes information. One needs to add some context to the raw data in order to create information and then have the ability to use it in order to build knowledge. *Data analytics* is the stage of the data value chain in which data is processed and analysed in order to find insights and produce useful information about the topic of interest. Data processing is the stage that focuses on the organisation of the data for the relevant analysis, according to the specified requirements. Processing transforms raw data into the desired format, facilitating the analysis. Data analysis involves the application of querying and statistical techniques to understand and interpret the data. This step transforms the

---

[1] https://www.stmvalidation.eu/ (accessed 12.4.19).

processed data into information, which supports the decision-making process and can be used in various business scenarios.

Depending on the desired outcome and the required decision to be made, data analytics may use different types of data and involve various forms of analysis so they can be classified in the following four categories:

1. *Descriptive* analytics answers the question 'What is happening?' Using historical data, it gives an overview of the past situation (including very recent past). Descriptive analytics is useful to present a holistic overview of the changes, performance and trends of the business. Descriptive analytics helps to answer questions like 'What is the current number of vessels in the port?', 'What is the average traffic in a specified area per day?' and 'Is this year fuel consumption higher or lower than the last year?'
2. *Diagnostic* analytics answers the question 'Why is it happening?' It helps to understand causal relationships and to discover anomalies of certain events. For example, diagnostic analytics can find why the fuel consumption is higher on certain routes.
3. *Predictive* analytics answers the question 'What is going to happen?' It takes historical data and, using probabilistic algorithms, forecasts possible outcomes of the future. Examples of predictive analytics may include a shipping company estimating the costs of fuel based on the past price variation and historic fuel usage data or a port estimating a vessel's arrival time based on its current route and sea conditions.
4. *Prescriptive* analytics answers the question 'What should I do now?' It allows users to produce guidelines about future decisions and quantify their outcomes. Prescriptive analytics describes what will happen and why it will happen, providing decision-makers with recommendations on the optimal outcomes. For example, it can provide recommendations on which vessel should enter the port first to reduce the waiting time of other vessels.

Data analytics allows decision-makers to understand many aspects of the maritime industry, including sea traffic, weather and surface conditions, environmental impact, etc. Thus, it enables better planning, operations and execution of tasks along the whole voyage process.

3 Spatiotemporal Data Properties

Spatiotemporal data sets are composed of two different types of data representing points in *space* and *time*. This composition of data lets analysts discover what happens at a specific location at a time point and interpret interactions between events to summarise their relationships for further analysis. While useful, this characteristic can be challenging to deal with and must be considered during the whole analytics process.

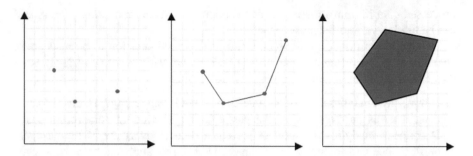

Fig. 1 Examples of spatiotemporal data representation. From left: points, line and polygon

Spatial data represent the locations of objects in space. Thus, they can be two-dimensional (e.g. geographic position of a ship watercraft) or three-dimensional (e.g. geographic position and keel depth of a ship watercraft below sea level). In spatial datasets, a set of coordinates determines the position of an object in space. Depending on the relationship between the coordinates, the object can be a point, a line or a polygon (see Fig. 1). For example, a set of geospatial coordinates (longitude and latitude) can represent the position of a vessel at sea (a point). Another set of geospatial coordinates can represent a coastline (a line) or a sea protected area (a polygon). By combining such sets of spatial data, it is possible to analyse the position of different objects in reference to each other.

Temporal data refers to time, and it records a temporal occurrence of a phenomenon. Time is unidimensional, and, thus, temporal data can represent past, present or (in case of forecasts) the future. It is important, however, to analyse the right temporal data. In most temporal databases, there are two types of time data. *Recorded* (or transaction) *time* is the time when an event was added to a database. *Actual* (or valid) *time* represents the time an event occurred in the real world. In some cases when the real-time data is stored, transaction and valid data might be almost the same, but they are always independent of each other. In most cases, data analyst uses the valid time.

Spatiotemporal data—the focus of this chapter,—is a particular type of data: it is a mix of both spatial and temporal data. Thus, they represent a spatial position of an object at a certain point in time. Analytics of spatiotemporal data allows interpreting changes in the positions of objects over time. For example, one can determine a route and time of arrival of a cargo vessel moving from port to port. Contrary to other data types in analytics, in the case of spatiotemporal data, it is possible to define observation units and their features in various ways (Atluri, Karpatne, & Kumar, 2018).

In general, we distinguish two types of spatiotemporal data. The first type is the observations about the same units (e.g. ships) at each time point (e.g. traffic control observing vessels' movement over time in order to avoid collisions). The second are observations assessing different units in each time period (e.g. movement of a group of fish in an area over time).

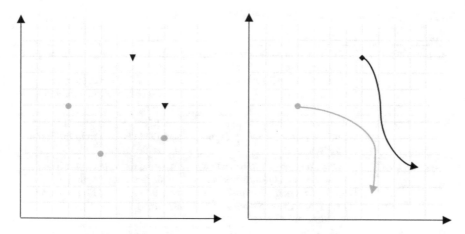

Fig. 2 Event and trajectory data representation

Atluri et al. (2018) classified spatiotemporal data into four most commonly used types applied in analytics. *Event data* represent distinct events occurring at a specific location at a point in time. Event data are typically represented as a point (see Fig. 2) but can also be represented as a line or polygon changing its position and shape in time (e.g. an oil spill can be represented as a polygon, showing the reach of the oil spill). *Trajectory data* represent a traced path of an object moving in space and time. Such data is usually collected from a device periodically transmitting an object's location. For example, data used in the Automatic Identification System (AIS) is streamed from vessels' transponders, transmitting the location of a vessel every 2–10 s (or every 3 min when at anchor).

Point referenced data represent continuous values measured by measurement objects (reference points) moving in space and time. For example, a set of weather satellites measures sea surface temperature on an hourly basis at various points on the Earth. *Raster data* represent the measurement of spatiotemporal data of fixed points at fixed locations. For example, a measure of sea traffic in a specific geographic area.

4 Spatiotemporal Data Analysis

To solve a decision-making problem, we can use several methods of spatiotemporal analysis, depending on asked questions and desired outputs. A query returns useful yet relatively simple output. Table 1 presents commonly used spatiotemporal queries and examples of their use in the maritime context.

In order to find more complex information, one needs to use more elaborate techniques. Thus, in order to find needed information, one needs to not only access

Table 1 Spatiotemporal data queries (Yuan and McIntosh, 2002)

Type	Description	Example
Simple query	– Presents the location of an object at a given time – Often additional data interferes with the results	– Tracking moving vessels or groups of animals – Factors like speed make the location of an object constantly changing
Range query	Analyses what happens to a region, represented by a polygon, at a given time	Identifying all the vessels within a specified distance from the port at a specified time
Behaviour query	Focuses on changes in behaviour and state of an object over space and time. Its outputs explain how the spatiotemporal changes affect the objects of interest	Tracking the state of perishable goods in a container during transport and its changes during the voyage
Relationship query	Answers the most complex questions. It concerns the relationships between different kinds of objects in space and time	Understanding how weather conditions affect changes in the fuel usage of a vessel

the right data but also apply the right technique for the given problem. In this section, we list some of the most common methods of spatiotemporal data analysis.

Spatiotemporal data *classification* is a technique that puts objects into categories, based on their known characteristics. It helps to understand their properties and phenomena related to them. To classify spatiotemporal data, features like location and shapes at different timestamps can be used to find similarities between points or polygons (Rao, Govardhan, & Rao, 2012). An example may be a classification of regions by the climatic conditions over time (Ganguly & Steinhaeuser, 2008). Such a classification can be useful for route planning or environmental protection initiatives. A similar technique is *clustering*, which groups the instances by the similarity of their attributes' values. While classification techniques rely on labels assigned to each instance, clustering identifies groups across observations based on their features. For example, clustering vessels by similarities of their trajectory during a time period has the potential for improving sea traffic control (Cazzanti & Pallotta, 2015; Laxhammar, Falkman, & Sviestins, 2009).

Patterns discovery helps to identify any regular and frequent occurrences or relationships in the dataset. Patterns can be observed in objects (e.g. a vessel's regular movement pattern) or events (e.g. an increase in traffic density due to seasonal weather conditions). Awareness of such patterns helps to detect *anomalies*, outliers, which are significantly different from the majority of the data set, or *deviations*—timestamps at which the behaviour of an object of interest variates from its expected behaviour. Pattern discovery and trajectory clustering proved to be useful tools in detecting sea traffic anomalies (Laxhammar et al., 2009).

Finally, spatiotemporal *causality analysis* helps to find information on the causal relationships between instances. A relationship can be an effect of both spatial and temporal causality. For example, extreme seasonal weather conditions may increase the risk of sea transportation in certain regions (Baksh, Abbassi, Garaniya, & Khan, 2018). Because of the existing interdependencies (see the next section), relationships between data points can be highly complex. For instance, the seasonal conditions on the Mediterranean Sea affect the traffic density, which in turn affects the animal population in the sea (Campana et al., 2017).

5 Challenges to Spatiotemporal Data Analytics

Due to the properties described in previous sections, the analytics of spatiotemporal data can be challenging. The algorithms used to analyse other types of data do not always prove to be useful in the case of spatiotemporal data analytics (Atluri et al., 2018; Ghaemi, Agard, Nia, & Trépanier, 2015).

Spatiotemporal data have two properties that make them particularly different from other data and create challenges to the analytics process (Atluri et al., 2018). First, observations made at nearby locations and time are not independent of one another. Having highly correlated observations is important in spatiotemporal data as it creates coherence in spatial observations and regularity of temporal observations. However, due to the correlation, many algorithms designed for independent data perform badly on spatiotemporal data. Second, spatiotemporal data are heterogeneous both in space and time at various levels. While classical data analytics assumes homogeneity, spatiotemporal data can demonstrate different characteristics, depending on the seasonality of data. For example, the maritime traffic is highly seasonal, and, depending on its intensity by season, it may affect pollution and animal populations in different ways (Campana et al., 2017). Observations about such phenomena will be distributed differently, according to the season.

Other challenges of spatiotemporal data analytics come from both the spatial and the temporal dimensions. Data about the same location and the same time are not always represented in the same way. It is extremely important to understand both the spatial and temporal measurement systems and make sure that all data are recorded in the same system. From the spatial side, data can be represented using various datums. Datum is a mathematical model representing the Earth. There are many sources of spatiotemporal data that do not always use the same datum. Coordinates on one datum do not match coordinates on another one. To analyse data coming from different sources, one must make sure that their formats are harmonised before performing analysis on such data. Related to this is the challenge of coordinates represented on different map projections, which is especially important for the correct visualisation of spatiotemporal data. A map projection is a mathematical process of representing the spherical shape of the Earth (and the particular datum being used) on two-dimensional maps. There are various projections in use (see Fig. 3). Analysis of data on an inaccurate representation of reality may diminish the results of the knowledge discovery process (Ladner & Petry, 2002).

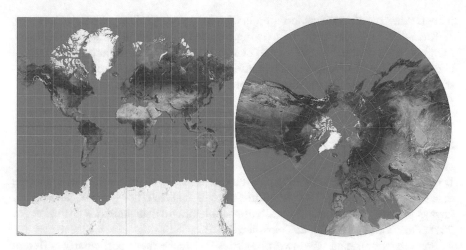

Fig. 3 Mercator projection (left) and Gnomonic projection (right) are two examples of map projections commonly used in navigation (images by Daniel R. Strebe, distributed under CC BY-SA 3.0 license)

The synchronicity of data points is a similar challenge posed by temporal data. Data representing time can be recorded at various time intervals. If sources of data use different time intervals, timestamp sets can be incompatible or irregular. Thus, it is important to transform the data in a unique format before running the analysis (Ladner & Petry, 2002).

Finally, spatial and temporal data are related, but their relationships are implicit. They are not explicitly encoded in the data, so they have to be extracted either during the preprocessing process or computed on the fly (Rao et al., 2012). For example, the neighbouring patterns of data can affect the pattern of interest—a storm and sea conditions can affect the sea traffic performance, even if the relationship between them is not explicitly expressed in the dataset.

6 Application Areas of Spatiotemporal Data Analytics in the Maritime Industry

The following section presents different application areas of spatial-temporal data analytics along a voyage process (see Fig. 4). Those examples are linked to the three primary goals of the maritime transportation industry—safety, sustainability and efficiency (European Commission, 2016). Specifically, five different use cases are presented, which emerge along a voyage process: (1) long-term route planning, (2) environment preservation and monitoring, (3) collision avoidance, (4) cargo tracking and (5) port call optimisation. These cases are underlined by the application

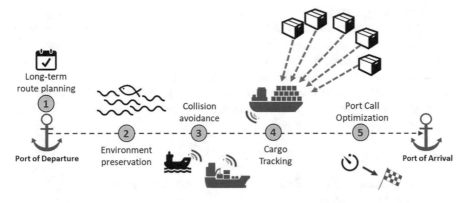

Fig. 4 Typical vessel voyage (own elaboration)

of graph data analysis as it has been proven to be an efficient way in dealing with spatiotemporal data analytics (George & Shekhar, 2008; Gunturi & Shekhar, 2017).

After giving a short introduction to each application area, more details on specific analytic concepts associated with those areas are elaborated. Alongside the exploration of those cases, it should become obvious that safety, sustainability and efficiency are usually complementing dimensions. Moreover, collaborative decision-making often not only has a positive impact on one of those categories but provides positive spillover to the other categories.

6.1 Application Area 1: Long-Term Route Planning

Accurate route planning involves the consideration of countless factors. Data consolidation from various actors and collaborative decision-making is the key to perform accurate and flexible route planning (Lind et al., 2015). The main actors involved in the planning process are port hubs and vessels owners (Lind et al., 2015). Within this process, a vessel gets assigned a planned time of departure from the port of origin, an estimated voyage duration and an estimated time of arrival (ETA) at the port of discharge.

Maritime shipping lanes are established routes in the oceans, which simplify the overall route planning process. Those lanes are designed to plan a voyage from its port of departure to its port of destination in the most efficient possible way. However, other potential disruption factors such as political no-go areas (possibly imposing the threat of piracy or restrictions from embargos) or environmentally sensitive ecosystems (e.g. reefs as a breeding ground for endangered species) need to be taken into account in the long-term route planning process. It is essential to constantly monitor such potential risk factors along a route.

Efficient long-term planning enables actors linked to a voyage to improve their related actions. Cargo owners can eliminate the uncertainty of time-related product availability further upstream in their supply chains (e.g. raw materials needed in the subsequent production process of a facility). Vessel owners can improve the crucial planning of their daily business, being the provision of a service to transport cargo across the oceans. Port operators are able to plan the resources needed for loading/unloading operations with higher accuracy, diminishing disruption risks in those processes (Lind et al., 2018).

6.2 Application Area 2: Environment Preservation and Monitoring

The route planning process ahead of a voyage is based on established principles and assumptions regarding the shipping conditions during a voyage. The longer the voyage, the higher the uncertainties associated with it are. The actual conditions experienced during the voyage can be very different from the assumed conditions in the long-term route planning process. For instance, extreme weather or strong currents can lead to changes in opting for the shortest route. As those factors can be subject to short-term changes, it is important for route optimisation processes to be able to dynamically take those circumstances into account (Lind et al., 2015).

An example of occurrences alongside a voyage, which might require short-term route adjustment, is the consideration of sensitive ecosystems. Sometimes, the geospatial data of sensitive ecosystems can be taken into account already at an early planning stage. However, sensitive ecosystems cannot always be seen as static, and their geographic characteristics can change with time (Campana et al., 2017). For instance, habitats of endangered species cannot be easily tracked and predicted at an early stage. In this case, a moving polygon must be considered when performing route optimisation based on environmentally sensitive areas.

6.3 Application Area 3: Collision Avoidance

Sea transportation is exposed to a large extent to the vagaries of nature. Vessels are highly isolated objects compared to other modes of transportation as they are travelling on the open sea. Thus, the desired safe harbour is often far away in the case of an accident in mid-ocean. Nevertheless, sea transportation has increased significantly and steadily over the last decades. Commonly used shipping routes, also known as maritime highways, in combination with the increasing volume of sea transportation, lead to critical traffic conditions, especially in maritime bottlenecks (John & Rizvanolli, 2016; Porathe, Brödje, Weber, Camre, & Borup, 2015). Given those circumstances, collision avoidance remains a major concern in the maritime context even in modern times (Porathe et al., 2015).

With the increasing number of vessels in high-traffic areas, an increasing need for early information exchange between vessels becomes vital. Standardised and automated information exchange between encountering vessels is a core element needed in order to increase safety on the sea and prevent critical collision situations.

6.4   Application Area 4: Cargo Tracking

Cargo owners often use third-party logistics providers to manage transportation. However, outsourcing shipping activities comes with the loss of control over the exact process flow (Ketler & Walstrom, 1993). Due to the complex networks of actors involved in transportation processes, problems such as clear warranty assignment for damaged goods become relevant. For instance, a damaged television screen can originate from the initial delivery leg to a port, from loading/unloading operations or from extreme weather at sea.

One approach to achieve transparency throughout a voyage can be affixing sensors to the transported goods themselves or to the container, in which the goods are transported. Various types of sensors exist, providing different functionalities and measuring different conditions such as geospatial data, lighting, radiation, shock or humidity (Pang, Chen, Zhang, Chen, & Zheng, 2010; Ruiz-Garcia, Barreiro, Rodríguez-Bermejo, & Robla, 2007). Each obtained observation is inseparably linked to spatiotemporal data, meaning that when a sensor streams data on the condition of a specific product, a timestamp and the geospatial information of the product are usually streamed with it.

6.5   Application Area 5: Port Call Optimisation

Vessels often experience severe delays in their loading/unloading processes in the case that ports could not set up the required nautical resources such as pilotage, tugboats or mooring in time. Such scenarios can be caused by internal congestion in the port area (see Fig. 5) or simply a misjudged estimated time of arrival of a vessel (Valenciaport Foundation, 2018).

Port calls involve a large number of actors with highly interconnected actions. Understanding the links between all actors is essential to establish a port call standard with clearly defined responsibilities, actions and alternative courses of action (Lind et al., 2015). This ensures a robust process and decreases the idle time of a vessel, a crucial indicator for the efficiency of a voyage.

The efficiency of ports can be measured in various ways: the average time needed for loading/unloading operations, the time a vessel spends at the port including idle time or a combination of both (Lind et al., 2018). Idle time in a voyage can

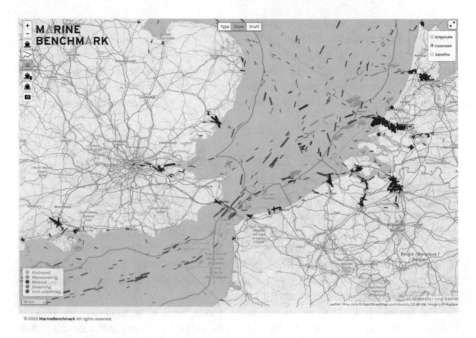

Fig. 5 Spatiotemporal data stream displayed on a map, demonstrating vessels' state and port congestions (by permission of Marine Benchmark, all rights reserved)

be described as a non-productive time where no actions can be performed, which would serve the process goal of arriving at the port of destination. Idle time usually appears in the form of waiting time of a vessel before entering a port area, e.g. due to congestion or unprepared berth operations (Lind et al., 2018). An idle time comes with high economic, social and environmental costs. While having to wait outside a port area, the time schedule of the subsequent supply chain processes is put under risk:

- The booked slot for the transportation from the port of destination to its intended destination may be missed due to delayed arrival.
- Unavailability of the transported goods at the destination further downstream the supply chain raises significant issues. For instance, a factory's production processes could be impaired if the required production parts run out of stock.

The conclusion is clear: as a vessel's idle time has a severe impact on subsequent supply chain processes and leads to negative consequences for related operations, the goal of port call processes should be to minimise this unproductive time and establish a standardised, predictable and robust process.

7 Examples of Spatiotemporal Data Analytics Using Graph Databases

As described in the previous section, maritime processes often involve a large network of interconnected actors and actions. The goal of this section is to demonstrate how to build a framework displaying relevant actors, the relationships among them, and to highlight the benefits of utilising spatiotemporal information in certain application areas. To cope with such complex network structures, we utilise the architectural benefits of graph databases.

7.1 Step 1: Continuous Spatiotemporal Data Stream from a Vessel on a Voyage

When leaving port, a vessel aims to follow a certain route to its desired destination, which was determined as an optimal route ahead of the voyage (Application Area 1). After the vessel left its port, it is continuously streaming spatiotemporal data. These streams can be displayed on a map like the one presented in Fig. 5. This constitutes the basis of our framework. While geospatial data streams serve as a fundament for all application areas described in the following steps, they do not contain value as long as they are not processed in a meaningful manner.

7.2 Step 2: Integration of the Instance 'Port Hub' as an Addressee

In order to improve route planning processes, a port hub node as a managing instance is created. It serves as an addressee of the spatiotemporal data streamed by the vessel but also consolidates relevant information from a vessel's macro environment such as data on environmentally sensitive areas or political no-go areas.

The communication between the vessel and port hub is bidirectional: while the vessel provides the port hub with continuously updated spatial data, the port hub can process this data based on the consideration of continuously changing external circumstances and propose route adjustments.

Such short-term route adjustments can have various reasons. For instance, a storm could impose risks on the vessel's safety or environmentally sensitive areas should be bypassed (Application Area 2).

7.3   Step 3: Ship-to-Ship Communication

While in the last decades, the shipping sector experienced continuous growth, this led to substantially more traffic in the oceans. Efficient ship-to-ship communication is essential to prevent collision risks at an early stage and avoid the need for critical last-minute manoeuvres. This requires an extended viewpoint on the maritime environment, accounting for the existence of other moving objects within a vessel's proximity. Spatiotemporal data points of vessels in a given area need to be constantly monitored to detect critical situations at an early stage (Application Area 3). When, from a technical viewpoint, two nodes inside a defined polygon are approaching each other and a certain minimum distance between those objects is infringed, an automated warning message should be triggered. In practice, the detection of critical situations with respect to collision scenarios is a complex matter in which many factors need to be considered. Geofencing in combination with route forecasting tools are a suitable solution to identify those situations.

Today's technical capabilities allow us to automatically communicate potential solutions such as route or speed adjustments to the involved vessels to prevent such critical situations at an early stage. In such cases, route optimisation does not only provide improvements for the safety on board but also has positive spillovers for fuel usage—going hand in hand with a decline in cost and emissions from fuel burned—and overall voyage efficiency.

7.4   Step 4: Combination of Sensor Data and Spatiotemporal Data

In this step, the communication of cargo-related data between vessel and cargo owner is integrated into the framework. When the right data is available, much more than just determining the status of a product at a certain time is possible.

A direct application area of spatial-temporal data is the domain of condition monitoring: the goal of this discipline is to constantly observe important information for a given item and derive useful actions based on the observed conditions. An example of condition monitoring is the processing of sensor data in combination with spatiotemporal data in cold chains (Tsang et al., 2017). The stringent fulfilment of keeping a cold chain at a certain temperature throughout the entire transport is key to deliver the product in the agreed condition.

Extremely sensitive goods such as medical goods may lose their potency and therefore their value even when experiencing only a short infringement of the required temperature range.

For other product types, a temporary deviation from the desired temperature may be correctable. For instance, when a container of fruits is transported, it is supposed to undergo a certain maturity process throughout the shipment. In some cases, the sensors embedded in the container not only can obtain data but can also trigger countermeasures to adjust the maturation process when predefined thresholds are exceeded, taking into account the remaining voyage duration based on spatiotemporal data. This way, the premature expiry of perishable goods can be prevented (Tsang et al., 2017).

Another example is the fact that tighter environmental regulations impose pressure on fuel efficiency and sustainable processes become a decisive factor in the market. As a result, a growing number of cargo owners preferably obtain services from shipping providers with a more sustainable fleet composition. In such circumstances, sensor data helps fleet owners to accurately measure the environmental performance of their fleets, e.g. in terms of fuel consumption and position themselves as a sustainable actor on the market.

Countless other use cases exist. Next to cargo owners, other stakeholders like transport buyers, forwarders, insurance companies, environmental organisations or other service suppliers may derive value out of such sensor data streams. Monitoring relevant Key Performance Indicators (KPIs) across time and establishing benchmark data for fleets of vessels or even single vessels help many stakeholders within the maritime domain to find best practices, establish good operations, increase energy efficiency and improve environmental footprints.

7.5 Step 5: Reflecting the Complexity of a Port Call Process

As previously outlined, idle time is a useful indicator to measure port call efficiency, and a delay of the vessel's arrival can have severe impacts for the entire supply chain. Causes for this phenomenon are manifold and include economic self-interest, conflicts of interest and information asymmetry (Lind et al., 2019).

Conflicts of interest and principal-agent behaviour lead to a highly fragmented industry, with its information systems being insufficiently integrated. However, there is a strong need for aligning processes to boost efficiency (Cerrini, 2015).

To resolve this problem, a clear understanding of all actors and relationships is essential (John & Rizvanolli, 2016). In order to acquire a clear picture of maritime actors, the EU-sponsored Sea Traffic Management (STM) Validation Project created a map showing all actors involved in a port call process and their relevant actions (see Karlsson, Haraldson, Lind, Olsson, & Andersen, 2020). This illustration shows nine main actors all fulfilling different functionalities along a vessel's port call process. In many cases, the actions of one actor depend on the fulfilment of the actions of at least one other actor. In this complex and sensitive network, not only the fulfilment of action but also its timing is crucial: actors of a port call often need to provide their service within a narrow time slot. In case a single actor is unable to deliver its service in the intended time slot, negative consequences for the entire port call process can emerge.

Openly communicating key figures among relevant actors, such as the estimated time of arrival (abbr.: ETA), the estimated time of departure (abbr.: ETD) and resource status changes could increase the predictability of when different states are reached, which enables actors of the process to optimally plan for their contribution to the ecosystem (Lind et al., 2015). Thus, we can conclude that a port call process involves a variety of actors, and its efficiency is determined by the interaction between them.

Given the complexity of a port call process, the vessel's ecosystem during a port call process is described by the various actors involved in the port call process and their subsequent relationships. Upon analysing every single relationship in detail, a specific plan should be developed on when to trigger certain events and how to communicate among the actors. When designing an efficient information system for this environment, spatiotemporal analytics techniques should be applied to detect event-based relationships, assessing the reliability of every single actor, their interdependencies and alternative solutions in case of deviation from the desired process.

We conclude that when a vessel approaches a port, a complex sequence of actions from various interdependent actors is required. Thus, having acquired a comprehensive understanding of the network dynamics is essential to ensure efficient port call processes.

7.6   Consolidating the Single Steps to One Framework for Spatiotemporal Data Analytics in a Maritime Environment

The previous sections were outlining various use cases where spatiotemporal analytics techniques can be applied in a maritime setting. Those different use cases focused on different phases of a voyage. They include both long-term route planning ahead of a voyage and short-term route adjustments due to unforeseen events such as no-go shipping areas (e.g. environmentally sensitive areas) or collision avoidance manoeuvres. Finally, we can consolidate the single focus areas and derive a more holistic picture of the spatiotemporal analytic opportunities arising throughout a voyage. As a result, we create a holistic framework of application areas for spatiotemporal data analytics along a vessel's voyage (Fig. 6). While the developed framework is sketched on a high level to give an overview of the before mentioned use cases, each single application area needs to be tackled considering many specific characteristics. Knowing the specificities of every single area in detail is essential to achieve an added value from spatiotemporal data analytics.

8   Conclusions

In this chapter, we have provided an overview of spatiotemporal data analytics for the maritime industry. We introduced the data analytics types and reviewed the properties of spatiotemporal data which cause challenges in the analytics process.

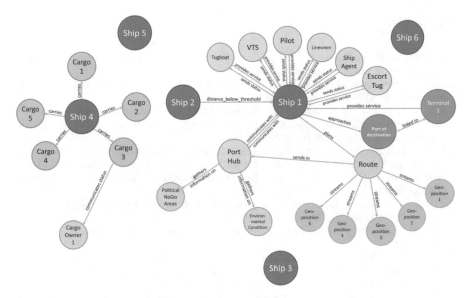

Fig. 6 Holistic framework of application areas for spatiotemporal data analytics along a vessel's voyage (own elaboration)

This allowed us to introduce some analytics methods and to introduce five use scenarios in the maritime context. Finally, an example of spatiotemporal data analytics along a typical vessel voyage was presented, using graph databases as a tool to optimise the process.

While this chapter focused mainly on scenarios around vessel-to-vessel communication, voyage planning and port call optimisation, it is important to highlight that spatiotemporal data analytics can also be extremely beneficial for stakeholders outside the described vessel and port operations such as cargo owners, transport buyers, forwarders, insurance companies, ship financing institutions, flag states, port states, environmental organisations, ship equipment suppliers, yards and other service suppliers. We reckon that the behaviour of cargo owners/transport buyers can be a decisive factor for the development of the maritime shipping industry as their demand has the power to reward efficient operations and sustainable fleet composition—in conjunction with thorough data analytics.

Both spatiotemporal data analytics and the maritime industry are very complex domains. In this chapter, we provide only a starting point to the knowledge discovery process in the context of maritime informatics. Yet, we show that spatiotemporal data analytics can support situational awareness on many levels, thus, making it a great tool to improve decision-making in the maritime industry.

References

Andrienko, N., & Andrienko, G. (2006). *Exploratory analysis of spatial and temporal data: A systematic approach*. Springer Science & Business Media.

Atluri, G., Karpatne, A., & Kumar, V. (2018). Spatio-temporal data mining: A survey of problems and methods. *ACM Computing Surveys (CSUR), 51*, 83.

Baksh, A.-A., Abbassi, R., Garaniya, V., & Khan, F. (2018). Marine transportation risk assessment using Bayesian Network: Application to Arctic waters. *Ocean Engineering, 159*, 422–436. https://doi.org/10.1016/j.oceaneng.2018.04.024.

Campana, I., Angeletti, D., Crosti, R., Luperini, C., Ruvolo, A., Alessandrini, A., & Arcangeli, A. (2017). Seasonal characterisation of maritime traffic and the relationship with cetacean presence in the Western Mediterranean Sea. *Marine Pollution Bulletin, 115*, 282–291. https://doi.org/10.1016/j.marpolbul.2016.12.008.

Cazzanti, L., & Pallotta, G. (2015). Mining maritime vessel traffic: Promises, challenges, techniques. In *OCEANS 2015-Genova* (pp. 1–6). IEEE.

Cerrini, C. (2015). *Defining sea traffic management*. The Current Situation (No. MONALISA 2 0_D2.1.1).

Duck, R. W. (2012). Marine spatial planning: Managing a dynamic environment. *Journal of Environmental Policy & Planning, 14*, 67–79. https://doi.org/10.1080/1523908X.2012.664406.

European Commission. (2016). *Mobility and transport – maritime* [WWW Document]. Maritime Mobility and Transport. Accessed April 12, 2019, from https://ec.europa.eu/transport/modes/maritime_en.

Ganguly, A. R., & Steinhaeuser, K. (2008). *Data mining for climate change and impacts* (pp. 385–394). Presented at the 2008 IEEE International Conference on Data Mining Workshops. https://doi.org/10.1109/ICDMW.2008.30.

George, B., & Shekhar, S. (2008). Time-aggregated graphs for modeling spatio-temporal networks. In S. Spaccapietra, J. Z. Pan, P. Thiran, T. Halpin, S. Staab, V. Svatek, P. Shvaiko, & J. Roddick (Eds.), *Journal on Data Semantics XI, Lecture Notes in Computer Science* (pp. 191–212). Berlin: Springer. https://doi.org/10.1007/978-3-540-92148-6_7.

Ghaemi, M. S., Agard, B., Nia, V. P., & Trépanier, M. (2015). Challenges in spatial-temporal data analysis targeting public transport. *IFAC-PapersOnLine, 48*, 442–447.

Gunturi, V. M. V., & Shekhar, S. (2017). *Spatio-temporal graph data analytics*. Springer. https://doi.org/10.1007/978-3-319-67771-2.

Harrald, J. R., Mazzuchi, T. A., & Stone, C. M. (1992). *Risky business: Can we believe port risk assessments?* (pp. 657–669). Presented at the Ports '92, ASCE.

John, O., & Rizvanolli, A. (2016). A concept for future shipping. *Baltic Transport Journal, 1*, 50–51.

Karlsson, M., Haraldson, S., Lind, M., Olsson, E., & Andersen, T. (2020). Data visualisation tools for enhanced situational awareness in maritime operations (Chapter 21). In M. Lind, M. Michaelides, R. Ward, & R. T. Watson (Eds.), *Maritime informatics*. Heidelberg: Springer.

Ketler, K., & Walstrom, J. (1993). The outsourcing decision. *International Journal of Information Management, 13*, 449–459.

Ladner, R., & Petry, F. (2002). Spatio-temporal data mining and knowledge discovery: Issues overview. In *Mining spatio-temporal information systems* (pp. 1–19). Springer.

Laxhammar, R., Falkman, G., & Sviestins, E. (2009). Anomaly detection in sea traffic-a comparison of the Gaussian mixture model and the kernel density estimator. In *2009 12th International Conference on Information Fusion* (pp. 756–763). IEEE.

Lind, M., Bergmann, M., Haraldson, S., Watson, R. T., Park, J., Gimenez, J., & Andersen, T. (2019). *From concept to implementation-an interplay between research and practice*. Concept Note.

Lind, M., Haraldson, S., Karlsson, M., & Watson, R. T. (2015). *Port collaborative decision making–closing the loop in sea traffic management*. 14th International Conference on Computer Applications and Information Technology in the Maritime Industries, Ulrichshusen, Germany.

Lind, M., Ward, R., Michaelides, M., Lane, A., Sancricca, M., Watson, R. T., Bergmann, M., Bjorn-Andersen, N., Haraldson, S., & Andersen, T. (2018). *Reducing idle time with collaboration and data sharing*. Notes 3, 5.

McAfee, A., & Brynjolfsson, E. (2012). Big data: The management revolution. *Harvard Business Review, 90*, 60–66, 68, 128.

Merrick, J. R. W., van Dorp, J. R., Mazzuchi, T. A., & Harrald, J. R. (2001). Modeling risk in the dynamic environment of maritime transportation. In *Proceedings of the 33rd Conference on Winter Simulation, WSC '01* (pp. 1090–1098). Washington, DC: IEEE Computer Society.

Pang, Z., Chen, J., Zhang, Z., Chen, Q., & Zheng, L. (2010). Global fresh food tracking service enabled by wide area wireless sensor network. In *2010 IEEE Sensors Applications Symposium (SAS)* (pp. 6–9). IEEE.

Pigni, F., Piccoli, G., & Watson, R. T. (2016). Digital data streams. *California Management Review, 58*, 5–25. https://doi.org/10.1525/cmr.2016.58.3.5.

Porathe, T., Brödje, A., Weber, R., Camre, D., & Borup, O. (2015). *Supporting situation awareness on the bridge: Testing route exchange in a practical e-navigation study*. https://doi.org/10.1201/b18514-12.

Rao, K. V., Govardhan, A., & Rao, K. C. (2012). Spatiotemporal data mining: Issues, tasks and applications. *International Journal of Computer Science and Engineering Survey, 3*, 39.

Ruiz-Garcia, L., Barreiro, P., Rodríguez-Bermejo, J., & Robla, J. I. (2007). Monitoring the inter-modal, refrigerated transport of fruit using sensor networks. *Spanish Journal of Agricultural Research, 5*, 142–156.

Sea Traffic Management. (n.d.). *About sea traffic management* [WWW Document]. Sea Traffic Management Validation Project – STM. Accessed March 12, 2019, from https://www.stmvalidation.eu/about-stm/.

Tsang, Y., Choy, K., Wu, C., Ho, G., Lam, H., & Koo, P. (2017). An IoT-based cargo monitoring system for enhancing operational effectiveness under a cold chain environment. *International Journal of Engineering Business Management, 9*, 1847979017749063. https://doi.org/10.1177/1847979017749063.

Valenciaport Foundation. (2018). *How STM measure and analyse results*. Sea Traffic Management Validation Project – STM. Accessed April 12, 2019, from https://www.stmvalidation.eu/news/how-stm-measure-and-analyse-the-results/.

Watson, R. T. (2013). *Data management: Databases and organizations* (6th ed.). eGreen Press.

Watson, R. T., Lind, M., Delmeire, N., & Liesa, F. (2020). Shipping: A self-organizing ecosystem (Chapter 2). In M. Lind, M. Michaelides, R. Ward, & R. T. Watson (Eds.), *Maritime informatics*. Heidelberg: Springer.

Yuan, M., & McIntosh, J. (2002). A typology of spatiotemporal information queries. In R. Ladner, K. Shaw, & M. Abdelguerfi (Eds.), *Mining Spatio-Temporal Information Systems. The Springer International Series in Engineering and Computer Science* (Vol. 699). Boston: Springer.

Data Visualisation Tools for Enhanced Situational Awareness in Maritime Operations

Mathias Karlsson (ID)**, Sandra Haraldson** (ID)**, Mikael Lind** (ID)**, Eddie Olsson** (ID)**,
Trond Andersen** (ID)**, and Miluše Tichavska** (ID)

1 Introduction

The world is globalised and freight transportation is a crucial supply chain component to enable efficient and environmentally friendly movements of freight and timely availability of such for society and industry (Crainic, 2003). Maritime transport is responsible for handling about 90% of the world's cargo. Historically, maritime transport has been considered to be a self-organised ecosystem (Kay, Regier, Boyle, & Francis, 1999; Watson, Lind, Delmeire, & Liesa, 2020), where each actor historically optimises their operations, often giving rise to inefficiencies on a holistic level. Over the past 20 years, we have seen how an increased degree of digitalisation has been central to altering previously "analogue" organisations. Today, it is possible to discern an alteration in how previously disparate organisations can work together to create and disseminate various services and products through increased digitalisation (Tilson, Lyytinen, & Sorensen, 2010). This

M. Karlsson (✉) · S. Haraldson · E. Olsson
Research Institutes of Sweden (RISE), Gothenburg, Sweden
e-mail: Mathias.Karlsson@ri.se; sandra@realsearchers.com; Eddie.Olsson@ri.se

M. Lind
Research Institutes of Sweden (RISE) and Chalmers University of Technology, Gothenburg,
Sweden
e-mail: mikael@realsearchers.com

T. Andersen
NOFO, Sandnes, Norway
e-mail: TA@Nofo.no

M. Tichavska
MarineTraffic, London, UK
e-mail: miluse.tichavska@marinetraffic.com

M. Lind et al. (eds.), *Maritime Informatics*, Progress in IS,
https://doi.org/10.1007/978-3-030-50892-0_21

digital transformation provides a means for enhanced transparency enabled by data sharing and situational awareness, contributing to better coordination and improved efficiency (Lind, 2018) for all actors involved. To create the means for such coordination, situational awareness needs to be established among involved actors empowered by digitalisation and principles for information sharing. By integrating information from maritime transport, a more sustainable and efficient transportation system should emerge. When several business activities are digitalised, new sources of information are generated and collected, which makes it possible for decisions based on real-time data (Jagadish et al., 2014; McAfee, Brynjolfsson, Davenport, Patil, & Barton, 2012), or as noted by McAfee et al. (2012, p.63) "Data-driven decisions are better decisions—it's as simple as that".

In this chapter, we elaborate on how to create meaningful data visualisations for decision support to enable distributed coordination in self-organised ecosystems. We visit applications of visualisations arising from different domains and put special attention towards one application in which we have been substantially engaged, visualisations for the test bed of Port Collaborative Decision Making (PortCDM), as one of the strategic enablers of the Sea Traffic Management (STM) concept.

Following this introduction, the chapter is divided into three sections. The first section covers visualisation in general, the second covers dashboards for visualisation, and the third covers dashboards for common situational awareness. We conclude the chapter with a brief summary highlighting the importance of context-specific visualisation.

2 Visualisation

Visualisation is not a new phenomenon. When our ancestors started creating cave paintings, they were attempting to communicate via images. In modern times, visualisations can be animations, images, videos or diagrams such as information about a performance management, a decision support or a business intelligence system. Information is often made understandable by the use of different types of graphics. Visualisation has numerous definitions, and one of the most used for digital visualisations is "the use of computer-supported, interactive, visual representations of data to amplify cognition" (Card, 1999).

Data visualisation is the graphical representation of data to help the viewer meaningfully interpret, analyse and understand large complex sets of data to support informed decisions. Visualisation tools must serve the purpose of the stakeholders who have a decision to make.

2.1   State-of-the-Art Associated with Visualisation Tools

Since most interfaces are built for web and mobile platforms (Puszynski, 2019), visualisation tools are often written in JavaScript, with the React framework being the most popular platform for current development. Most tools focus on standard visualisations, such as charts and graphs, but typically support the creation of more advanced visualisations, such as in Fig. 1.

There are also visualisation frameworks for geographical information data, mostly geared towards the rendering of Web Feature Layer (WFL) data, as served by most GIS platforms for web publishing. For those that want to go beyond flat visualisation, there are a number of fully developed 3D platforms that support everything from simple 3D rotatable bar charts to full 3D rendering with physics engines, particle systems, materials and real-time lighting for fully interactive animations. With today's browser capabilities and software tools, we can literally visualise anything we like, any way we like (see, e.g. Fig. 2). That being said, any available technology is, at best, an enabler of good visualisation.

The purpose of a visualisation is not always best approached by doing what is possible; rather the focus needs to be on what best helps the decision-maker interpret the data. This also means that a certain set of data may need different visualisations, not only for different people but for each person's specific needs and diversity of the tasks that they face. For example, the same data that in one visualisation shows a simple graph of how many ships are expected to be in a port during the coming 5 days may also be used to indicate which berths are beyond capacity during that same period by means of a color-coded map. Both of these visualisations can be displayed side by side in a dashboard to make both perspectives available without any need for navigation between views.

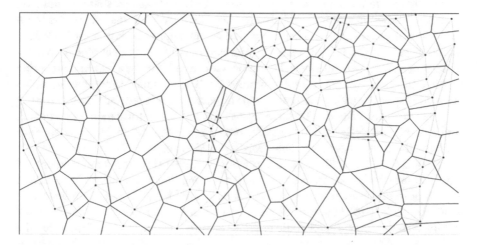

Fig. 1 Delaunay/Voronoi Tessellation example from Nivo (https://nivo.rocks/)

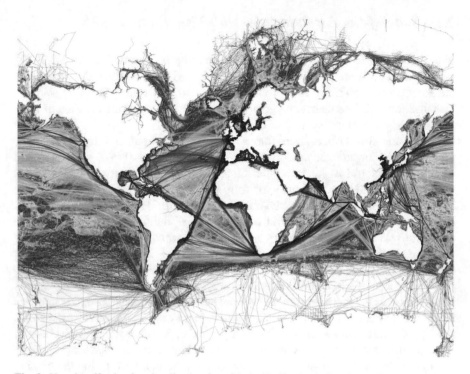

Fig. 2 Vessel traffic density visualisation from MarineTraffic (https://marinetraffic.com)

3 Using a Dashboard for Visualisation

When organisations, public and private, need to collaborate and share information with each other in order to effectively solve their tasks, a dashboard can be a good way of visualising information, which was an approach chosen for the Future Airports and the GOTRIS II projects. The Future Airports project took a door-to-door perspective, which involved the processes from booking a trip to completing a round-trip journey from origin to destination. This included synchronised multi-modal transport, as well as activities at the airports to be visited and possibly the use of other means of transport. Different ways of visualising information were studied, and a dashboard design was chosen for passengers, with the ability to personalise the visualised information for their decision-making needs.

The GOTRIS (Göta älv River Information Services) II project was a demonstration platform for collaborative information-sharing and coordination by different means of transportation, where relevant actors provided and received information that was critical to their operations. The core idea was that by knowing other actors' intentions, each actor could optimise their own actions and performance. The GOTRIS platform supported services for the various actors, including the operator in charge of the railway traffic crossing a river, ships movement on the river for

Fig. 3 Visualisation tool for pilots in GOTRIS II

the pilots and captains in ships and river Vessel Traffic Service (VTS) information for those operating the locks on the river and some of the bridges crossing the river (Holmberg, 2015). One of those services was a dashboard built for a tablet computer and used by the pilots on the ships travelling on the river Göta älv, in order to support the pilot with information such as when the bridges crossing the river could be opened for passage of the ship, speed suggestions to arrive at the bridges on time, where they could expect to meet other ships and weather-related information such as visibility, since fog is a challenge for river traffic. The information about the real-time water flow on the river was also provided, which the pilots used when manoeuvring a ship. Figure 3 shows the dashboard in use on a ship and a screenshot of it.

The operators in charge of railway movements in the area around Gothenburg and the railway bridges crossing the river also had access to a dashboard where they could see the forecast of when a ship on the river is expected to arrive at specific railway bridges. The GOTRIS platform automatically tries to find an empty slot where a ship will not interfere with railway traffic. The platform takes into account the time required for bridge openings and for a ship's passage under the bridge to find available windows when there are no railway movements. The railway operator can use their dashboard to reject or to give permission for a ship's passage to the pilot on board the vessel. Figure 4 shows two different views of the railway operator's dashboard.

Traditionally, dashboards have been used for measurement control systems and have been limited to the governance of a single organisation (Bose, 2006). Dashboards can usefully support decision-makers when they combine multiple information sources into a single screen, as defined by Few in Few, 2006 and referred to by Yigitbasioglu and Velcu (2012, p.44) "A dashboard is a visual display of the most important information needed to achieve one or more objectives; consolidated and arranged on a single screen so the information can be monitored at a glance". Using dashboards provides the possibility to provide several different methods of visualisation to support decision-making (Lind & Haraldson, 2015).

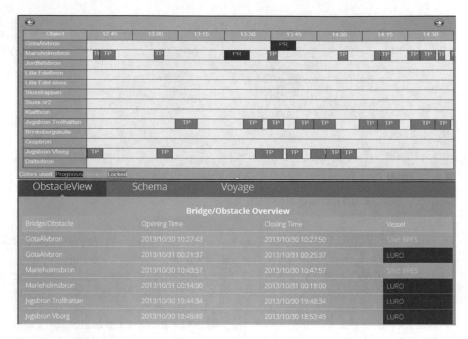

Fig. 4 Visualisation tool for the railway operator in GOTRIS II

Decision quality is likely to increase when the different actors involved in a port call are shown appropriate visualisations of the same information to provide them with the situational awareness relevant and customised for their needs.

3.1 Spatial-Temporal Data Visualisation

Spatial data refers to location (or space), for example, a specific berth in a port; or it could be information providing directions to different locations (see Fig. 5 below). Temporal data refers to time, such as when a ship berthed.

Combining spatial data with temporal data, so-called spatial-temporal data refers to data containing both the time and the location of an object or its status. This makes it possible to reference according to a certain location and time. For example, in the information statement: "*Mare Liberum* was first published in 1609 in the Netherlands" (Wikipedia, 2020), "1609" is temporal data, and "Netherlands" is spatial data. Spatial-temporal data can also be used to give directions, for example, "the ship arrived at berth 519 in the Port of Gothenburg at 17:15", or "Flight SK144 departs from gate 19A at 07:00", as shown in Fig. 6.

Since 2005, most ships engaged on international voyages, together with many others engaged on coastal passage, must be equipped with an Automatic Identification System (AIS) (IMO, 1974). The AIS laid the ground for the digitalisation

Fig. 5 Spatial data visualisation at a Spanish airport

0635	Reykjavik	LH621	13		Check-In Kiosk	
0650	Brussels	FI385	15		Check-In Kiosk	
0655	Copenhagen	SN2324	UA9916	-		
0655	London LHR	SK433	-		Check-In Kiosk	
0700	Stockholm ARN	BA803	20B			
0700	Stockholm BMA	SK144	19A		Check-In Kiosk	
0700	Chania	TF005	12			
0700	Heraklion	TOM3424	11A		Check-In Kiosk	
0715	Stockholm ARN	DK1788	11B		Check-In Kiosk	
0715	Oslo	DY4072	17		Check-In Kiosk	
0730	Prague / Hamburg	WF325	18C			
0735	Karpathos	OK545	18E			
0740	Paris CDG	SK7817	16		Check-In Kiosk	
0755	Mahon	AF1553	UX3614	18F		
0800	Warsaw	BLX501	11A		Check-In Kiosk	
		LO496	-		Check-In Kiosk	
0820	Stockholm BMA	TF011	13			
0825	London LGW	DY4439	19B		Check-In Kiosk	
0830	Krakow	FR4011	12			
0850	Helsinki	AY862	15			
0855	Düsseldorf	EW9221	18D			
0855	Warsaw	W61506	14			
0910	Belgrade	W64206	20B			
0930	Östersund Åre	NFA134	-			

Fig. 6 Spatial-temporal data showing flight information

of shipping—see Watson et al. (2020), as it is able to provide spatial-temporal data related to a ship's movements in different time intervals, such as the identity of the ship, its position, speed and heading. AIS information is now regularly incorporated into a ship's radar display and shown on its electronic chart display and information system (ECDIS) to visualise other ships' position in real time, thereby increasing the safety of navigation (Fig. 7).

The presentation of AIS data on the ECDIS navigational chart display enables officers in a ship to visualise the presence of other ships in their vicinity. It can also be used by those working at VTS stations to monitor ship movements in their control areas. Since AIS has become mandatory for a majority of ships and the implementation of the AIS technology has matured significantly, some companies have started providing online ship tracking and maritime intelligence services. This

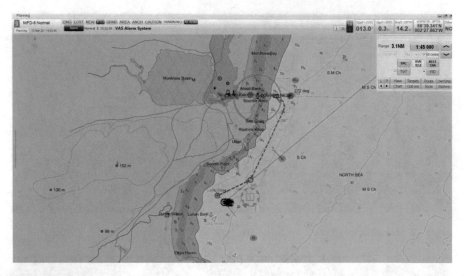

Fig. 7 Visualisation of a ship at anchor outside Luna Bay and its route out from Montrose

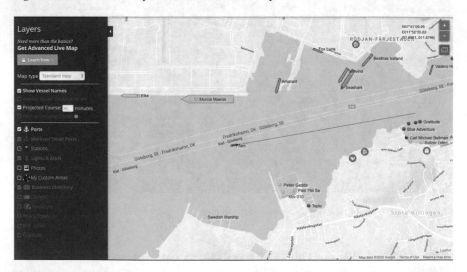

Fig. 8 Vessel position visualisation in the port of Gothenburg (https://marinetraffic.com)

sometimes includes free-of-charge basic accounts allowing the visualisation of ship movements by positioning them on maps (see Fig. 8).

Tracking AIS information could be useful for actors within a port who want to see the present position of a ship that they are anticipating, in order to calculate when they can expect it to arrive, especially when they have doubts about the accuracy of data provided previously by other means.

In the GOTRIS project, AIS information is used as one source for calculating when a vessel can be expected at certain locations, such as bridges or locks, but

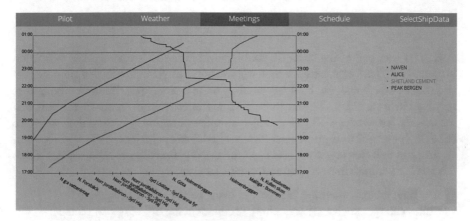

Fig. 9 Meeting predictions presented on the GOTRIS dashboard

it was also used for calculating where different ships in the river can expect to meet each other. Figure 9 shows one of the views, called "Meetings", which is based on spatial-temporal data from AIS and other sources visualised on the pilot's dashboards. It predicts where and when the pilots can expect such meetings.

In the "just-in-time" project, led by several Norwegian ports, machine learning and artificial intelligence was used on AIS data to predict different events, such as the predicted accuracy of the ETA (estimated time of arrival) being approximately equal to the ATA (actual time of arrival). Project data could then be used to trigger a warning if the deviation in a certain pattern from routes already mapped with standard and maximum deviation vectors occurred. This supports services such as VTS services. The same information, when made available for visual presentation to stakeholders, can support common situational awareness.

In the SELIS project, Living Lab 7 (LL7) explores the use of standardised data models and pipeline data exchange principles in the context of cross-border movements of goods. LL7 demonstrates how the early collection of supply chain data, including positional information of vessels (via AIS), and the use of pipeline or data exchange principles, can enhance risk analysis and facilitate e-compliance.

Finally, in the BigDataOcean project, AIS data feeds are used in the project use case on maritime security and anomaly detection. This identifies vessel routes based on their motion patterns to act proactively and minimise threats at sea. Through anomaly detection, a number of anomalies including route deviations, proximity events, sailing in shallow or dangerous waters and AIS signal loss, among others are identified and visualised for the closer monitoring of high-risk vessels and areas at sea.

4   Using Dashboards for Common Situational Awareness

PortCDM was one of the strategic enablers within the EU-funded STM validation project. PortCDM enables enhanced coordination of port calls based on common situational awareness enabled by sharing of real-time data between the actors involved in a port call. Within PortCDM, the international standard for port call messaging, known as S-211 (Fig. 10) within the common maritime data structure (CMDS), emerged to support such standardised data exchange.

The port call message format is used for coordination of port calls, during which the involved actors share critical status data, such as:

- The time when something is expected to happen or when it happened
- Status changes such as if something is commencing or being completed
- The location of a state, such as where it is happening
- When it was shared

A visualisation of these data creates a shared situational awareness among port call actors (Fig. 11).

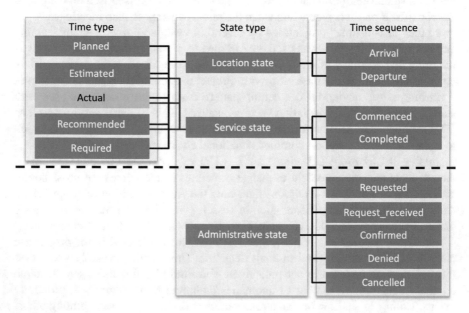

Fig. 10 The different components of a timestamp according to the S-211 standard

Fig. 11 Shared situational awareness

4.1 Visualisation of a Port Call Using a Metro Map

To optimise a port call, the different required actions need to be synchronised, and the involved actors need to be able to trust that the prediction and achievement of each episodic tight coupling of events is shared (Lind, Haraldson, Karlsson, & Watson, 2015; Lind, Haraldson, Karlsson, & Watson, 2016). In order to visualise the dependencies of these episodes, a "Metro Map" (Fig. 12) visualisation has been developed to show the complexity and the interdependencies involved in a port visit. The Metro Map shows, for example, that in order for a towage operation to start, a ship and a tug need to be organised and synchronised to be at the same location at the same time.

The Metro Map provides an easy to understand presentation of the important coordination points in a port call process. A *station* (a white round circle) on the Metro Map is where there is an episodic tight coupling. In order to reach these coordination points, information needs to be exchanged before reaching a station, which are illustrated as lines on connecting small grey ringed white circles, such as the coordination between a tugboat operator and a ship's master.

4.2 Coordination of Port Calls Through Visualisation

The visualisations chosen for PortCDM were inspired by the dashboard thinking of Few (2006) and Yigitbasioglu and Velcu (2012), where the principle is that presented information should fit on a computer screen and be configurable. When

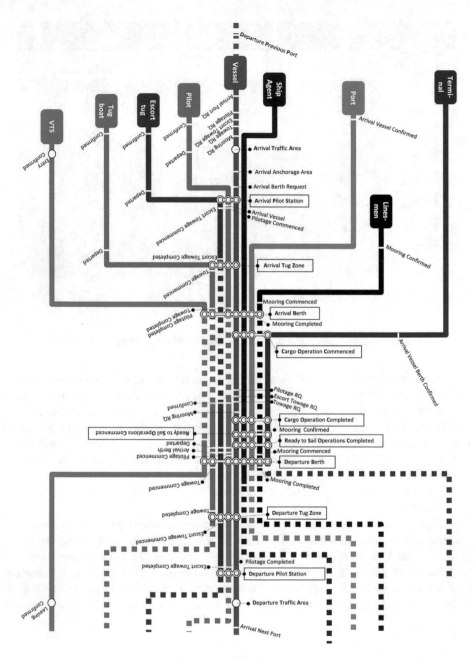

Fig. 12 Visualisation of a port call through a Metro Map

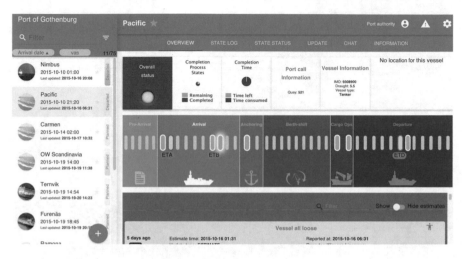

Fig. 13 Situational awareness

Fig. 14 Gantt timeline

PortCDM was tested and validated, the visualisation tool allowed a choice between different predefined applications, or widgets presenting the same information using different visualisation techniques in order to meet different needs.

For the MONALISA 2.0 project, a dashboard like web-based application was developed for visualising port call-related information (Fig. 13).

Based on the feedback, a Gantt timeline (Fig. 14) was developed to show planned, ongoing and terminated parallel operations of a port call. Each line on the Gantt timeline can be clicked to show more information about an event. The timeline uses different colours to indicate who has reported information thereby supporting the coordination of actions.

Two widgets were developed: "Data Sources", which gives an overview of the system or reported information for a specific port call and the "Statement Log" which reports the progress of a port call in a tabular format (the same information can also be viewed in a Gantt timeline) (Fig. 15).

Fig. 15 Statement log visual

Fig. 16 Visualisation of port call and weather data

Following another request, a widget providing a geographical view of Marine Traffic (Fig. 16) was created to combine and compare information from the Gantt timeline and statement log with a geographical view. In addition, it is also possible to add weather and oceanographic data.

To keep track of several port calls at once, a widget called "Portcall Multiview" was created. This view reports the status of multiple specified port calls (Fig. 17). Clicking on any port gives more detailed information of a port call. Figure 17 shows the widgets "Portcall Multiview" and "Portcall Overview".

To support mobile port employees, a PortableCDM for smartphones and tablets was developed (Figs. 18 and 19).

In the port call list, the port calls of interest can be designated as "favourites", and tapping a port call retrieves a timeline. A Gantt chart is not ideal for a smartphone, so a timeline similar to those in many public transportation applications was created. Horizontal red lines on the timeline indicate present operations, and tapping on the timeline reveals the information creating the visualisation. All the times on the

Fig. 17 Portcall Multiview

Fig. 18 PortableCDM, showing menu, available port calls and a port call timeline

timeline are also marked including estimates and actuals. The app also raises an alarm when there are possible discrepancies in the timing of events.

There is also a need to visualise the performance of port call operations by reporting a port's key performance indicators (KPIs) for different stakeholders (Fig. 20).

To monitor a port's digital data streams, a dashboard is useful (Fig. 21). This enables technical support staff to identify problems.

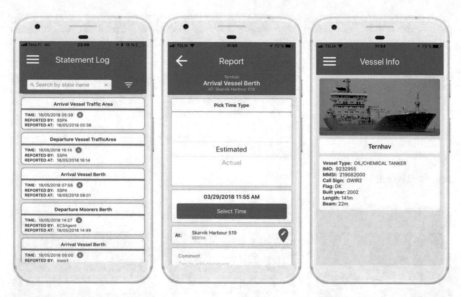

Fig. 19 PortableCDM, showing statement log, how to report times and information about the ship

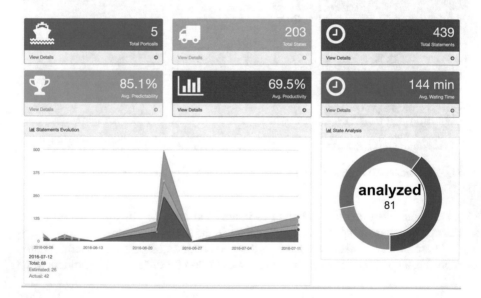

Fig. 20 A visual for Port analytics

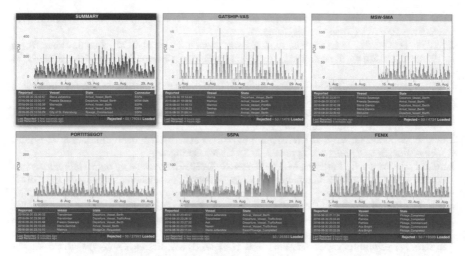

Fig. 21 Monitoring dashboard for digital data streams

5 Conclusions

This chapter highlights efforts to provide suitable visualisations for common situations during one or more port calls. It reveals how different modes of visualisation can be used to engage with stakeholders to fine-tune their different needs. Visualisations for common situational awareness provide insights on how spatial-temporal dimensions can be represented.

We are at an early stage with respect to visualisations to support maritime decision-making and planning. It is important that Maritime Informatics researchers develop and deploy new forms of visual data representation as they gain access to more data about voyage and port operations and learn how various forms of visualisation improve decision-making.

References

Bose, R. (2006). Understanding management data systems for enterprise performance management. *Industrial Management & Data Systems, 106*(1), 43–59. https://doi.org/10.1108/02635570610640988.

Card, M. (1999). *Readings in information visualization: Using vision to think.* Morgan Kaufmann.

Crainic, T. G. (2003). Long-haul freight transportation. In R. W. Hall (Ed.), *Handbook of transportation science* (Vol. 56, pp. 451–516). Kluwer Academic. https://doi.org/10.1007/0-306-48058-1_13.

Few, S. (2006). *Information dashboard design: The effective visual communication of data* (1st ed.). O'Reilly.

Holmberg, P. (2015). *GOTRIS demonstration project—Final report, Part 1.* Viktoria.

IMO. (1974, November 1). *International convention for the safety of life at sea (SOLAS)* (Vol. 1184, p. 278). UN Treaty Series, London.

Jagadish, H., Gehrke, J., Labrinidis, A., Papakonstantinou, Y., Patel, J. M., Ramakrishnan, R., & Shahabi, C. (2014). Big data and its technical challenges. *Communications of the ACM, 57*(7), 86–94.

Kay, J. J., Regier, H. A., Boyle, M., & Francis, G. (1999). An ecosystem approach for sustainability: Addressing the challenge of complexity. *Futures, 31*(7), 721–742.

Lind, M. (2018, November). Digital data sharing in maritime transport chains. *Digital Ship*, p. 6. Retrieved from www.thedigitalship.com.

Lind, M., & Haraldson, S. (2015). (Air) port innovations as ecosystem innovations. In *BPM-driving innovation in a digital world* (pp. 193–213). Cham: Springer.

Lind, M., Haraldson, S., Karlsson, M., & Watson, R. T. (2016). *Overcoming the inability to predict a PortCDM future*. 10th International Harbor Masters' Association Congress–Global Port & Marine Operations.

Lind, M., Haraldson, S., Karlsson, M., & Watson, R. T. (2015). *Port collaborative decision making–closing the loop in sea traffic management*. 14th International Conference on Computer Applications and Information Technology in the Maritime Industries, Ulrichshusen, Germany.

McAfee, A., Brynjolfsson, E., Davenport, T. H., Patil, D., & Barton, D. (2012). Big data: The management revolution. *Harvard Business Review, 90*(10), 60–68.

Puszynski, A. (2019). These are the best JavaScript chart libraries for 2019. Retrieved from https://www.freecodecamp.org/news/these-are-the-best-javascript-chart-libraries-for-2019-29782f5e1dc2/

Tilson, D., Lyytinen, K., & Sorensen, C. (2010). *Desperately seeking the infrastructure in IS research: Conceptualization of "digital convergence" as co-evolution of social and technical infrastructures* (pp. 1–10). 2010 43rd Hawaii International Conference on System Sciences.

Watson, R. T., Lind, M., Delmeire, N., & Liesa, F. (2020). Shipping: A self-organizing ecosystem (Chapter 2). In M. Lind, M. Michaelides, R. Ward, & R. T. Watson (Eds.), *Maritime informatics*. Heidelberg: Springer.

Wikipedia Contributors. (2020, January 24). *Mare Liberum*. Wikipedia, The Free Encyclopedia. Retrieved February 15, 2020, from https://en.wikipedia.org/w/index.php?title=Mare_Liberum&oldid=937348672.

Yigitbasioglu, O. M., & Velcu, O. (2012). A review of dashboards in performance management: Implications for design and research. *International Journal of Accounting Information Systems, 13*(1), 41–59.

Intelligent Maritime Information Acquisition and Representation for Decision Support

Ioannis Kyriakides ⓘ, Daniel Hayes ⓘ, and Pavlos Tsiantis ⓘ

1 Introduction

The complexity of the natural marine processes and the rapidly increasing human maritime activity call for enhanced data acquisition and meaningful, timely collection and provision of information to human users for decision support. The resource constraints imposed by the complex, wide-area, limited connectivity maritime environment prohibit the collection and processing of a set of data that could satisfactorily represent the information needed by operators in that environment. Moreover, decision support systems that allow manual requests for existing data cannot provide the amount of information needed to build a common operational picture to support informed decisions related to the rapidly evolving maritime activity. Existing data sets and operational observing platforms are improving coverage in time, space, and parameter year after year with the advance of processors, power systems, connectivity and communications, and data infrastructure, but the ocean is still vastly under-observed for operational purposes. Therefore, a paradigm shift is needed for maritime informatics and decision support that will employ a method of information collection and representation that considers the needs of specific operational scenarios and coordinates available human and cyber-physical capabilities towards collecting and interpreting maritime information.

Innovation in maritime information production and representation will be achieved by the combination of smart management and agile response capabilities

I. Kyriakides (✉) · P. Tsiantis
University of Nicosia Research Foundation, Nicosia, Cyprus
e-mail: kyriakides.i@unic.ac.cy; tsiantis.p@unic.ac.cy

D. Hayes
Cyprus Subsea Consulting and Services C.S.C.S. Ltd., Lakatamia, Cyprus
e-mail: hayesdan@cyprus-subsea.com

M. Lind et al. (eds.), *Maritime Informatics*, Progress in IS,
https://doi.org/10.1007/978-3-030-50892-0_22

of cognitive systems. Cognitive systems, equipped with perception, reasoning, learning, action, and intelligent resource allocation capabilities are able to actively enhance situational awareness under resource constraints. Novel maritime informatics for cognitive decision support systems will excel compared to traditional systems in that they will actively seek missing information to enhance situational awareness via intelligent configuration of human and cyber-physical resources. Intelligent configuration will then address the specific challenges found in the maritime domain that include wide-area coverage, continuous operation, scarce power availability, limited processing and communication rates, limited platform capability of repositioning, and modelling of a highly complex dynamic environment.

Cognitive systems will utilise modern machine learning theory and algorithms that will optimally configure data acquisition systems. Such a network of data acquisition systems will have advanced capabilities, including repositioning, selecting the type of processing of raw data on-board of sensing nodes to generate sufficient statistics, adjusting communication rates while operating under limited or intermittent power, sensor node intentional or accidental failure due to cyber or physical tampering. The improved data acquisition methods will contribute to understanding the complex maritime natural environment and complex dependencies between maritime activities including coastal tourism, water sports, fishing, shipping and maritime transport, and off-shore infrastructure, delivering advanced maritime spatial planning capabilities to human users.

The vision of intelligent information collection and representation is to bring to the human user a common operational picture for decision support that adapts to specific scenarios via intelligent collection, interpretation, and meaningful presentation of maritime data. The cognitive decision support system will enhance information quality and quantity in the maritime space via efficient coordination of human and cyber-physical resources forming a symbiotic relationship.

This chapter reviews sensing systems available for information collection and types of data collected specifically for the maritime domain. It also examines cognitive systems that have the potential to dynamically evolve to select specialised information based on the application considered and the capabilities and constraints available.

2 Maritime Data and Intelligent Sensing Systems

The Global Ocean Observing System (GOOS), an international framework for collecting and managing data from the world's oceans and seas, is executed by the Intergovernmental Oceanographic Commission-UNESCO (IOC-UNESCO) and dozens of organisations and people devoted to coordinating knowledge of the ocean, from remote sensing systems like satellites and coastal radars, to computer models, and direct or in situ observations. Since remote sensing systems and models cover nearly 100% of the surface of the world's oceans, we focus on in situ observations, the most difficult to collect and share, which is why IOC and the World Meteorological Organization (WMO) founded the Joint WMO-IOC Technical Commission for Oceanography and Marine Meteorology (JCOMM) in situ Observations Programme Support Centre (JCOMMOPS). Coordinated groups are centred around regions (e.g. EuroGOOS) and particular observation platforms at various stages of maturity and legal status (e.g. Argo for profiling floats, European Multidisciplinary Seafloor and water column Observatory (EMSO) for seafloor observatories, OceanGliders for autonomous underwater gliders). Many of these systems are supported by governmental funding and implemented by consortia of specialists, and all are meant to provide free, known-quality maritime data for socially relevant purposes following the Findable Accessible Interoperable and Reusable (FAIR) principle (Wilkinson et al., 2016), now widely encouraged for oceanographic data (Tanhua et al., 2019).

Traditionally collected by ships, ocean data are increasingly collected by autonomous systems, driven by the high costs of dedicated research vessels, and by limited coverage and availability of ships of opportunity. Before dismissing the value of ships in ocean observing it is critical to understand that research vessels provide unequalled opportunities in many ways, such as the ability to collect water for extremely precise and detailed measurements and to support seafloor exploration through the use of specialised equipment like Remotely-Operated-Vehicles. In terms of coverage in time and space, the most valuable, unique ship data sets are being produced by a global network of ships of opportunity: FerryBoxes (EuroGoos, 2017), Expendable BathyThermographs-XBT (Goni et al., 2019), and Continuous Plankton Recorders (Continuous Plankton Recorder (CPR) Survey, n.d.). While indispensable, it is widely accepted that ships alone will not be able to meet society's need for marine data, and that autonomous systems should play a large part. Commercially available autonomous maritime platforms that can host sensor nodes and are suitable for the maritime area include Autonomous Stationary Systems (ASSs), Autonomous Underwater Vehicles (AUVs) and gliders, Autonomous Surface Vehicles (ASVs), Deep Profiling Floats (DPFs), and Autonomous Aerial Vehicles (AAVs). Autonomous Vehicles (AxVs) often have the characteristic of long endurance and complementary capabilities in terms of motion, which, when functioning as swarms in a cognitive sensor network, makes them invaluable assets for achieving coverage in the maritime domain.

ASSs include coastal stations, cabled observatories, buoys (e.g. Fig. 1), moorings (Norweagian Ocean Observation Laboratory, n.d.; Ocean Observatories Initiative, n.d.; OceanSITES, n.d.), and sensor arrays mounted on the sea-bed that can utilise renewable energy for long-term operation. AxVs include ASVs (Autonaut USV, n.d.; Liquid Robotics' Wave Glider, n.d.; Sailbuoy USV, n.d.) which traverse the ocean surface, with sensors in the upper ocean and lower atmosphere and often utilise renewable energy to provide propulsion and solar photovoltaics to provide long-term power autonomy at sea via rechargeable batteries. ASVs allow remotely programmable piloting to either travel paths or to remain at an approximately stationary position without mooring. Communications are typically achieved via satellite communication, providing a robust and secure link to the land-based station

Fig. 1 Meteorological/Oceanographic buoy with sensors. Credit: Daniel Hayes

(e.g. Iridium RUDICS system). AUVs such as those in Fig. 2 use propellers to move quickly and with precision over confined distances (a few kilometres) and short times (a few hours) before recharging. Underwater gliders (Fig. 3) with buoyancy engines, on the other hand, are capable of long-term missions at sea thanks to their proven energy efficient buoyancy propulsion mechanism, although at much slower speed (half-knot) and less navigational precision (100 m). Multi-month missions are common with gliders currently available and have been shown to reach an acceptable 90-day mission success probability (BRIDGES, n.d.; Brito, Smeed, & Griffiths, 2014; Eriksen et al., 2001; Hayes, 2016; Stanway, 2011). Like the above platforms, AUVs carry environmental sensing modules such as acoustic, temperature, salinity, and optical probes, even though much more limited in payload size and available power. Passive acoustic sensing is known for its low power, environmental friendliness, and ability to provide information on background noise, marine mammals, and sea-borne vessels based on engine sound. Moreover, innovative AUVs have emerged with flexible modular structures allowing a wide range of underwater operations (The Eelume Concept, n.d.). Deep Profiling Floats (Argo Autonomous Profiling Float, n.d.), as shown in Fig. 4, complement other nodes due to their lower cost and their capability of longer-term unattended presence in an oceanographic basin. Since floats can be programmed to rest on the seafloor and rise to the surface to transmit collected data at defined intervals, they can

Fig. 2 URRready4OS project experiment: Underwater Robotics Ready for Oil Spills—URready4OS (ECHO/SUB/2013/661056—URready4OS http://ocean.upct.es/urready4os). Surface vehicle (centre): PlatyPOS from LABUST for acoustic and WiFi communications between the AUVs (back, left, and right) and drone (front). Credit: Universidad Politécnica de Cartagena (UPCT)

remain at an approximately stationary position and provide dense coverage of areas and require less maintenance at the expense of flexibility of repositioning and communication frequency. In general, however, they are freely drifting (Lagrangian) platforms, as opposed to fixed systems (Eulerian), or AUVs and ASVs (typically following user-determined transects or semi-Lagrangian). Although deep floats will not provide near-real-time measurements in case of an incident, they are valuable assets providing long-term data that improve the system's learning process to improve performance. Finally, in the global drifter program (DBCP, n.d.; PhOD, n.d.) freely-drifting platforms remain on the surface and collect information on currents and upper ocean/lower atmosphere conditions as in Fig. 5. New designs also collect wave information. Significant areas have been covered and continue to be seeded with drifters, although as an operational tool, they are also used for short-term local studies or emergency operations (search and rescue or oil spill tracking). A summary of widely used platforms, including their time and space coverage, data repositories, unique capabilities, and their significant drawbacks are provided in Table 1.

AAVs can also be used in the maritime domain for long range missions requiring fast response and can be fitted with customised sensing packages (LSTS Systems, n.d.; Undersea, n.d.; Underwater Radio, n.d.). A recent example of using an

Fig. 3 Underwater glider in the surface communication position. After the pilot on shore confirms satellite communication, commands the glider to begin the dive-climb cycle, which will deflate/inflate an oil-filled bladder while steering with dead-reckoning and recording ocean properties. Credit: Jerald Reodica

homogeneous network of platforms for operational pollution response, including real-time UAV, USV underwater communications and AAV WiFi relays, is described at (López-Castejón & Gilabert, 2019; Vasilijevic et al., 2015). Therefore, recent advances in the technology of autonomous stationary, underwater, surface, and aerial vehicles, swarm and artificial intelligence, low power sensing, processing, communications systems, and energy harvesting indicate that the use of cognitive systems for wide maritime area monitoring is a feasible target for the near future. Moreover, functional systems currently exist that need to be further promoted for greater area coverage, cognition, and longer-term persistence (URready4OS, n.d.).

Progress achieved in intelligent systems theory and practical applications for the maritime domain can be found in Champion and Joordens (2015), Franco, Magni, Parisini, Polycarpou, and Raimondo (2008), Joordens and Jamshidi (2009), and Miskovic, Nad, and Rendulic (2015). Practical cognitive systems include a low-cost robotic platform solution (Costa, Duarte, Rodrigues, Oliveira, & Christensen, 2016) designed and developed inexpensive light autonomous robotic maritime units that included on-board processing, communications, and sensing. In Vasilijević, Nad, Mandi, Miškovi, and Vukić (2017), environmental monitoring is addressed via a cooperative robotic system consisting of an AUV and ASV where the design and implementation of the cooperative robotic system and a human-in-the-loop approach is described. In Elkins, Sellers, and Monach (2010), The Future Is

Fig. 4 Profiling float (ARGO). Performs the dive-climb cycle while drifting and recording ocean properties. Credit: Stavros Stylianou

Fig. 5 Surface drifter. The cloth visible in the distance is the drogue which will slowly sink to approximately 15 m depth and ensure the drifter follows currents, with minimum wind effects. Credit: Jerald Reodica

Table 1 Ocean observing platform typical characteristics

Platform	Unique capabilities	Significant drawback	Typical depth range	Spatial/linear range	Latency for summary data	Data/information source
Ships of opportunity	Water samples, ROV support	Running costs, weather limitations	0–10,000 m	Limited by fuel and weather	Seconds	DBCP (n.d.)
Observatories, moorings, buoys, coastal stations	High temporal resolution	Low spatial coverage	0–1000 m	Single point, but possible connected by 1000+ km of cable	Seconds for cables, satellite comms. Months for moorings	OceanSITES (n.d.), National Data Buoy Center (n.d.), Global Sea Level Observing System (n.d.)
Autonomous underwater vehicles (propeller)	High spatial and temporal resolution	Low endurance, high dependence on ship support	0–6000 m	100+ km	Seconds for cables, sat comms., months for moorings	No public source
Autonomous underwater vehicles (gliders)	Long endurance with high vertical resolution	Slow speed, medium spatial resolution	10–1000 m	1000+ km	Hours. Depends on surfacing frequency	Ocean Gliders (n.d.)
Surface vehicles	Real-time control and data	High initial cost	0–20 m	Unlimited if renewable energy used	Minutes	No public source
Profiling floats (Argo)	Very long endurance, deep measurements	Freely drifting	1–2000 m	1000+ km, 1–5 years	Days. Depends on surfacing frequency	Coriolis Operational Oceanography (n.d.)
Surface drifters	Very long endurance, inexpensive	Freely drifting	0–30 m	1000+ km, 1–5 years	Minutes. Depends on configuration	DBCP (n.d.)

Now (n.d.), a combination of sensors, hardware, and software was used to enable autonomy of autonomous surface vehicles with the goal for plug-and-play capability when used as a modular system that can be placed on existing platforms.

3 Data Assimilation, Data-Driven Modelling, and Forecasting

Before data can be used for meaningful analysis and decision-making, quality control needs to take place. There are several ways this can be done: from automatic real-time checks to delayed-mode human-driven controls. Besides marking data points with quality flags, estimates of accuracy and precision should be calculated. Any data-driven model will need these estimates in order to evaluate how much "weight" to place on a given observation when it invariably confronts a difference between the observation and the predicted values. Secondly, data need to be in a format that contains both observations and metadata about those observations (information about quality control procedures and flags, about the sensor and platform, the time and place, etc.). Without metadata, reusability and data longevity are drastically reduced. This format or standard should be commonly used in order to allow easy sharing (interoperable). Organisations that collect data often share with regional or global data assembly centres for wider sharing, sometimes with an embargo period to allow for exclusive scientific analysis and publication by the initial owners. When data are finally shared, and meet these standards, they are known as FAIR. Marine data can be found of all levels of "FAIR"-ness, but adoption of FAIR principles is now strongly encouraged by many funding agencies, governments, and international bodies.

Observations of known accuracy and quality are particularly important when simulating a chaotic, under-observed system such as the ocean with its circulation laws and heat and property budgets. Consider that a typical operational coastal ocean forecasting system with spatial resolution of about 1 km, with a grid of 256 by 256, and 25 vertical layers (such as Hayes, Dobricic, Gildor, and Matsikaris (2019)) has about 1.5 million grid points. At each grid point, the model solves deterministically for 3-D variables of temperature, salinity, eastward velocity, northward velocity, and 2-D variable of sea surface height (upwards of six million points). While it is relatively straightforward to write the equations governing the evolution of this ocean model, they can only be solved numerically, and the slightest perturbation or difference in initial or boundary condition could result in a different solution. Like atmospheric forecasting centres, oceanographers turn to observations to constrain their forecasts, not just evaluate them, through a procedure known as data assimilation: producing an optimal ocean state estimate, given a set of observations and a model state (Cummings, 2005; Moore et al., 2019). There are dozens of approaches, but in each one, it is accepted that only a very small fraction of the model variables is actually measured. Even so, minimising the differences between the measurements and the model variables can result in much different, and improved, operational forecasts. In situ observations can also be used in a non-operational sense (i.e. months or years after being collected). For example, performing data assimilation on a larger data set over a long period produces a re-analysis which can be useful as a background state for off-shore operators. Knowing the statistical properties like expected conditions and probability of an extreme event related to ocean parameters like currents or waves helps the operators plan their activity. It should be emphasised that this can be done even at locations where measurements were never actually collected, because the modelling procedure fills in the gaps, while maintaining the consistency with the measurements and the physical laws mandated by the model equations.

A practical implementation of merging observations and deterministic modelling (data assimilation) has been carried out in the eastern Mediterranean. An autonomous underwater glider collected and sent profiles of temperature and salinity in near real time over a 6 month long mission south of Cyprus. An operational forecast of ocean currents, temperature, and salinity (Zodiatis et al., 2008) combined with a data assimilation system (Dobricic & Pinardi, 2008) was used to ingest these profiles and produce an optimised, daily re-analysis, and updated daily forecast (Hayes et al., 2019). This sort of up-to-date, operational current information is important for authorities to respond effectively to various situations. In this case, the control run (a typical forecast without local observations) misrepresented the strength and position of a large oceanographic eddy feature detected in the observations. This is because the model (or the low resolution model used to initialise it) is apparently missing the key natural formation and evolution processes of this feature. If pollution were released in that area, the predictions of its trajectory would be very different if the control run was used, obviously influencing the decision-making process for containment and response. Similarly, for search and rescue, man-overboard, or drifting vessel incidents, knowledge of the surface current is one of the most important factors for the decision maker to lead a successful recovery campaign. The currents derived from this analysis may also be useful for routing ships: the surface currents differ by more than two knots (see Fig. 6).

Data assimilation is also done at larger scales and in many other regions for real-world applications. Using currents re-analysis for ship routing is one application, although in situ data are limited in the open ocean (possibly profiling floats or ships of opportunity). Remote sensing and ocean and atmosphere numerical modelling are used to produce current maps of these regions, (Copernicus Marine Environment Monitoring Service, n.d.; ECMWF, n.d.; Operational Forecast System, n.d.) are all examples, and optimisation routines may not be using the most accurate currents available, often relying on historical or forecast models or even constant weather (Walther, Rizvanolli, Wendebourg, & Jahn, 2016). The latest algorithms seem to emphasise waves and winds over currents in terms of weather (Bentin et al., 2016). It should be noted that even weather forecasts are less reliable in the open ocean, since atmospheric data assimilation is also hindered by a lack of in situ weather data. In this way, ships of opportunity can also be helpful by providing lower atmosphere observations to forecasting centres, something encouraged for decades by the WMO

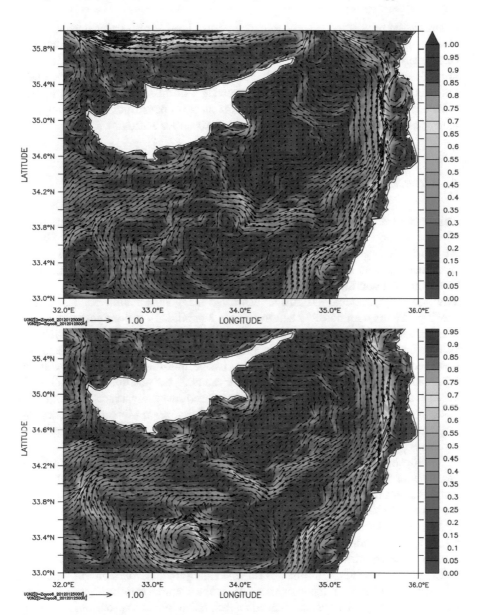

Fig. 6 Current direction and magnitude (m/s) at 1 m for day 50 (24 January 2012) for control run (top) and data assimilative run (bottom)

through the Marine Meteorology and Oceanography Programme (MMOP) (MMOP, n.d.) and specifically the International Convention for the Safety of Life at Sea (SOLAS) (WMO Maritime Services, n.d.). Having better maps of ocean properties, like the heat content and surface temperature in turn helps weather forecasting centres better predict the strength and trajectory of large storms or hurricanes as they interact with the ocean, obviously much safer to achieve with autonomous platforms like underwater gliders or surface vehicles (New Storm Chasers, n.d.). While these are off-shore processes affecting ships en route, they certainly impact operations in and around marine ports, so accurately knowing a storm's properties and trajectory before it makes landfall would allow for the most proper response (avoiding false alarms as well as providing more time to prepare and/or evacuate).

4 Cognitive Fusion Methods

This section reviews cognitive methods for intelligent information collection and decision support that utilise the capabilities of cognitive systems (Haykin, 2006b). An emphasis is given to the improvement in the estimation of the evolving state of dynamical systems which include, for example, moving vehicles or changing environmental conditions and the resulting improvement of situational awareness. The state of dynamical systems is estimated using information collection from sensing systems with possibly heterogeneous capabilities and configurable settings. The state consists of variables such as the position, velocity, and acceleration of a vehicle or the temperature, salinity, and sea currents in a maritime area and it is observed through measurements that may have a non-linear relationship with the state and contain stochastic parameters. For example, the position and velocity of a vehicle is observed using delay and Doppler measurements by a radar sensor. In this case, the relationship between measurements and state is non-linear since delay and Doppler measurements are functions of the range and range-rate that are non-linear functions of the vehicle and radar sensor positions and velocities.

Improvement in evolving state estimation performance is achieved through the adaptive configuration of settings of the sensing system. The configuration of system settings aligns the system's limited information acquisition capabilities to observing the specific values that the state may take in the immediate future. A prediction of the value of the state is based on information by past measurements and the state evolution model. Systems using such adaptation based on past observations are referred to as cognitive systems (Guerci, 2010; Haykin, 2005, 2006a, 2006b, 2012, 2013) which provide capabilities of understanding the environment via sequential estimation of the state of the natural environment or human activity. Practical implementations of cognitive systems that adapt their behaviour to improve observation of their environment are now possible due to advancements in hardware and software. Adaptive capabilities of cognitive systems include reconfigurable transmission (Sira, Papandreou-Suppappola, & Morrell, 2009), agile sensing (Xue & Morrell, 2002), reconfigurable processing (Kyriakides, Morrell, & Papandreou-Suppappola, 2008b), adaptive communications (Haykin, 2013), or power allocation (Saksena & Wang, 2008). Parameters in cognitive systems can, moreover, be configured in a cognitive method to maximise information gain under the constraint of limited system resources (Fishler et al., 2006; Hero & Kreucher, 2007). Another example of a cognitive approach is path planning of a network of underwater gliders. Given a heat map in a parameter of interest such as uncertainty or error and a map of sea currents, a cognitive approach calculates path waypoints for gliders to visit to reduce uncertainty within the mission time available. The method has been applied for the optimisation of temperature measurements in the eastern Mediterranean (Rossides, Georgiou, & Hayes, 2017). The planning can be completed before any glider is deployed; however, in a cognitive approach, the path planning process can be repeated regularly with updated currents and updated sensor information.

For a practical implementation of a cognitive framework, the Bayesian methodology can be used for cognitive sequential state estimation (Haykin, 2006b). The Bayesian method estimates the value of an evolving state related to the natural environment or human activity based on prior information. Such prior information is obtained from the state evolution model and past measurements. The cognitive method utilises prior information to configure parameters of sensing nodes in a sensor network to proactively improve information acquisition. The configuration of parameters is necessary to intelligently utilise the constrained resources of information acquisition systems to provide improved observations of the estimated values. After measurement collection the Bayesian method updates the prediction using newly arriving measurements (Haykin, 2006b). State estimation applications using cognition include cognitive radar (Haykin, 2006b; Haykin, Zia, Arasaratnam, & Xue, 2010). Applications in target tracking using the Bayesian methodology are found in Bell, Baker, Smith, Johnson, and Rangaswamy (2014, 2015) and methods using adaptive waveform design are found in Haykin, Xue, and Davidson (2008), Kershaw and Evans (1997), and Sira et al. (2009).

Additionally to cognition, the use of heterogeneous nodes is highly beneficial to estimation performance as cognitive heterogeneous nodes both observe the state from varying viewpoints and efficiently allocate system resources. When using heterogeneous nodes, however, the challenge lies in configuring multiple types of nodes and fusing heterogeneous measurements (Lahat, Adali, & Jutten, 2015). The measurements may have a non-linear relationship to the state and contain varying amount of information on the state. Moreover, the information provided refers to different estimated characteristics, for example, the identity or kinematic properties of a vehicle being tracked. Moreover, the non-linear relationships between measurements and the state (Arulampalam, Maskell, Gordon, & Clapp, 2002; Gustafsson, 2010; Kreucher, Kastella, & Hero, 2005; Kyriakides, Morrell, & Papandreou-Suppappola, 2008a; Orton & Fitzgerald, 2002) result to a non-Gaussian posterior probability distribution of the estimated state. In addition, the configuration of heterogeneous sensing nodes becomes a complex problem due to the diverse configurable characteristics of nodes. Cognitive parameter estimation that utilises heterogeneous sensing nodes for information acquisition is, therefore, a challenging problem that requires both the efficient fusion of data from heterogeneous sensing nodes and the configuration of individual nodes based on information from multiple heterogeneous nodes.

A methodology utilising heterogeneous cognitive sensing nodes to improve estimation performance is cognitive fusion (Kyriakides, 2019). Cognitive fusion adaptively configures sensing node settings and handles non-linear, non-Gaussian scenarios achieving heterogeneous data fusion. The types of configuration parameters handled are related to sensing, processing, communication, actuation, and power depending on the type and capabilities of each sensing node. The goal is to improve information acquisition by, for example, increasing signal-to-noise ratio, reducing measurement ambiguity function sidelobes, and selectively increasing resolution in subsets of the measurement space. The resulting outcome of cognitive fusion is the improvement in information acquisition that is achieved by utilising heterogeneous sensing nodes to provide diverse information about the estimated state. Cognitive fusion utilises the Bayesian Sequential Monte Carlo (particle filtering) (Arulampalam et al., 2002; Gustafsson, 2010; Kreucher et al., 2005; Orton & Fitzgerald, 2002) framework to deal with measurements that are non-linearly related to the estimated state and where the posterior distribution of the state is non-Gaussian. A simple form of particle filtering, the Sampling Importance Resampling (SIR) particle filter, takes samples from the state evolution model that may be learned using data-driven modelling methods, to form hypotheses on the future values of the parameters (Arulampalam et al., 2002; Gustafsson, 2010). For estimating high-dimensional states or when using measurements from high resolution sensors advanced sampling methods are used to represent the peaked measurement likelihood and high-dimensional sets of estimated parameters (Kreucher et al., 2005; Orton & Fitzgerald, 2002).

Utilising the methods described above, cognitive information acquisition via heterogeneous node configuration and data fusion for maritime applications is made possible. Data from heterogeneous nodes such as underwater acoustic, image, and chemical can be fused to provide diversity in information on estimates of states that, for example, can include the number of people present in a maritime area, the position and velocity of a maritime vehicle, the characteristics of the natural environment, and pollution spread. Moreover, the configuration of the sensing, processing, communications, and actuation parameters of nodes allows the intelligent allocation of limited resources when operating in the maritime domain to enhance situational awareness.

5 Conclusions

A new generation of cognitive heterogeneous nodes with capabilities of repositioning, communication link re-routing, and adaptive sensing and processing provide a diversity of information and adaptively allocate their resources to improve information acquisition for decision support in maritime applications. However, the fusion of heterogeneous data and adaptation of configuration settings of heterogeneous sensing nodes is challenging due to the often non-linear and varying relationship between the estimated parameter values and collected measurements. Cognitive methods for intelligent information acquisition and decision support have the potential to offer an agile response to the challenge of understanding the complex and rapidly changing maritime environment by enabling heterogeneous data fusion and capability integration. Cognitive systems actively seek missing information and provide a common operational picture to human users to facilitate decision support. Utilising the potential of cognitive systems, a cognitive decision support framework is envisioned that provides an ecosystem for the symbiosis of cyber-physical and human capabilities. The integrated capabilities will provide an agile response to modern challenges in information collection in the maritime environment. The symbiotic system will combine the speed and accuracy of cyber-physical systems for tactical decisions and while allowing human users to make strategic decisions and empower entities to *make sense* of the complex maritime environment.

References

Argo Autonomous Profiling Float. (n.d.). http://www.argo.net/

Arulampalam, M. S., Maskell, S., Gordon, N., & Clapp, T. (2002). A tutorial on particle filters for online nonlinear/non-Gaussian Bayesian tracking. *IEEE Transactions on Signal Processing, 50*(2), 174–188. Retrieved from http://ieeexplore.ieee.org/document/978374/. https://doi.org/10.1109/78.978374

Autonaut USV. (n.d.). Retrieved from http://www.autonautusv.com/

Bell, K. L., Baker, C. J., Smith, G. E., Johnson, J. T., & Rangaswamy, M. (2014, May). Fully adaptive radar for target tracking part I: Single target tracking. In *2014 IEEE Radar Conference* (pp. 0303–0308). IEEE. Retrieved from http://ieeexplore.ieee.org/lpdocs/epic03/wrapper.htm?arnumber=6875604. https://doi.org/10.1109/RADAR.2014.6875604

Bell, K. L., Baker, C. J., Smith, G. E., Johnson, J. T., & Rangaswamy, M. (2015). Cognitive radar framework for target detection and tracking. *IEEE Journal of Selected Topics in Signal Processing, 9*(8), 1427–1439. Retrieved from http://ieeexplore.ieee.org/document/7181639/. https://doi.org/10.1109/JSTSP.2015.2465304

Bentin, M., Zastrau, D., Schlaak, M., Freye, D., Elsner, R., & Kotzur, S. (2016). A new routing optimization tool-influence of wind and waves on fuel consumption of ships with and without wind assisted ship propulsion systems. *Transportation Research Procedia, 14*, 153–162. Retrieved from http://www.sciencedirect.com/science/article/pii/S2352146516300515 (Transport Research Arena TRA2016). https://doi.org/10.1016/j.trpro.2016.05.051

BRIDGES: Bringing Together Research and Industry for the Development of Glider Environmental Services. (n.d.). http://www.bridges-h2020.eu/

Brito, M., Smeed, D., & Griffiths, G. (2014). Underwater glider reliability and implications for survey design. *Journal of Atmospheric and Oceanic Technology, 31*(12), 2858–2870. https://doi.org/10.1175/JTECH-D-13-00138.1

Champion, B. T., & Joordens, M. A. (2015, July). Underwater swarm robotics review. In *2015 10th System of Systems Engineering Conference, SOSE 2015* (pp. 111–116). Institute of Electrical and Electronics Engineers Inc. https://doi.org/10.1109/SYSOSE.2015.7151953

Continuous Plankton Recorder (CPR) Survey. (n.d.). https://www.cprsurvey.org/

Copernicus Marine Environment Monitoring Service. (n.d.). http://marine.copernicus.eu/

Coriolis Operational Oceanography. (n.d.). http://www.coriolis.eu.org/Data-Products/Data-Delivery

Costa, V., Duarte, M., Rodrigues, T., Oliveira, S. M., & Christensen, A. L. (2016, June). Design and development of an inexpensive aquatic swarm robotics system. In *Oceans 2016 - Shanghai*. Institute of Electrical and Electronics Engineers Inc. https://doi.org/10.1109/OCEANSAP.2016.7485496

Cummings, J. A. (2005). Operational multivariate ocean data assimilation. *Quarterly Journal of the Royal Meteorological Society, 131*(613), 3583–3604. Retrieved from https://rmets. onlinelibrary.wiley.com/doi/abs/10.1256/qj.05.105. https://doi.org/10.1256/qj.05.105

DBCPData Buoy Cooperation Panel. (n.d.). http://www.jcommops.org/dbcp/

Dobricic, S., & Pinardi, N. (2008). An oceanographic three-dimensional variational data assimilation scheme. *Ocean Modelling, 22*(3–4), 89–105. Retrieved from http://www.sciencedirect. com/science/article/pii/S1463500308000176. http://dx.doi.org/10.1016/j.ocemod.2008.01.004

Ecmwf. (n.d.). https://www.ecmwf.int/

Elkins, L., Sellers, D., & Monach, W. R. (2010). The autonomous maritime navigation (AMN) project: Field tests, autonomous and cooperative behaviors, data fusion, sensors, and vehicles. *Journal of Field Robotics, 27*(6), 790–818. https://doi.org/10.1002/rob.20367

Eriksen, C. C., Osse, T. J., Light, R. D., Wen, T., Lehman, T. W., Sabin, P. L., et al. (2001). Seaglider: A long-range autonomous underwater vehicle for oceanographic research. *IEEE Journal of Oceanic Engineering, 26*(4), 424–436. https://doi.org/10.1109/48.972073

EuroGoos. (2017). *FerryBox WhiteBook.* http://eurogoos.eu/download/publications/EuroGOOS_ Ferrybox_whitepaper_2017.pdf

Fishler, E., Haimovich, A., Blum, R. S., Cimini, L. J., Chizhik, D., & Valenzuela, R. A. (2006). Spatial diversity in radars - Models and detection performance. *IEEE Transactions on Signal Processing, 54*(3), 823–838. Retrieved from http://ieeexplore.ieee.org/document/1597550/. https://doi.org/10.1109/TSP.2005.862813

Franco, E., Magni, L., Parisini, T., Polycarpou, M. M., & Raimondo, D. M. (2008). Cooperative constrained control of distributed agents with nonlinear dynamics and delayed information exchange: A stabilizing receding-horizon approach. *IEEE Transactions on Automatic Control, 53*(1), 324–338. Retrieved from http://ieeexplore.ieee.org/document/4459797/. https://doi.org/ 10.1109/TAC.2007.914956

Global Sea Level Observing System. (n.d.). https://www.gloss-sealevel.org/data.

Goni, G. J., Sprintall, J., Bringas, F., Cheng, L., Cirano, M., Dong, S., et al. (2019). More than 50 years of successful continuous temperature section measurements by the global expendable bathythermograph network, its integrability, societal benefits, and future. *Frontiers in Marine Science, 6*, 452.

Guerci, J. R. (2010). Cognitive radar: A knowledge-aided fully adaptive approach. In *2010 IEEE Radar Conference* (pp. 1365–1370). IEEE. Retrieved from http://ieeexplore.ieee.org/document/ 5494403/. https://doi.org/10.1109/RADAR.2010.5494403

Gustafsson, F. (2010). Particle filter theory and practice with positioning applications. *IEEE Aerospace and Electronic Systems Magazine, 25*(7), 53–82. Retrieved from http://ieeexplore. ieee.org/document/5546308/. https://doi.org/10.1109/MAES.2010.5546308

Hayes, D. (2016). *Physical oceanography from Seaglider mission CNCY201114910.* Tech. Rep. Oceanography Center.

Hayes, D. R., Dobricic, S., Gildor, H., & Matsikaris, A. (2019). Operational assimilation of glider temperature and salinity for an improved description of the Cyprus eddy. *Deep Sea Research Part II: Topical Studies in Oceanography, 164*, 41–53.

Haykin, S. (2005). Cognitive radio: Brain-empowered wireless communications. *IEEE Journal on Selected Areas in Communications, 23*(2), 201–220. Retrieved from http://ieeexplore.ieee.org/ document/1391031/. https://doi.org/10.1109/JSAC.2004.839380

Haykin, S. (2006a). Cognitive dynamic systems [Point of View]. *Proceedings of the IEEE, 94*(11), 1910–1911.

Haykin, S. (2006b). Cognitive radar: A way of the future. *IEEE Signal Processing Magazine, 23*(1), 30–40. Retrieved from http://ieeexplore.ieee.org/document/1593335/. https://doi.org/10.1109/ MSP.2006.1593335

Haykin, S. (2012). Cognitive dynamic systems: Radar, control, and radio [Point of View]. *Proceedings of the IEEE, 100*(7), 2095–2103. Retrieved from http://ieeexplore.ieee.org/document/ 6218166/. https://doi.org/10.1109/JPROC.2012.2193709

Haykin, S. (2013). Cognitive networks: Radar, radio, and control for new generation of engineered complex networks. In *IEEE National Radar Conference Proceedings*.

Haykin, S., Xue, Y., & Davidson, T. N. (2008, October). Optimal waveform design for cognitive radar. In *2008 42nd Asilomar Conference on Signals, Systems and Computers* (pp. 3–7). IEEE. Retrieved from http://ieeexplore.ieee.org/document/5074349/. https://doi.org/10.1109/ACSSC.2008.5074349

Haykin, S., Zia, A., Arasaratnam, I., & Xue, Y. (2010). Cognitive tracking radar. In *2010 IEEE Radar Conference* (pp. 1467–1470). IEEE. Retrieved from http://ieeexplore.ieee.org/document/5494383/. https://doi.org/10.1109/RADAR.2010.5494383

Hero, A. O., & Kreucher, C. M. (2007, July). Network sensor management for tracking and localization. In *2007 10th International Conference on Information Fusion* (pp. 1–8). IEEE. Retrieved from http://ieeexplore.ieee.org/document/4408181/. https://doi.org/10.1109/ICIF.2007.4408181

Joordens, M. A., & Jamshidi, M. (2009). Underwater swarm robotics consensus control. In *Conference Proceedings - IEEE International Conference on Systems, Man and Cybernetics* (pp. 3163–3168). https://doi.org/10.1109/ICSMC.2009.5346165

Kershaw, D. J., & Evans, R. J. (1997). Waveform selective probabilistic data association. *IEEE Transactions on Aerospace and Electronic Systems, 33*(4), 1180–1188. Retrieved from http://ieeexplore.ieee.org/document/625110/. https://doi.org/10.1109/7.625110

Kreucher, C., Kastella, K., & Hero, A. O. (2005, October). Multitarget tracking using the joint multitarget probability density. *IEEE Transactions on Aerospace and Electronic Systems, 41*(4), 1396–1414. Retrieved from http://ieeexplore.ieee.org/document/1561892/. https://doi.org/10.1109/TAES.2005.1561892

Kyriakides, I. (2019). In Spanias, A. (Ed.), *Cognitive fusion for target tracking*. Synthesis Lectures. San Rafael: Morgan and Claypool.

Kyriakides, I., Morrell, D., & Papandreou-Suppappola, A. (2008a). Sequential Monte Carlo methods for tracking multiple targets with deterministic and stochastic constraints. *IEEE Transactions on Signal Processing, 56*(3). https://doi.org/10.1109/TSP.2007.908931

Kyriakides, I., Morrell, D., & Papandreou-Suppappola, A. (2008b). Using a configurable integrated sensing and processing imager to track multiple targets. In *IEEE Aerospace Conference Proceedings*. https://doi.org/10.1109/AERO.2008.4526446

Lahat, D., Adali, T., & Jutten, C. (2015). Multimodal data fusion: An overview of methods, challenges, and prospects. *Proceedings of the IEEE, 103*(9), 1449–1477. Retrieved from http://ieeexplore.ieee.org/document/7214350/. https://doi.org/10.1109/JPROC.2015.2460697

Liquid Robotics' Wave Glider. (n.d.). http://liquidr.com/

López-Castejón, F., & Gilabert, J. (2019). Underwater robotics ready for oil spill. Technical Paper URready4OS Project, 98.

LSTS Systems, Underwater Systems and Technology Laboratory. (n.d.). http://lsts.fe.up.pt/vehicles/x8

Marine Meteorology and Oceanography Programme (MMOP). (n.d.). https://www.wmo.int/pages/prog/amp/mmop/index_en.html

Miskovic, N., Nad, D., & Rendulic, I. (2015). Tracking divers: An autonomous marine surface vehicle to increase diver safety. *IEEE Robotics and Automation Magazine, 22*(3), 72–84. https://doi.org/10.1109/MRA.2015.2448851

Moore, A. M., Martin, M. J., Akella, S., Arango, H. G., Balmaseda, M., Bertino, L., et al. (2019). Synthesis of ocean observations using data assimilation for operational, real-time and reanalysis systems: A more complete picture of the state of the ocean. *Frontiers in Marine Science, 6*, 90. Retrieved from https://www.frontiersin.org/article/10.3389/fmars.2019.00090. https://doi.org/10.3389/fmars.2019.00090

National Data Buoy Center. (n.d.). Retrieved from https://www.ndbc.noaa.gov/

Norweagian Ocean Observation Laboratory. (n.d.). https://oceanlab-no.weebly.com/observatory.html

Ocean Gliders. (n.d.). https://www.oceangliders.org/achievements/

Ocean Observatories Initiative. (n.d.). https://oceanobservatories.org/

OceanSITES. (n.d.). http://www.oceansites.org/

Operational Forecast System. (n.d.). https://tidesandcurrents.noaa.gov/models.html

Orton, M., & Fitzgerald, W. (2002). A Bayesian approach to tracking multiple targets using sensor arrays and particle filters. *IEEE Transactions on Signal Processing, 50*(2), 216–223.

PhOD - Global Drifter Program. (n.d.). https://www.aoml.noaa.gov/phod/gdp/

Rossides, A. K., Georgiou, G., & Hayes, D. R. (2017, June). Mission planning optimization for fleets of underwater gliders to increase the accuracy of hydrodynamic forecasting systems. In *Oceans 2017 - Aberdeen* (pp. 1–5). https://doi.org/10.1109/OCEANSE.2017.8084798

Sailbuoy USV. (n.d.). http://www.sailbuoy.no/

Saksena, A., & Wang, I.-J. (2008). Dynamic ping optimization for surveillance in multistatic sonar buoy networks with energy constraints. In *2008 47th IEEE Conference on Decision and Control* (pp. 1109–1114). IEEE. Retrieved from http://ieeexplore.ieee.org/lpdocs/epic03/wrapper.htm?arnumber=4739329. https://doi.org/10.1109/CDC.2008.4739329

Sira, S. P., Li, Y., Papandreou-Suppappola, A., Morrell, D., Cochran, D., & Rangaswamy, M. (2009). Waveform-agile sensing for tracking. *IEEE Signal Processing Magazine, 26*(1), 53–64. Retrieved from http://ieeexplore.ieee.org/document/4775880/. https://doi.org/10.1109/MSP.2008.930418

Sira, S. P., Papandreou-Suppappola, A., & Morrell, D. (2009). *Advances in waveform-agile sensing for tracking*. San Rafael: Morgan and Claypool.

Stanway, M. J. (2011). Dead reckoning through the water column with an acoustic Doppler current profiler: Field experiences. In *Oceans'11 MTS/IEEE* (pp. 1–8). Retrieved from http://ieeexplore.ieee.org/document/6107136/

Tanhua, T., Pouliquen, S., Hausman, J., O'Brien, K. M., Bricher, P., de Bruin, T., et al. (2019). Ocean fair data services. *Frontiers in Marine Science, 6*, 440.

The Eelume Concept. (n.d.). http://eelume.com/

The Future Is Now: Navy's Autonomous Swarmboats Can Overwhelm Adversaries. (n.d.).

The new storm chasers? Unmanned ocean gliders go deep to help improve hurricane forecasts. (n.d.). https://www.noaa.gov/stories/new-storm-chasers-unmanned-ocean-gliders-go-deep-to-help-improve-hurricane-forecasts

Undersea navigation and positioning system development to begin for U.S. Navy. (n.d.). www.baesystems.com

Underwater Radio, Anyone? (n.d.). http://www.darpa.mil/news-events/2016-12-16

URready4OS: Autonomous Underwater vehicles ready for oil spill. (n.d.). http://www.upct.es/urready4os/

Vasilijevic, A., Calado, P., Lopez-Castejon, F., Hayes, D., Stilinovic, N., Nad, D., et al. (2015, September). Heterogeneous robotic system for underwater oil spill survey. In *MTS/IEEE Oceans 2015 - Genova: Discovering Sustainable Ocean Energy for a New World*. Institute of Electrical and Electronics Engineers Inc. https://doi.org/10.1109/OCEANS-Genova.2015.7271492

Vasilijević, A., Nad, D., Mandi, F., Miškovi, N., & Vukić, Z. (2017). Coordinated navigation of surface and underwater marine robotic vehicles for ocean sampling and environmental monitoring. *IEEE/ASME Transactions on Mechatronics, 22*(3), 1174–1184. https://doi.org/10.1109/TMECH.2017.2684423

Walther, L., Rizvanolli, A., Wendebourg, M., & Jahn, C. (2016). Modeling and optimization algorithms in ship weather routing. *International Journal of e-Navigation and Maritime Economy, 4*, 31–45. Retrieved from http://www.sciencedirect.com/science/article/pii/S2405535216300043. https://doi.org/10.1016/j.envi.2016.06.004

Wilkinson, M. D., Dumontier, M., Aalbersberg, I. J., Appleton, G., Axton, M., Baak, A., et al. (2016). The FAIR guiding principles for scientific data management and stewardship. *Scientific Data, 3*, 160018.

WMO Maritime Services. (n.d.). https://mcanet.mcga.gov.uk/public/c4/solas/solas_v/Annexes/Annex04.htm

Xue, Y., & Morrell, D. (2002). Adaptive foveal sensor for target tracking. In *Asilomar Conference on Signals, Systems and Computers* (pp. 848–852). https://doi.org/10.1109/ACSSC.2002. 1197298

Zodiatis, G., Lardner, R., Hayes, D., Georgiou, G., Sofianos, S., Skliris, N., et al. (2008). Operational ocean forecasting in the Eastern Mediterranean: Implementation and evaluation. *Ocean Science, 4*(1), 31–47.

AIS Data Analytics for Intelligent Maritime Surveillance Systems

Xiuju Fu (iD)**, Zhe Xiao** (iD)**, Haiyan Xu** (iD)**, Vasundhara Jayaraman** (iD)**,
Nasri Bin Othman** (iD)**, Chye Poh Chua** (iD)**, and Mikael Lind** (iD)

1 Introduction

With the advance in sensors and other devices in the Internet of Things (IoT), the bulk of big data are machine-related data besides social data and transactional data. Valuable because of the tremendous amounts of information that it contains, big data refers not only to the size or volume of data but also to its variety and the velocity or speed of data accrual (Fadel M. Megahed & Allison Jones-Farmer, 2015). Generated incessantly, big data keeps stretching and challenging analytical methodologies, computational resources, and storage due to its increasing volume, variety, and velocity.

Recording recognizable and varying physical properties of objects, big data forms are various, such as numbers, symbols, text, image, sound, etc. Among big data sets, spatial-temporal data are increasing popular which are related to variations in space and time. Large volumes of spatial-temporal data from location-aware sensors, devices, and satellite location systems (GPS) can be used to represent the trajectories of moving objects, including human beings, robots, cars, airplanes, and

X. Fu (✉) · Z. Xiao · H. Xu · V. Jayaraman · N. B. Othman
Institute of High Performance Computing, A*Star, Singapore, Singapore
e-mail: fuxj@ihpc.a-star.edu.sg; xiaoz@ihpc.a-star.edu.sg; xuh@ihpc.a-star.edu.sg;
jayaramanv@ihpc.a-star.edu.sg; othmannb@ihpc.a-star.edu.sg

C. P. Chua
ShipsFocus Group, Singapore, Singapore
e-mail: ccp@shipsfocus.com

M. Lind
Research Institutes of Sweden (RISE) and Chalmers University of Technology, Gothenburg, Sweden
e-mail: mikael@realsearchers.com

M. Lind et al. (eds.), *Maritime Informatics*, Progress in IS,
https://doi.org/10.1007/978-3-030-50892-0_23

vessels. This allows to perceive deeper insights of modern systems, by addressing the four basic elements (4Ws) (ICA's 67th Annual Conference Panel, 2017): *Who does What at When and Where*, beyond the limit of traditional research methods (e.g., survey, experiment, and content analysis).

2 Maritime Traffic Surveillance Systems

In the maritime sector, spatial-temporal data are becoming increasingly available for tracking maritime traffic. A Vessel Traffic System (VTS) paradigm together with AIS, Long-Range Identification and Tracking (LRIT) system, coastal radar, and satellite-borne synthetic aperture radar (SAR) is illustrated in Fig. 1 (Xiao, Ponnambalam, Fu, & Zhang, 2017). Terrestrial AIS and coastal radars support vessel traffic surveillance in port waters, while LRIT, S-AIS, and SAR are primary instruments used for open oceans. These main information systems are introduced below, by which the corresponding traffic or sensor data containing spatial-temporal information is collected for ship tracking, monitoring, port operation visibility, maritime traffic surveillance, and safety management.

Automatic Identification System (AIS) AIS is a self-reporting system, which has been widely applied in maritime traffic surveillance (Tetreault, 2005). The data may be shown on the AIS display or Radar/Electronic Chart Display and Information System (ECDIS) equipment and used for many other purposes in maritime logistics systems besides traffic safety. AIS allows the exchange of both the navigational information (like position, velocity, course, etc.) and vessel information such as (Maritime Mobile Service Identity (MMSI), length, breadth, and draught etc.,) in-between ships and between ships and shore-based AIS stations using very high-

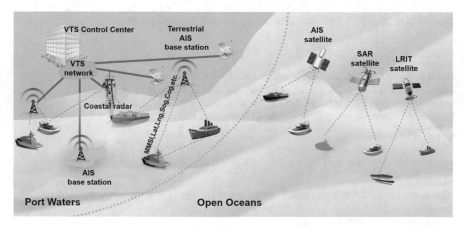

Fig. 1 Overview of maritime surveillance networks, information systems (Xiao et al., 2017)

frequency (VHF) radio transmission. Land-based AIS, i.e., terrestrial AIS, relies on shore-based monitoring stations to receive signals; airborne AIS, i.e., satellite AIS (S-AIS) employs satellites to collect signals (BigOceanData, 2016; Carson-Jackson, 2012; Holsten, Tobehn, & Borowy, 2009; Høye, Eriksen, Meland, & Narheim, 2008) thus is capable of tracking vessels in the open oceans. AIS data transmit interval depends on the vessel's navigational state, specifically, every 2–10 s for sailing vessels and around 3–6 min for vessels at anchoring vessels. From July 1, 2002, AIS is compulsory for all passenger vessels and vessels larger than 300 gross tonnage (GT) (International Maritime Organization (IMO) n.d.). As of now, most commercial vessels are equipped with an AIS transmitter, serving as an important technique part of collision avoidance and maritime traffic safety enhancement.

Long-Range Identification and Tracking (LRIT) LRIT is a non-automatic reporting system that requires the active participation by both the vessel and the vessel owner. In 2006, the IMO established the LRIT system in order to complement other information systems to enhance maritime awareness (European Maritime Safety Agency n.d.). LRIT is a satellite-based vessel position reporting system (U.S. Coast Guard Navigation Center n.d.). According to regulation, all passenger ships, cargo-carrying ships, high-speed craft of 300 GT and above, and mobile offshore drilling units need to report their position at least every 6 h. LRIT comprises several essential components including the transmitting device and satellite communication equipment, communication and application service providers, data centers, data distribution plan, and the International Data Exchange (MI News Network, 2019). Both S-AIS and LRIT allow for ship detection from space but have different mechanisms, and they can complement each other. A comprehensive comparison of S-AIS and LRIT has been reviewed in the previous literature (Y. Chen, 2014).

Coastal Radar Coastal radar is a shore-based system that provides sensing imagery data for VTS to detect and track vessels in port waters, harbours and busy waterways. Coastal radars mainly support maritime traffic safety and security in the covered area. Many commercial radar products are available in the market (Furuno n.d.; Terma n.d.). Nowadays, the high-frequency surface wave (HFSW) radars (groundwave radar) have attracted a growing interest because of their wider coverage (Braca, Maresca, Grasso, Bryan, & Horstmann, 2015; Grosdidier, Baussard, & Khenchaf, 2010). The performance assessment of HFSW radars with the multi-target tracking setup have been investigated in recent studies (Braca et al., 2015; Maresca, Braca, & Horstmann, 2013; Maresca, Braca, Horstmann, & Grasso, 2014; Vivone, Braca, & Horstmann, 2015).

Satellite-Borne Synthetic Aperture Radar (SAR) SAR has a widespread utilization for maritime surveillance (Koppe, Bach, & Lumsdon, 2014). The high-resolution SAR imagery data supports detecting ships over a wide water area under any weather conditions (Brusch et al., 2011; Wang et al., 2017). SAR allows for oceanographic observations and extends the coverage beyond coastal systems. In the research community, novel signal processing techniques were proposed to enhance the detection performance using SAR images (Biondi, 2016, 2018, 2019). Some of the well-known satellite-borne SARs include RADARSAT (Stasolla, Mallorqui, Margarit, Santamaria, & Walker, 2016), ENVISAT ASAR (Greidanus, 2008), Sentinel-1 (Greidanus & Santamaria, 2014; Santamaria et al., 2017), COSMO-SkyMed SAR (Marco Martorella, Berizzi, Pastina, & Lombardo, 2011; Martorella, Pastina, Berizzi, & Lombardo, 2014), TerraSAR-X (Bentes, Velotto, & Tings, 2017; Paes, Lorenzzetti, & Gherardi, 2010; Pitz & Miller, 2010; Velotto, Bentes, Tings, & Lehner, 2016), and TanDEM-X (Moreira et al., 2004).

Besides the aforementioned systems, optical satellites are also used for vessel tracking and monitoring (Máttyus, 2013). In comparison with SAR, optical satellite images allow for more frequent revisit times and a higher spatial resolution to detect smaller objects (Máttyus, 2013). In practical use in VTS, the information systems mentioned above are used complementarily, in order to avoid possible disruptions caused by a single system's failures, like potential hardware breakdown, communication interruption (Poḷevskis, Krastiņš, Korats, Skorodumovs, & Trokšs, 2012), or detection limitations (blind spots) (Uchacz & Galor, 2013), and to enhance the system-level surveillance performance. To coordinate data from multiple sources, data fusion (Bar-Shalom, Willett, & Tian, 2011) serves as one of the indispensable components. Many data fusion technologies have been proposed for radar and AIS data fusion (Guerriero, Willett, Coraluppi, & Carthel, 2008; Brusch et al., 2011; Mazzarella, Vespe, & Santamaria, 2015; Vieira et al., 2016) and AIS, radar, and SAR data fusion (Carthel, Coraluppi, Grasso, & Grignan, 2007; Vespe & Sciotti, 2008). The Ornstein-Uhlenbeck (OU) process is also applied to improve the association of AIS with HFSW radars and SAR data (Vivone, Millefiori, Braca, & Willett, 2017) (Gaglione, Braca, & Soldi, 2018).

The traffic sensing data stream from multiple systems is eventually gathered at the VTS center to assist managers and operators in performing maritime traffic management, maritime operation monitoring, and efficiency enhancement. The traffic sensing data captured by individual systems first needs to be decoded. For instance, the raw AIS messages are encoded, so they need to be decoded to obtain information such as the vessel's position, course, and velocity, among others. Some of the most popular decoding toolkits include "AISmessages" (Thomas Borg Salling, 2017), "decoder for AIS" (Kurt Schwehr, 2014), and "AisDecoder" (Neal Arundale, 2018). AIS data has been applied for investigating the vessel's motion behavior, cargo movements, traffic patterns, logistics and trade across the sea (Alessandrini, Mazzarella, & Vespe, 2019; Chen et al., 2016; Millefiori, Zissis, Cazzanti, & Arcieri, 2016; Perera, Oliveira, & Guedes Soares, 2012; Rajabi, Khodadad Saryazdi, Belfkih, & Duvallet, 2018), as well as traffic safety management (Eriksen et al., 2010; Page, 2017). Because the AIS transmitter on vessels transmits location, speed, course, heading, and destination information of the vessels every few seconds or minutes (Xiao et al., 2017), the volume of available AIS data is huge and growing (Pallotta, Vespe, & Bryan, 2013b).

Besides the increasing size, the received data contains information for all the vessel traffic in the target zone; thus data formation is often required to structure the traffic data to be vessel-based (or other traffic feature-based) as a preparatory step before further processing. Meanwhile, it is not possible to achieve absolute system reliability, due to possibly missing or low-quality (i.e., noisy) data. Taking AIS data as an example, MMSI is likely to be shared by different vessels (Mazzarella et al., 2013), which requires either eliminating or correcting the error data in such cases (Mazzarella, Vespe, Damalas, & Osio, 2014; Pallotta, Vespe, & Bryan, 2013a). Data pre-analysis or processing is therefore vital to augment the quality of the data. Some common processing includes data cleaning, noise and outlier removal, etc. In many applications, interpolation is also needed to make data structured in a reasonable and unified time frame to facilitate the visualization and processing. While the preprocessing algorithm ensures better data quality, it also introduces data redundancies which can further increase the volume of the already sizeable AIS data.

3 Preprocessing Framework for Big AIS Data

Data footprint is an important consideration for data sharing among maritime stakeholders. With the boom of digital intelligence applications worldwide, there is a growing awareness, emphasis, and pressure in the maritime sector for collaboration and data-sharing to reduce inefficiencies and redundancy (Lind et al., 2019a). The increased transmission overhead and storage cost for larger volumes of data requires greater efforts for reducing redundant information. Here, we present a framework (Xu et al., 2019) that enables the speedy access and transfer of AIS data across networks and systems while generating aggregated data for easier access, further analysis by practical applications.

The first aim of the framework is realized through a lossless compression algorithm (Xu et al., 2019) which converts the AIS data into compressed archives in binary form. The AIS data is partitioned in batch (e.g., daily records), and each AIS data batch is converted into several matrices in which each value is stored using its native fixed-sized binary representation, and a symbol table is used to connect original strings and their integer indices in the matrices. The matrices are then sorted, column-major transposed, "XOR-difference" (Fletcher, 1997) processed, and finally LZ4 (Kiselkov, 2013) compressed. The output is a collection of compressed archives which are independent of each other and properly indexed. Hence, each archive can be individualistically decompressed on demand in order to reduce the use of disk memory, the decompressed contents are cached to favor fast subsequent access, and parallel operation can also be applied to speed up the processing. This algorithm provides significant performance gain and benefits the typical workflows especially for AIS data which contains lots of strings and duplicate information.

The second aim of the framework is to generate data that contains the key information of vessel movement that can be easily accessed by common users. To achieve this objective, each binary file is decomposed and aggregated to grid-based data with key information retained and/or derived, which compresses the data further. The grid and key information are customized based on the application use case.

In the following sections, we introduce the lossless compression algorithm, the aggregation algorithm for extra data compression, and the application and evaluation of the framework.

3.1 Lossless Compression Algorithm

Vessels transmit AIS information every few seconds or every few minutes. If we batch these incoming transmissions by vessel ID (MMSI) and date, then each batch will have redundant information, i.e., the vessel's signature such as MMSI, IMO, and vessel name will remain the same and therefore become redundant between each subsequent transmission. The duplicated information, especially string data, may occupy a large storage space. Lossless compression algorithms (Li, Drew, & Liu, 2014) use a statistical model to summarize the input data and then apply this model to map input data to bit sequences in such a way so that frequently encountered data will produce a shorter output than the original data. In this section, a lossless compression algorithm is proposed to compress the AIS data for efficient storage and analysis.

Our proposed lossless compression algorithm consists of two parts. The first part pertains to "compression," while the second is related to "access."

In the first part, we process the input files into compressed archives. Each input file represents a batched partition of data (e.g., daily records) and is processed independently. The input file is assumed to be a tabular data source with rows of entries and columns of attributes, such as a CSV file.

The processing flow of the lossless compression algorithm is illustrated in Fig. 2, and details of steps can be found in (Xu et al., 2019). It is worth mentioning that the XOR-difference is a common preprocessing step employed by compression algorithms. Our implementation of the XOR-difference is somewhat simpler than the implementation in the time series compression algorithm in gorilla (Pelkonen et al., 2015) since we run the stream through the LZ4 compression algorithm.

3.2 Access and Decompression Algorithm

When preprocessed against all input files, the output is a collection of compressed archives that can be analyzed efficiently. To access a single sub-matrix, the following algorithm can be used:

Step 1 Determine the corresponding compressed archive that contains the sub-matrix, and decompress it using LZ4. Decode the metadata block. Cache the

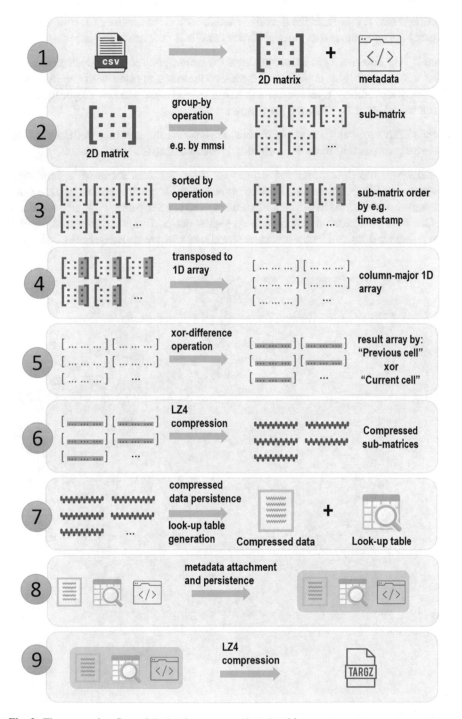

Fig. 2 The processing flow of the lossless compression algorithm

decompressed archive and the decoded metadata block in memory for future access.
(Note: LZ4 decompression is much faster than hard disk read speeds.)

Step 2 The sub-matrix is extracted from the decompressed archive using the sub-matrix lookup table. It is then decompressed and then applied with the inverse of the "XOR-difference" operation and then transposed back into row-major form. The extracted sub-matrix is cached for future access.

Step 3 The user can then perform their analysis on the sub-matrix directly. Note that string values will have to be obtained by consulting the symbol table.

Likewise, the decompression processing flow for data retrieval is intuitively illustrated in Fig. 3. Caches are used to allow fast subsequent accesses into the same data structures. Entries in the cache can be evicted based on user-defined conditions.

Our data compression scheme yields significant performance gain and benefits for typical workflows. First, since most workflows involve numerous calculations on

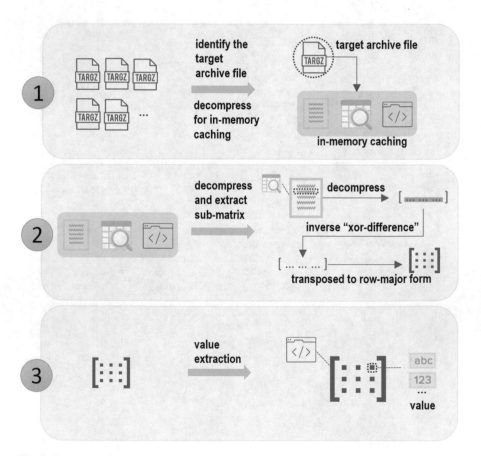

Fig. 3 Decompression processing flow for data retrieval

related data clusters iteratively, the batch partitioning and the sub-matrix decomposition offer rapid indexing into the relevant data and decent cache locality. Second, the compressed sub-matrices are only decompressed when needed, reducing disk and memory requirements. Third, decompressed contents are cached so that subsequent accesses are fast. Fourth, the output files are self-contained archive files and can be replicated across a computing cluster for parallelism. We emphasize that the scheme is flexible and can be adapted for general-purpose data compression, provided the original data can be represented in a tabular format.

3.3 Aggregation for Further Data Compression

After lossless compression, the binary files of the AIS data can be efficiently stored, speedily accessed, and easily transferred. Accommodating the domain application requirements, we then perform an aggregation of the data in the compressed binary files to improve searching and indexing of data by vessel ID, date, etc. Grid-/lattice-based aggregation is a way for further data compression (Xiao et al., 2017).

In order to study the vessels' activities within the port, we overlay a rectangle of evenly spaced horizontal and vertical lines on the map covering the port boundaries, with every cell formed by the cross section of intersecting lines forming cells with dimensions that are determined by the resolution required. For our purposes, we chose cells measuring 278 m × 278 m. Each cell is assigned a grid code that uniquely identifies the row and column ID to which it belongs. The location information (latitude and longitude) in the AIS data is used to determine the row and column IDs of the grid as shown in the Eqs. (1) and (2) below and assign the corresponding grid code to the row. Vessels not within the grid are assigned the code "−1". Variables presented in Eqs. (1) and (2) are illustrated in Table 1.

$$\text{RowID} = \text{round}\left(\frac{y - y_{\min}}{y_{\max} - y_{\min}} M, 0\right) \tag{1}$$

Table 1 Definition of variables used in Eqs. (1) and (2)

Symbol	Definition
x	Longitude of the vessel
y	Latitude of the vessel
$x_{\min}$	Minimum value of latitude within the 2D Grid Matrix
$x_{\max}$	Maximum value of latitude within the 2D Grid Matrix
$y_{\min}$	Minimum value of longitude within the 2D Grid Matrix
$y_{\max}$	Maximum value of longitude within the 2D Grid Matrix
M	Number of rows in the grid
N	Number of columns in the grid

$$\text{ColID} = \text{round}\left(\frac{x - x_{\min}}{x_{\max} - x_{\min}} N, 0\right) \tag{2}$$

A spatial-temporal aggregation algorithm is applied to the compressed data as follows. For vessels within port entering any grid cell, its location, timestamp, and course of entry of the grid cell are recorded along with other information such as minimum, maximum, and median/average speed of the vessel within the grid cell. For vessels dwelling within a grid cell, in addition to the entry point into the grid, the midpoint location of the vessel within the cell is also recorded. A time window is applied to work together with the grid code during aggregation. When vessels are out of the grid area, aggregation is done based on the time window. A time window also works to further remove outliers and derive other interested information regarding the vessels' activities within the port. For example, based on the speed recorded within each time window, we can determine if the vessel is in the "MOVING" state or in a "SLOW SPEED/STATIONARY" (S3) state at each time stamp simply by applying a minimum speed threshold within the port, and then by comparing the occurring frequency of each state, we can properly classify the vessels within each time window. This also helps narrow our focus onto the S3 state where the vessel is more likely to be performing loading/unloading, anchoring, or bunkering activities. Understanding vessels' location and duration in the S3 state leads to better perception of a port's occupation statistics and congestion area and thus better port management.

The aggregated data for each vessel, identified by its unique MMSI, is stored together organized by date for easy indexing and search. The aggregation algorithm applied thus achieves a higher compression rate while retaining the necessary information, provided that the aggregation algorithm is carefully designed (e.g., selection of attributes, grid cells' size, length of time window, etc.).

4   A Practical Case for Implementing the Preprocessing

Singapore is one of the busiest ports in the world. We demonstrate how to use our algorithm to efficiently generate easily accessible AIS data for vessels at the Singapore port. The proposed framework is evaluated considering the saving of storage space and processing duration and the retaining of key information.

4.1   Input Data

The AIS transmitters on vessels record location, speed, course, heading, and destination information, at regular time intervals, from a few seconds to a few minutes. This information is organized in data files, with each file containing movement information for one vessel during a single day. The recorded AIS data is then preprocessed to remove outliers, with gaps in the data removed through interpolation using the course, speed, and heading fields. The preprocessing algorithm thus yields a dataset containing spatial-temporal information in a tabulated form for a single vessel's movements near and within the port boundaries with 1 s resolution. Thus, the number of rows in each file cannot exceed 86,400 (the number of seconds in 1 day). Depending on the quality of the data, these files may be anywhere between a few kilobytes and a few megabytes in size. This is possible, especially if the gaps in the dataset are too big for any interpolation algorithm to accurately determine the missing positions.

4.2 Lossless Compression and Access

The above AIS files are then fed into the lossless compression algorithm described in Sect. 3.1 in chapter "Preprocessing Framework for Big AIS Data" to generate archives of the AIS files. From our dataset, we have been able to achieve a data compression ratio of up to 42 times (we were able to compress 302 GB of AIS data files into 7.1 GB). While the time taken to convert each of these csv files into the corresponding binary (.bin) files is around 6–15 s depending on the size of data in each file, the read time of all these files is less than 1 s for each file. It is possible to read multiple binary files very quickly since the data is only decompressed as needed and otherwise retained in memory in their compressed form. Since the compression is only done once and the archives are available for future referencing, this method seems ideal for our purposes. Time taken to read multiple binary files into the memory depends on the specifications of the computer being used. Smaller memory computers may take longer, as the data is loaded into the memory for fast access. On a computer with a 2.8 GHz core, 64-bit processor, and a 32 GB RAM, an AIS data file of size 21 MB takes about 10.76 s to be loaded into the memory, and the compression algorithm with simultaneous write-to-file takes about 7.7 s. Time taken to read the resulting compressed binary file of size 670 KB (~32 times compression rate) was about 0.3 s. The resulting file encodes all the relevant information in the original AIS data file (Xu et al., 2019).

4.3 Vessel Movement Classification and Spatial-Temporal Aggregation

AIS data aggregation is used to further improve data compression and accessibility. Grid information as described in Sect. 3 in chapter "Intelligent Maritime Information Acquisition and Representation for Decision Support" is applied to enable fast analysis on vessel position.

Vessel's moving speed is an important indicator for the vessel's activities. For example, "SLOW SPEED/STATIONARY" (S3) state may indicate that a vessel is berthing, anchoring, or even doing some unauthorized activities. As such, it is essential to identify a speed threshold so as to identify the vessel's movement state. Here we study the speed of vessels near known anchorage locations in Singapore port. We use a piecewise linear function to fit the logarithm of vessel's speed frequency against the vessel's speed (see Fig. 4). In this figure, points A, B, C, and D with speed 1.0, 10.7, 13.9, and 14.2 knots, respectively, are the changing points. The points are obtained from the segmented linear function (we set parameters in the function such that seed equals to 2 and the initial values of the four speeds are 0.5, 1, 10, and 15 knots, respectively) from segmented package in R 3.4.4. One knot is then used as the threshold speed to classify the vessel's state between the S3 state and the MOVING state. Note that the same speed threshold (one knot) is also used by (Patroumpas et al., 2017) to identify if a vessel's movement state is in the S3 state. Vessel's movement state is another attribute of interest added to the file.

We propose the use of a time window for data aggregation outside grid area and for classifying vessels' movement state given the proposed threshold. During aggregation, by observing the number of records within each time window, we classify the vessel state within the time window (e.g., 10 min are used here) as either S3 or MOVING.

With S3 state identified, the nature of activities in which the vessel is participating will be analyzed. Tagging the known locations of anchorages and berths in Singapore onto the grid, the anchorage and berth to every vessel based on distance can be then determined.

The aggregated file thus records vessel movement across the grid. Detailed information includes entry location and timestamp into the grid cell and midpoint location, duration, movement state, average and median of course and minimum, maximum, average, and median values of speed within the grid cell. If the movement state is S3, the aggregated file also records a berth ID if the vessel is close to the berth within a given distance threshold, or it records an anchorage ID if the vessel is in the anchorage.

After aggregation, the binary files (7.1 GB) are further compressed into csv files (639 MB~11 times compression rate) including additional derived information, such as the movement state and the berth/anchorage ID. If we discard the files related to vessels that do not enter the Singapore port in a whole day, the resulting size of effective aggregation files is only 54 MB.

4.4 An Application Case of Aggregated AIS Data: Vessel Voyage Event Detection

To check if relevant information is retained in the aggregation data, we applied the aggregated vessel movement data in the Singapore port waters to identify the

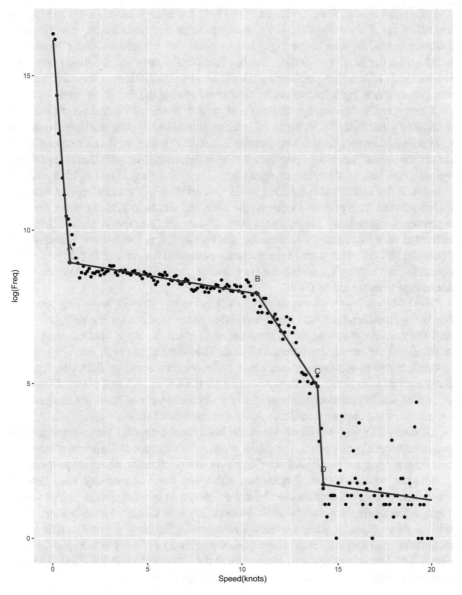

Fig. 4 Logarithm speed frequency of a type of vessels at anchorage area of Singapore port with piecewise linear fitting (Xu et al., 2019)

berth where a vessel stayed for operations or waited for operations and derived the duration of stay at the anchorage or berth.

We compared the detected vessel voyage event details (who, when, where, and duration) against available port operation data for a few vessels within Singapore and observed that 95% of berths and 99.5% of berth stay duration were correctly identified for 88 journeys in 2017. Among berth detection cases, the 5% mis-detected cases, in which the right berths were not recognized but detected as neighboring berths, are caused due to the close proximity of neighboring berths and the variation of satellite positioning for different vessels. More research is needed and other supporting information for further enhancing the detection accuracy.

The current vessel voyage detection algorithm developed based on offline AIS data has a great potential in terms of offering maritime big data intelligence. It can also be used for real-time vessel voyage event detection, i.e., it can automatically detect the vessel's current operation and also determine the port activities of this vessel right before the current operation (i.e., following a series of operation events). If the algorithm is applied to detect and trace all vessels' operations and traffic patterns in a port, the information obtained can help achieve real-time port monitoring through a "bird's eye view" of the port's activity. In addition, the extracted vessel operation event chains can be utilized to predict the vessel's next operation and the corresponding port resources needed for performing the particular operation, for example, leaving the port, moving to the next berth, or returning to anchorage with the aid of pilots.

The wide variety of maritime services (Lind et al., 2019b), including berthing, bunkering, maintenance, and repair as well as other services for the ship, the crew, and the movement of cargo, all have to be in place during a port call and often must take place over a short period of time. This often needs high visibility of port operations which requires in turn close collaboration, complex data sharing, and communication between the crew, owner, agent, the terminal, and others. However, such data sharing mechanism is not fully established yet due to either the existing resistance in the current maritime systems or the lack of timely digital information. Maritime intelligence based on maritime big spatial-temporal data, leveraging on preprocessing algorithms as the ones presented here, sheds light on alternative solutions for supporting digital coordination and optimization of vessel port calls.

The port visibility (vessel operation status and berth availability, etc.) derived from maritime intelligent models based on maritime big data, such as our vessel voyage event detection, can be shared among relevant maritime stakeholders. This will be very helpful to increase transparency and efficiency of port operations for eventually realizing full data sharing among relevant parties towards just-in-time operations. For achieving that, international data standards like the S211 port call message format (Lind et al., 2019a) will be of importance.

5 Conclusion

In this chapter, we reviewed the key maritime information systems for maritime vessel traffic management and highlighted the importance and potential values of maritime big spatial-temporal data and the challenges of dealing with such data. We presented a computational framework to enable the preprocessing and aggregation of big AIS data for research development and practical applications.

Based on the experimental and evaluation results presented, the proposed computational framework achieves a good data compression performance, while the volume of large-scale AIS data could be reduced significantly for storing, retrieval, and analysis, and essential information of the original large-scale data is retained for the subsequent development of intelligent models for industrial applications and scientific research tasks.

The emergence of big spatial-temporal data in maritime and many other sectors helps generate new insights and understanding of traditional operations and system management. It also sheds light for applying digital technology to provide intelligence for transforming the traditional operations and enhancing safety and operation efficiency from diversified angles. The proposed data preprocessing approach can be applied to efficiently store, retrieve, and analyze big AIS data with reduced computational cost. It can then be fused with other sources of digitalized data to facilitate big data intelligence development towards innovation processes and applications, not only in the maritime but also in other domains.

References

Alessandrini, A., Mazzarella, F., & Vespe, M. (2019). Estimated time of arrival using historical vessel tracking data. *IEEE Transactions on Intelligent Transportation Systems, 20*(1), 7–15.

Arundale, N. (2018). *AisDecoder by Neal Arundale*. Accessed April 7, 2020, from https://arundaleais.github.io/docs/ais/ais_decoder.html.

Bar-Shalom, Y., Willett, P. K., & Tian, X. (2011). *Tracking and data fusion: A handbook of algorithms*.

Bentes, C., Velotto, D., & Tings, B. (2017). Ship classification in TerraSAR-X images with convolutional neural networks. *IEEE Journal of Oceanic Engineering*. https://doi.org/10.1109/JOE.2017.2767106.

BigOceanData. (2016). *Satellite AIS – addressing some misconceptions*. Accessed April 7, 2020, from http://www.bigoceandata.com/news/satellite-ais-addressing-some-misconceptions/.

Biondi, F. (2016). Low Rank plus Sparse Decomposition of Synthetic Aperture Radar Data for Maritime Surveillance. In *4th International Workshop on Compressed Sensing Theory and Its Applications to Radar, Sonar and Remote Sensing (CoSeRa)* (pp. 75–79). Aachen.

Biondi, F. (2018). Low-rank plus sparse decomposition and localized radon transform for ship-wake detection in synthetic aperture radar images. *IEEE Geoscience and Remote Sensing Letters, 15*(1), 117–121.

Biondi, F. (2019). A polarimetric extension of low-rank plus sparse decomposition and radon transform for ship wake detection in synthetic aperture radar images. *IEEE Geoscience and Remote Sensing Letters, 16*(1), 75–79.

Braca, P., Maresca, S., Grasso, R., Bryan, K., & Horstmann, J. (2015). Maritime surveillance with multiple over-the-horizon HFSW radars: An overview of recent experimentation. *IEEE Aerospace and Electronic Systems Magazine, 30*(12), 4–18. https://doi.org/10.1109/MAES.2015.150004.

Brusch, S., Lehner, S., Fritz, T., Soccorsi, M., Soloviev, A., & Van Schie, B. (2011). Ship surveillance with TerraSAR-X. *IEEE Transactions on Geoscience and Remote Sensing, 49*(3), 1092–1103. https://doi.org/10.1109/TGRS.2010.2071879.

Carson-Jackson, J. (2012). Satellite AIS – developing technology or existing capability? *Journal of Navigation, 65*(2), 303–321. https://doi.org/10.1017/S037346331100066X.

Carthel, C., Coraluppi, S., Grasso, R., & Grignan, P. (2007). Fusion of AIS, RADAR, and SAR data for maritime surveillance. In *Proceedings of the SPIE, Image and Signal Processing for Remote Sensing XIII* (Vol. 6748). Florence, Italy. https://doi.org/10.1117/12.737334.

Chen, Y. (2014). Satellite-based AIS and its comparison with LRIT. *TransNav, International Journal on Marine Navigation and Safety of Sea Transportation, 8*(2), 183–187. https://doi.org/10.12716/1001.08.02.02.

Chen, L., Zhang, D., Ma, X., Wang, L., Li, S., Wu, Z., & Pan, G. (2016). Container port performance measurement and comparison leveraging ship GPS traces and maritime open data. *IEEE Transactions on Intelligent Transportation Systems, 17*(5), 1227–1242. https://doi.org/10.1109/TITS.2015.2498409.

Eriksen, T., Skauen, A. N., Narheim, B., Helleren, Ø., Olsen, Ø., & Olsen, R. B. (2010). *Tracking ship traffic with space-based AIS: Experience gained in first months of operations* (pp. 1–8). 2010 International WaterSide Security Conference, Carrara.

European Maritime Safety Agency. (n.d.). *LRIT CDC – legal basis.* Accessed April 7, 2020, from http://www.emsa.europa.eu/lrit-main/lrit-home/legal-basis.html.

Fletcher, W. I. (1997). *An engineering approach to digital design* (1st ed.). Upper Saddle River, NJ: Prentice Hall PTR.

Furuno. (n.d.). *TZ coastal monitoring.* Accessed April 7, 2020, from http://www.furuno.com/en/systems/coastal-monitoring/.

Gaglione, D., Braca, P., & Soldi, G. (2018). Belief propagation based AIS/radar data fusion for multi-target tracking. In *1st International Conference on Information Fusion (FUSION)* (pp. 2143–2150). Cambridge.

Greidanus, H. (2008). Satellite imaging for maritime surveillance of the European Seas. In *Remote Sensing of the European Seas* (pp. 343–358). https://doi.org/10.1007/978-1-4020-6772-3_26.

Greidanus, H., & Santamaria, C. (2014). First analyses of sentinel-1 images for maritime surveillance. *JRC Science and Policy Reports., 2014.* https://doi.org/10.2788/132810.

Grosdidier, S., Baussard, A., & Khenchaf, A. (2010). HFSW radar model: Simulation and measurement. *IEEE Transactions on Geoscience and Remote Sensing.*https://doi.org/10.1109/TGRS.2010.2047022.

Guerriero, M., Willett, P., Coraluppi, S., & Carthel, C. (2008). Radar/AIS data fusion and SAR tasking for maritime surveillance. In *11th International Conference on Information Fusion* (pp. 1–5). https://doi.org/10.1109/ICIF.2008.4632409.

Holsten, S., Tobehn, C., & Borowy, C. (2009). Global maritime surveillance with satellite-based AIS. In *OCEANS 2009-EUROPE* (pp. 1–4). Bremen. https://doi.org/10.1109/OCEANSE.2009.5278192.

Høye, G. K., Eriksen, T., Meland, B. J., & Narheim, B. T. (2008). Space-based AIS for global maritime traffic monitoring. *Acta Astronautica, 62*(2–3), 240–245. https://doi.org/10.1016/j.actaastro.2007.07.001.

ICA's 67th Annual Conference Panel. (2017). *Temporal and spatial analysis of mobility data.* ICA's 67th Annual Conference. Accessed April 7, 2020, from http://tinyurl.com/hpw4buw.

International Maritime Organization. (n.d.). *Regulations for carriage of AIS.* Accessed April 7, 2020, from http://www.imo.org/en/OurWork/safety/navigation/pages/ais.aspx.

Kiselkov, S. (2013). *LZ4 Compression – Illumos – Illumos Wiki.* Accessed from https://wiki.illumos.org/display/illumos/LZ4+Compression.

Koppe, W., Bach, K., & Lumsdon, P. (2014). Benefits of TerraSAR-X – PAZ constellation for maritime surveillance. In *10th European Conference on Synthetic Aperture Radar* (pp. 1413–1416). Berlin.

Li, Z.-N., Drew, M. S., & Liu, J. (2014). *Texts in computer science: Fundamentals of multimedia* (2nd ed). Springer International. Accessed from www.springer.com/gp/book/9783319052892.

Lind, M., Chua, C. P., Bergmann, M., Fu, X., Adams, A., Nair, S., & Lim, M. (2019a). Enabling efficient tanker operations. *Informa Connect.* Accessed April 7, 2020, from https://informaconnect.com/enabling-efficient-tanker-operations/.

Lind, M., Ward, R., Bergmann, M., Haraldson, S., & Zerem, A. (2019b). *UNCTAD transport and trade facilitation Series No. 13 – Digitalizing the port call process.* Accessed April 5, 2020, from https://unctad.org/en/PublicationsLibrary/dtltlb2019d2_en.pdf.

Maresca, S., Braca, P., & Horstmann, J. (2013). Detection, tracking and fusion of multiple HFSW radars for ship traffic surveillance: Experimental performance assessment. In *International Geoscience and Remote Sensing Symposium (IGARSS)* (pp. 2420–2423). https://doi.org/10.1109/IGARSS.2013.6723308.

Maresca, S., Braca, P., Horstmann, J., & Grasso, R. (2014). Maritime surveillance using multiple high-frequency surface-wave radars. *IEEE Transactions on Geoscience and Remote Sensing, 52*(8), 5056–5071. https://doi.org/10.1109/TGRS.2013.2286741.

Martorella, M., Berizzi, F., Pastina, D., & Lombardo, P. (2011). Exploitation of COSMO SkyMed SAR images for maritime traffic surveillance. In *IEEE National Radar Conference Proceedings* (pp. 113–117). https://doi.org/10.1109/RADAR.2011.5960511.

Martorella, M., Pastina, D., Berizzi, F., & Lombardo, P. (2014). Spaceborne radar imaging of maritime moving targets with the cosmo-SkyMed SAR system. *IEEE Journal of Selected Topics in Applied Earth Observations and Remote Sensing, 7*(7), 2797–2810. https://doi.org/10.1109/JSTARS.2014.2321708.

Máttyus, G. (2013). Near real-time automatic marine vessel detection on optical satellite images. *International Archives of the Photogrammetry, Remote Sensing and Spatial Information Sciences – ISPRS Archives, 40*(1W1), 233–237.

Mazzarella, F., Alessandrini, A., Greidanus, H., Alvarez, M., Argentieri, P., & Nappo, D. (2013). Data fusion for wide-area maritime surveillance data fusion for wide-area maritime surveillance. In *Proceedings of the Workshop on Moving Objects at Sea* (pp. 1–5).

Mazzarella, F., Vespe, M., Damalas, D., & Osio, G. (2014). Discovering vessel activities at sea using AIS data: Mapping of fishing footprints. In *17th International Conference on Information Fusion (FUSION)* (pp. 1–7). Salamanca.

Mazzarella, F., Vespe, M., & Santamaria, C. (2015). SAR ship detection and self-reporting data fusion based on traffic knowledge. *IEEE Geoscience and Remote Sensing Letters, 12*(8), 1685–1689. https://doi.org/10.1109/LGRS.2015.2419371.

Megahed, F. M., & Allison Jones-Farmer, L. (2015). Statistical perspectives on "Big Data". In S. Knoth & W. Schmid (Eds.), *Frontiers in statistical quality control* (Vol. 11, pp. 29–47). Cham: Springer International.

MI News Network. (2019). *The long range tracking and identification (LRIT) system: Tracking and monitoring ships.* Accessed April 7, 2020, from https://www.marineinsight.com/maritime-law/the-long-range-tracking-and-identification-lrit-system-tracking-and-monitoring-ships/.

Millefiori, L. M., Zissis, D., Cazzanti, L., & Arcieri, G. (2016). *Scalable and distributed sea port operational areas estimation from AIS data* (pp. 374–381). 2016 IEEE 16th International Conference on Data Mining Workshops (ICDMW), Barcelona.

Moreira, A., Krieger, G., Hajnsek, I., Hounam, D., Werner, M., Riegger, S., & Settelmeyer, E. (2004). TanDEM-X: A TerraSAR-X add-on satellite for single-pass SAR interferometry. *IGARSS 2004 IEEE International Geoscience and Remote Sensing Symposium, 2*(C), 2–5. https://doi.org/10.1109/IGARSS.2004.1368578.

Paes, R. L., Lorenzzetti, J. A., & Gherardi, D. F. M. (2010). Ship detection using TerraSAR-X images in the Campos Basin (Brazil). *IEEE Geoscience and Remote Sensing Letters, 7*(3), 545–548.

Page, C. E. (2017). Maximizing maritime safety and environmental protection with AIS: (Automatic identification system). In *OCEANS 2017 – Anchorage* (pp. 1–4). Anchorage, AK.

Pallotta, G., Vespe, M., & Bryan, K. (2013a). Traffic knowledge discovery from AIS data. In *Proceedings of the 16th International Conference on Information Fusion (FUSION)* (pp. 1996–2003). Istanbul.

Pallotta, G., Vespe, M., & Bryan, K. (2013b). Vessel pattern knowledge discovery from AIS data: A framework for anomaly detection and route prediction. *Entropy, 15*(6), 2218–2245. https://doi.org/10.3390/e15062218.

Patroumpas, K., Alevizos, E., Artikis, A., Vodas, M., Pelekis, N., & Theodoridis, Y. (2017). Online event recognition from moving vessel trajectories. *GeoInformatica, 21*(2), 389–427. https:// doi.org/10.1007/s10707-016-0266-x.

Pelkonen, T., Franklin, S., Teller, J., Cavallaro, P., Huang, Q., Meza, J., & Veeraraghavan, K. (2015). Gorilla: A fast, scalable, in-memory time series database. *Proceedings of the VLDB Endowment, 8*(12), 1816–1827. https://doi.org/10.14778/2824032.2824078.

Perera, L. P., Oliveira, P., & Guedes Soares, C. (2012). Maritime traffic monitoring based on vessel detection, tracking, state estimation, and trajectory prediction. *IEEE Transactions on Intelligent Transportation Systems, 13*(3), 1188–1200. https://doi.org/10.1109/TITS.2012.2187282.

Pitz, W., & Miller, D. (2010). The TerraSAR-X satellite. *IEEE Transactions on Geoscience and Remote Sensing, 48*(2), 615–622. https://doi.org/10.1109/TGRS.2009.2037432.

Poḷevskis, J., Krastiņš, M., Korats, G., Skorodumovs, A., & Trokšs, J. (2012). Methods for processing and interpretation of AIS signals corrupted by noise and packet collisions. *Latvian Journal of Physics and Technical Sciences, 49*(3), 25–31. https://doi.org/10.2478/v10047-012-0015-3.

Rajabi, A., Khodadad Saryazdi, A., Belfkih, A., & Duvallet, C. (2018). *Towards Smart Port: An application of AIS data* (pp. 1414–1421). IEEE 20th International Conference on High Performance Computing and Communications; IEEE 16th International Conference on Smart City; IEEE 4th International Conference on Data Science and Systems (HPCC/SmartCity/DSS), Exeter, UK.

Salling, T. B. (2017). *AISmessages*. Accessed April 7, 2020, from https://github.com/tbsalling/aismessages.

Santamaria, C., Alvarez, M., Greidanus, H., Syrris, V., Soille, P., & Argentieri, P. (2017). Mass processing of sentinel-1 images for maritime surveillance. *Remote Sensing, 9*(7). https:// doi.org/10.3390/rs9070678.

Schwehr, K. (2014). *C++ decoder for automatic identification system for tracking ships and decoding maritime information*. Accessed April 7, 2020, from https://github.com/schwehr/libais.

Stasolla, M., Mallorqui, J. J., Margarit, G., Santamaria, C., & Walker, N. (2016). A comparative study of operational vessel detectors for maritime surveillance using satellite-borne synthetic aperture radar. *IEEE Journal of Selected Topics in Applied Earth Observations and Remote Sensing, 9*(6), 2687–2701. https://doi.org/10.1109/JSTARS.2016.2551730.

Terma. (n.d.). *Coastal surveillance radar*. Accessed April 7, 2020, from https://www.terma.com/surveillance-mission-systems/radar-systems/coastal-surveillance-radar/.

Tetreault, B. J. (2005). Use of the automatic identification system (AIS) for maritime domain awareness (MDA). In *Proceedings of MTS/IEEE OCEANS* (pp. 1590–1594). Washington, DC. https://doi.org/10.1109/OCEANS.2005.1639983.

U.S. Coast Guard Navigation Center. (n.d.). *Long range identification and tracking (LRIT) overview*. Accessed April 7, 2020, from https://www.navcen.uscg.gov/?pageName=lritMain.

Uchacz, W., & Galor, W. (2013). *Optimization model of radar stations location in vessel traffic system* (pp. 426–429). Methods and Models in Automation and Robotics (MMAR), 2013 18th International Conference On. https://doi.org/10.1109/MMAR.2013.6669946.

Velotto, D., Bentes, C., Tings, B., & Lehner, S. (2016). First comparison of Sentinel-1 and TerraSAR-X data in the framework of maritime targets detection: South Italy case. *IEEE Journal of Oceanic Engineering, 41*(4), 993–1006. https://doi.org/10.1109/JOE.2016.2520216.

Vespe, M., & Sciotti, M. (2008). Maritime multi-sensor data association based on geographic and navigational knowledge. In *IEEE Radar Conference* (pp. 1–6). Rome. https://doi.org/10.1109/RADAR.2008.4720782.

Vieira, F. M., Vincent, F., Tourneret, J., Bonacci, D., & Gare, D. (2016). *Ship detection using SAR and AIS raw data for maritime surveillance* (pp. 2081–2085). Signal Processing Conference (EUSIPCO), 2016 24th European. https://doi.org/10.1109/EUSIPCO.2016.7760615.

Vivone, G., Braca, P., & Horstmann, J. (2015). Knowledge-based multitarget ship tracking for HF surface wave radar systems. *IEEE Transactions on Geoscience and Remote Sensing, 53*(7), 3931–3949. https://doi.org/10.1109/TGRS.2014.2388355.

Vivone, G., Millefiori, L. M., Braca, P., & Willett, P. (2017). Performance assessment of vessel dynamic models for long-term prediction using heterogeneous data. *IEEE Transactions on Geoscience and Remote Sensing, 55*(11), 6533–6546. https://doi.org/10.1109/ TGRS.2017.2729622.

Wang, Y., Zhang, Z., Li, N., Hong, F., Fan, H., & Wang, X. (2017). Maritime surveillance with undersampled SAR. *IEEE Geoscience and Remote Sensing Letters, 14*(8), 1423–1427. https:// doi.org/10.1109/LGRS.2017.2717459.

Xiao, Z., Ponnambalam, L., Fu, X., & Zhang, W. (2017). Maritime traffic probabilistic forecasting based on vessels' waterway patterns and motion behaviors. *IEEE Transactions on Intelligent Transportation Systems, 18*(11), 3122–3134. https://doi.org/10.1109/TITS.2017.2681810.

Xu, H.-Y., Jayaraman, V., Fu, X., Othman, N. B., Zhang, W., Yin, X. F., Zhai, D., & Mong Goh, R. S. (2019). Efficient compression and preprocessing for facilitating large scale spatiotemporal data mining – A case study based on automatic identification system data. In *2019 IEEE International Conference on Industrial Engineering and Engineering Management (IEEM)* (pp. 354–358). https://doi.org/10.1109/IEEM44572.2019.8978767.

Index

Printed in the United States
by Baker & Taylor Publisher Services